University of Plymouth
Charles Seale Hayne Library
Subject to status this item may be renewed
via your Voyager account

http://voyager.plymouth.ac.uk
Tel: (01752) 232323

Japanese Multinationals in the Changing Context of Regional Policy

MAN-HEE HAN

Avebury

Aldershot · Brookfield USA · Hong Kong · Singapore · Sydney

Published by
Avebury
Ashgate Publishing Limited
Gower House
Croft Road
Aldershot
Hants GU11 3HR
England

Ashgate Publishing Company
Old Post Road
Brookfield
Vermont 05036
USA

British Library Cataloguing in Publication Data

Han, Man-hee
    Japanese Multinationals in the Changing
    Context of Regional Policy
    I. Title
    338.880952
ISBN 1 85628 867 6

Library of Congress Cataloging-in-Publication Data

Han, Man-hee 1956–
    Japanese multinationals in the changing context of regional policy
    / Man-hee Han
        p.cm.
    ISBN 1-85658-867-6 (hbk) : $68.95 (U.S. : approx)
    1. International business enterprises--Japan--Location--Decision
    making. 2. Corporations, Japanese--Great Britain. 3. Corporations,
    Japanese--Korea (South)   I. Title
    HD2907.H25 1994   94-8714
    338.8'8952--dc20   CIP
Reprinted 1995

Printed and bound by Athenæum Press Ltd.,
Gateshead, Tyne & Wear.

Contents

Lists of Tables and Figures ix
List of Appendices xvi
List of Abbreviations xvii
Synopsis xix
Preface xxi
Acknowledgements xxii

Introduction 1

The Aim of the Study 1
The Scope of the Study 3
Method 5

Part I: **The Locational Behaviour of Japanese Multinational Companies in the Changing Context of Regional Policy : Theoretical Framework**

Chapter 1 The World Economy in a Changing Context **8**

1.1 Introduction 8
1.2 The World Economy : Its Changing Figures and
    Conceptualization 9
1.3 National and International Geography in the Changing
    World Economy 23
1.4 Japanese Capital in the Changing Context of the World Economy 26

**Chapter 2 The Nature and Influence of Multinational
    Companies** 37

2.1 The Nature of the Multinational Company and Foreign Direct
Investment 37
2.2 Multinational Company Activities and the Nation State 47
2.3 Foreign Direct Investment in the UK, Korea and Japan 53

Chapter 3 The Causes and Effects of Industrial Location **65**

3.1 Approaches to Industrial Location 65
3.2 Industrial Location Theory 66
3.3 Empirical Location Analysis 73
3.4 Locational Decisions of MNCs and Their Impact on Host Regions 80
3.5 Framework of Location Analysis in This Study 81

**Chapter 4 Regional Policy and the Location of
Multinational Companies** **84**

4.1 Introduction 84
4.2 Regional Policy in the UK and Korea 85
4.3 Regional Policy and the Location of MNC 100

**Part II. The Locational Behaviour of Japanese Multinational
Companies in the Changing Context of Regional
Policy : Empirical Evidence**

Chapter 5 Methodology **107**

5.1 Introduction 107
5.2 The Analysis of Locational Distribution Using Descriptive
Statistics 108
5.3 Locational Factor Analysis Through Regression Analysis 109
5.4 Locational Factor Analysis Through Survey 115

**Chapter 6 Empirical Evidence I : The Geographical Distribution
of Japanese Multinational Companies in the Two Host
Countries** **125**

6.1 The Geographical Distribution of Japanese Multinational
Companies in Great Britain 125
6.2 Locational Distribution of Japanese Multinational
Companies in Korea 135
6.3 Comparison between Britain and Korea 141

Chapter 7 Empirical Evidence II : Factors Influencing the Locational Choices of Japanese Multi-national Companies - Regression Results 147

7.1 Significant Geographical Factors in Great Britain 147
7.2 Significant Geographical Factors in Korea 169
7.3 Comparison between the Regression Results
   of the Two Host Countries 185

Chapter 8 Empirical Evidence III : Factors Influencing the Locational Choices of Japanese Multinational Companies - Survey Results 188

8.1 Significant Locational Factors in Great Britain 188
8.2 Significant Geograpical Factors in Korea 212
8.3 Comparison between the Two Countries 233

Part III : Interpretation of Empirical Evidence in the Light of the Theoretical Framework and the Policy Implications

Chapter 9 The Interpretation of the Empirical Evidence within the Context of a Worldwide Managerial Strategy ... 238

9.1 Introduction 238
9.2 The Main Findings of the Empirical Analyses 239
9.3 The Locational Behaviour of Japanese Multinational
   Companies in Terms of Their Managerial Strategy 246
9.4 Summary 247

Chapter 10 The Implications of the Locational Behaviour of Japanese Companies for Regional Policy in the Host Countries 259

10.1 Regional Policy and the Response of Japanese
   Multinational Companies 259
10.2 Policy Implications 271
10.3 Summary 278

Chapter 11 Final Conclusion 283

11.1 Theoretical Framework : Overview 283
11.2 Methodology Reconsidered 285

11.3 Findings and Policy Implications 287

Notes 291
Appendices 310
Bibliography 342

List of tables and figures

I. List of Tables

1.1   The comparison between Fordism and post-Fordism   15

1.2   The comparison between organized and disorganized capitalism   20

2.1   Total net direct overseas investment in the UK   54

2.2   Total net direct overseas investment from and into the UK   55

2.3   Annual FDI flow into Korea   57

2.4   Total outward investment of Korean MNCs   58

2.5   The total stock of Japanese outward direct investment   59

2.6   The distribution of the total stock of Japanese outward direct
      investment   60

2.7   The distribution of Japanese FDI in major European countries . .   60

4.1   Position of Seoul in Korea   94

4.2   Gross regional product per capita   98

4.3   Net population movement to Seoul   98

4.4   Comparison of the geographical boundary of AAs   101

5.1   Dependent and Independent Variables (British Case)   116

5.2   Dependent and Independent Variables (Korean Case) 120

6.1   Regional distribution of Japanese manufacturing companies
in Britain in 1990 126

6.2   The current mean size of Japanese companies 130

6.3   Current mean size of Japanese manufacturing companies
in each region 131

6.4   The operating fields of Japanese manufacturing companies
in Britain 133

6.5   Distribution of the operating fields of Japanese
manufacturing companies between regions in Britain 134

6.6   Regional distribution of Japanese manufacturing companies
in Korea 135

6.7 Current investment size distribution of Japanese
manufacturing companies between regions in Korea 138

6.8 The operating fields of Japanese manufacturing
companies in Korea 140

6.9   Distribution of the operating fields of Japanese
manufacturing companies between regions in Korea 140

6.10 Statistics of the geographical distribution of Japanese manufacturing
companies between regions in Korea and Britain 143

7.1   The variables which have high correlation
coefficients with X_{21} 156

7.2   Important variables chosen by the regressions
including and excluding X_{21} 157

7.3   The significant variables chosen in static and
change analysis (Britain) 158

7.4   Variables constructing the indices of locational
factors (Britain) 160

7.5   The significant explanatory variables for the
      locational decisions of Japanese manufacturing
      companies in each period (Britain) 168

7.6   The significant variables chosen in static and
      change analysis (Korea) 177

7.7   Variables selected for the construction of indices (Korea) 178

7.8   The significant explanatory variables for the
      locational decisions of Japanese manufacturing
      companies in each period (Korea) 184

8.1   The size and establishment year of companies
      surveyed by questionnaire (Britain) 189

8.2   The industrial distribution of companies surveyed
      by questionnaire (Britain) 190

8.3   The locations of the companies surveyed by
      questionnaire (Britain) 190

8.4   The profile of the companies interviewed 191

8.5   Position and origin of the interviewees 191

8.6   Main markets of the companies surveyed (Britain) 192

8.7   Push factors in Japan resulting in overseas
      investment (Britain) 193

8.8   Important locational factors for the Japanese
      companies surveyed (Britain) 195

8.9   Unsatisfactory locational factors for the Japanese
      companies surveyed (Britain) 198

8.10 The influence of government assistance on the
      location decisions of Japanese companies (Britain) 200

8.11 The influence of government assistance on the
      location decisions of Japanese companies by region
      (Britain) 201

8.12 The measures of assistance provided by the host
     government (Britain) 201

8.13 Important measures of government assistance in
     each region (Britain) 202

8.14 Relationship between the measures of government
     assistance and their influence on the location of
     Japanese companies 203

8.15 Alternative countries considered in the world to Britain 205

8.16 The important factors which caused the rejection of
     alternative locations in other countries (Britain) 206

8.17 Relationship between the rejected alternative
     locations and unfavoured locational factors 207

8.18 Alternative areas considered in the UK 208

8.19 The important factors which caused the rejection
     of alternative areas in the UK 208

8.20 Relationship between the rejected areas and
     unfavoured locational factors (Britain) 210

8.21 The size and established year of companies
     surveyed by questionnaire (Korea) 213

8.22 The industrial distribution of companies surveyed
     by questionnaire (Korea) 214

8.23 The locations of the companies surveyed by
     questionnaire (Korea) 214

8.24 Main markets of the companies surveyed (Korea) 215

8.25 Push factors in Japan resulting in overseas
     investment in Korea 216

8.26 Important locational factors for the Japanese
     companies surveyed (Korea) 218

8.27 Unsatisfactory locational factors for the Japanese
companies surveyed (Korea) 220

8.28 The influence of government assistance in the
location decisions of Japanese companies (Korea) 222

8.29 The influence of government assistance on the
location decisions of Japanese companies by Do (Korea) 223

8.30 The measures of assistance provided by the host
government (Korea) 224

8.31 Important measures of government assistance in
each area (Korea) 224

8.32 Relationship between the measures of government
assistance and its influence on the location of
Japanese companies (Korea) 225

8.33 Alternative countries considered in the world to Korea 226

8.34 The important factors which caused the rejection of
alternative locations in other countries (Korea) 228

8.35 Relationship between the rejected alternative
countries and unfavourable locational factors (Korea) 229

8.36 Alternative areas considered in Korea 230

8.37 The important factors which caused the rejection of
alternative areas in Korea 231

8.38 Relationship between the rejected areas and
unfavoured locational factors (Korea) 232

8.39 The comparison of main survey findings in the two
host countries 235

9.1 Comparison of the main findings from the empirical
analyses 240

10.1 Japanese companies in AAs and non-AAs by date of arrival ... 262

10.2 Financial assistance received by Japanese companies   265

10.3 Japanese companies in the IEs and non-IE areas by
      date of arrival   269

II. List of Figures

4.1 Assisted Areas in the UK 89

4.2 Prosperous and Lagged Regions in Korea 95

6.1 The increase in Japanese manufacturing companies
in Great Britain 127

6.2 The increase in the number of Japanese manufacturing
companies in Great Britain 128

6.3 The percentage share of each region in the
cumulative number of Japanese manufacturing
companies in Great Britain 129

6.4 The increase in Japanese manufacturing companies in Korea . . . 132

6.5 The percentage share of each region in the
cumulative number of Japanese manufacturing
companies in Korea 137

6.6 The geographical distribution of Japanese
manufacturing companies between regions in Korea
and Britain 142

10.1 The AAs in 1979 and the locations of Japanese
companies arriving before 1981 263

10.2 The AAs in 1982 and the locations of Japanese
companies arriving 1982-1984 263

10.3 The AAs in 1984 and the locations of Japanese
companies arriving 1985-1990 263

10.4 The coverage of AAs and the proportion of Japanese
companies in the AAs 264

List of appendices

Appendix 1 : Derivation and Sources of Variables (British Case) . . . 310

Appendix 2 : Derivation and Sources of Variables (Korean Case) . . 318

Appendix 3 : Questionnaire Form 322

Appendix 4 : Interview Questions 327

Appendix 5 : Indices of Locational Factors (Britain) 332

Appendix 6 : Indices of Locational Factors (Korea) 340

List of abbreviations

AA	assisted area
AJEI	Anglo-Japanese Economic Institute
CIPFA	Chartered Institute of Public Finance and Accountants
DA	development area
DTI	Department of Trade and Industry
MNC	multinational company
E(E)C	European (Economic) Community
ERDF	European Regional Development Fund
EZ	enterprise zone
FDI	foreign direct investment
HCI	heavy and chemical industry
IA	intermediate area
IBB	Invest in Britain Bureau
IBJ	Industrial Bank of Japan
IDC	industrial development control
IEs	industrial estates and Free Export Zones
IFMP	Institute of Fiscal and Monetary Policy
IMF	International Monetary Fund
JEI	Japanese Economic Institute
JETRO	Japan External Trade Organization
KRIHS	Korea Research Institute for Human Settlement
KTA	Korea Trade Association
LDC	less developed country
MITI	Ministry of International Trade and Industry
MOC	Ministry of Construction
MOF	Ministry of Finance
MPR	metropolitan region
NICs	newly industrialising countries
NIDL	new international division of labour
OECD	Organization for Economic Co-operation and Development
R&D	research and development

RDG	regional development grant
REP	regional employment premium
RSA	regional selective assistance
RSA	Regional Studies Association
SDA	special development area
SME	small and medium sized enterprise
TTWA	travel-to-work area
TDC	Telford Development Corporation
UN	United Nations
WDA	Welsh Development Agency
WMDA	West Midlands Development Agency

Synopsis

The geography of a country, or a region, has been increasingly influenced by international market forces, which itself is experiencing a drastic change. On the other hand, the locational choices of multinational companies (MNCs), which form the main part of the international market forces, are understood as the products of the interaction between the geography of host countries, or host regions, and the dynamic managerial strategies of the companies.

Given this context, this study aims to link directly the geography of host countries (especially, regional policy) and the worldwide managerial strategy of Japanese MNCs. Firstly, this study tries to infer the worldwide managerial strategy of Japanese MNCs through the locational behaviour of these companies in the two host countries, the UK and Korea. And, secondly, by investigating the responsiveness of Japanese MNCs based on their worldwide managerial strategy to the changing context of regional policy, this study aims to estimate the effectiveness and to search for the future direction of regional policy in the two countries. For this purpose, this study implemented various analyses including descriptive, regression and survey analyses.

Through these analyses the following aspects were clarified. Firstly, Japanese MNCs have been highly responsive and flexible to changes in locational factors in host countries in order to maximize their own profit and the main features of the worldwide managerial strategy of Japanese companies can be summarised as 'the division of the world market into smaller market areas' and 'the flexible utilisation of the circumstances in each market area'. And, secondly, British regional policy has been successful in attracting mobile Japanese firms mainly due to the coincidence of the changing content of British regional policy with the managerial objectives of Japanese MNCs, while regional policy in Korea has failed to take advantage of incoming Japanese companies because of the lack of government effort in coordinating these two influential forces.

From these findings, it became evident that the locational behaviour of Japanese companies in each host country is consistent with, and is able to be explained by, the worldwide managerial strategy of these Japanese companies. And, therefore, it is claimed that there should be a renewed emphasis on the importance of changes in international market forces, including the activities of foreign MNCs, in discussing the direction and measures of regional policy in each country. This is much more so in this era of 'post-Fordism' or 'disorganized capitalism'.

Preface

The geography of a country, or a region, has been increasingly influenced by international market forces, which itself is experiencing a drastic change. On the other hand, the locational choices of multinational companies(MNCs), which form the main part of the international market forces, are understood as the products of the interaction between the geography of host countries, or host regions, and the dynamic managerial strategies of the companies.

In order to clarify this inter-relationship, this book focuses on the activities of Japanese MNCs in host countries. Japanese companies were chosen with the recognition of the growing influence of these companies and their investment on the regional economy as well as on the national and world economy. In choosing the host countries to be examined, it was natural to decide on Korea where I was born and the UK where I studied.

By investigating the behaviour of Japanese MNCs in different host countries, this book aims to link directly the geography of host countries (especially, regional policy) and the worldwide manageiral strategy of Japanese MNCs. For this purpose, this study implements various analyses including descriptive, regression and survey analyses.

In preparing this book, I owe an enormous debt to many people in various ways. First of all, Mrs Barbara M.D. Smith at the Centre for Urban and Regional Studies, University of Birmingham, should be appreciated for her wholehearted guidance and encouragement throughout my research. I am also greatly indebted to Choong-Bae Lee, who is also doing his research in the University of Birmingham, for his help with revisions and proof reading. My gratitude should be sent to the managers in Japanese companies who kindly replied to my questionnaire and interview. And, finally, it is my own responsibility for any errors of fact or judgement remain in this book.

Acknowledgements

The author and publishers are grateful to the following who have kindly given permission for the use of copyright material:

Lancaster Regional Group - P. Bagguley The Post-Fordism Enigma: Theories of Labour Flexibility, Lancaster 1989; Hodder and Stoughton - D. Massey and J. Allen, Uneven Re-Development: Cities and Regions in Transition,1988; British Chamber of Commerce - Business Briefing, 19.June,1992; HMSO - Regional Trends, 26 (1991); Regional Studies Association - R.L. Martin 'Monetarism Masquerading as regional policy? The Government's New System of Regional Aid', Regional Studies,19.4,1985; CLES - J. Tomaney 'Japanese Inward Investment: North East Experiences' resented to the CLES conference on 'Japanese Inward Investment in the UK', Matlock 1991; Penguin Books - H. Radice (ed.) International Firms and Modern Imperialism, Harmondsworth 1975; Leiden - E. Thielemans 'The Multinational Enterprise', in J.S. Wilson and C.F. Scheffer (eds.) Multinational Enterprises: Financial and Monetary Aspects, Sijthoff 1974; Routledge and Kegan Paul - M. Brech and M. Sharp Inward Investment: Policy Options for the UK, London 1984; Macmillan - M.E. Porter The Competitive Advantage of Nations, London 1990; Harper Collins - P. Dicken and P.E. Lloyd Location in Space, New York 1990; United Nations - World Investment Report 1991: The Triad in Foreign Direct Investment, New York 1991; Harvester Wheatsheaf - Thomsen S. and Nicolaides The Evolution of Japanese Direct Investment in Europe, Hemel Hemstead 1991.

Every effort has been made to trace all the copy-right holders, but if any have been inadvertently overlooked the publishers will be pleased to make the necessary arrangement at the first opportunity. . . . .

Introduction

The aim of the study

In most countries, central governments have made great efforts to improve the economic situation in those regions suffering from particularly high unemployment, low income levels, high migration, etc. and, thus, to accomplish a balanced national growth. For this purpose, governments have tried to mobilize all the policy measures available such as grants, tax cuts and incentives, industrial development controls and the like.

With regard to the goal of regional policy, there has been a growing concern about the cause and effect of the locational shift of large, multinational companies (MNCs) during the last decades. This concern is mainly caused by the fact that the decisions of these companies are very important in terms of their impact on employment and income at both national and regional level. Moreover, often, a major part of the drastic changes in the world economy are said to be attributable to the activities of these MNCs.

It is broadly agreed that the investment (or disinvestment) decisions of MNCs are a part of their worldwide strategies for pursuing profit maximization and have significant implications for many regions and nations. Often, the locational decisions of these large MNCs have caused conflicts with the policy efforts of individual governments. Although the governments possess legal power to confront these international corporate forces such as to introduce tariffs, tax cuts and exchange rate controls, they are unlikely to have much success in controlling the companies or in preventing the impact of changes in the decisions of MNCs. In this circumstance, it seems imperative to make explicit the relationship between the government industrial or regional policy in a country and the locational decision-making of MNCs in that country.

In general, these activities of MNCs are understood as a part of the foreign direct investment (FDI) process (Hood and Young, 1983,p.1)[1]. Santiago classified empirical studies of FDI into three types of approach. According to him, one approach concentrates on any causal relationship between the industrial structure of the host countries and the behaviour and performance of

1

MNCs. Another approach emphasizes the specific features of MNCs compared to those of indigenous firms. And, another different group of studies tries to identify the locational features in the host countries (Santiago,1987,p.317).

Basically, the present study develops the standpoint of the third approach, especially in implementing the empirical analyses. Therefore, investigating the relationship between the geographical, or locational, forces in a country and the flow of international market forces with this inevitably involving the management decisions of MNCs becomes the main issue of concern in this study. Within this aim, the particular focus is directed at Japanese MNCs and towards their FDI in Britain and Korea, and its relationship with regional policy in each country.

With its growing economic power, Japan has increased its overseas investments during the last twenty years. By the same token, the overseas activities of Japanese companies have substantially expanded in a variety of ways. As a result, there has been a growing concern in many countries about the behaviour of these multinationalized Japanese companies. Needless to say, like most multinationalized companies, Japanese companies try to maximize their profit in overseas markets by taking advantage of available opportunities to the greatest extent possible[2]. Therefore, the investment or disinvestment decisions of Japanese MNCs should be interpreted in this context.

During the last several decades, Japanese companies have been the largest source of foreign investment in Korea. On the other hand, they have invested a large amount in a number of developed countries, and, here, the UK is one of the most important recipients. However, it seems likely that there are many differences between the Japanese investments in the two countries, Korea and the UK, not only in the amount but also in the type of and strategy behind these investments. In particular, the two patterns of locational behaviour are expected to be substantially different from each other because the locational decision-making behind the investments in the two countries is a part of the overall management strategy of the Japanese parent companies. In similar vein, with respect to regional policy in Korea and Britain, with this policy being different in its objectives and measures in the two countries, the reaction of Japanese capital to the need to accommodate itself either to the policy or to policy changes is likely to vary.

Against this background, the present study aims at identifying the characteristics and the global strategies of Japanese MNCs as reflected in their locational behaviour in the two host countries and at searching for its policy implications for the two host countries. Therefore, the following three objectives become the main focus of the study: firstly, to identify the characteristics of the geographical distribution of Japanese investment in each country; secondly, to explore the unique strategies of Japanese MNCs, especially in the changing context of the world economy, represented by their locational behaviour and by the main geographical factors influencing their

2

distribution; and, thirdly, to investigate how the regional policy in the two countries can make best use of the mobile Japanese FDI.

In short, this study tries to look for the relationship between the locational behaviour of Japanese MNCs and geographical factors present in the two countries under the different circumstances operating in each. These include the forms of regional policy. In other words, this study attempts to identify the worldwide managerial strategy of Japanese MNCs by examining geographical factors and to find the implication of this strategy for the future geography of the two host countries.

The scope of the study

As mentioned above, this study tries to connect the geographical factors, including regional policy, with the location of Japanese MNCs behaving as a main market force in the world economy. Therefore, the following four issues emerge as the most important theoretical areas for study; namely the world economy, MNCs, industrial location and regional policy.

The study of MNC activities can hardly be carried out without considering the context of the world economy. MNCs tend to respond sensitively to changes in the structure and forces of the international economy. Conversely, the dynamic activities of MNCs often cause substantial changes in national and international economies. In other words, the world economy can be said to be both a motivator and a reflector of MNC activities[3]. This relationship has been reinforced in parallel with a series of dramatic changes in the world economy since the late 1960s, which are often called 'post-Fordism' or 'disorganized capitalism'. During the process, the Japanese economy and Japanese MNCs appeared as the main actor in the changing world economy. Therefore, this study, before discussing the activities of Japanese MNCs, investigates first the nature of this changing world economy and the role of Japanese capital in the process of change.

Next, in examining the behaviour of Japanese MNCs, an investigation of the general features of MNCs becomes a prerequisite for the study. However, the ever growing and diversifying activities of MNCs prevent any single way of explanation or prediction. Moreover, it is difficult to generalize the global locational behaviour of Japanese investments only through exploring the examples in the two countries.

There have been large numbers of approaches to explaining the activities of MNCs, in particular those of Japanese MNCs, according to different standpoints. This study, after examining the general theories of MNCs, will move on to a discussion of Japanese MNCs, mainly from the viewpoint that the activities of Japanese MNCs reflect both the profit maximizing processes of private concerns and the well planned breakthrough of the Japanese economy within the fluctuating international economy.

3

Regarding industrial location, there have been a number of viewpoints through which authors try to explain the actual location and movement of industry. According to the viewpoint on which the theory is based, industrial location theories have been classified into several groups. Among these, neoclassical theory, behavioral theory and structural theory provide the main streams. From each point of view, authors have done a lot of empirical studies to investigate the cause and effect and the nature of locational movement. These empirical studies can be divided into two main strands; the one is locational factor analysis comprising the analyses of push and pull factors and the other is locational shift pattern analysis. Each emphasizes a different stage in the sequential process of locational movement.

The empirical analysis in Part II of this study includes locational factor analysis largely focusing on pull factors. The study of the push factors that cause FDI flows outward is restricted because of the difficulty in collecting relevant data, especially published data at the macro-level, in so far as the push factors arise largely outside the host country and outside the MNC's corporate strategy. Therefore, the discussion about the push factors in Japan will be limited to the findings revealed from the answers of Japanese managers to the related questions during the survey in this study.

As discussed above, locational decisions of Japanese MNCs are considered as being made basically as part of the strategy of worldwide profit maximization. However, these decisions of Japanese MNCs based on the profit or rationality maximization in this study is never identical with that of neoclassical location theory. In other words, the concept of profit maximization in this study involves long-term intangible profit as well as short-term financial profit. Also, the general features of the locational behaviour of Japanese MNCs will be considered both at micro (local and regional)- and macro (national)-level. This means that, on the one hand, the behaviour involved in selecting a suitable site in a given country is examined at the micro-level. On the other hand, the causes that lead to the choice of a specific host country among all the countries available is considered at the macro-level. In the process, a number of organizational and structural constraints on Japanese MNC choice will be taken into account.

Regional policy has long been investigated and discussed by many authors and by governments themselves, notably in the U.K. However, since this study is proceeding in the form of comparative analysis, there arises a problem of defining the concept and content of regional policy unambiguously when the policy is implemented in different ways and with different purposes in the two countries studied. In addition there is a need to realign and confirm the policy measures throughout each country's overall industrial policy. In this respect, the term, regional policy, should be defined more broadly and more flexibly. (Therefore, in several parts of this study, European Regional Development Fund [ERDF] and the newly introduced spatial policy measures of the British

4

government are included in this broader concept of British regional policy.)

Regional policy in Korea was mainly initiated in the early 1970s. However, the policy has not been established and undertaken in a unified systematic way like that in the UK. Therefore, in this study, the policy measures to be examined will not be confined to the initiatives under the name of regional policy, but will include various kinds of policies related to the development of regions even though they are introduced for the purpose of national economic growth. On the other hand, with regard to time scale, in order to maintain the consistency of this research, the British case will also be examined mainly after the beginning of the 1970s.

The industry studied here will be confined to the manufacturing sector. This is because manufacturing industry is regarded as a basic sector for both the regional and national economy. Also, regarding overseas investment, manufacturing has been drawn attention to, since it is the investment form to be identified most clearly and the one with the most significant effects on the economies of host countries[4].

Method

This study consists of three main parts, the investigation of the theoretical framework, the exploration of the empirical evidence and the interpretation of the empirical results. In total, this is a comprehensive study concerned with the identification of the main features of the given situation (i.e. the locations of Japanese companies) and the development of hypotheses on the basis of raw data collected for this study as well as published information. Sources or literature will be collected on four main issues as mentioned in the previous section; the world economy, MNCs, industrial location and regional policy. In the first part, the examination of general theories on the above four fields becomes the main effort. Therefore, this part is provided to introduce the major theories and to compare them for the purpose of this study.

After examining the theoretical viewpoints, analyzing the empirical evidence of the locational behaviour of Japanese MNCs becomes the main concern of the second part of this study. In the process, since MNCs change their locations frequently according to their overall strategy and since this study, being a comparative analysis, necessitates two kinds of empirical data, collecting a sufficient amount of data is the most crucial issue for the analysis.

Collected data, in the first place, will be systematized and aligned in such a way that they can show the unique features of the geographical distribution of Japanese companies in each host country. Specifically, the present characteristics of the Japanese companies in the two host countries such as the size, type and the industrial field of the capital investment, and the historical change of these characteristics are the focal points of the effort.

Given the data on the geographical distribution of the Japanese companies and the locational factors including regional policy, the relative significance of these factors for the location of Japanese companies will be tested using both methods of regression and survey analyses. The more specific explanation of the methodology for the empirical study will be displayed in Part II.

After examining the empirical evidence using regression and survey analyses, this study will move on to its concern with comparison of the results in the two countries. In short, this study is a typical comparative study between two countries. The main reason for taking this kind of approach is to demonstrate the locational pattern of Japanese companies more clearly by comparing different cases in different circumstances, and to identify the more relevant causes of locational decisions in this wider context.

It may be thought that the comparison between Korean and British experience has no significant relevance or interrelationship as the countries are so diverse. However, it is considered that the comparison of the two countries' experience is meaningful in that the UK is one of the largest recipients of Japanese FDI in the developed countries while Korea is similarly placed amongst Asian developing countries. Specifically, the notable characteristics of the two countries can be listed as follows:

Firstly, there are a set of similarities: 1) they have both experienced a large trade deficit with Japan during the last decade; and 2) their population, resources, territory, etc. are to a certain extent similar.

Secondly, a number of aspects that differ between the two make the comparison more meaningful as follows: 1) while the British economy has experienced a serious decline since the 1970s, the Korean economy in total has developed rapidly during the last three decades in spite of its struggle in recent years; 2) while Britain has a limited relationship with Japan largely confined to trade, Korea historically has had several kinds of relationship with Japan involving political, economic and cultural aspects; 3) the primary objective of British regional policy is different from that of Korean policy which is implemented within, and confined by, the context of national security and national economic growth; 4) the power and influence of central government on the economy is much stronger in Korea than in Britain; and 5) there is a tremendous deviation in the geographical distance from Japan of the two countries.

In short, these two countries are selected and analyzed as representatives of the developed and Asian developing countries respectively for outward Japanese FDI. By adopting this comparative analysis, it is thought that the identification of the overall strategies of Japanese FDI and MNCs becomes more feasible.

And, as a concluding part, after the empirical analysis explained above, an effort will be made to figure out the meaning and the spatial policy implications of the worldwide managerial strategy of these companies which are identified in the locational behaviour of these companies in the two countries studied.

1 The world economy in a changing context

1.1 Introduction

After the Second World War, the capitalist economy, under the strong regulation and intervention by the state in economic fields, met a golden era showing a consistent prosperity (Castells,1989,p.22). Manufacturing production in major developed countries sharply increased and the improvement of communications and transportation ran in parallel with the development of technology. Also, during this time, international trade and the activities of MNCs increased remarkably alongside the increasing specialization of labour and production within countries. As many authors assert, this postwar boom can be said to be a fruit of the cooperation between Fordist mass production and Keynesian mass consumption (Hirst and Zeitlin,1991,p.9).

The world economy, however, began to be shaken from the mid-1960s demonstrating a series of disruptions. Certainly, there has appeared a group of symptoms signalling the advent of structural change: namely, 1) the sharp rise of unemployment and inflation in advanced economies; 2) the spatial dispersion of manufacturing industry; 3) the growth of the share of service sector employment in contrast to the declining share of manufacturing employment; and 4) the oil crises and worldwide recessions in the 1970s and 1980s (Massey,1988,p.48; Allen,1988b,p.97)[5]. This dramatic change in the world economy has resulted in socio-economic restructuring in individual countries, especially in the advanced countries.

Indeed, the world began to witness a transition to a new structure or order for both the national and international economies. Witnessing this changing world economic order, scholars have been busy exploring and identifying its causes, actors and effects. Although the arguments of these scholars differ from each other according to their viewpoints, and although each of these arguments

8

contains limitations, they have in common the signalling of an important issue; that of a marked structural change in the world economy since the mid-1960s and, more drastically, since the 1970s[6].

At the same time, confronting this structural change in the world economy, people in advanced countries have begun to consider more seriously the influence of Japanese capital in shaping the present world economy and that capital's leading role and position in the future world economic order. Regarding this, many authors, based on their own research efforts, predict that the role of Japanese capital, with its competitiveness and flexibility, will continue to grow and that its influence in forming the new socio-economic order will be crucial.

However, such a new socio-economic order is unlikely to be completed without any painful process of adjustment with the old order. In particular the old traditional contexts of either the world economy or the domestic structure in Japan itself will continue to hamper the development of new world economic order given the leading role of Japan and her capital.

The sufficient understanding of this structural change in the world economy seems to be essential for the purpose of this study, i.e. the examination of the relationship between the behaviour of a specific international market force (Japanese capital) and the geography of its host countries (Britain and Korea). Therefore, this chapter, in order to illuminate the trend and future directions of worldwide structural change, will examine some of the issues which are thought to be crucial to these developments in turn. Although considered one at a time for convenience, they are of course all closely related. Firstly, in the next section, the features and nature of recent structural change will be explored. After that, the main efforts to conceptualize the structural changes in the world economy will be elucidated.

1.2 The World Economy : Its Changing Figures and Conceptualization

1.2.1 Structural change in the world economy

1.2.1.1 Recognition of structural change

In order to move forward the discussion on the nature of structural change, it seems most necessary to explore the main features of this structural change. In brief, what kinds of factors are constructing the structural change that has occurred over the past two decades which is even called the 'crisis of mass production' or the 'crisis of Fordism' (Meegan,1988,p.136), or even the 'crisis of capitalism' (Marshall,1987,p.1; Peet,1987, p.9)?

In some respects the present kinds of changes have been occurring often in human life over the centuries. In other words, the current structural change in the capitalist economy can be said to be one of the products which capitalism, especially the capitalism emphasizing the role of the state based on the Keynesian economic theory, itself has implied[7]. However, the strength and influence of the changes since the mid-1960s, which have disrupted the way of thinking about social and economic formulae, seem to be much more severe than before.

In identifying and indicating the main features of structural change, scholars tend to vary according to their own analyses. (Obviously, their separate analyses share many features.) Among those, Allen and Massey, defining a structural economic change as one that represents a fundamental shift in the way that the economy has hitherto been organized, pointed out the following interweaved aspects to be the main features of recent fundamental structural change: 1) the shift in the economy from the manufacturing to the service sector; 2) the decline of cities as the centres of productive activity; 3) the strengthening of the dominance of multinational companies in the world economy; and 4) the shift in the balance of the labour market from male, full-time employment towards female, part-time employment (Allen and Massey, 1988,pp.2-3).

Similarly, Lash and Bagguley listed internationalization, de-industrialization, and the growth of service occupations, as the main features of current structural change (Lash and Bagguley, 1987,pp.6-7). Harris, on the other hand, arguing that the structural change of each individual economy is determined by the structural changes in the world economy, identified internationalization and multilateralism as the main characteristics of the changes in the international economy (Harris,1988,pp.23-25). Combining these arguments, we can summarize the common points forming the recent structural change as follows.

1.2.1.2   The main features of structural change

Firstly, the international monetary system constructed under the pivotal role of the US began to lose its ground with the deterioration of the US economy and the growing importance of the Euro-dollar in the world financial market. This resulted in the break down of the post-war monetary system in the late 1960s culminating in the ending of the Bretton Woods agreement in 1971. Fixed exchange rates based on the dollar were replaced by floating exchange rates, and the control of the gold standard and the International Monetary Fund (IMF) lost their persuasive power. These shifts meant the international monetary system became more vulnerable to a sudden disruption in the financial system of one country and to the conflicts caused by the severe competition between countries surrounding not just trade and finance but, notably, currency speculation and manipulation. Eatwell attaches importance to the failure to develop a new 'big spender' with political clout in the world as well as economic power after the demise of first Britain and then the US

(Eatwell,1982,p.98).

Secondly, the leading role of the US in the international political and economic scene has been threatened and, in some respects, eroded. In international politics, the threat came from the European Community and increasing nationalism in Third World countries. In its economic aspect, the threat came from the expansion of Japanese and German (or European) capital, the competitiveness of the newly industrializing countries (NICs) in the world economy and the American balance of payments deficit (Castells,1989,p.304). In particular, the growing size of the deficit in American government finance and trade is regarded as a major threat to the stability of the world economy[8].

Thirdly, world economic activity became increasingly dominated by multinational companies (MNCs). At the same time, with the development of communications and transport technology, the organizational structure of these MNCs became more centralized in terms of decision making with regard to production and finance (Castells,1989,p.320; Julius,1990,pp.4-5).

Fourthly, the development of technology began to accelerate, especially after the 1970s. The continuous advancement in electronics and computer science has led this technological development. Incessantly developing communications and transportation facilities have enabled people to overcome the barriers of time and space. As a result, the issue of industrial location choice, which had significant implications for manufacturing and services, withered in importance in many product fields. The international division of labour, thus, became feasible even if not yet established. On the other hand, the development of information technology has strengthened capital's bargaining power against labour by providing management with a variety of measures, such as automation of jobs, decentralization of production facilities and sub-contracting of production with which to challenge labour in addition to rising and often long term unemployment (Castells,1989,p.189).

Fifthly, there has been a substantial shift between industries. The long established emphasis on manufacturing has weakened and, instead, some service sectors have occupied its place. This shift has been mainly caused by the increase in public sector and personal service jobs, the displacement of manual labour by brain power and machinery/robots, the social tendency towards professionalism and the growing importance of the research and development function. Consequently, the service sector, in particular producer services and information technology related services, became the main producer of jobs, national income and output in most advanced countries including the UK (Allen,1988b). However, it is still relevant to emphasize that manufacturing is the engine of national growth in many developing and under-developed and possibly still in developed countries, with much service development tied to manufacturing (and, often, indeed, simply hived off from manufacturing concerns as functions devolved and dispersed)[9].

Finally, and largely interrelated with the fifth issue, the occupational

11

structure has changed in the direction of diversification, feminization and both de-skilling and multi and re-skilling. Briefly and crudely speaking, female, part-time and producer-service non-manual jobs substituted for male, full-time and manufacturing manual jobs (Nielsen,1991,pp.46-48). This change has significant implications for government employment policies, for the pattern of life in households, for education and training requirements and for polarization tendencies in society.

In summary, the recent structural changes involve the development of technology and the consequent shift from manufacturing to the service sector in industrial structure (which is often called a process of deindustrialization). Also involved has been the shift from mainly male, full-time employment to more female part-time employment in the occupational structure, the decline of the importance of big cities as the centres of productive activity in the spatial structure and the restructuring in the international financial system and world economic market followed by the major changes in economic management policies.

This structural change entails a series of transformations in the production process which have determined the tempo or pattern of the world economy and, thus eventually, the way of life of people. As a result, these broad changes have been seen even as a collapse of existing regulation both at the international and national level (Harris,1988,p.43).

To tackle these emergent changes, a bundle of research efforts has been undertaken. According to approach, different kinds of diagnoses and remedies have been suggested. In particular, many researchers have focused on the issue of the organization of production (from mass production to flexible specialization or post-Fordism) as the source or nature of the structural change. The next section examines these approaches.

1.2.2 The theoretical context

1.2.2.1 Post-Fordism versus disorganized capitalism

Since the late 1970s, various striking terms or phrases have been employed to explain the nature of recent structural change and, particularly, of the new production system. Some subtle nuances seem to distinguish the terms used. 'Neo-Fordism' (Aglietta,1979) or 'post-Fordism' (Bagguley,1989, etc.), 'flexible specialization' (Piore and Sabel,1984), 'disorganized capitalism' (Lash and Urry,1987), 'new competition' (Best,1990) and 'lean production' (Womack et al.,1990) are the main terms mobilized to expound the present structural change. Among these, post-Fordism and disorganized capitalism are likely to be the most commonly used terms by authors to forward their arguments.

The terms of 'post-Fordism' and 'disorganized capitalism' have in common that both refer to the general features of the socio-economic structure in

12

industrial capitalism which has been changed fundamentally by the various forces discussed above. It is difficult to make a clear distinction between the boundaries and meanings of these two concepts through the expressions of their authors. In reality, authors usually present their arguments without providing a clear distinction between the two. Often, 'disorganized capitalism', 'post-Fordism' and 'flexibility' intermingle with each other to express the changed form of industrial capitalism from that based on mass-production. Nevertheless, a certain type of distinction can be made by configurating the arguments of authors.

Basically, the approaches using the concept of 'post-Fordism' try to explore and characterize the present structural change by postulating *a change in basic manufacturing organization* from Fordism to post-Fordism. By contrast, 'disorganized capitalism' is the concept formed by shedding light on *the changing feature of the existing organized capitalism*. Of course, the changed mode of production and the flexibility, which are the central norms in discussing Fordism and post-Fordism, also play a significant role in understanding the disorganization of capitalism. However, these two concepts, 'post-Fordism' and 'disorganized capitalism', are different in their starting points.

Here, the theoretical perspectives on recent structural change will be examined from these two different points of departure, respectively 'post-Fordism' and 'disorganized capitalism'.

1.2.2.2 Perspectives on post-Fordism

Post-Fordism is compared or contrasted with the main features of its predecessor, Fordism. Fordism consists of two central parts, namely mass production and mass consumption. Mass production can be achieved by maximizing the activities of labour and automated facilities within the complicated framework which is planned by the management. Under Fordism, labour needs neither skilful craft nor positive attitude to improve the automated and sub-divided working process. Therefore Fordism is criticized by scholars, especially those of the standpoint of Marxism, in that it downgrades the value of labour[10].

Nowadays, 'Fordism' is used as a concept envisaging not only a mode of production but also the social and economic patterns related to this mode of production. From this viewpoint, Murray, pointing particularly at the UK government over the past decades, criticizes the Fordist state which accommodates the Fordist and Taylorist idea in its own operation in that it lacks variety and, thus, that its work organization is characterized by a divided and deskilled labour force and a centralized and information-heavy administration (Murray,1991,p.22)[11].

Like Fordism, post-Fordism centres around, first of all, the mode of production. After that, the term comprises other related aspects which the mode of production directly implies, for example the impact of the mode of production on wage levels, consumer markets and employee behaviour. In this process, flexibility appears as the central criterion to distinguish the mode of production under Fordism from that under post-Fordism. In contrast to Fordism, which is characterized by the pre-determined and invariable mass production process, post-Fordism is discussed as mainly based on the flexible production process, especially to meet diversifying consumer patterns.

In short, a certain kind of consensus has been reached about the main features of post-Fordism, namely flexibility in production, labour participation in decision making about the production process through quality circles, etc. and decentralization of the production function in the industrial organization. The differences between Fordism and post-Fordism are summarized in Table 1.1.

However, scholars are contradictory when it comes to the nature or sources of post-Fordism. Three groups of writers stand out amongst others in discussing this issue.

The regulationists' approach

There is a group of French writers usually called the regulationist school. Aglietta and Lipietz are the best-known representatives. They try to explain the changes in the capitalist economy or social relations mainly by the interaction between the modes of regulation, which define the rules of the game in a given period of time in the capitalist economy, and regimes of accumulation, which are organised systematically by production, income distribution, product exchange and consumption (Dunford, 1990,pp.303-308; Painter,1991,pp.23-26).

For them, the process of capital accumulation is the main source of the evolutionary change in capitalism encompassing the crisis of the capitalist system, the resolution of this crisis and the transformation of the mode of production during the process. They see structural change, or the crisis of Fordism, as the collapse of one mode of regulation, mainly caused by its mismatch with a regime of accumulation, and the shift towards developing a different kind of regulation at the national and international level. In this theory, the changing social organization of production or the changing labour process is the core of the changing regime of accumulation (Harris,1988,p.33; Massey,1988, p.80).

They think the main impetus behind transition is the production function. Therefore they, especially Aglietta, assert that most problems which Fordism has encountered can be resolved by the introduction of a more developed production system. As a result, in their assertion, instead of Fordism, neo-Fordism is being introduced. Neo-Fordism, which is characterized by the use of automated machines in a total system of operating and organizing and by

14

the more centralized control of capital over the labour process, is the solution to the crisis of Fordism. One thing to be noted is that Aglietta, differently from other approaches, believes that job flexibility can be achieved through a strengthened deskilling rather than multi-skilling (Aglietta, 1979, p.126; Lash and Bagguley,1987,p.10).

Table 1.1 The comparison between Fordism and post-Fordism

	Fordism	Post-Fordism
Markets	mass consumption	fragmented 'niche' markets
Technology	dedicated	general
Production	assembly-line	batch
Workers	semi-skilled	multi-skilled
Management	Taylorist	hunam relations
Unions	general/industrial	absent/company unionism
Industrial relations	centralized	decentralized
Spatial pattern	decentralized	centralized

Taken from Bagguley (1989,p.5).

However, the argument of the regulationists, especially that of Aglietta, is attacked for over-generalizing the labour process, for its belief in restructuring by capital and for its neglect of the significance of gender, of the service sector and of the demand side in internationalized economies (Bagguley,1989,p.12; Dunford,1990,pp.316-317). Consequently, this approach is evaluated by some as an intermediary step from Fordism to post-Fordism or flexible specialization (Wood,1989,p.23).

Piore and Sabel's approach[12]

Piore and Sabel, concentrating their focus on the transition of the production system or the model of industrial development, argue that:

"... the present deterioration [since 1973] in economic performance results from the limits of the model of industrial development that is founded on

15

mass production..." (Piore and Sabel,1984,p.4).

According to them, the market and technological conditions appropriate for mass production have changed and disappeared. Therefore, they claim that managements should reflect diversified market demand and the flexibility of the new technology in designing their work organization (Wood,1989,pp.11-12).

They identify two alternative ways for companies to confront the present economic disruption. The one is through the extension of mass production, and the other is through the introduction of flexible specialization. The latter can be achieved by endless innovation based on flexible equipment, skilled workers and the escape from competitive circumstances available for those favouring innovation (Piore and Sabel,1984,pp.16-17). Furthermore, they argue that, whether firms move towards flexible specialization or stick to the existing mass production, is determined by the degree of mass production in their countries.

When compared with the regulationists' arguments, Piore and Sabel's view is different in its emphasis on the importance of market demand and of social struggles during the process of transition and on the appearance of small firms and industrial districts as the basis of flexible specialization (Bagguley,1989, p.13). However, this theory, together with that of Storper and Scott (1989), is criticized for the ambiguity of both the notion and the necessary level of flexible specialization, for over-confidence in the manipulation of demand and for over-concentration on new technology (Wood,1989,pp.14-19; Amin and Robins,1990,p.12). Moreover, its ignorance on the racial and gender aspect in labour relations and its over-simplification of society into mass production and flexible specialization is criticized (Bagguley,1989,pp.17-20; Best,1990, pp.9-10)[13].

Atkinson's approach

Atkinson believes that the goal of 'flexibility' can be achieved through managerial strategy or the 'flexible firm'. He argues that the 'flexible firm' can be feasible mainly through labour utilization and subcontracting. As to labour utilization, he acknowledges the duality in the labour market; i.e. a core and peripheral labour force. According to Atkinson, the core labour force is a group of workers who take the central part in the firm's activities with their high or multi-skill and permanent contracts. On the other hand, the peripheral labour force covers those who are mainly part-time, semi- or non-skilled workers and who are thought to be more vulnerable to organizational changes than the core workers.

Also Atkinson thinks that the flexibility of the firm is obtained through control of the numbers employed by utilizing part-time and female workers, etc. (numerical flexibility), through the adjustment and deployment of the skills of the firm's employees to meet the necessities from changing work conditions (functional flexibility), through the replacement of employment contracts by commercial contracts in using labour (distancing) and through the wage increases paid to enhance the productivity of the firm (pay flexibility) (Atkinson,1989,pp.1-6; Wood,1989,p.1).

Atkinson's approach is under criticism for its neglect of increased market volatility and increased competition, technological change and the reorganization of production, and the industrial atmosphere as factors influencing the introduction of flexibility plus the importance of gender relations in the dualistic labour market. Furthermore, the variability of 'core workers' and its over-reliance on the management's coordinated pursuit are pointed out as other weakness of this approach (Bagguley,1989,pp.22-25; Wood,1989,5-8).

Comment

The decline of systems constructed under Fordism and the emergence of post-Fordism have been declared by numbers of scholars as above. In general, they have attempted to herald the fundamental change in the basis on which the various ways of life are formed and maintained, mainly from mass production to flexible specialization. Due to their efforts, people have begun to recognize the change, so-called, from Fordism to post-Fordism. However, some questions arise from their arguments.

In particular, there is a question whether the changes occurring these days deserve to be called post-Fordism. This question is closely related to the development stages of capitalism. Most scholars mentioned above carry their arguments forward by dividing the development of capitalism into craft production before the early nineteenth century, mass production represented by Fordism during from the nineteenth century to the early 1960s and flexible production these days. The problem is that consensus on the actual advent of post-Fordism has not yet been reached.

There is still controversy as to whether flexible production can be an independent stage equivalent to craft production and mass production, and further as to whether it can replace the dominance of mass production or not. It is not entirely clear whether there is a sharp distinction between Fordist mass production and post-Fordist flexible production (Sayer,1989,p.671; Amin and Robins, 1990,p.13; Ettlinger,1990,p.69). Flexibility could be pursued even in Fordist mass production. In order to produce diversified final goods through flexible manufacturing, some parts of intermediate goods still need to be produced through standardized mass production. As Hirst and Zeitlin express this:

"... neither model [i.e. mass production or flexible specialization] could ever be wholly predominant in time or space. ...firms in most countries and periods deliberately mix elements of mass production and craft or flexible production because they are acutely aware of the dangers involved in choosing an unalloyed form of either model" (Hirst and Zeitlin,1991,p.6).

Therefore it could be interpreted that the present flexibility on which authors concentrate their research efforts is a kind of complementary management strategy, especially of MNCs, for the mass production system to fulfil the goal of maximization of profits by means of high-technology and of politics in the management-labour relationship (Nolan and O'Donnell, 1991,pp.114-123).

In other words, although there is an important shift towards a diversification in production and in the labour process, it is hard to call it decisively the transition of a technological paradigm towards a new post-Fordist flexible regime of accumulation. On the contrary, these changes could be interpreted as changes in the capacity of management in managing facilities and the labour force (Hudson,1988,pp.161-162). This means that more crucial and predominant features need to emerge and be configured in order to replace the mass production system by post-Fordism thoroughly. Moreover, these theorists are criticized for the fact that they take no account of the problems of labour market fragmentation and that, in treating flexibility, they ignore the differences between countries or 'the significance of the national state dimension' (Lash and Bagguley,1987,pp.29-30; Sadler,1992,p.252).

In short, the characteristics of flexible production and the flexible labour market have not really been manifested sufficiently yet to be considered a substitute for Fordism. Consequently, from this viewpoint, Lovering's remark below on the efforts of other scholars trying to support their arguments with practical evidence seems to be worth considering:

"Flexible specialization may be but one of several coexisting forms in which capital accumulation can take place.... The post-Fordist debate has not yet generated the new scientific paradigm which can give birth to a new spate of Kuhnian 'normal science'" (Lovering,1990,pp.169-171).

1.2.2.3 Perspectives on disorganized capitalism

As described before, the focus of the assertions about disorganized capitalism is concentrated on the changes which have appeared in every part of organized capitalism.

Briefly speaking, organized capitalism is characterized by concentration, magnification, regional industrial specialization, strengthening of the power of the nation state and collective forces, and the influence of management. In other words, organized capitalism means the capitalism which shows concentration of power in the hands of collective organizations including the state, trade unions, management and bureaucracies (Lash and Urry,1987, pp.3-4). Therefore, with the development of organized capitalism, capitalist society and economy tends to be dominated by a sort of 'logic of power', hence, for example, organization rather than individual, centralization rather than decentralization, homogenization rather than diversification. This organized capitalism, in the case of the US and UK, although there are some differences between countries, has continued or been strengthened until the mid-1960s, when 'disorganized capitalism' appeared (ibid,p.6).

As 'organized capitalism' is the term made to expound the whole system of capitalism involving politics, economy and society, 'disorganized capitalism' also can be traced by investigating capitalism as a whole, with special accentuation of the political, in particular the capital-labour relationship, and the economic features of capitalism. In Lash and Urry's perspective, disorganized capitalism is depicted as having the tendencies or inclinations opposed to the characteristics of organized capitalism. Therefore, the major characteristics of disorganized capitalism can be summarized as internationalization, decline of the size of most plants, decentralization of control and power, diversification of products, etc. In particular, the main features of disorganization in employment are the new flexibility of job tasks in work organization and the increased worker participation in management through, for instance, quality circles and in ownership through employee equity holdings (ibid,pp.5-7).

Lash and Bagguley, indicating the difference in the actors and patterns of disorganization of capitalism between countries, assert that the changes in British capitalism have been led by the state and that trade unions have been sluggish in terms of reacting to labour flexibility. According to them, the fragmented unions and manufacturing capital allowed the government, especially the Thatcher government, to play a crucial role in decentralizing and disorganizing British society as revealed in the anti-union legislation, the privatization of nationalized industries and the introduction of market rules into the policies of the welfare state (*ibid,*pp.24-26).

Explaining the British brand of disorganization, Martin summarizes the changes in the field of industry, employment, etc. by comparing the features between the periods before and after the mid-1970s as shown in Table 1.2.

Certainly, capitalism in these days has a lot of different features compared to the late nineteenth or early twentieth century or even in the post-war boom period. The whole change cannot be attributed to a particular factor or group of factors. It is plausible to say that the changes have resulted from the complicated interaction between the forces composing international politics and the economy.

In short, disorganized capitalism means the changed status of capitalism

Table 1.2 The comparison between organized and disorganized capitalism

Characteristics	Organized	Disorganized
[Accumulation regime]	[monopolistic]	[flexible]
Industry	monopolistic; increasing concentration of capital	rationalization andmodernization of established sectors
Employment	full employment	persistent mass unemployment
Consumption	rise and spread of mass consumption norms	differentiated consumption patterns
Production	economies of scale	economies of scope
[Socio-institutional structure]	[collectivistic]	[competitive-individualist]
Labour market	collectivistic	competitive
Social structure	organized mainly by occupation	increasingly hierarchical
Politics	aligned with occupation and labour; regionalist	de-alignment from socio-economic class ; localist
State intervention	Keynesian-liberal collectivist	free-market conservative
Space economy	convergent; narrowing regional disparities	divergent; widening regional disparities

Constructed from Martin (1988,p.213 and p.219).

which has experienced, and is experiencing, a series of fundamental restructurings which cause the shift from the systems of, and even the attitude of people in, organized capitalism towards flexibility, diversification and efficiency by the interaction of individual forces constructing capitalism at the national and international level. This shift of capitalism from the organized to the disorganized can be said to be the result of the combined activities of politics, the economy and society in capitalism pursuing the maximization of the production function by means of flexibility and diversity[14]. Here, the norm of flexibility plays another crucial role in announcing the significant changes in capitalism.

However, Hirst and Zeitlin criticize this approach on the ground that: 1) it uses the notion of flexible specialization as the product of exogenous forces instead of as the product of deliberate management strategy; 2) it emphasizes more the organization of national, macro-economic and intra-firm patterns rather than those of regional and inter-firm forms; 3) it takes no account of the importance of specific patterns of regional collaboration and regulation; and 4) overall, the approach ignores the role of flexible specialization in analyzing modern economies and their forms of governance (Hirst and Zeitlin, 1991, pp.13-14).

1.2.2.4 Other perspectives

Besides the perspectives mentioned above, there are some other research efforts trying to interpret the structural change occurring recently. Long-wave theory and world-systems theory are among these.

A group of writers attempt to explain the present structural change by referring to the Kondratiev's 50 year cycle of the capitalist economy and the Schumpeterian innovation theory (Marshall,1987; Hall,1988)[15]. From this standpoint, it can be said that the capitalist economy, which experienced slump in the late 1920s and the beginning of 1930s and found its way to recover and to reach the prosperity from the 1930s to the 1960s by the help of Keynesian theory, began to encounter another slump in the 1970s and 1980s: the slump phase of the fifth Kondratiev cycle (Dunford, 1990,p.298).

Scholars in this strand argue that, located in this slump phase, the capitalist economy can be returned to the boom phase by introducing a bunch of technological innovations (Hall quoted in Massey and Allen,1988,pp.83-85). Therefore, this theory focuses on the causes of technological change and technology's role in the wider system (Dunford,1990,p.299). The problem with this theory is that it leaves further questions such as how and why long waves appear and what are the relationships between international structure, innovation and the internationalization of industries (Harris,1988,p.29).

Then there is world-systems theory. A group of writers, Wallerstein is a representative among them, explain that structural change in an individual economy results from that of the world economic system. These days the growth of the available labour force in Third World countries, the division of the production process to the greatest level and the development of communications and transport facilities have caused the broadening of the market sphere and the intensification of the activities of multinational companies. These developments result in frequent movements of manufacturing

21

facilities and funds in order to pursue the maximization of profit. This level of increased movement causes structural change towards the core - semi-periphery -periphery configuration and, thus, recession in specific regions and eventually the expansion of instability at the world economy level. However, this theory is criticized for lack of sufficient explanation of the relationship between the national and the worldwide dimensions and of the nature, distribution and interrelationship of the labour process across the globe (Harris,1988,pp.30-31; Henderson,1989,pp.25-26).

So far, the structural change in the world economy has been explored theoretically. Briefly speaking, the development of technology and other socio-economic systems has broadened the boundary of capitalism in terms of time and space. During the process, there has been a series of up and downs in both the world and national economies mainly due to the unbalanced development of these technologies and systems. However, the change which we have experienced over the past two decades is the most dramatic one over all. As a result, every part of the world economy is said to be meeting some kind of crisis. This crisis of the world economy has been recognized by many authors and is, as discussed above, often called the emergence of post-Fordism or disorganized capitalism. However, it is hardly a simple task to describe the nature, and to predict the future direction, of this change. Therefore, there has come out a volume of arguments trying to expound this structural change as discussed here.

Confronting this drastic change in the national and international economies, individual governments have exerted their efforts at ameliorating the present bitterness and on preparing a sound condition for the coming years of stable prosperity. The supply side economic policy, which is contrasted with the Keynesian demand side policy and is being implemented in the UK and US, can be said to be one of the strategies introduced for this purpose.

1.2.3 The world economy in the 1990s

The drastic changes in the world economy, which happened during the last two and a half decades, and which have been discussed so far, resulted in a different facade in the economic relationship between countries. At the end of the 1980s, the structure of the international economy can be summarized as the tripolarization of world economic power comprising the US, Europe and Japan. This relationship was established mainly by the diminishing economic power of the US and the growing importance of Japanese capital and industry in the world economy achieved by the strong competitiveness of Japanese products in the world market.

At the same time, the structure of the world economy is characterized by the intensified international division of labour, the increased activities of MNCs and FDI, the shift of emphasis from manufacturing to the service sector resulting in the movement of jobs between industrial sectors and between regions and the growing importance of medium- and small-sized firms as a driving force towards innovation and flexible production (Julius,1990, p.16)[16].

In aggregate, the period of the late 1980s and onwards is showing and will show another series of drastic changes in the international economy such as: 1) the accelerated cross-border movement of capital and manufacturing either aiming at the unified market of Europe in 1992 or to circumvent protectionism[17]; 2) the severe competition between blocs and between countries; 3) the increased transformation of industry in individual countries by the adoption of the new management ideology named say, post-Fordism or flexible specialization to meet challenges in the international economy; and 4) the continued disorganisation of capitalism by the growing tendency of liberalization, diversification and decentralization of economic activities in both developed and developing countries.

The continued structural change in the 1990s as predicted above is rendered feasible by the rapidly developing information technology, on the one hand, and by the ever-increasing competition and interaction between countries in the world market, on the other. From a different point of view, which sees the upswings of the Kondratiev cycle as being generated by technological innovation and the technological development in the 1980s as making industry prosperous, the future period after 1990 is expected to see another dramatic upswing in the world economy (Freeman and Perez quoted in Hirst and Zeitlin,1991,p.15).

As a summary, the world economy, which previously had followed an ever-expanding way, has experienced fluctuations since the mid-1960s for various reasons and in various shapes. And the accelerating development of technology and the interaction between countries will continue to result in unceasing structural change in the national and international economies far into the 1990s. Now it is time to turn the focus of this research to the changing national and international geography in this worldwide restructuring.

1.3   National and International Geography in the Changing World Economy

The recent structural change in the world economy results in, or accompanies, a significant impact evident in a different geography for that impact in different countries and even in different regions. This implies that the spatial division of labour in the era of post-Fordism, or flexible accumulation, appears in different forms from that in the Fordist era (Oberhauser,1990, pp.212-218). Therefore, it is necessary to analyze geographical changes by reference to the transition in world capitalism.

The activities of MNCs and the increasing flow of FDI prompted the structural change in the world economy and thus in the economic geography at national and international level[14]. Here, the particular influence of the structural change in the world economy especially on the geography of technology, manufacturing and services are sorted out in turn.

1.3.1 The geography of technology

The recent structural change in the economy and the development of technology have influenced each other reciprocally. Since the early 1970s technology has leaped forward remarkably, based mainly on the development of knowledge in the field of electronics and computer science. On the other hand, the world economy has experienced a drastic structural change during this period. These simultaneous changes are enough to manifest that there exists a close relationship between the development of technology and structural change.

In particular, the development of information technology and that industry[15] has played a crucial role in the drastic change taking place in both national and international economies, and thus in the geography, of a nation or a region. This means that restructuring has proceeded in different ways in different regions or nations according to the particular level of technological development. For instance, in the US, the existence of information industries and researchers in the areas of California and Massachusetts adjacent to the leading military sector in the 1960s and, later, the clustering of those firms in Silicon Valley and around the Boston area following the commercialisation of this industry in the 1970s illustrate this situation (Castells,1989, pp.292-295).

Furthermore the growing competition and restructuring in the international market, in particular between Japanese and American producers, in the 1980s had different consequences for economic geography at the international and national level. At the international level, there appeared a new international division of labour (NIDL). Compared to the previous period, which was ruled by the simple division of function between countries, the world market which is related to information technology and industry these days is dominated by an intensification of labour market division showing the increase of professional and technical workers in certain areas with the unchanged number of semi- and under-skilled workers elsewhere. In other words, there appeared the development of the technical division of labour in the world (Henderson,1989,pp.33-34; Sadler,1992,p.5).

At the national level, the development of the new information technology industries, which require professional and technical labour forces in high-wage level jobs and the new kind of production facilities, inevitably resulted in green field sites for these industries far from the old urban areas (Nielsen,1991, p.44). The location of high technology industries in the Silicon Valley near Stanford University (US) and along the Cambridge-Reading-Bristol axis (UK) provides a good example (Castells,1989, pp.3-4; Storper and Scott,1989,p.28).

Such a locational pattern made the inner city problem of old, big cities deteriorate further. Overall, this geographical feature in technology is directly related to the regional and urban transformation and to the modification of the socio-economic system.

1.3.2 The geography of manufacturing

The worldwide structural change has had to do with the re-distribution of international and national manufacturing and its impact on the areas and people concerned. As Peet expresses it:

"The geography of production can be comprehended as a particular part of a general theory of modes of production ..." (Peet,1989,p.40).

This means that the changes in the world economy have influenced different regions at different levels especially in the field of manufacturing. With the development of technology and the growth of the activities of MNCs, regions which had enjoyed the wealth produced by traditional manufacturing began to encounter a difficult situation. The difficulty is characterized by the weakening competitiveness of the manufacturing in the international market, declining profit followed by the closure of plants or firms and the outward movement of people and firms to gain opportunities for new jobs and new circumstances for management. As a result, some regions became prosperous by attracting this increasing labour force and their jobs at the expense of a sudden downfall in the long established industrial regions or cities.

International economic forces, including the activities of MNCs in the world market and the growing FDI, accelerated and fortified this process. The economic forces running worldwide are more sensitive to the international and national changes and more prompt in locating in or dislocating from the critical nations and regions. The most eloquent examples in the UK are the decline of the North West and West Midlands following the diminishing competitiveness of the textile and motor vehicle industry based in these regions respectively and the prosperity of mid-Scotland and the South East created by the clustering of the semiconductor industry and productive services in these regions[16].

This procedure makes manifest the fact that the national and regional economy came under the direct influence of international economic forces, and thus of the restructuring of the international economy.

1.3.3 The geography of services

One of the most important features of the worldwide restructuring today is the growth of the service sector in most countries (see above 1.2.1.2). The growth of service industries and employment has significant implications for national economic geography.

In the case of the UK, as with other developed countries, the shift of the labour force from manufacturing to services is regarded as one of the main features of deindustrialization and restructuring (Fothergill et al.,1988,p.68). However, there has been a sharply uneven development of the service sector between regions in terms of employment and occupation. In particular, producer services which provide most service sector employment are found to be concentrated more in the South East region than in any other regions. While the south in the UK, involving the South East, South West and East Anglia, has been experiencing the growth of service jobs refilling the position of manufacturing, the remaining north and west regions have suffered from an insufficient increase of service jobs compared to their large decline of manufacturing (Allen,1988b,pp.122-125; Townroe and Martin,1988,p.9).

The impact of the uneven development of service industries is heightened by the fact that the new manufacturing industries tend also to be attracted to the areas where a sufficient level of high-quality service industries is found (Wood,1988,pp.94-95; Townroe and Martin,1988,pp.9-10). Allen explained this centralization of service industries near London and the Southeast region as 'a reworked north-south division', and the division of the labour market into high-status professional groups and low-paid casualized groups as a 'class polarization of the labour market' (Allen,1988a,pp.130-132).

In aggregate, the development of technology, the appearance and increase of new information industries at the expense of traditional manufacturing and the diversification and professionalization of service activities have played a significant role in the restructuring of world economic order. However, on the contrary, the procedure of worldwide restructuring has also influenced the geography of technology, manufacturing and services enormously.

One thing should be noted is that these spatial changes tend to aggravate regional problems rather than to improve the situation (Massey,1988,p.60). Industry, which has a propensity for searching for the best location where it can make the best profit, tends to utilize the existing uneven development and, thus, to create a new and deteriorated spatial division of labour. Now it is necessary to scrutinize the relationship between worldwide restructuring and the development of Japanese capital for the purpose of this study.

1.4 Japanese Capital in the Changing Context of the World Economy

Recently, with the growing power of the Japanese economy, the role of Japanese capital in the changing world economy and in the changing economic geography has attracted much attention in the world. In other words, it has come to be believed that the recent changes in the world economy have had a special relationship with Japan and Japanese industry. Therefore, the rest of this chapter examines the role of Japanese capital in the changing world economy.

1.4.1 The changing features of Japanese capital

Since about the time when the international economy experienced severe recession in the 1970s, the Japanese economy has been conceived as one of the most advanced and prosperous economies. However, the path through which the Japanese economy has developed is far from a stable one. There have been some fluctuations during the process summarized as follows:

1) Japan was no more than a closed feudalistic country before the opening of the nation to the outer world coercively by the black ships of Commodore Matthew C. Perry of the US and the Meiji Restoration in the mid-nineteenth century (Macpherson,1987,pp.25-27);

2) From the late nineteenth century to the early twentieth century Japan became a fully industrialized country and emerged as 'a new kind of colonial power'. Growing Japanese imperialism and expansionism inevitably brought about wars with other countries such as China and Russia and, eventually, with the US and Britain in World War II (Wilkinson,1983,pp.57-64; Nester,1990, p.47);

3) After the defeat in World War II, the Japanese government and people had to pour their every effort until the early 1950s into restoring their devastated economy. During the process US aid played a crucial role in the reconstruction of the Japanese economy (ibid,pp.48-54);

4) From the early 1950s, the Japanese economy began to show a steady and consistent growth. The Korean War, which broke out in 1950 and continued for three years, increased the demand for Japanese products and, consequently, boosted the Japanese economy back to the pre-war level by 1955[17]. In addition, the opening of the UK and US markets to the Japanese investment, which was begun with the commercial treaty between the UK and Japan in 1962 and the success of the Tokyo Olympics in 1964, ignited the dramatic development of the Japanese economy (Kunio,1986,pp.18-26);

5) In 1965, the Japanese economy met a kind of trigger-point. Between 1965 and 1973, every field of the economy exhibited dramatic growth, e.g. a 10.2% average annual rate of real GNP growth, a 2.2 times increase of real GNP and a change in the emphasis of industry from light engineering to heavy machinery. Furthermore, during this period, the Japanese economy was literally transformed into an internationalized

economy characterized by export-led expansion. This expansion of the Japanese economy was mainly due to a series of policy efforts by the Japanese government to stimulate the staggering economy after the Tokyo Olympics (Wakabayashi,1988,p.14)[18]

6) From 1973 to the mid-1980s the Japanese economy, similarly to the economies of other developed countries, suffered from the recessions following the two oil crises. However, the impact of these recessions was less substantial for the Japanese economy compared to others. After this tough period, Japanese industry became stronger in its efficiency and competitiveness rather than weaker. This, however, led to more severe trade conflicts between Japan and other developed countries (ibid,pp.18-24). In short, in the 1980s and since, the Japanese economy not only has dominated but also has been influenced, or has complied with, the worldwide structural changes. Furthermore, the attack from the US and Europe on the Japanese closed market and business culture prophesy a further restructuring in the Japanese economy.

In aggregate, Japan emerged as one of the great powers in the world economy within a short period of time from the disaster of the Second World War. In relation to the development of the Japanese economy, two issues need to be clarified. One is the main factors of that economic development and the other is the inclination to internationalization of Japanese capital.

Main factors of Japanese economic development

A number of factors have been listed by researchers as the major forces which brought about the economic success of Japan after the 1950s. The factors listed most frequently are the successful economic policy of the Japanese government, the unique style of management, a wider dissemination of flexible manufacturing strategies compared to other countries and advantageous circumstances in the world economy[19].

Among these factors, the main actor in the economic success of Japan has been controversial. Some authors accentuate the crucial role of the Japanese government in the economic development of Japan, while others emphasize the superiority of Japanese management. Indeed, the influence of the government or bureaucracy on Japanese society seems to be even more crucial than imagined. Without the strong influence of the government in the economy, the kind of unified and coordinated behaviour of Japanese enterprises in absorbing the impact of the high rise of the yen and in implementing the effective restructuring of its industry would be improbable. Therefore, these authors label the development of the Japanese economy as a government-led development[20].

Here, a question arises about whether the term 'government' comprises both politics and bureaucracy, or bureaucracy only. For long, the role played by the bureaucrats, especially those of Ministry of International Trade and Industry (MITI), has been recognized as substantial. By contrast, the influence of the Japanese politics, which have been marked by instability and corruption, is far from unambiguous, and even thought by some to be an obstacle to the development of the Japanese economy. However, the role played by Japanese politicians should not be under-estimated compared to that of the bureaucrats. In fact, the leadership of politicians, large numbers of whom came from the bureaucracy, has determined the direction of Japanese economic policy and provided a continuous driving force in spite of the fluctuations within the political arena. In other words, the 'conservative policy line (hoshu honryu)' of the ruling Liberal Democratic Party, which has the characteristic of close interdependence between politics and big business, has played a crucial role in the remarkable achievements of the Japanese economy. Therefore, it seems proper that 'government' as the term used here comprises both the politics and bureaucracy of Japan (Muramatsu and Krauss,1987,pp.516-554).

On the other hand, a group of writers, criticizing the above argument of a strong government role, assert that the development of the Japanese economy during this period is the product of managerial strategies or market forces, or the political ability of firms to acquire supportive rules or resources in the given circumstances. Porter claims that:

"Japan is an economy driven by firms, not government. ... Aggressive domestic rivalry, demanding buyers, cooperative suppliers and rapid upgrading of factors of production are the more decisive advantages" (Porter,1990,p.420).

In short, they argue, market forces or the political astuteness of firms account for most of the exceptional achievement of the Japanese economy rather than government policy[21].

In aggregate, it seems to be most plausible to conclude that the Japanese economic success in this period is the product of the efforts of Japanese government and industry including financial institutions, largely guided by the government, to coordinate their activities most swiftly and flexibly in order to exploit, in their own and the national interest, the given circumstances in the international economic structure to the greatest extent[22]. Therefore, it seems most appropriate to expound that:

"Japanese economic success is based upon an institutional complex of large firms ... vertical tiers of ever smaller firms, and industrial policy agencies of the central government" (Best,1990,p.25).

The inclination to the internationalization of Japanese capital

As demonstrated above, the Japanese economy has developed steadily, although it has experienced some frustrations and bitterness. In this developing process, the Japanese economy or, more specifically, Japanese capital has changed its characteristics in accordance with changes in domestic and international circumstances.

Broadly speaking, Japanese capital has shown a strong inclination towards internationalization and outward movement. This is not new. For centuries before the 1970s, the inclination leading to actual outward movement of Japanese capital had arisen from the internal forces that comprise domestic politics (e.g. local-based politicians, radical rightists, etc.) and the economy and their complicated power relationship. The Japanese colonization of Korea in 1910 and the involvement in the Pacific War in the late 1930s were examples representative of this process[23].

Since the 1970s Japanese capital has shown a positive outward surge to develop overseas markets. The outward movement of Japanese capital and industry in the forms of MNCs and FDI has intensified remarkably, especially since the mid-1980s. However, this time, the impetus behind the movement is not the domestic context of politics and the economy but international economic circumstances. The friction over the Japanese trade surplus, the mounting pressures from foreign countries demanding that Japan open its economy and liberalize its financial system and the movements of other developed countries towards regional trade blocs all promoted the internationalization of Japanese capital[24]. At the same time, the structure of the Japanese economy experienced, and is still experiencing, a drastic restructuring procedure (Ogata,1989,p.3). Social attitudes have also been transformed. As a result, the manufacturing plants using a low level of technology have been sent out of Japan to developing countries and the industries based on higher technology and R&D activities have taken over the central place in the Japanese economy.

In short, the internationalization of Japanese capital and the restructuring of Japanese industry since the 1970s, in contrast to previous years, are characterized by the strong influence of international market forces. An important point is that Japanese capital has proved able to respond swiftly and effectively to the changing circumstances of the world economy. However, this does not mean that Japanese capital has always been simply a reactor to international market forces. Conversely, Japanese capital has begun to act as one of the main actors in the changing structure of the worldwide economy especially in the recent internationalization of that economy.

1.4.2 Japanese capital : A main factor of structural change

As described in the previous section, the world economy has experienced a series of changes building up into one overall structural change. With regard to the causes of this structural change, the role of Japanese capital and industry has attracted the attention of people worldwide. The main issue is how far Japanese capital has played a crucial role in provoking the restructuring of the world economy.

The influence of Japanese capital on the world economy can be identified by tracing two contrasting aspects. The one is the quantitative influence that Japanese capital exerts on the numeric volume of the world economy, such as manufacturing capacity, trade volume or surplus, and foreign exchange rates. The other influence is the qualitative one. This qualitative influence is related to the behaviour and ideas of management, labour and government. With the continuing strength of Japanese capital and industry, people began to concentrate their attention more on the qualitative influence, in particular on the nature and advantages of Japanese style management and management-labour relationships. Recently, many firms in other developed countries are greatly attracted by the advantages of Japanese style management and are eager to learn the core of Japanese management and its relations with its workforce.

The main characteristics of the Japanese style of management and of management-labour relationships are represented by the terms 'flexibility' and 'pursuit of perfection'. The characteristics of Japanese style management involved, first, the 'kanban'(just-in-time) system or zero-inventory; second, consensus management involving 'bottom-up' and group-centred decision-making processes (quality circles); third, total quality management or zero-defect and, finally, endless product variety (economy of scope). Most of these are closely related to the increase in, particularly, the flexibility and perfection of the system (Wakabayashi,1988,p.53; Womack et al.,1990,p.3; *Financial Times*, 9 Mar. 1992)[25]. As Tomaney claims;

> "Increased labour flexibility across tasks and flexibility over time lie at the heart of Japanese work methods. Flexibility agreements and single union deals can be seen as central to their success" (Tomaney,1991,p.13).

As the economic power of the Japanese economy has strengthened over the last two decades, this Japanese style management, pursuing maximum flexibility and perfection, became a catalyst in the debate on 'post-Fordism' and 'disorganized capitalism'.

This means that the ever-strengthening Japanese capital and industry have played a major role in the structural change in the world economy from Fordist mass production to post-Fordist flexible production. Indeed, the western economy is now facing an urgent need to make the greatest effort to achieve

31

style management.

Thus, overall, it seems certain that Japanese capital has been one of the major factors effecting structural change in the world economy since the 1970s by means both of its ever-growing numerical magnitude and of the singularity in its nature.

1.4.3   Japanese capital and an inflexible blockage

Certainly, Japanese capital has begun to be recognized as one of the main factors which determine the direction and nature of structural change in the world economy. However, an important problem is that there still remain some issues to be resolved before Japanese capital can become a full leading force in world capitalism. More specifically, a number of blockages or impediments are waiting for relaxation before flexible Japanese capital can become the model for capitalism worldwide. These blockages can be divided into two; internal and external blockages.

Internal blockages for flexible Japanese capital come from Japanese society and from Japanese capital itself. The lack of basic science, the irrational customs of Japanese society resisting the access of foreign people and industry, the immature strategy in overseas markets, etc. are indicated to be the main blockages within Japan (*Financial Times*, 2 Jan. 1991 and 4 Jun. 1991). Moreover, the lack of semi-skilled labour at a reasonable wage level and soaring land prices have placed serious restraints on the flexibility of Japanese capital and have made it move offshore (Munday,1990,p.12).

However, the most substantial internal blockage may be the fact that Japanese style management cannot, by its nature, be easily accessible to foreign capital. In other words, the strength of the Japanese style management and management-labour relationships should not be explored solely in terms of managerial rationality or efficiency. Although the techniques and methods of Japanese management can be imitated, the flexibility and accuracy of Japanese enterprises seem in practice to be difficult to achieve to the same extent in other countries.

This must mean that, besides the technological and managerial advantages and the effectiveness of Japanese industrial policy, there exists in the background a cultural aspect to the strength of Japanese enterprises. Overtime working, the requirement of labour to be multi-skilled, the priority given to group objectives or collective goals, the quasi-legalised power of government administrative guidance, mainly that of MITI, the close government-management relationship, etc. cannot be easily replicated in other countries. Therefore, the clue to the strength of Japanese management and enterprise should be found in the national traits which Japanese people possess by inheritance (Nester,1990,p.235; Best,1990,pp.144-146)[26].

32

"The loyalty to organization or the group-centred pattern of value orientation of the Japanese is invariably alluded to when describing Japanese-style management" (Kumazawa and Yamada,1989,p.107).

"These singularities have not only stimulated much sociological debate but have also queried the relevance of the Japanese experience as a model for less developed countries (LDCs) and the viability of importing Japanese labour practices to British and American car plants" (Macpherson, 1987,p.12).

With respect to industrial policy, also, the key to the successful industrial policy lies in the systemic factors of Japanese society, or political economy, rather than in the distinctiveness of the policy measures. As Okimoto expounds:

"In Japan's case, the relative efficacy of the policy instruments used for the promotion of high technology has depended on the distinctive nature and structure of Japan's political economy" (Okimoto,1989,p.11).

In short, the nature of Japanese capital and of the economy shows a dualistic structure, i.e the highly flexible management strategy at the micro-level and the highly organized and rigid socio-economic system at the macro-level which enables the former to be probable. Moreover, this highly flexible management strategy operates in practice in several manufacturing sectors only in the whole economy. In this regard, the management and industrial policy in other countries cannot, and should not, follow the Japanese style management without taking account of the Japanese 'internal context' and the prerequisites of that country's system and culture and without modifying the management and policy concepts to accommodate to their own national cultures (Juergens, 1989,p.205; Okimoto,1989,pp.237-238; Sayer,1989,p.691; James, 1989,p.126; Lever-Tracy,1990,p.194; Sadler,1992,p.169) or, in theory at least, modifying the latter to accept and fit the Japanese model.

On the other hand, the main external blockage comes from the conflicts between Japan and other countries surrounding Japan's trade, FDI and MNC activities. Various trade barriers of other developed countries led by the US, the movement of groups of countries (and their markets) towards regional blocks, the unilateral demand for Japan to lessen its trade surplus without being able to indicate specific problems hampering free trade into Japan, etc. form the main elements in the external blockage for flexible Japanese capital (Womack et al.,1990).

In aggregate, therefore, there are many problems for the world economy before it can be fully restructured by means of flexibility. Although Japanese capital has come nearest to this objective, a number of blockages produced by both internal and external forces are preventing even Japanese capital from playing a full leading role in the world economy.

1.4.4   Future perspective

The structural change in the world economy which began in the mid-1960s is continuing in the late 1980s and early 1990s. Although recently the world economy is showing a kind of growth as if it is going to follow the Kondratiev's cycle, the restructuring of the world economy in relation to the adoption of flexibility is unlikely to be completed quickly.

The management style of the major developed countries has not changed significantly and flexible management is still in the introductory stage. It cannot be valid for countries to criticise the trade surplus of Japan without making sincere efforts to change their own structure and behaviour (Friedman,1988,pp.220-223; James,1989,p.39; *Financial Times*, 10 Jun. 1991). As Maswood claims:

> "Instead of adjusting to global structural changes, much energy [of the US] was devoted to fighting the current of change through protection ..." (Maswood,1989,p.206).

Japanese capital is also likely to fail to provide the world economy with a new model of capitalist production or a reference point for behaviour in capitalism. Japanese style management is still largely dependent on the unique tradition and nature of Japanese society including submission to group regulation, obedience to seniors and abandonment of private life for the sake of the prosperity of the organization. Indeed the interesting question is whether the inevitable 'modernization' or 'westernization' of Japanese society will not destroy the Japanese miracle from within. Japanese youth are already challenging these key tenets of their industrial society (Best,1990,p.160; *Financial Times*, 13 May 1992).

Thus, after all, the norm of Japanese style management has failed to separate thoroughly itself from Fordist mass production (Sayer, 1989,pp.681-690; Sadler,1992,pp.21-23). Often it has been devalued as a sort of Fordist mass production, motivating employees fully with the stimulus of merit, responsibility and social regulation. For instance:

> "The loyalty to the company is neither spontaneous nor absolute. It is a hierarchical segmentation of the nation's working population which generates the dependence the privileged minority have on the company" (Kumazawa and Yamada,1989,p.107).

> " ... it is widely accepted that the success of Japanese production methods

34

are based, in their essence, on an intensive exploitation of labour, which has been described as a sophisticated form of Taylorism. ... these practices translate into a production system which requires a highly intensive rate of effort on the part of workers, with little or no collective defence against speed-up or rationalization measures" (Tomaney,1991,pp.11-14)[27].

"Toyotism is simply the practice of the organisational principles of Fordism under conditions in which management prerogatives are largely unlimited" (Dohse et al. quoted in Lever-Tracy,1990,p.182).

As Hudson concludes, Japanese style management may not mean a transition from Fordism but a corporate strategy to maintain Fordist mass production (Hudson,1988,p.152).

Capitalism has continued, and will continue, to develop in the direction of diversification and flexibility as Lash and Urry analyzed. However, so far, it seems that in this process all the countries, including Japan and the US, have failed to fully adopt the new norm, or new mode of regulation, in their economy and society. In particular, in order to become a worldwide regulation of management and management-labour relationships, Japanese style management needs to be supplemented by several important aspects including the changes in the participation of labour in the production process from nominal to real terms and the promotion of group autonomy from the central control of organization. The present repressive control of capital over labour needs to be transformed into a more democratic form to be transferable to other countries (Juergens,1989,p.216)[28]. In addition, basically, Japanese society, where Japanese style management is formed, should modify its conservative behaviour and become more tolerant to, and coordinated with, other peoples and countries (Ogata, 1989,p.14). The escape from the 'sense of international vulnerability' or 'sense of isolation', which is not compatible with the magnitude or influence of its economy in the world economy, seems to be the most imperative agenda for the Japanese management, government and people (Okimoto,1989,pp.32-33).

Owing to the decline of the key role of the US and the immaturity of Japan to substitute for the US, the present world economy seems likely to continue unstable. Moreover, if Japan, based on its strength in the sphere of the international economy, appears as another superpower in international politics and military security, the world order will ultimately encounter a different kind of instability. This fact provides a dilemma for the leading developed countries, especially the US, seeking a prompt settlement of the present instability in the world order (Maswood,1989,p.196)[29]. In these regards, another substantial period of time will be necessary to reach the real 'disorganized capitalism' or 'post-Fordist' era.

Based on the discussion so far, the next chapter examines the FDI flows and MNC activities which have been the main driving forces of structural change in the international economy over the last two decades. This explanation focuses especially on the situation in three countries, the UK, Korea and Japan.

2 The nature and influence of multinational companies

The previous chapter delineated the nature and causes of the structural change in the world economy and the role of Japanese capital during the process. Based on the above discussion, this chapter examines the nature of the MNC and FDI, the main strategies of the MNC and their effects, and the positions of the UK, Korea and Japan respectively in MNC activities and, in particular, their FDI flows.

2.1 The Nature of the Multinational Company and Foreign Direct Investment

2.1.1 Definitions

It is by no means an easy task to define the nature of MNCs and their FDI in brief words, since these firms contain very broad and diversified features. One writer listed a number of features of MNCs and their activities from the perspective of a political economist as follows:

"[MNCs] 1) ... are large; 2) ... tend to be found in more concentrated or oligopolistic industries; 3) ... are mostly rather national in terms of ownership and still more in terms of control; 4) ... are subject to highly centralized strategic decision-making through complex management structures and information systems; 5) ... are supported by a growing internationalisation of banks and of service companies of all kinds; 6) ...[are showing a shift] from portfolio to a direct form of foreign investment flow; 7) ... increasingly internalize flows of goods and money; and 8) ... clash with economic and other goals of states and classes" (Radice,1975,p.11).

In general, as discussed in chapter one, MNC activity is understood through the process of, and in close relationship with, FDI. Accordingly, it is considered that the growth of MNCs is part of a broader process of internationalisation of capital which, usually, operates to bring about a more integrated world economy (Jenkins,1987,p.34).

Basically, a MNC is a type of business form which operates in more than two countries. Most briefly, and rather broadly, it is defined as:

" ... a firm which owns and controls income-generating assets in more than one country" (Clegg,1987,p.3).

Thielemans adds a nationalistic element in his definition of a MNC by saying that:

" [A MNC is] one in which all operations with foreign countries - as regards both structure and policy - are on the same footing as domestic operations, and the management is prepared to use the available resources for the company's purposes, without thereby paying attention to national borders. Ownership and central management are in the hands of persons from the country of origin of the multinational company; its decisions are therefore nationally inspired" (Thielemans,1974,p.15).

On the other hand, FDI refers to a financial flow abroad in the management process, especially in that of the MNC. Parry regards FDI as a particular kind of response by MNCs to imperfect markets (Parry,1980,p.15). *British Business*, citing the definitions of the International Monetary Fund (IMF) and the Organization for Economic Co-operation and Development (OECD), defines FDI as:

" ... investment that adds to, deducts from, or acquires a lasting interest in an enterprise operating in an economy other than that of the investor, the investor's purpose being to have an effective voice in the management of the enterprise" (*British Business*, 6 Jun. 1986,p.464).

Configurating these definitions, we find that the concepts of the MNC and FDI respectively represent a static business identity and its dynamic activity, especially in terms of financial flows.

Nowadays, FDI is central to the activities of the MNC. Of course the impact of MNC activities both on the world and individual economies cannot be solely accounted for by FDI flows, since there are various other forms of MNC activities including exporting, licensing management contracts, turnkey contracts, portfolio investment and so on (Santiago,1987,p.318; United Nations [UN], 1988,p.74). However, unlike other types of activities, FDI is the capital involvement form which most directly influences the foreign economy in its employment, production and income. It introduces foreign technology and management style as well as foreign capital (see 2.2.3). FDI in general is implemented in two distinctive forms; the one is the establishment of a new venture and the other is the acquisition of an existing firm. Compared to the latter, the former tends to provide more employment and production potential to the host nation.

The motives which lead the MNC to invest overseas are various. Brech and Sharp list a group of specific motives as follows:

" ... to reduce production costs by using cheaper foreign inputs; to eliminate foreign competitors through take-over; to supply a market that is closed to imports through trade restrictions; to avoid 'distance' factors associated with exporting from the home country...; or to reduce transaction costs between interdependent activities located in different countries" (Brech and Sharp,1984,pp.27-29).

On the other hand, Flaherty and Raubitschek argue that MNCs aim to improve their competitiveness, or to increase the preference of local consumers for their products, through the establishment of foreign manufacturing configurations (Flaherty and Raubitschek, 1990,pp.301-308).

In short, the FDI activity of the MNC can be said to be a form of direct involvement of capital in a foreign economy aiming to utilise the investment as a platform for achieving the ultimate goal of profit maximization across the whole world. However, regarding the nature of MNC activities, or the causes of FDI, the views of scholars have been diverse. There have appeared large numbers of theories from different viewpoints. At the end of this section, these theories about MNCs are examined and the standpoint of this study is clarified. Before that, the historical and spatial context of MNC activities is portrayed briefly.

2.1.2 Historical and spatial context

Since the beginning of the twentieth century, the activities of MNCs have attracted the attention of people in many advanced countries. Although these MNCs can be said to involve a changed form of the international trading companies that developed in the mercantilist period in the eighteenth century, MNCs in this century have taken a great leap forward both in the boundaries of their activity and in the nature of their management[1].

Moreover, the large and multinationalized corporations which have appeared in more hierarchically structured form with global headquarters[2] in this century have begun to dominate and influence the everyday life of people more directly than ever did the social class and hierarchy which dominated in the mercantilist period (Hymer,1972,pp.115-117). This means that the MNC has appeared as one of the most influential forces which have essentially determined the nature and boundary of people's lives in the recent world. The evolution of MNCs in the twentieth century can be divided into the following four stages:

1) before the First World War, production and trade became concentrated in the hand of a small number of European MNCs culminating in the outbreak of the First World War;
2) from 1914 to 1954, the scope of MNCs in the world economy declined markedly mainly because of the two World Wars, the nationalization of economic activities in the socialist countries and the trend of decolonization in the Third World;
3) from 1954 to the mid-1970s, the activities of MNCs, in particular those that were US-based and in the field of manufacturing, have grown remarkably in line with the growth of world trade;
4) in the 1980s and 1990s, despite the worsened economic environment, the importance of MNC activity is continuing to grow with the constellation of MNC affiliates originating from various countries (Hamilton, 1985, pp.3-4; Dicken,1992,pp.51-54)[3].

In particular, the 1970s saw the beginning of, or transition to, a much wider development of MNCs. MNCs expanded their range of activities both geographically and conceptually showing the 'inter-penetration of national markets'. The development of computers, telecommunications and management science has enabled them to diversify their activities and to concentrate their controls over subsidiaries and affiliates. Also, in addition to the trade in products in the form of exports and imports, MNCs have come to recognize the importance of fiscal or monetary flows in undertaking their global strategies. These forces have brought about the increased movement of capital all over the world (Taylor and Thrift,1982,pp.1-2; Dunning,1988b,pp.88-90).

On the other hand, in the 1970s, with the decline of the power of US in the world economy, the political aspect of MNC activity in the form of FDI came to the fore as a matter of public interest (Nye,1983,pp.13-16; Heininger,1986,pp.351-362). MNC activities or FDIs which were not harmonized with government foreign policy, and questions about the morality of MNCs operating in developing countries attracted more attention, especially in the US, than the managerial aspects of MNC activities such as exporting, profitability, cost effectiveness, and so on. Although this interest declined in the 1980s[4], the political aspect of MNC activity still remains as an important factor in assessing the overall performance of MNCs.

The spatial distribution of FDI indicates that there has been major shifts since the late 1970s.

Firstly, with the growth of European- and Japanese-owned MNCs, the dominance of US-owned MNCs in the total has declined. At the same time, instead of EC countries and Canada, the US has emerged as the most important host country of FDI. The US's share of total world inward investment in developed countries increased from 14.7% in 1960 to 44.0% in 1979 falling to 38.9% in 1985[5]. This shift has been concurrent with the decline of its share of total world outward investment, from 71.7% to 51.7% in the period of 1960 to 1979 and further to 25.4% in 1985 (UN,1983,p.34 and 1988, pp.76-77; O'hUallachain, 1985,p.152).

Secondly, there has been a remarkable growth of Japanese FDI since the mid-1970s. By March 1991, Japan's direct investment overseas totalled $ 352.4 bn. (*JEI Report*, 19 Jun. 1992). Literally, Japan became the second largest source country for FDI after the US. In 1978, the FDI stock of the US and that of Japan were $ 168.1 bn. and $ 26.8 bn. each and these expanded to $ 250.7 bn. and $ 83.6 bn. in 1985 (UN,1983 and 1988). With the rapid growth of Japanese FDI in recent years, this gap is predicted to have narrowed to only a slight margin. Also, considering its continuing trade surplus and its growing trade conflict with other developed countries, Japan's share in FDI is expected to continue to grow substantially for the time being. The decline of US-owned MNCs and the upsurge of Japanese-owned ones has brought about a situation of 'interpenetration' of capitals in line with the changing features of the world capitalism as mentioned in chapter two. Recently, there is a tendency to analyze the relationship between the capitals of US, Europe and Japan using the concept of 'triad power' (Ohmae,1985; Rugman and Verbeke,1990).

And, thirdly, in recent years (up to the breakdown in eastern Europe at least), there has been a decline of outward investment by MNCs placed in the newly industrializing countries (NICs) and in the socialist countries, where such investment peaked in the early 1980s. Although, the MNCs from NICs have played an important role in sourcing the international capital flow with their rapid growth of economic power, their activities have not been able to match those from developed countries. On the other hand, the proportion of total inward FDI locating in developing countries decreased from two thirds in 1914 to below one fourth of total capital flow in the 1980s, specifically 25% in 1980-1985 and 17% in 1986-1990 (Hamilton,1985,p.7; UN,1988, pp.24-25; *Financial Times*, 15 Jul. 1992). These facts mean the traditional pattern of FDI flow, from developed countries to developing or less developed countries, has been changed into a more diversified pattern of capital flow between countries including developed ones[6].

2.1.3 Theories about the MNC[7]

Theories about the nature of MNCs and their activities have come from various standpoints and interests. Historically, the focus of theorists has been transferred from resource-based and macro-economic ones to company-specific factors and internal operations (Hutton,1988,p.25; Bartlett et al.,1990,p.5). Broadly speaking, the views on MNCs can be divided into two groups; the one group includes those explaining the positive aspects of MNC activities in the global economy and the other group are those criticizing the problems produced by MNCs. While classical economic theories, orthodox models of MNCs such as those produced by Vernon and Dunning, internalisation theory, etc. are included in the former group, political economists and radicals writing on MNCs are placed amongst the latter group of views (Radice,1975,pp.12-13; Jenkins,1987,pp.17-32).

Here the major theories on MNCs which have contributed to identifying the nature of MNCs are examined in turn: namely, the classical theory of international capital flows; location theory; market imperfection theory; internalization theory; the eclectic paradigm; and the political economy view[8].

2.1.3.1 The classical theory of international capital flows

Writers from the classical viewpoint such as Floyd (1969) and Branson (1970) have thought that overseas investment is determined by two forces, the marginal rate of return on capital and the rate of interest. They explain broad investment without taking into account any differentials between investment forms. They also assume a perfect market. According to this theory, the flow of private capital, driven by interest rates and rate of return differentials, has effects on income and welfare not only in the home and host countries but also in all the countries around the world (Dunning,1973,p.299). However, it became apparent that there are other factors. In particular, this approach cannot explain the newly emerged pattern of capital flows since the 1970s, which is characterised by the overseas investment flows between developed countries rather than or as well as from developed to developing countries (Root,1990, p.620; Cantwell,1991,p.20). Therefore, since the early 1960s, a number of theories and empirical studies have been presented to investigate further the determinants of foreign investment.

2.1.3.2 Locational theory and international investment

Some authors, mainly geographers including A. Lösch and A. Weber, have made an effort to expand location theory to cover the international aspect. This theory emphasizes country-specific characteristics including geographical factors and market demand (Santiago,1987,p.318). For these writers, the supply and demand forces of an industrial location are thought to be applicable to the spatial distribution of investment across national boundaries (Dunning,1973, p.308). On the other hand, an effort has been made to combine location theory and market failure, in particular by Buckley and Casson (1976), taking account of proprietary knowledge.

However, two main problems are left unsolved by this theory. The first is that the theory assumes that there is no significant difference between foreign investment and domestic investment in the process of locating plants. This has been questioned in that there are many restrictions and cultural complications in investing in other countries. The second is that, although this location theory examines the motive behind investment as a push factor for a company, the purpose and process of specifically overseas investment by a firm basically remains untackled (Dunning,1979a,pp.272-273).

In short, this theory can be said in effect to explain the activities of MNCs by location-specific forces rather than by the internal motives of MNC. Although criticized mainly for the above reason, this approach has some implications for the studies which try to relate MNC activities and location-specific characteristics like the present study.

2.1.3.3 Market imperfection theory

Gradually, for one group of theorists such as Caves (1971), Williamson (1975) and Magee (1977), the imperfection of the market has been recognized as the main cause of the overseas direct investment of a firm. This market imperfection has been considered and examined in various ways. Among these, trade barriers, restrictions on factor movement, unfixed rent of knowledge and oligopolistic industrial structures comprise the main parts of the theory.

Firstly, it is thought that MNCs, confronted with trade barriers either of national policy or of natural restriction, respond with direct investment either defensively in the existing market or positively in the new market (Horst,1971,pp.1065-1068). Trade barriers, such as tariffs and trading blocs, are conceived of as one of the main factors which impede the access of foreign firms to a market and eventually generate investment decisions of MNCs to open plants in the market.

Secondly, restrictions on the movement of factors have been taken as one of the main determinants of international investment. In particular, an impediment blocking the financial returns of a firm such as host government policy, including tariffs and exchange controls, has been considered to be central in deciding on overseas investment (Dunning,1973,pp.329-330).

Thirdly, the issues surrounding the transfer of knowledge and its rent have been conceived of as being another important force which leads to MNC overseas investment. The product life cycle (PLC) model of Vernon (1966) and others, which has provided a forceful theoretical basis for international investment, is largely concerned with this problem[9].

And, fourthly, some authors such as Caves (1971) and Hymer (1972, 1976), look for the theoretical clue in the imperfect competition derived from the very nature of an effective industrial organization. They assert that it is the possession by a firm of a unique asset involving know-how, scale economies, etc., which was produced by a certain market structure, that leads the firm to invest directly in overseas markets (Parry,1980,p.29; Dunning, 1989,p.59).

2.1.3.4 Internalization theory

Internalization theory postulates that the MNC is:

" ... an organization which uses its internal market to produce and distribute products in an efficient manner in situations where a regular market fails to operate" (Rugman, 1982,p.11).

Because of the imperfection of a range of markets such as the financial market, the raw material market, etc., MNCs try to internalize various functions using their own subsidiaries rather than depending on the existing market processes. Internalization theory consists of a number of elements such as industrial organization, international market structure, and so forth. Accordingly, assertions in this theory vary in their focus of explanation.

One group of writers led by Buckley and Casson (1981), Kay (1983) and Hennart (1989), and originally Coase (1937), who form the main stream of internalisation theory, emphasizes the minimisation of transaction cost through the internalisation of markets. They assert that the low transaction cost of administered exchange compared to those made in a market produce the internalisation of markets and, thus, the internationalisation of production of firms (Cantwell, 1991,p.23; Hennart,1991,p.83).

A different group of writers, including Magee and Young (1983), stresses the importance of the knowledge factor in explaining internalization. In other words, the market imperfection in measuring and capitalizing on know-how, which is normally developed by investing a large amount in R&D, makes the firm protect its proprietary knowledge by means of internalization of the generation and use of that R&D within the firm.

On the other hand, a third group of writers attempts to explain overseas investment in terms of the effort of firms to win in the international competition and, thus, to increase their market share. The new version of Vernon's production cycle model (1974) and the technological accumulation approach by Pavitt (1987), Cantwell (1991), etc. are involved in this category[10]. The main feature of this approach is the emphasis on the competitiveness of firms in the international market mobilizing either trade barriers or ownership advantages which are mainly produced by technological accumulation.

All these approaches, although each emphasizes different aspects of MNC activities, are closely associated with each other and construct a sequence in the internalisation process as a whole. In this regard, the expression of

Horaguchi and Toyne seems to expound the nature of MNC activities, or FDI, more accurately, configurating all these arguments:

" ... just as general price theory needs the concept of supply and demand, the general theory of FDI needs the concept of managerial resources [administrative, technological, marketing, organizational know-how, etc.] and transaction costs" (Horaguchi and Toyne,1990,p.492).

2.1.3.5 The eclectic paradigm

As a kind of offshoot of internalization theory, amongst another set of writers, there is an effort to integrate a number of factors determining the overseas investment of the MNC into a single theoretical framework. The eclectic theory, and later the eclectic paradigm[11], presented by Dunning (1977,1979a, 1988) is the most prominent one. The main contents of this theory can be summarized as that the FDI activities of an enterprise are normally determined by three conditions; these are ownership advantages, the feasibility of internalization and location advantages[12].

First of all, in order to invest overseas, the company is required to possess competitive advantages or productivity assets which make the enterprise stand out from others (ownership-specific advantages). Secondly, it is necessary that producing or servicing the above assets by the company itself and its subsidiaries is more advantageous than licensing or selling them to others (internalisation of market). Thirdly, the condition that producing or servicing in the foreign country is much more profitable than doing it in the home country or by export has also to be fulfilled (location-specific advantages).

The configuration of these factors determines the propensity of a country (as an accumulation of companies) to engage in outward and inward investment. In other words, the propensity of a country to engage in overseas activities can be different from that of other countries at the same stage in their development paths according to the different configuration of the three factors (Dunning,1991,p.130). Empirical studies such as those of Dunning (1979b) and Santiago (1987) support the argument of this theory.

However, this approach is criticized mainly by the theorists of internalization in that the 'ownership advantage' overlaps with the other two concepts and is, thus, redundant (Itaki,1991,p.445).

2.1.3.6 The political economy view

Political economists regard an MNC as a form of capital operating across any natural or political boundary to maximize its surplus. Therefore, two basic terms, 'internationalization of capital' and 'accumulation of capital' are essential for the theory.

According to these economists, a capital (or company) has to increase its surplus value to the greatest extent possible. Otherwise, the capital itself cannot maintain its position in a given capitalist structure. As a writer asserted:

"Interclass relations, between capitalist producers, are thus increasingly characterised by enhanced competition between multinational corporations operating on a global scale" (Peet,1987,p.16).

In order to accumulate more surplus, capital has come to depend on the worldwide division of labour or the internationalization of capital. The term 'internationalization of capital' implies the export of capital by way of state loans, financial participation, financing foreign enterprises, credit between banks and the buying of foreign stocks (Bukharin,1975,p.25). An attribute of this highly internationalized capital is that it will bring about sharp conflict between national interests. At the same time, the enhanced forces of these internationalized MNCs tend to create conflicts with national planning by individual governments as the latter aim to correct the inequality brought in by the MNCs (Hymer,1972,p.126).

Overall, political economists argue that the MNC brings about permanent trends involving uneven development between regions and countries, uneven development between the forces of classes, the overflow of capitalism across national boundaries and, eventually, the internationalization of class struggle (Mandel,1975, pp.154-157).

2.1.3.7 Comment and the standpoint of this study

As discussed above, theories relating to MNCs have been presented from various viewpoints. However, theories are not, in reality, divided so clearly, since they share assumptions and contents. This is especially the case in recent studies of market imperfection theory and internalization theory.

Today, studies based on the internalization theory seem to form the main stream of the discussion (Johanson and Mattsson,1988, p.306; Pitelis and Sugden,1991,p.9). Most studies of FDI have concentrated on the motivational behaviour of MNCs which is caused by market imperfections and domestic factors rather than by structural factors such as the globally constructed profit maximising system. However, although internalization theory successfully illuminates the basic forces of MNCs' overseas investment, it seems improper to accept the assertion made by internalization theory that it is applicable to all overseas investments in any kind of circumstances (Fieldhouse,1986,p.25; Dunning,1991,p.120).

Furthermore some writers, especially those from the structural viewpoint, criticize internalization theory in that the theory has not fully reflected the importance to the investment of MNCs of either the multinational system or the network relationships in an industrial market (Kogut,1983,p.42; Johanson and Mattsson,1988,pp.308-309).

Indeed, the diverse fields of MNC activity and the changing environment of overseas investment will probably never allow a single all-encompassing interpretation of the nature or operating process of MNCs. In this respect, the studies which have tried to integrate various approaches such as that of Dunning (1979a,1988) and Kogut (1983) are worth noting.

This study is performed mainly on the basis of location theory (location-specific advantage in Dunning's framework) supplemented by the internalisation theory above. In particular, the location advantages of each of the two host countries become the major matter of concern. Needless to say, there are some difficulties in depicting the overall nature of MNCs by using the location- oriented approach. However, since this study tries to examine the distinctive locational features of a specific group of MNCs in the given host countries and, thus, to interpret the strategy of international market forces by means of these geographical features, the approach focusing on location-specific factors is likely to provide a better explanation than other approaches.

2.2 Multinational Company Activities and the Nation State

For the purpose of this study, apart from the nature of the MNC and FDI, the relationship between the activities of MNCs and the nation state policies needs to be clarified. However, there is still no consensus on many features related to the activities or strategies of MNCs. Among these, the following issues need to be investigated more specifically - namely, the comparison between licensing and direct investment; the worldwide division of labour; and transfer pricing and intra-firm trade by MNCs. Based on this discussion, the relationship between the individual state and MNCs is examined at the end of this section.

2.2.1 The main strategies of MNCs

2.2.1.1 Licensing or FDI

The MNC uses a number of ways to gain access to foreign markets such as trade, licensing or selling proprietary assets, portfolio investment and FDI. Among these, the direct investment route has expanded its significance amongst the activities of MNC in recent days. Licensing proprietary assets is one of the most frequently considered alternatives to FDI. Therefore, the characteristics of FDI can be traced more clearly by comparing it with other forms of MNC activity, in particular licensing.

It is argued that the MNC will tend to be motivated towards licensing

47

under certain circumstances, such as where the barriers of entry prevent the firm from investing directly in the market; when technology is changing rapidly; where the cost for arranging licenses or the opportunity cost is not too high; or where there exists a high risk to direct investment and so forth (Caves,1982a, pp.261-262). The findings of Clegg, which show the highest level of inward licensing transactions into Japan and the lowest level of outward licensing contracts by Japanese firms among five developed countries, are consistent with and back up the above argument (Clegg,1987,p.71).

Under given circumstances, the MNC weighs and calculates the predictable profits and costs in both cases of direct investment and licensing or selling the proprietary assets. In other words, a comparison between market transaction costs (licensing) and internal organization costs (FDI) is conducted. If it is difficult to expect a sufficient rate of return from direct investment (i.e. the cost of FDI is higher than the cost of licensing) in a certain period of time in the foreign market, licensing rather than direct investment will be chosen (Hennart,1989,pp.215-217). In this case, in order to compensate for the risk of diffusion of their technology, MNCs tend to require a large amount of premium, or royalty, from licensees.

In short, a direct investment by the MNC is the consequence of a complicated process of calculation between different ways of obtaining access to foreign markets under the aim of profit maximization.

2.2.1.2   The worldwide division of labour

The MNCs operate over the whole world across national boundaries even if many only operate in a limited number of countries. Their decisions are made in terms of the interest of each corporation at the global scale. As a result, they tend to allocate their managerial functions, such as procurement, production and sales, between countries according to which distribution is considered most appropriate to meet their managerial goals (Adam,1975, pp.90-92). Here, the issue of the 'worldwide division of labour' arises.

This division of labour consists of two kinds; the one is the horizontal division of labour and the other is the vertical division of labour. In order to take advantage of given circumstances and to confront a sudden change in production, the MNC may disperse the whole function of each stage in the overall production process over a large number of small scale plants across the world. This activity has been called horizontal integration or the horizontal division of labour. By contrast, the vertical division of labour arises where the MNC attempts to maximize the advantages of internalization in a market through the coordination of different stages of production following 'upstream' and 'downstream' activity (Casson,1986,p.11). This is characterized by the flow of intermediate products either between subsidiaries and the headquarters or between subsidiaries and the dispersed repetitive manufacturing plants.

This latter phenomenon, compared to the former, has produced more vividly the problem of branch plant economies all over the world. In this system, each nation is destined to be one of either the providers of raw materials, the manufacturers of intermediate or finished products, or even the markets for finished products. As a result, although individual plants and regional offices may make their own decisions in a limited range of ordinary activity, higher level decision-making and control over these worldwide branches are concentrated in the headquarters usually located in one of the major cities of the developed countries. Therefore, in many cases, important decisions, including the closure of subsidiaries, are made in the headquarters without necessarily any prior notice to the management of the subsidiary (McDermott,1989, p.17).

This division of function within MNCs has often been indicated as the cause of uneven development between regions or between nations (Hymer, 1972,p.129; Jenkins,1987,p.191). On the other hand, the divided production process encourages cooperative production between different countries by, for example, trade or exchange of intermediate products between small scale manufacturers located in different countries to make a finished product. Empirical studies on intra-firm trade and vertical integration have concluded that Japanese MNCs have a greater tendency than others for intra-firm trade and vertical integration (Lecraw,1985,p.25; Casson,1986, p.229). This tendency, with the transfer pricing which is described below, provides an important element in depicting the overall nature of Japanese MNCs.

2.2.1.3 Transfer pricing and intra-firm trade

Transfer pricing is one of the main features of the MNC as it tries to maximise its global profit. The term transfer pricing means:

> " ... the price used for internal sales of goods and services between the divisions of a business enterprise" (Rugman and Eden,1985,p.1).

In general, transfer pricing is introduced in an effort to minimize the tax burden (or government intervention) with which the MNC headquarters and subsidiaries will be charged in all countries within which they are operating mainly by exploiting the taxation differentials between countries. Along with this, the MNC may depend on transfer pricing in order either to overcome restrictions in financial markets or to equalize profits in each host country (Parry,1980, pp.100-103; Jenkins, 1987, pp.117-118; Abdallah, 1989, pp.29-48; Al-Eryani et al., 1990, p.422)[13].

It is common that transfer pricing tends to appear in the process of intra-firm trade, especially that of major components (i.e. internalization of components sourcing). It has been argued that intra-firm trade, which is one

49

of the main characteristics of MNC activities, constitutes about 30-40% of the total manufacturing products trade and that this ratio reaches even higher in industries in which MNCs play a dominant role (Dunning,1988b,p.98). During the process, the MNC, given its quite common position as a monopolistic supplier, can easily utilize transfer pricing[14]. However, the major problem to the commentator is that empirical studies are unlikely to succeed in providing obvious evidence of the presence of transfer pricing because of the confidentiality of the operation (Dicken,1992, pp.390-391).

One of the most crucial issues regarding transfer pricing is whether it increases overall efficiency and world welfare or not. While, in general, the transfer pricing of MNCs tends to be conceived of as lessening global welfare, some writers stress the positive function of transfer pricing, arguing that it alleviates the inefficiency caused by government intervention in world trade (Diewert,1985,pp.77-79; Aliber, 1985, p.96). This argument originated chiefly with the microeconomic analysis of transfer pricing.

It is difficult to confirm the plausibility of these arguments by using empirical evidence. However, it seems certain that, when one explains transfer pricing from the standpoint of the interest of a particular country, the negative aspect of transfer pricing rather than the positive one tends to become more prominent. Japanese MNCs have been criticised for having a greater tendency to fall back on non-market based transfer prices in the South East Asian countries than MNCs from other countries (Lecraw,1985, p.229). The recent debate surrounding the tax evasion of Japanese companies, provides further evidence to this argument (*The Sunday Times*, 22 Mar. 1992).

In short, the introduction of transfer pricing by the MNC between subsidiaries in different countries is a significant feature of the MNC, and such pricing will influence adversely the host country's economy as much as it contributes to the total profits of the MNC.

2.2.2 The relationship between state policy and MNC activities

2.2.2.1 Influence of the national state on MNC activities

Since the MNC is distinguished from domestic firms most obviously by its transcendence over national boundaries, the relationship between individual states and MNCs operating worldwide has been a significant matter of concern[15]. In particular, with the growing interest in political aspects of MNCs since the 1970s, this issue has been an important subject of the discussion regarding MNC activities.

Scholars insisting on an orthodox approach to MNCs tend to concentrate on the relationship between national state policy and an MNC's international management strategy. For example, the efforts of governments to promote or control MNC activity and the response of MNCs to these policies occupy most of these studies. By contrast, political economists have tended to look upon the relationship between individual states and international MNCs as a kind of tension, or a power relationship (Jenkins,1987,p.120). They consider this matter in conjunction with the international division of labour and territorial non-coincidence between expanding capital and its home state. Palloix states:

" ... the internationalization of capital itself means that the reproduction of the capital of any nation is constantly crossed with the reproduction of other capitals on an international scale" (Palloix,1975,p.76).

However, with regard to the relative power of a state and multinational capital, political economists diverge in view. Some think existing states have often suffered through the increased power of internationalized MNCs (Murray,1975; Jenkins,1987); some others see most internationalization or expansion of the economy as the consequence of national planning, especially that of the home country (Warren, 1975)[16].

On the other hand, the relationship between government policy and the activities of MNCs has been examined by many authors over many years[17]. In particular, whether remedial policies to restrain the selfish activities of MNCs are fully effective or not has been the major matter of concern. Under the condition of market imperfections, MNCs attempt to utilize their firm-specific advantages, or monopoly power, through, for example, transfer pricing and, thus, to maximize their global profits. Against these activities of MNCs, host governments tend to depend on supplementary and remedial policy measures to limit the monopolistic profits of MNCs and to secure the benefit or welfare of domestic customers and firms. However, because of the lack of criteria for assessment and because of the conflict between policies within the nation, these secondary policy measures have tended to fall short of this goal (Parry,1980,pp.150-154; Rugman et al.,1986, pp.260-265; Hennart,1989, pp.218-230). Regardless of their success or failure, the policies of host governments have been one of the most influential factors resulting in the increasing international distribution of MNC activity (Dunning, 1988b,p.87).

With the growing restriction of less-developed country (LDC) governments on the entry of MNCs (to varying degrees) and the increasing control of outward investments in developed countries to maintain employment and production, the conflicting relationship between nation states and international firms is predicted to continue.

2.2.2.2 The influence of MNC activities on the national economy

The MNC's activity has significant influence on the world economy by means of, for example, the increase in international trade, the changes in the balance of payments of each country, mainly in favour of the MNC's home country, etc. (Ghertman and Allen,1984, Ch.3). However, it seems that writers' concern has largely been concentrated on the influence of MNCs on the national economy of both the home and host countries.

With regard to the economy of the MNC's home country, the influence of MNCs was initially considered from the viewpoint of the balance of payments of the home country. In the early 1970s, concern moved to the employment problem of the home country which was associated with the surge of outward investment often by MNCs. In brief, it is argued that the direct overseas investment of MNCs increases production and employment in foreign countries at the expense of that in the home country[18].

This issue tends to be more controversial in the countries which have powerful trade unions. In the case of the UK, the overseas activities of British multinationalized companies especially have been questioned (Morgan,1979,p.87; Massey and Meegan,1979,p.171; Gaffikin and Nickson, 1984,Ch.4; Lloyd and Shutt, 1985,p.42), even though this has not been proved satisfactorily by empirical evidence to be one of the main causes of the restructuring process in the UK economy (Keeble,1989,p.8). Other issues, which have been mentioned frequently, are the taxation of MNC profits and the general income distribution between MNCs and internally operating companies and their employees, etc.

In the host country, the activities of MNCs have created a dilemma by generating influences in opposite directions (Hennart,1989, p.211). While, on the one hand, MNCs can act as the motivator of the economic prosperity of the host country, on the other hand, they are often criticized for the fact that the host country is degraded to the level of a branch plant economy and to being a stepping-stone for MNCs' global strategies.

As a stimulus to the host country economy, the MNCs have impacts in various ways. Most directly, the MNCs increase the employment[19], national output and income of the host country. During the process, the host country enjoys the benefits of an improved balance of payments[20], increased domestic fixed capital formation, etc. Indirectly, the host country can expect some enhancement of its competitiveness with the technological and managerial spill-overs and resource transfer effects of the MNC (Brech and Sharp,1984,p.33). Indeed, the MNC plays the role of producer of technical knowledge. This function contains all the stages related to technology from the invention of new technology to its diffusion. Although the R&D function tends to be concentrated in the area near MNC headquarters rather than in foreign markets, production and selling in foreign countries necessarily results in technology transfer effects in the host country mainly through the training of manpower and the movement of experienced local workers (Caves,1982b, pp.263-265; Dicken,1992, p.392).

Often, this technology transfer gives rise to the debate about the 'boomerang effect' between the advanced countries and the highly competitive developing countries such as NICs. For instance, the Japanese government and industry, having experienced the rapid growth of the competitiveness of Korean industry in the world market using the technology developed by Japanese, now tend to resist technology transfers to, or even co-operative activities with, Korean industry (James,1989,p.151; Nester,1990,p.227).

The extent to which the MNC uses local supplies in its products has been another important matter of concern. This issue arises not only in the developing countries, but also in the developed countries such as EC countries facing the massive arrival of foreign MNCs, especially those of the Japanese (Dicken,1986). Sometimes, by way of excuse, the MNCs point out the low quality of local products and the lack of efficient local suppliers. Apart from whether this argument is right or not, the efforts of the MNC and the host country on this issue run in different directions and often end up with the host country imposing legal and administrative restrictions on the extent of non-domestic content. In this regard, the announcements made by Japanese car manufacturers, namely Toyota, Nissan and Honda, forecasting that their local content in Britain will be over 80%, or in one case 90%, and the news announcing that the local content of Cannon in France will be over 60% are worth noting (*Financial Times*, 8 Jan. 1991 and 13 May 1992).

In sum, a writer emphasizes the positive aspects of MNCs mainly from the standpoint of LDCs as follows:

" Like any other firm, the MNCs contribute to economic growth and development by creating demand for productive factors of host countries, and transforming materials into more useful (utility-generating) forms" (Ahiakpor,1990, p.29).

However, on the contrary, the activities in the developing countries of the MNCs from developed countries often give rise to criticism for the exploitation of the low-cost labour force of the host country (Sadri and Williamson, 1989,pp.182-183). Furthermore, since MNCs tend to move easily from one country to another in which they can take advantage of a labour force at a lower cost, the position of workers in the existing host countries tends to become unstable.

As described so far, the MNC activities have been assessed both in positive and negative ways. Recently, in spite of the negative aspects listed above, especially the problem of the branch plant economy, most countries seem to regard the inward investment of MNCs as being advantageous as a whole for their economies and, thus, show a competition to attract FDI into their own territory. (Even France, which had maintained the most reluctant attitude towards Japanese investment, began to participate in this competition.) Discussion about policy implications in this study in chapter eleven will also be made from this viewpoint. Having set out the theory and the main issues of MNCs relevant to the study, the focus moves on to FDI in the three countries with which the study is concerned.

2.3 Foreign Direct Investment in the UK, Korea and Japan

2.3.1 Position of the three countries

2.3.1.1 U K

For over a century, FDI has been an important factor in the UK economy. Not only as a source country, but also as a host country, the UK has played a significant role in the international flow of capital. Since the early 1970s, there has been a large increase in outflows from the UK. The relative overvaluation of sterling and the removal of exchange control in 1979 were conceived of as one of the important causes (Brech and Sharp,1984,p.3).

Recently, the position of the UK in the international capital flow has been challenged by the major shifts discussed in the previous section (2.1.2). Nevertheless FDI, both into and from the UK, has grown steadily during the last decades. In practice, employment by foreign-owned firms reached 4.3% of total employment in 1979 and 13% in 1987 (Hood and Young,1983, pp.51-53; *Lloyds Bank Economic Bulletin*, Jun. 1990)[21].

Table 2.1 Total net direct overseas investment in the UK[22]   (£ m)

	1985	1986	1987	1988	1989	1990	1991p[+]
(Outward direct investment)							
Investment(A)	8,442	11,783	19,198	20,880	21,454	9,596	10,810
Net earnings from total investment(B)	7,732	7,802	10,938	13,852	16,656	15,905	13,819
(Inward direct investment)							
Investment(C)	4,506	5,837	9,455	11,893	18,675	18,593	11,958
Net earnings paid out on inward investment(D)	7,572	5,293	7,043	8,666	9,226	7,007	6,438
Net contribution of earings to current account(B-D)	160	2,509	3,895	5,186	7,430	8,088	7,381
Net outward investment (A-C)	3,936	5,946	9,743	8,987	2,779	-8,997	-1,148

[+] p: provisional
  Includes miscellaneous
Source : *Business Briefing* (19 Jun. 1992).

Table 2.1 summarizes the features of recent FDI flows into and out of

54

the UK. This table shows that both inward- and outward- direct investment had grown until 1989 and began to decline in 1990. According to the figures, the UK has enjoyed a substantial amount of net earnings from outward FDI, although taking into account the growing expenditure which should be paid out on the inward investment of foreign companies.

Table 2.2 shows the main host countries for the outward investment of the UK firms and the main home countries of the inward investment in the UK. In total outward investment in 1990, the largest share (63%) was oriented to the European countries and the second largest one (33%) went to other countries. By contrast, European countries (43%) and the US (27%) provided most of the inward investment.

However, the investment flow from and into North America, especially the US, was crucial at least until 1989 for the position of UK FDI from the fact that these flows were not only large in their amounts, but also growing steadily. Indeed, the UK had long been the most important destination for the outward investment of US capital.

On the other hand, the FDI flow between the UK and Western Europe has been increasing consistently and substantially. Both outward and inward investment have increased markedly since 1988. Japanese investment, although increasing rapidly in recent years, has not provided a significant part of the UK inward investment.

Table 2.2 Total net direct overseas investment from and into the UK[23] (£ m)

	1986	1987	1988	1989	1990
(Outward investment)					
US	7,558	12,591	10,413	11,876	-530
Japan	119	-24	102	230	253
Europe	1,431	2,939	5,772	5,616	6,002
Australia	690	563	1,789	654	675
Others	1,985	3,129	2,804	3,078	3,196
Total+	11,783	19,198	20,880	21,454	9,596
(Inward investment)					
US	1,261	1,598	1,324	6,287	5,080
Japan	43	856	1,013	1,426	1,705
Europe	3,048	3,529	7,294	7,920	7,923
Australia	84	919	1,575	846	1,232
Others	1,401	2,553	687	2,196	2,653
Total+	5,837	9,455	11,893	18,675	18,593

+ Including miscellaneous.
Source : *Business Briefing* (19 Jun. 1992).

Dunning analyzed and explained the trends in UK inward and outward investment using the concepts mentioned earlier of 'ownership advantages' and 'location advantages'. A main finding of his analysis was that the UK outward/inward capital stake in the UK's gross national product had decreased during the 1960s and 1970s (Dunning,1979b,p.19). This was interpreted as a consequence of the improved international competitiveness of UK firms and the growing tendencies to direct production and supply in foreign markets (in place of exports to those markets from the home country).

On the contrary, it was found that European MNCs had a tendency to depend more on export rather than direct investment to reach British domestic markets. These tendencies were summarized as the result of increasing ownership advantages and declining location advantages for foreign investment in the UK (ibid,p.20). However, since the mid-1980s, the relevance of the result has been challenged, and should be modified, by the changed pattern of overseas investment. In other words, with the growing inward investment into the UK both from Japan and European countries in the latter half of 1980s, location advantages for inward investment are more conspicuous than ownership advantages.

With regard to the characteristics of inward investment, the aforementioned study of Hood and Young identified a number of features as follows (and these findings are still thought to be relevant in the late 1980s) - 1) the importance of the US as a source country for FDI in the UK is reaffirmed; 2) contrary to the previous view, such as that of Yannopoulus and Dunning (1976), foreign firms are equally attracted by certain locational factors as indigenous firms; 3) because of the high fixed costs of foreign investment, foreign-owned companies tend to be much larger in average size of plant than their indigenous counterparts; and 4) while foreign inward investment to the AAs continuously prefers to establish there on new greenfield sites, acquisition or take-over is growing in other areas of Britain (Hood and Young, 1983,pp.56-72)[24].

2.3.1.2 Korea

Korea has achieved a considerable economic development during the last three decades. GNP growth has reached 8-10% per annum. During the process, foreign loans and FDI have taken a crucial role in that they have provided the financial basis for the economic development of Korea. A lot of incentives such as tax holidays and profit guarantees have been provided to attract large foreign investors into Korea (Koo,1984,pp.6-8). Recently, in consequence of this economic growth, the outward investment of Korean MNCs has begun to increase rapidly.

As seen Table 2.3, the inflow of FDI increased steadily until 1988[25]. It should be noted that FDI in 1987 and 1988 tripled that of the average of 1983-1986. The liberalization policy of opening the domestic market to foreign investments and the brightening forecast for business activities in Korea were pointed to as the main causes of the sharp increase of inward investment. However, this trend has been reversed since 1989. Since that year, the FDI flow into Korea has declined sharply, making the figure of 1990 two thirds that of 1988. The drastic increase in production cost, led by wage levels, the soaring value of the Won and the instability of the labour- management relationship in Korea have been pointed out as the main causes of the fall (*Financial Times*, 27 Nov. 1989 and 16 May 1990).

Table 2.3   Annual FDI flow into Korea(1983-90)   ($ m)

	1983-86	1987	1988	1989	1990	%share
(Source)						
Japan	836	497	696	462	235	46.9
US	481	255	284	329	317	28.6
Europe	177	210	243	212	207	18.0
Others	85	101	60	87	44	6.5
(Industry)						
Manufacturing	806	772	738	727	583	62.3
Chemicals	81	153	237	173	218	14.8
Pharmaceuticals	56	34	43	37	36	3.5
Metals	18	18	13	13	13	1.3
Machinery[+]	292	206	108	243	154	17.2
Electronics	230	206	268	116	89	15.6
Others[++]	129	155	69	145	73	9.9
Services	765	287	533	359	219	37.2
Others[+++]	8	4	12	4	1	0.5
Total	1,579	1,063	1,283	1,090	803	100

[+]   Includes light engineering and vehicles.
[++]   Includes textiles, foods, etc.
[+++]   Includes agriculture, mining, etc.
Source : Ministry of Finance (Korea) (31 Dec. 1990).

Japan and the US have taken the lion's share of total inward investment in Korea; these two countries accounted for over three quarters of the total amount. However, the investment of Japan has declined dramatically, showing one third of the level of 1988 investment in 1990. This sharp decline of Japanese FDI in Korea has significant implication for investigating the managerial or locational strategies of Japanese MNCs in the changing context of the world economy. On the other hand, the investment has been mainly concentrated in services and in technology-intensive industries.

Outward direct investment by Korean firms began to increase from the beginning of the 1980s, with the internationalisation of the Korean economy, the outward FDI from Korea has increased markedly over the last decade.

Table 2.4 illustrates the overall features of Korean outward investment.

Table 2.4 Total outward investment of Korean MNCs   ($ m)

	1968-83 (% share)		1968-90 (% share)	
(Host countries)				
US	104	26.9	807	34.6
Canada	61	15.8	299	12.8
Japan	19	4.9	51	2.2
Europe	9	2.3	152	6.5
Australia	45	11.7	76	3.2
Others	148	38.4	950	40.7
(Asian developing countries)	(123)	(31.8)	(715)	(30.6)
(Industry)				
Mining	149	38.6	447	19.2
Manufacturing	60	15.5	1,061	45.4
Non-manufacturing	177	45.9	827	35.4
Total	386	100	2,335	100

Source : The Bank of Korea (1984,1991); Koo and Lee (1985).

In terms of host country distribution, Asian developing countries have taken a large share, nearly one third, of Korean total investment 1968-1983 and 1968-1990. This reflects the endeavour of Korean MNCs to take part in the development of overseas natural resources. However, in gross figures, investment in developed countries accounts for a larger share (61.6 and 59.3%) than that in developing countries. Until the early 1980s, it interpreted as the consequence of a number of Korean-owned large-scale coal mining development projects in Australia, Canada, and of trade and service-related investment in developed countries (Koo and Lee,1985,pp.11-15).

Since the mid-1980s, with the growing competitiveness of Korean manufacturing industry, the emphasis of the outward FDI of Korean firms has shifted from securing natural resources towards the operation of manufacturing firms in developed countries, among which the US is the prime destination. This trend has been accelerated by the increasing conflicts between Korea and market countries over Korea's trade surplus. On this ground, a writer names the recent outward FDI of Korean firms as 'defensive direct investment' (Jung,1990,p.187).

In conclusion, inward investment of foreign capital has played an important role in the economic development of Korea during the last two decades. However, the overseas investments into Korea, especially those from Japan, have begun to decline substantially since 1989. Recently, Korean outward investment has begun to increase considerably and is expected to grow consistently mainly in the field of manufacturing.

2.3.1.3 Japan

Recently, the trend to increasing Japanese overseas investment has become a significant matter of concern for both developed and developing countries. This concern is mainly due to the fact that, first, the shift from the traditional Japanese dependence on the export of finished goods to the export of capital is proceeding with remarkable speed, and that, second, this shift will necessitate a different kind of policy response in host countries already suffering from the bulk of their trade deficit with Japan.

In statistical terms, Japan has emerged as one of the most important source countries of FDI. Table 2.5 illustrates the remarkable growth of Japanese FDI since the 1970s.

Table 2.5 The total stock of Japanese outward direct investment   ($ bn.)

	1977	1982	1986	1987	1988	1989	1990	1991[+]
Total	21.2	53.1	106.0	139.4	186.4	253.9	310.8	352.4
Net increase	31.9	52.9	33.4	47.0	67.5	56.9	41.6	

[+] This figure represents the cumulative total of outward   investment at the end of March 1992.
Source : Institute of Fiscal and Monetary Policy (IFMP) (1986); *Financial Times* (24 Nov. 1987 and 7 Dec. 1988); *JEI Report* (15 Jun. 1990, 21 Jun. 1991 and 19 Jun. 1992).

In particular, total Japanese FDI doubled between 1982 and 1986, and further became seven-times as large at the end of 1991 (more precisely, March 1992), reaching the total then of $ 352.4 bn.

Table 2.6 shows the geographical distribution of Japanese FDI in every second year from 1984 and the total for 1951-91. The figures in this table illuminate the fact that, while Japanese investment in Asia, Latin America and Africa is declining or stagnating, that in North America and Europe is increasing remarkably. In particular, the US has appeared as the most important country for Japanese outward investment in these years, even more so than 1951-91.

This trend has a close relationship with the increasing trade barriers in the US and Europe. In other words, trade friction with these countries has urged Japanese industry to shift its traditional pattern of trade and FDI, and to seek for a horizontal integration within developed countries (Economic Planning Agency, Japan, 1984,p.116; *The Japan Economic Review*, 15 Jul. 1990).

Among European countries, the UK has taken the largest share of Japanese direct investment. This situation is indicated in Table 2.7. Although the

Netherlands has received the second largest amount of Japanese investment during 1951-1991, the UK enjoys the predominantly leading position in the cumulative total of Japanese FDI and the gap is getting larger.

In total stock 1951-91, 26.7% of Japanese overseas investment is attributed to the manufacturing sector though the proportion was on a declining trend from 1982 (32.7%) and 1985 (29.2%). However, the manufacturing share in recent years, ranging from 25 to 30%, is on a recovering trend from a level of less than 20% in the mid-1980s (*The Japan Economic Review*, 15 Feb. 1990). In the non- manufacturing sector, banking, finance and insurance (27.9%), real estate (21.7%), services (15.9%) and trade and sales (14.5%) are the important sectors where outward investment was performed between 1951-91 (IFMP,1986,p.74; *JEI Report*, 19 Jun. 1992, p.11)[26].

Table 2.6 The distribution of the total stock of Japanese outward direct investment   (%)

	1984	1986	1988	1990	1991	Cumulative total(1951-90)
North America	34.9	46.8	47.5	47.8	45.3	43.8
(US)	(33.1)	(44.5)	(46.2)	(45.9)	(43.3)	(42.2)
Europe	19.1	15.5	19.4	25.1	22.6	19.5
Asia	16.0	10.4	11.8	12.4	14.3	15.2
Latin America	22.6	21.2	13.7	6.4	8.0	12.4
Oceania	1.5	4.5	5.7	7.3	7.9	6.1
Africa	3.2	1.4	1.4	1.0	1.8	1.8
Middle East	2.7	0.2	0.5	0.0	0.1	1.0
Total	100.0	100.0	100.0	100.0	100.0	100.0

Source : IFMP (1986); *Financial Times* (7 Dec. 1988); *JEI Report* (21 Jun. 1991).

Table 2.7 The distribution of Japanese FDI in major European countries   (%)

	1984	1986	1988	1990	1991	Cumulative total(1951-90)
UK	16.2	28.4	43.4	47.6	38.3	38.2
Netherlands	23.6	18.8	25.9	19.2	20.9	21.5
Luxembourg	16.2	31.5	7.2	1.6	2.8	8.6
West Germany	12.6	6.1	4.5	8.7	11.9	8.5
France	6.3	4.4	5.1	8.8	8.7	7.2
Switzerland	12.0	2.6	5.0	4.7	0.7	3.7
Belgium	3.7	1.4	1.8	2.6	2.4	2.8
Others	9.9	6.8	7.1	6.8	14.3	9.5
Total	100.0	100.0	100.0	100.0	100.0	100.0

Source : IFMP (1986); *Financial Times*(19 Apr. 1989); *JEI Report* (21 Jun. 1991)

Inward investment of foreign capital into Japan has been a marginal figure, and the institutional and non-institutional restrictions in Japan towards foreign investment have been severely attacked abroad. Actually, FDI in Japan is negligible in terms of both amount and number of examples. In 1991, the amount of inward FDI into Japan was only $ 3.9 bn., not more than 10% of outward investment, albeit increased markedly from below 5% in 1990 (*Japan Economic Almanac*,1991,p.254 and 1992,p.223).

In general, the increase in Japanese FDI has the following three causes. The first and the most important reason is that FDI has been necessary to support export activities in industries which have been suffering from trade barriers, especially in developed countries. The second is to obtain natural resources with which Japan is poorly endowed. And the third is to transfer out of Japan those businesses which have become no longer profitable unless performed in developing countries with an abundant and therefore low cost labour force (Landaburu,1985,p.xiv). The sharp appreciation of the yen since 1985 and the lack of low cost labour in Japan have strengthened, and continue to strengthen, these causes in the beginning of the 1990s (*Financial Times*, 15 Jul. 1991). Porter summarizes this situation as follows:

"[FDI] is proceeding rapidly in many internationally successful Japanese industries, and will boost productivity by shifting less sophisticated activities elsewhere. This will not only help deal with protectionism but will make the Japanese economy less vulnerable to domestic factor costs. It will also allow Japanese firms to be better able to compete in a range of industries when local proximity is important" (Porter,1990,p.704)[27].

In conclusion, Japanese FDI, mainly caused by the appreciation of the yen, the increasing labour shortage in Japan and, most notably, the growing trade friction with the US and with European countries, has increased dramatically during the last decade. In particular, 'the growing interpenetration of capital' among these advanced countries represents most eloquently the recent activities of Japanese capital and MNCs. Given the general picture of the three countries' FDI position above, the rest of this chapter briefly outlines the features of Japanese MNCs which have been found and claimed by many authors[28].

2.3.2 Features of Japanese MNCs

The main features of Japanese MNCs which differentiate them from the MNCs of other countries may be examined largely in terms of the following three aspects of outward investment: its geographical distribution, the low technology level of production and the role of small and medium sized manufacturers in that investment.

2.3.2.1 Geographical distribution

By the early 1980s, Asia and Latin America had come to take a substantial part of overall Japanese MNCs' activities and FDI. In particular, NICs, which are characterized by low labour costs, fast growth and an export-oriented economy, have been the most important foreign sites for Japanese MNCs (Franko,1983,p.xi; Billet,1990,pp.12-13). During the 1980s, roughly one fifth of cumulative total Japanese outward investment has been placed in these Asian developing countries in a one way flow[29]. In contrast, in the case of investment flows between the US and Europe, each side's MNCs have taken the lion's share of the counterpart's inward investment.

Indeed, Japanese MNCs have invested in a large number of developing countries to take advantage of the abundant raw materials and cheap cost labour forces in these countries and to export the manufactured products made there either to major markets direct or to other plants of their own to make them into finished products (IBJ,1988,p.31; Dicken,1992,pp.78-81)[30]. During the process, the benefit from intra-firm sourcing has been pursued by Japanese firms by providing intermediate goods to the subsidiaries in these countries. This also means that Japanese MNCs have largely depended on export not only of finished products but also of intermediate components to, rather than direct investment in, the major markets in the developed world (Kotabe and Omura,1989,p.26; Kotabe and Murray,1990,pp.387-388).

Recently, however, the type of FDI of Japanese MNCs is being changed. Mainly due to the growing trade conflict with major developed countries, especially with the US, Japanese FDI has begun to move to North America and Europe. Today, North America is the largest destination for Japanese FDI, far surpassing Asia. On the other hand, it is also found that the Japanese FDI flow into North America and Europe is skewed towards the commercial and financial sectors, while the sectoral distribution in Asian countries is spread evenly (Dicken,1988,pp.636-638). This fact strongly indicates that the outward movement of Japanese manufacturing industry is still largely dependent on Asian developing countries rather than North America and Europe[31].

2.3.2.2 The low technology level of outward investment

It is often said that, compared to American and European MNCs, those of Japan concentrate their R&D function and high technology production in the home country rather than allocate these functions to suitable host countries. In other words, Japanese MNCs establish subsidiaries operating mainly standardized and less skilled labour production in the host countries, especially in those countries possessing low cost labour forces (Ozawa,1979, p.54; Franko,1983,p.xi; James,1989,ch.20; Dicken,1992,p.80).

The concentration of the R&D function in the home country or near to headquarters has been usual in most MNCs mainly in order to keep secret the proprietary knowledge or to secure scale economies in R&D activities[32]. However, Japanese MNCs stand out from those of US and Europe in the strength of this tendency to keep R&D in Japan (Ozawa,1979,pp.52-54; Westney,1990,p.297). This means Japanese MNCs carry relatively labour-intensive and technologically standardized manufacturing plants abroad. Although there are some exceptions, such as the production of 1 megabit semiconductors in a Scotland plant by NEC, the provision of design autonomy in the Komatsu plant at Birtley, the planned operation of independent vehicle development teams of Honda in the US, Japan and Europe and the increasing R&D work in Wales (Nonaka,1990, pp.88-89; *Financial Times*, 12 Aug. 1991 and 19 Jun. 1992), the strength of this tendency forms a unique feature of Japanese FDI differentiating it from that of other countries.

In a recent study of the influence of firm-specific strategy on the behaviour of Japanese semiconductor firms, it was asserted that, although highly tentative, there is a significant relationship between the Japanese firm's technological lead in a particular field and the involvement in FDI in advanced countries (Kimura,1989,p.310). Another statistical analysis also backed up this result by showing the highest R&D intensity by Japanese MNCs operating in the US compared to American-owned firms and other foreign-owned firms (Kim and Lyn,1990,pp.47-48). From these results, it seems reasonable to infer that the recent upsurge of Japanese investment in advanced countries is a result of the enhanced technology level of Japanese MNCs coming out of their own territory (Dunning,1990a,p.208).

In short, the ever increasing R&D expenditure, the concentration of the R&D function in the Japanese home country, the diffusion of standardized less-skilled production processes to developing countries, and the maintenance of profits through the export of the output of the plants in these developing countries on the behalf of Japan have been the sequential characteristics related to the Japanese MNCs' distribution of functions at home and abroad, even though a set of changes has begun to appear in this pattern.

2.3.2.3 The role of small and medium sized manufacturers

Another important feature of Japanese MNCs is that small and medium sized parent companies[33] take a large share of Japanese outward investment (Dicken,1992,p.77). Ozawa asserts that the overseas investment of these firms tends to locate in the countries nearest to Japan. As evidence, he declares that 70.0% of total investment of Japanese capital in Korea and 82.3% of that in Asia has been made by these small and medium sized firms (Ozawa,1979,pp.27-28).

These two phenomena are quite different from US or European based MNCs which are generally both large companies and operate large plants in far located countries. (The exception is US investment in Canada and Mexico.) By contrast to Japan, it is thought that American and European MNCs operating in foreign countries tend to be larger in average size than indigenous firms because of their large fixed costs (Hood and Young,1983,p.66).

However, these days, with their strengthened competitiveness in the world market, the small and medium sized firms in Japan have increased their overseas activities in distant countries such as the US and Europe (Munday,1990,p.15). The interpretation put on this is that, since Japanese manufacturers are highly related to each other by vertical integration, the FDI of the main companies has brought about a flood of overseas investment by these related small size manufacturers. In practice, a large part of recent Japanese inward investment into the UK has been undertaken by intermediate suppliers following the large finished goods manufacturers such as Nissan, Honda, Toyota, etc. into the UK. One of the most vivid examples of this is provided by Toyota. The decision of Toyota in choosing Burnaston, which is located just on the outskirts of the West Midlands Region, for its manufacturing plant, has resulted in the subsequent arrival of car part suppliers and banks in the West Midlands region centring on Birmingham and Telford.

With regard to the overall features of Japanese FDI, Kojima suggested a Japanese model of MNC activity (Kojima,1978 and 1986). He insisted that, unlike American MNCs which are characterized as large, high-technology based and with a monopolistic market structure, Japanese MNCs can be explained as marginal firms feeling pressure to build plants overseas in order to utilize lower cost labour within the developing countries. The proportion of the overseas investment going to developing countries in the whole Japanese FDI (55-57% in the latter half of 1970s, just over 45% in mid-1980s and around 30% in the late 1980s) was much higher than that of Western developed countries (showing a 20-30% range i.e. 21.0% of the US and 23.4% of Germany in 1981, and 10-22% range in 1985 i.e. 22.6% of the US, 16.1% of the UK and 14.9% of Germany) (Beal,1982,p.13; Hood and Young,1983,p.16; Kojima,1986, p.75; UN,1988,pp.518-520).

Ozawa (1979) also presented a macroeconomic model which regards Japanese FDI as a product of domestic factor shortages, insecurity of supply of industrial resources and environmental constraints. These are some push factors arising in Japan. Although there is an argument which explains Japanese FDI in the framework of the internalization theory discussed above (Giddy and Young,1982, pp.64-65), the assertions of Kojima and Ozawa seem to depict Japanese FDI and MNC activities more precisely[34].

Having examined the general features of MNCs, in particular those of Japanese MNCs, the concern now turns to the issue of the relationship between the geographical factors of a nation or a region and the locational decisions of MNCs, especially those of Japanese MNCs, to come close to the objective of this study. The next chapter illuminates this issue.

64

3   The causes and effects of industrial location

Having described the changing structure of the international economy and, within this context, the increasing role of MNCs, especially those from Japan, in the previous chapters, this chapter examines the background of and the effects of the locational decisions of individual firms. In particular, various perspectives on industrial location and the specific geographical factors which bring about locational choice are the major issues of concern.

3.1   Approaches to Industrial Location

To formulate a general rule or theoretical model of industrial location is far from an easy task. The difficulty is caused by the fact that the factors or forces influencing location decisions are diversified according to the circumstances which confront decision makers seeking for appropriate locations for their firms (e.g. size and type of the firm, characteristics of investment, competition with other firms, etc.) (Alperovich and Katz,1988, pp.243-244; Chisholm,1990,p.163).

For a long time, writers have tried to generalize the framework of industrial location which leads to the change in geographical distribution of firms. Industrial location analysis is summarized as:

> " ... the study of the spatial arrangement of industrial activity. ... The concern is with the general circumstances determining industrial location ... the location of the single productive facility is of critical importance in the search for the reasons behind what is observed" (Smith,1981, pp.4-5).

In general, the locational shift of a firm follows a sort of sequence in which various factors and forces interact with each other. In other words, a number of sequential stages construct the locational shift process of a firm; namely,

65

recognition of the necessity to shift, decision-making, final location choice, implementation and evaluation and so forth. In this sequential process of locational movement, the factors or forces influencing each stage vary. However, particular factors such as labour supply and land availability have been taken into consideration in most stages of the process. These locational factors and the issue of the firm's decision-making process have been the major objects of industrial location analysis.

The analytical or theoretical standpoints of authors have seldom been identical. Some stick to the possibility of firms finding optimal locations; some concentrate their focus on the cause and effect of the locational shift; and another group of writers try to elucidate the influence of higher level (corporate and social) systems than the individual production facility. Surrounding the various methodological approaches to industrial location, Massey and Meegan properly drew attention to the fact that different methodological standpoints make for differences in the understanding of the underlying forces of locational change and lead to different policy recommendations (Massey and Meegan,1985, p.4).

Regarding this matter, there have been several efforts to distinguish various approaches to location analyses in a more consistent way. Some authors distinguish industrial location analyses roughly by dividing them into deductive approaches and inductive ones according to whether the analysis starts with some basic propositions or with empirical enquiries. Smith argues from this standpoint that, whereas geographers have been interested in empirical study to derive the general characteristics through case studies, economists have emphasized the highly theoretical deductive approach (Smith,1981,p.2). Also, there is a classification which divides industrial location analysis, in particular those concerned with decision-making, into normative models, analytical models and descriptive models according to their characteristics and measures (Cooper,1975).

However, it seems to be quite common to classify these viewpoints on industrial location according to the ideology possessed by each analyst; to recognise the standpoint of neoclassical economists, of behaviourists, of structuralists and of political economists (Watts,1987,pp.14-16; Healey and Ilbery,1990,pp.19-30). In particular, the first two standpoints have been said to provide tangible frameworks for the analysis of industrial location and movement (Keeble,1976,Introduction). On the other hand, empirical analyses of industrial location tend to be classified practically into the following two categories according to the points in the sequential process of locational shift on which they focus; the two are locational factor analysis and locational shift pattern analysis.

The next section first delineates major location theories based on ideological standpoints. After that, the examination of actual location analyses, factor analysis and shift pattern analysis, will follow.

3.2 Industrial Location Theory

As just mentioned, existing theories of industrial location can be categorised into three very broad groups; they are neoclassical location theory, behavioral theory and structural theory[1].

3.2.1 Neoclassical location theory

There have been a group of writers who have attempted to find an optimum location for either a footloose company or a newcomer. They believe that a company can find the optimum location which minimizes costs, hence maximizes profit of the company, and that there exists one suitable place which fulfils this need. They also believe that it is possible to build a general analytical framework or a normative model for this purpose.

Generally, these writers have attempted to explain the existence of an optimum location with reference to neoclassical economic theory. Accordingly, their location theory involves a number of the assumptions and postulates that neoclassical economic theory needs. Among these, the assumptions of 'economic man' with full rationality and of perfect market conditions are the most important two. Because of this, works with this standpoint have been said to involve the theory of rationality or normative theory (Chapman and Walker,1990,p.19), or even an abstract model (Massey, 1979b,p.59).

Many authors have contributed to the development of neoclassical location theory. However, few would object to calling Alfred Weber the founder of industrial location theory. Indeed Weber's book *Über den Standort der Industrien* published in 1909 was a more comprehensive and deductive work than anything else in this field which had emerged until then (Smith,1981,p.68; Dicken and Lloyd, 1990,p.85). Weber has always been the theoretical point of departure for other authors in this field of study. This is so in spite of the existence of the negative appraisal of some writers (Carr,1983,p.391).

For Weber, transport cost is the most important factor influencing manufacturing location. He tried to find the location where transport cost becomes minimum on the argument that it is there that manufacturing plants would choose rationally to locate[2]. Since the means of transportation were not developed and, thus, transport costs were critical in making location decisions at that time, it was relevant for Weber to concentrate on transport cost in explaining industrial location. The necessity to consider the geographical variation of transportation cost in choosing the location of firms and in deciding policy measures has been argued until now by researchers and managers (Tyler and Kitson,1987, pp.61-73; Fingleton and Tyler,1990,p.440). In short, with this theoretical framework based on neoclassical economic theory, Weber constructed a well-shaped location model and has provided a solid theoretical basis in the field of industrial location.

After the presentation of Weber's theory, the industrial location analysis based on economic deductive theory developed remarkably. Great efforts have been poured into refining the analytical method and into widening its scope of explanation by, for example, T. Palander, A. Lösch, W. Christaller, etc.[3].

Basically, there are two strands of study in this model; theories of cost-minimization and theories of locational interdependence (Smith,1981,p.91). The main difference between these two strands is that, while the former deals purely with the cost aspects of location, the latter emphasizes demand aspects as well as cost aspects[4]. However, in these two different approaches, the assertion of the one actually operates as the major limitation of the other.

Confronting this theoretical separation, there appeared another group of theorists including M.L. Greenhut and W. Isard who attempted to integrate these two different approaches. They intended to consider all the possible factors influencing industrial location choice such as cost, demand and personal factors in their models. In particular, Isard attempted to explain as many factors as possible by using a substitution framework (Norcliffe,1975,pp.27-29; Dicken and Lloyd,1990,pp.93-97). This means that the scope of the theory was expanded by increasing the number of variables to be taken into account.

On the other hand, Smith (1970 and 1981) tried to reform the Weberian model, in the process confronting serious attacks from other standpoints, by introducing the two concepts of sufficient profit and welfare maximization (Carr,1983,p.392). Although being improved and modified, these analyses nevertheless share a common character in that, first, they are all based on the set of assumptions presented by neoclassical economic theory and that, second, they try to search for an optimum location in a given situation.

A number of criticisms have appeared pointing out the shortcomings of this theory in parallel with the criticisms of neoclassical economic theory. The main points of the criticisms can be summarised as follows. Firstly, the assumption of rational 'economic man' is unrealistic and, rather, limited rationality in a decision-maker is common in the real world. Secondly, it is almost impossible to find an optimum location because of various external reasons not included in the model. Thirdly, in this theory, only a few limited variables can be modelled. And, lastly, the theories are basically static. Thus, they have been appraised to have a weakness in application to the ever-changing circumstances and variables of the real world (Middlesex Polytechnic, 1979,pp.11-12; Carr,1983,pp.368-388)[5].

As a result, fresh approaches to explain industrial location using different theoretical frameworks have appeared. In particular, behavioral theory is the most visible thrust among these frameworks.

3.2.2 Behavioral approaches to industrial location

The behavioral approach in industrial location has increased over the last few decades. During that period, behavioral theory has largely ruled over the field of industrial location with its theoretical conceptualization and empirical analysis.

This means that the reliance on the deterministic explanation of locational decision-making based on neoclassical economic theory has decreased and that an alternative style of empirical research has been emphasised. The behavioral approach, begun with criticisms of classical location theory[6], has developed in two large strands; the theory of bounded rationality and the systems approach.

The theory of bounded rationality concentrates on company organization, decision-making processes and economic factors. According to the authors following this approach, single optimum locational decision-making is hampered by several constraints. These constraints come either from the decision-maker himself or from the organization in which the decision-maker is involved.

The major constraints preventing rational decision-making are satisficer behaviour on the part of decision-makers, psychic income, the quality and quantity of data, etc. (Hoare,1983,p.45). In particular, decision-makers have incomplete information to make a decision optimally, especially in respect of time and space. In addition, apart from bounded rationality, existing social norms, or procedures, and the personal judgement of the decision-maker have begun to be recognized as important factors which limit the causality of rationalistic industrial location model (Townroe, 1991,pp.386-392). Therefore, according to them, a decision-maker (or, more often, nowadays, decision-makers) behaves as a person of bounded rationality rather than of perfect rationality, as a satisficer rather than an optimiser (Devine et al.,1976, pp.115-117)[7]. In short, authors in this approach try to incorporate the limitations of the decision-makers with the complexity of the circumstances in the process of locational decision-making (Cooper,1975,p.17).

On the other hand, another group of behavioral theorists concentrates on the relations between a company and the larger economy in terms of the relations between the two 'systems'. Like other applications of the systems approach, there are three major elements in the system of industrial location; namely the structure of the system (locational requirements and linkage patterns), the system's process (the growth motive of a firm and its transformation into practice) and the system's environment (the force of the long-run development of the wider industrial system impacting on the individual firm) (Storper,1981,pp.20-26).

The systems approach, on the whole, provides the theoretical background to expanding the scope of location analysis from the micro-level of optimization theory to the macro-level. Authors in this approach, stressing the importance of the systems approach, claimed that a systems approach might help to develop general models of spatial behaviour (Hamilton and Linge,1979,p.1). Recently, with the growing complexity of company organization, the impetus or constraints coming from the organization tend to be conceived as the major force(s) determining the location of firms. In particular, the relationship between the organizational structure of a firm and its targeting strategy has become the main focus of analysis. As Dicken and Lloyd (1990) put it:

"this shifting process of integration and disintegration [of corporation functions] is of great significance in the changing geography of economic activities" (p.272).

"locational requirements [of corporate production units] vary considerably, depending on the specific organizational and technological role they play within the organization and the geographic distribution of their specific inputs and outputs" (p.313)[8].

One of the most important characteristics of behavioral location theory may be its recognition of the overall economic changes outside a firm and their influence on the location choice of the decision-maker(s) of the firm (Wood,1987,p.39)[9]. In practice, most empirical studies of the locational decision-making process in manufacturing companies have been undertaken from the standpoint of behavioral theory.

However, a number of doubts have also been cast against the behavioral framework. Firstly, the influence of irrationality and of personal factors in the process of decision-making tends to be over-emphasised. Secondly, it is difficult to relate the meaning of decision-making at the level of a company to the higher level of the economy. Thirdly, behaviourists tend to over-stress the importance of management in the way that they attribute the cause of growth or decline of a firm or industry to decision-making (Carr,1983,pp.397-398; Wood,1987,p.38). As a result, empirical studies based on behavioral theory are said by some to be no more than a description of a given situation (Wood,1974,p.46; Massey,1984,p.4)[10].

3.2.3 Structural theory

The appearance of structural theory in the 1970s was mainly caused by discontent with existing theory for some on the inability of existing theories to explain the problem of an economy and to indicate future direction.

In particular, the most rigorous influence leading to the emergence of structural theory came from political economic theory. Political economists interpret industrial location change as basically a product of the complex web of cause and effect relationships within capitalism. In essence, they understand spatial change as the conjunction of modes of production (capitalism) and the concept of space (geography). For them, the locational change of a firm is regarded as part of the process of surplus maximization by capital against the will of labour. Since capital accumulation is accomplished through the production of sufficient surplus value relative to the capital invested, capital must be restructured continuously to increase the rate of surplus value. The spatial movement of a firm is simply an aspect of this production process which necessarily reflects and causes conflict between the classes (Dunford,1977,pp.513-517). Therefore, it is asserted that:

"location theory has to be seen as part of investment theory and investment

70

theory as part of a general theory of capitalist accumulation" (Dicken and Lloyd,1990,p.366).

Critically, the basic argument of structuralists is that a company should not be considered as isolated from the economy as a whole. This is caused by the fact that most important factors for the company, such as the prices of particular products, investment, trading markets, etc., are determined and defined at either the international or national level with the company itself having only a modest and mainly responsive influence on these factors. Therefore, for structuralists, the spatial level at which the analysis should start is the level of the international economy (Kafkalas,1982,pp.2-4). This means that the activities of a company should not be considered as purely the result of internal forces within the company but also as the result of often over-riding external forces reflecting and caused by changes in its economic environment.

From this viewpoint, the locational change of a firm is explained in the context of the international structure of industry and the economy. The economic policies of other countries, or of other companies, and fundamental changes in demand, etc. become, therefore, major factors in general locational change and in the locational behaviour of individual companies. Chapman and Walker emphasize the role of the structural approach in industrial location theory by saying that:

" ... the most significant contribution of the structural approach lies not in its mode of explanation, but in its challenge to the ideological basis of industrial geography" (Chapman and Walker,1990,p.29).

The painstaking work of Massey and Meegan on the restructuring process of capital is the most famous among studies presented from this standpoint. They analyzed the restructuring process of British manufacturing industry and identified three forms of restructuring: these are intensification, investment and technological change and rationalization (Massey and Meegan,1982, pp.17-18). Whichever form a restructuring took, the process was regarded as an effect of international market forces. Also, any geographical change in a firm in this process was interpreted in this broader context. This means that:

" ... different spatial structures of production imply different forms of geographical differentiation and spatial inequality" (Boddy,1987,p.62).

In short, locational decision-making in structural theory is characterized as substantially a product of the activities of the external economy chiefly at the international level but also at the national and regional level, the essential point being that the decisive forces operate outside the firm and through its markets and competitors there.

However, structural theory is also criticized in the aspect that: firstly, it overemphasizes the influence of the macro-economy; secondly, it under-estimates the role of industrial firms and decision makers; and, thirdly, it neglects the geographical shifts of economic activity by sticking to the characteristics of overall economic change (Healey and Ilbery,1990,p.29).

On the other hand, in the last few years, the role of local activities or initiatives based on the historical and political background of each locality has been emphasized in the formation and transformation of local economies and firms within the context of given, or ever increasing, national and international forces (Massey,1984,p.300; Cooke,1989,pp.296-305). This means that the location of firms and the regeneration of deprived local economies are determined by the conjuncture of internal and external forces rather than solely external forces.

3.2.4 Comparison between theories

It can be said that locational decision-making theories have developed from static and micro-economic approaches to dynamic and macro-economic ones. The simple and optimalist model at the initial stage of location theory has been modified and expanded into the broader and more complicated ones which encompass a wider range of factors. This process can be said to be a reflection of the changes in circumstances which locational decision-makers have had to confront.

At the time when neoclassical theory was initiated, cost factors, in particular transport costs, were crucial for the location of a firm and, incidentally, linked to transport costs inter alia, competition was often more localised. The distance from raw material or market was the critical determinant of either success or failure for the concern. Thus, writers including Weber, concentrated on the problem of cost minimization or profit maximization, and tried to generalize the framework of optimum location using economic theory.

However, the development of science and technology, such as the improvement of transport equipment, especially motor lorries, the generalized use of electricity and the introduction of machinery replacing labour skills, has made firms more footloose. As a result, behavioral factors could come much more to the fore in industrial location decisions. Whether seeking to explain or predict, it appeared to be impossible to determine locational decision-making outcomes precisely without considering behavioral factors such as personal and organizational ones.

The situation was changed once again by the widening of markets to the international level and by the growing competition between companies. Firms and markets were becoming more and more internationalized and, thus, structural factors began to emerge as the most significant force in locational decisions. A reduction in the differences in costs between places resulting from the increased mobility of capital accelerated this trend.

However, this development does not mean that other models outside structural theory are meaningless in explaining industrial location (Dicken and

Lloyd,1990,p.11). Although behaviourists refuse to accept the single objective of profit maximization, firms basically try to increase their profits. The ideal of an optimum location still remains in a changed shape. The problem is that finding an optimum location through such an obvious route as neoclassical theorists postulated is not possible any more (if it ever was). Therefore, it seems most proper to draw the conclusion that, due to the constraints on location choice generated by personal, organizational and wider structural reasons, the goal of profit maximization is accomplished at best at the satisficing level. Overall, only by configuring all the points emphasized in each theory does it seem possible to delineate the general picture of locational change in the real world.

3.3 Empirical Location Analyses

3.3.1 Locational factor analysis

Few works have been published in the field of industrial location without mentioning that there exist a number of factors which influence, and even determine, the locational decisions of companies. Writers, in particular those of the behavioral approach, have attempted to demonstrate the factors which are considered to be important for locational decision-making mainly through empirical analysis. Most analyses rely for discerning the important factors on the survey results which are obtained from contact with the decision-makers who are responsible for the locational movement of the firms. Through such surveys, using the questionnaire or interview method, many factors have been identified as being important in location decisions. These factors tend to be classified into several groups in accordance with the purpose of the explanation.

3.3.1.1 Classification of locational factors

The forces determining the spatial location of whole industries can be divided into two categories, internal and external forces. The internal forces mean the specific factors internal to industries which cause factories in an industry to cluster or disperse such as organizational structure and external economies of scale[11]. The external forces of location are those of the area characteristics attracting the companies in an industry (Spiegleman,1968,p.19; Townroe,1969,pp.18-22). Although these concepts are introduced to analyze the locational pattern of industrial sectors, it is thought that these concepts have similar implications for the analysis of individual company movements.

On the other hand, factors which influence the locational shift of manufacturing companies are also divided into two categories; push factors which make a company move from an existing site and pull factors which attract the company, which is on the move, to an area. External forces and pull factors are likely to be related to geographical locations more directly, although sorting out purely geographical factors is never an easy task. On the other hand, push factors tend to imply both geographical and non-geographical motives in industrial location. Internal factors are largely conceived of as being other aspects of the decision-making process within an organization. The rest of this section examines briefly general features of push and pull factors respectively. The actual impact of locational factors on the location choice of Japanese MNCs is analyzed in Part II of this study, giving more emphasis to the external and pull factors than to others.

3.3.1.2 Main locational push factors

A push factor underlies the need for a company either to move from its existing site or to decide on a new location possibly for an additional branch factory. In other words, it is mainly an impetus which makes a company recognise the necessity of moving from its existing location. Therefore, the recognition of problems at the existing site is the direct origin of push factors. Several causes have been listed as push factors in empirical studies on the movement of manufacturing companies. Among these, the shortage of space for expansion at the existing premises has been found to be the most significant one in causing a move. Keeble (1969), Smith (1971), Townroe (1972), Fothergill and Gudgin (1982), etc. have backed up this fact in their studies.

On the other hand, labour supply problems, including wider aspects like militancy, skill, etc., and government controls, in particular in Britain the industrial development certificate (IDC) control, have also been found to be crucial push factors. Other factors which have been proposed are changes in the supply of raw materials or components away from local supplies, new management or technology and a bad environment, vandalism, etc., at the existing site. In the case of the UK, 'the old problems of high rents, shortage of skilled employees, costly staff turnover and the overheads imposed on working in the overcrowded and congested south-east' have been pointed out as the main push factors in that region (*Financial Times*, 30 Apr. 1992). Recently, with the growth of companies, e.g. multi-branch companies and MNCs, organizational factors such as the overall strategies of headquarters appear to be an important push factor for branch plants.

The push factors affecting the Japanese companies now operating in the UK and Korea originate in Japan in the main. The wage cost increase in the home country, the difficulty in securing raw materials there and the necessity to secure a foreign sales network and to access foreign markets, etc. are listed as the main motives of Japanese overseas investment (Economic Planning Agency,Japan,1984,pp.114-116; *The Japan Economic Review*, 15 Jul. 1990; *Financial Times*, 15 Jul. 1991).

3.3.1.3 Main locational pull factors

Unlike push factors, pull factors normally work to help a company in deciding on one location among several alternative sites rather than to make a firm move directly (Cooper,1975,p.41). Not so many empirical studies have been done about the actual influence of individual geographical factors, with the exception of regional policy, in attracting footloose firms to particular places. This is mainly due to the fact that locational decisions are normally the compounded results of many factors so that it is difficult to compute the exact influence of any particular factor. Furthermore, the fact that the critical factors making firms locate in certain places vary according to the very nature of the firms prevents writers from drawing an easy conclusion on this issue (*Financial Times*, 4 Jan. 1991).

Regarding this issue, many researchers assert that firms which intend to move or open a new plant tend to make location decisions through the following three stages; the selection of a certain region, the selection of a certain local area within the region and the choice of a specific site in the local area (Stafford,1979,p.102; Haigh et al.,1989,Part 3; Haigh,1990,pp.22-31; Walker and Greenstreet,1991,p.15). As a result, the important location factors which firms take into consideration are said to be different according to the geographical scales of search, i.e. national, regional or local (Wheeler,1981,pp.134-145; Schmenner et al.,1987,pp.83-104; Walker and Calzonetti,1990,pp.15-30).

For instance, Schmenner (1982) and Schmenner et al. (1987) identify a group of important location factors through extensive interviews. Firstly, at the region/state level, those important factors are a favourable labour climate, nearness to markets and an attractive place for engineers and managers to live. On the other hand, at the site level, access to rail services and motorways, the special provision of utilities to the firm and a rural area were found to be important location factors.

By comparing all the factors mentioned by each author, a group of factors can be derived as the most important pull factors of industrial location. They include the supply and price of labour (favourable labour climate); the supply and price of land and premises; market accessibility (nearness to market); the quality of infrastructure (access to railway services, motorways and utilities); government policy; and an attractive environment and living circumstances (rural area).

Here, it seems meaningful to examine briefly the concept of each factor and related issues in order to be able to provide criteria for selecting the explanatory variables required later in the study[12]. While the qualities and aspects of these factors are referred to here in isolation, it is actually their relative quality, individually and collectively, as a 'package' that is crucial (e.g. relatively lower wage costs than in alternative locations, etc.).

Firstly, labour availability. The importance of labour supply has been proposed and confirmed in most empirical studies including Townroe (1971), Stafford (1974), Haywood (1979), Schmenner (1982), Haigh et al. (1989) and Galbraith et al. (1990). In general, there are several issues which should be considered in relation to the labour supply problem. These are the skill, wage level, productivity and militancy of the labour force in the area. In the case of the firms in high technology industry, a highly skilled labour force becomes an even more important pull factor for their location (Rabino,1989,p.205). Recently, a sufficient number of young age workers available has begun to be recognized as another important pull factor for industrial location, especially for foreign companies (WMDA,1989,p.68; *Financial Times*, 4 Jan. 1991). It is expected that many Japanese MNCs operating in Korea have been influenced by this latter factor.

In addition, if it is difficult to expect an area to have a sufficient volume of labour to meet all these requirements, then the mobility of labour either between regions (geographical mobility) or between industries in the same region (occupational mobility) becomes important (Hoare,1983,pp.27-30). In particular, a company may wish to transfer some employees who must be willing to move to the new area.

Secondly, land and premises. Availability of land and premises, in particular of land, have long been recognized as an indispensable factor for mobile companies or newcomers. This covers availability, size of site, or premises, quality, cost, future price and so on (Bale,1976,p.33). The growing preference for single-floor plants and extra space for lorry-turning, car parking and welfare facilities makes companies that are searching for new facilities to be more interested in bigger sites. As a result, obtaining suitable land becomes more difficult than before. Again, the importance of available land and premises was emphasized by Townroe (1971), Haywood (1979), Slowe (1981) and Fothergill et al. (1987) and by the operations of bodies like English Estates.

Thirdly, market accessibility. This has been listed as another important factor in industrial location. Market accessibility is emphasized on the grounds that the market is not only the place where products are sold but it also provides crucial information such as product price changes, entry of new competitors and so on. Recently, the concept of the market has become extended with the growth of company activities from the regional to the national and international levels. Many empirical studies, including the works of Townroe (1971), House of Commons (1973), Schmenner (1982) and Chapman and Walker (1990), have showed the importance of this factor. In the study of Haigh et al, proximity to market was found to be the most important factor for the plant-location decisions of the foreign companies coming into the US (Haigh et al.,1989,pp.36-37). In similar vein, Swamidass reports in his analysis of the location strategies of foreign and domestic manufacturers in the US that the market accessibility factor is more important for foreign companies than for their domestic counterparts (Swamidass,1990,p.311). In particular, many companies open branch plants to assist entry to and supply of new markets distant from their main plant, and this seems to be the case of Japanese MNCs locating in the UK[13].

Fourthly, government policy. Government policy influencing the location of manufacturing firms encompasses not only regional policy but also tax holidays, advice, town planning, etc. Among these, the conducive regional policy is the main object of this study. However, in parallel with the diminishing role of regional policy, the importance of other types of government assistance is growing[14]. In addition, the positive activities of local authorities have played a crucial role both in decreasing the force of central government policy and in broadening and diversifying public policy instruments (Haigh,1990,pp.22-31; also see chapter eleven). There have been large numbers of empirical studies on the impact of government policy on industrial location (see chapter five). And, mostly, they have proved the importance of regional policy in location decisions. Among policy measures, the industrial development control (IDC) (1947-1979) was found to be one of the most powerful measures, however, as a push factor for indigenous firms - though, for a Japanese or inward investing company prior to the abolition of the IDC, this would have worked as a *negative* pull factor stopping them from building factory floor space in particular parts of Britain.

The most important pull factor inducing company investment in the assisted areas (AAs) has been the regional financial incentives in existence since 1945. These financial incentives comprise regional development grant (RDG), which was abolished recently, and regional selective assistance (RSA). Other assistance at times promoted training, labour (selective employment tax/regional employment premium)(SET/REP), premises, etc. The question about which measure has been the more influential one has been controversial. Although RDG is considered to be more convenient than RSA for firms, it seems to be difficult to find a considerable difference in effect between the two measures (McGreevy and Thomson,1983,p.355). On the other hand, the inconsistency of policy and the reduction of the coverage of AAs after 1981 have been pointed out as lessening the influence of regional policy in recent locational decision-making (Regional Studies Association,1983,pp.12-16; Begg and McDowall,1987, p.469)[15].

Fifthly, infrastructure. The concept of infrastructure here involves road and communication facilities, banking, education and training up to and including university level, etc. Included too is a supply of industrial components and services and, indeed, all those things that used to comprise agglomeration and urbanisation economies. The importance of infrastructure as a pull factor in location decisions is expressed by many decision-makers and writers (House of Commons,1973; Schmenner,1982; Henry et al.,1989; Basset et al.,1989; Wheatley,1991; *Financial Times*, 30 Apr. 1992)[16]. In particular, this factor is thought to be more important in developing countries compared to the fully developed countries (Galbraith et al.,1990,p.46). Recently, with the growing tendency for a dispersion of R&D facilities, the proximity to a university is getting to be a more crucial factor[17].

And, lastly, *environment and living circumstances.* A pleasant environment such as nice weather, clean air and water and green fields is now frequently considered as an important factor in industrial location (Archer,1970,p.5; Stafford,1974,p.179)[18]. Especially, companies in the field of high technology employing large numbers of researchers and white collar workers have a tendency to consider this factor to a greater extent than traditional manufacturing firms employing many semi-skilled workers (Begg and Cameron,1988,pp.374-375; Galbraith et al., 1990,pp.35-36). However, writers seem to have experienced difficulty in measuring the importance of this factor relative to other factors chiefly due to the fact that this factor is largely related to subjective personal preferences (Cooper,1975,p.42). It is also a relatively new factor in industrial location reflecting the greater freedom now available from the constraints of the earlier influences like transport costs.

3.3.2 Locational shift pattern analysis

3.3.2.1 Approaches to locational shift pattern

There are a group of studies focusing on the shift pattern of locational change and on its relationship with motives and pulling factors behind company movements. As this type of study is concerned with the overall process of locational change, such studies tend to comprise works on locational factors and locational decision-making processes. However, it seems that these studies are different from other forms of analysis in that they base their emphasis on the aggregated features of locational change of industry in general or of an industry at the national (or international) level.

Most studies concerned with employment change between regions are included in this category. They try to explain the causes of major employment changes and to identify the implications of the changes for public policy. These studies are largely dependent on the theoretical framework of the behavioral approach using empirical surveys to test a specific hypothesis relating to industrial location by statistical analysis. Frequently the measures used are components of change analysis, shift-share analysis and entropy index (Keeble,1976,pp.31-34). In particular, shift share analysis has provided a useful framework for identifying the major features of change in a vast range of studies[19].

On the other hand, in this type of study, there are two approaches to empirical analysis; the one is a micro-level approach and the other is a macro-level approach. While the former investigates industrial location change through data acquired directly from each manufacturer, the latter tests an established hypothesis by statistical analysis of published aggregate data series (ibid, pp.4-5). In Britain, although there has been a sharp debate between two approaches, the former approach seemed more popular in the early 1970s (Massey and Meegan eds.,1985; Begg and McDowall,1987), though the latter has substantial exponents in Keeble (1976), Pounce (1981), Fothergill and Gudgin (1982), Moore et al. (1986) and Begg (1990).

3.3.2.2 The locational pattern in the UK

The overall trend in British manufacturing is termed a process of de-industrialization (Blackaby,1979). The manufacturing sector has been declining relatively, and even absolutely, in the 1970s and especially in the early 1980s in employment terms if not in output. Growing international competition and the weakness of British industry in the international market at existing exchange rates and the world recession have been pointed out as the main causes of this change. As a result, a number of changes have occurred within the manufacturing sector such as changes in the industrial structure (mix, size and ownership of manufacturing concerns), and in the types of labour required and in industrial concentration (Hoare,1983,p.15; Lever,1991,pp.983-985). A large proportion of the locational shifts in British manufacturing industry have been accounted for by this de-industrialisation process which is closely related to worldwide structural change (Massey and Meegan,1982,pp.3-6).

In the British locational shift pattern, three trends have been identified by these empirical studies as important. Firstly, after 1960, especially in the later 1960s, there has been a reversal of the traditional trend for manufacturing to concentrate in the major conurbations. The dispersion to peripheral regions and parts of regions began to substitute for the concentration of manufacturing industry and employment in the cities (counter-urbanization). As a result, there has been a remarkable manufacturing employment growth in hitherto underdeveloped regions. In particular, regions neighbouring major conurbations, such as East Anglia, the East Midlands and South West, have been major beneficiaries of this trend (Law,1980,Ch.2; Keeble,1987, p.11)[20]. This trend continued into the 1970s and 1980s.

Secondly, since the latter half of the 1970s, there has appeared a fundamental change in the structure of the national and international economy and this change has had an uneven impact upon different regions. In brief, the phenomenon of the north-south divide between regions reappeared with the weakening trend of urban-rural shift and with the increasing share of favoured regions, i.e. the South East, East Anglia, East Midlands and South West, in manufacturing employment (ibid,pp.12-14). Moreover, the restructuring, which is prevalent among large multiplant enterprises pursuing profit maximization, has aggravated rather than improved any disparity between regions. For instance, in some regions, it became more difficult to find newly established independent companies (except as very small concerns). Rather, branch plants or subsidiaries of large companies began to constitute a larger proportion of manufacturing industry in these regions. The growth of service sector and high technology industry in the 1980s has reinforced rather than weakened this trend of regional imbalance (Goddard and Thwaites,1987,pp.103-107; Begg, 1991,pp.962-963) at least until the current slump.

And, thirdly, the dramatic change in British manufacturing industry in the 1970s has produced another significant problem in British geography. This is the inner city problem. The process of restructuring in manufacturing industry, inevitably as matters stood, resulted in depressed areas in old urban cities where the bulk of social, physical and economic problems intertwined with each other in a way that could hardly be solved. The locational shift of manufacturing companies and employment from their old urban sites on which they had long been based left an undermined urban economy as well as derelict land and premises. As a consequence, both the direction and effectiveness of traditional spatial policy began to be seriously attacked (Fothergill et al., 1985,pp.40-42; Fingleton and Tyler,1990,pp.433-445).

In short, the results of these locational pattern analyses made people recognise the necessity of more comprehensive analysis and treatment of these fresh geographical problems.

3.4 Locational Decisions of MNCs and Their Impact on Host Regions

In general, the impact of MNC location on the regional economy has been thought to be mainly in line with that on the host country national economy[21]. MNCs influence the regional economy in various ways. However, the influences can largely be divided into two: positive aspects and negative ones.

The nature of the positive impact can be set out as follows (Blackbourn,1982,pp.153-157; Roberts and Noon,1987,pp.167-169; Young et al.,1988,pp.67-100), though any particular MNC project will not necessarily have all of these impacts:

Firstly, in general, the movement of MNC affiliates into a regional economy increases employment levels in the region. Although the scale of the job creation effect has often been challenged, especially in the case of capital intensive industry and rationalized production, the increase of employment has long been a presumption for continuing regional policy and local authority economic initiatives[22]. In the meantime, a change in the labour relations in the host country mainly through the introduction of the management style and customs from the home country has been expected by authors and policy-makers (Dohse, 1987,pp.124-145).

Secondly, the location of a MNC in the region will provide the region with an opportunity for contact with new technology and innovation and, therefore, will enhance indigenous growth. Although the lack of R&D facilities in MNC branches in assisted regions has been pointed out, MNCs generally introduce, and transfer to a less extent, a step higher technology or more innovative products to the region than those already present[23].

Thirdly, MNC affiliates, by using the products of indigenous firms, will enable local firms to expect increased scale economies, and this will bring about an further increase in indigenous invention and innovation.

And, fourthly, overseas inward investment tends to have multiplier effects in the region through increased inter-industry linkages. Either through direct investment and attraction of component suppliers from their home countries or through the purchase of labour and intermediate products, MNC plants generate substantial effects in the regional economy[24].

Against these benefits, as in the case of the national economy, overseas investment into a region is condemned in that it results in increased external control and, thus, a branch plant economy or a loss of structural autonomy. Firn, investigating the effect of overseas investments in the Clydeside conurbation, suggested the negative impact of external control that resulted from inward investment; namely reduction of local linkage, diminishing R&D activities and skilled labour employment and prevention of local initiatives (Firn,1975,pp.410-412). In a similar vein, the vulnerability of the host country economy to international demand and supply conditions resulting from MNC activities was presented by Dunning (1985,pp.47-48).

It is difficult to draw a firm conclusion about whether a MNC location will be beneficial or malign to the regional economy without taking into account all the costs and benefits caused by the attraction of the investment. As O'hUallachain properly indicated, since the inward overseas investments to a region are an integration of widely diverse economic interests, only through focusing on the complexity of products and process of investment flow, can we understand the exact role of that investment in the regional economy (O'hUallachain,1986,p.160).

In general, the spatial policy of a country tends to be implemented under the postulation of one dominant aspect out of these two. Here, the following questions arise in proceeding more on to regional policy, the next section briefly outlines the framework of location analysis in this study.

3.5   Framework of Location Analysis in This Study

This study, as described earlier, tries to investigate the locational behaviour of Japanese MNCs. In order to figure out the behavioral features of Japanese companies, this study depends upon descriptive analysis in identifying the features of their geographical distribution and upon regression analysis and upon survey in finding out specific locational factors influencing substantially the locational movement of the firms. However, the results will be interpreted in a broader structural context rather than sticking either to the neoclassical or the behavioral approach. Therefore, the main framework of this study concerned with industrial location will be on the three elements set out below.

Firstly, this study assumes that Japanese MNCs basically attempt to maximize their profit in host countries. However, their profit will be considered in the longer-term incorporating non-financial factors such as the growth of good-will for Japanese companies among British or Korean people. In addition, it is necessary to extend the geographical boundary of this profit as broadly as possible rather than confine it simply to profitability in British or Korean territory. This is because MNCs, in particular those of Japanese origin, will not invest in a foreign country just in order to secure the market of the country but have wider motives in mind and consider the profitability of the whole MNC[25].

Secondly, the statistical analysis in this study will depend on both published data and individual survey results. This means that the present study relies not only on a macro-level approach but also on a micro-level approach. The main reason for taking both a macro- and micro-level approach in this study is that, as Japanese companies operating in Britain and Korea are the consequences of complex interactions among various factors, it is difficult to obtain sufficiently reliable results by simply using either approach on its own. Therefore, the macro-level approach using regression analysis, the micro-level approach using questionnaire and interview survey and, finally, the aggregation of the results of these two approaches are adopted to infer the influence of locational factors on the actual location decisions of Japanese companies that have given rise to plants in particular locations in the two countries.

The locational factors to be considered here are mainly pull factors. Important pull factors are identified in both approaches, while push factors are considered only in the micro-level approach. This is because Japanese MNCs' movements between regions within the host countries are rare and the pushes arise in Japan and, to that extent, there is a limitation on the ability to acquire relevant macro-level data to find push factors in Japan.

One thing which should be considered here with regard to the identification of important locational factors is that this study mainly concentrates its focus on the factors which influence the location decisions at regional (County) level among different levels of location decisions. This is based on the grounds that location factors which affect national and local level decisions are difficult to identify by analyzing published data for macro-level analysis and, therefore, can only be found out partially in the expressions of decision makers found in the individual surveys. In addition, the identification of different locational factors which influence in each stage of location decisions, as asserted by Wheeler, Schmenner, etc., is seldom an easy task in the British and Korean case in contrast to the American case on which the theory is based. This is due to the fact that the features of regions in Britain and Korea influence or are closely related to the choice of these countries among larger areas like European and East Asian countries and the choice of a specific local area in a given region. Therefore, the locational factors influencing national and local level location decisions are considered as supplementary to the regional level location decision.

Thirdly, the interpretation of results will be made largely from the viewpoint of structuralist theory. This is because Japanese investments in the UK or Korea are typical instances of the operation of international market forces[26], and it is meaningless to confine consideration to purely the regional or national level in either country. This means that an additional effort is needed to relate the locational behaviour of Japanese MNCs found in the two host countries to the national and international circumstances including the changing structure of the world capitalism which Japanese MNCs confront. In addition, this effort will have to include a special emphasis on the connection of the findings of these analyses with the managerial strategy of the Japanese companies at the worldwide level, which is considered to be the outcome of the integrated action of international circumstances and Japanese culture. In short, this study is a 'closer alignment of behavioral research with structuralist thinking', such as Wood and Boddy mentioned (Wood,1987,p.52; Boddy,1987,p.63).

Having indicated the study's interest in the locations of MNCs and important locational factors, the next chapter examines the relationship between the locational decisions of MNCs and spatial policies in host countries, as the latter are one of the most important locational factors.

4 Regional policy and the location of multinational companies

4.1 Introduction

As indicated at the end of the previous chapter, the identification of the relationship between the regional policy in the host countries, the UK and Korea, and the location of Japanese MNCs are the major concerns of this study. As the last pillar for building the theoretical framework, several issues about regional policy are considered here.

Regional policy varies between countries in its concept and measures. In the UK, regional policy is usually defined as:

" ... [a set of government efforts] to encourage manufacturing industry to move to designated [AAs], in order to create jobs in those parts of the country suffering persistently high rates of unemployment" (Ashcroft and Taylor,1979,p.43).

UK regional policy has used investment incentives as the most important instrument to achieve this goal. By contrast, in a broader context, regional policy refers to all the policy measures concerned either with encouragement or prevention of development in certain regions. Therefore, the concept implies various kinds of activities such as physical planning and development activities and tax concessions as well as investment incentives[1]. Regional policy in Korea is largely understood as this wider concept.

Comparing regional policy in these two countries using the same ruler looks likely to be very difficult, and even impossible because of the complexity of the measures involved. Nonetheless, in order to find out and compare the locational patterns of Japanese MNCs in these two host countries, an effort at rearranging regional policy in Korea as if it is being implemented in the same way as that of

84

the UK is made in this study (4.2).

The relationship between regional policy and MNC location can be examined in two ways. On the one hand, it can be considered in terms of the existing regional *incentives* of host governments and the location of MNC plants in designated assisted regions to take advantage of the provided incentives. On the other hand, a series of policy *responses* to MNC activity can be considered such as the restriction of the use of foreign manufactured intermediate products or of foreign personnel and the complementary policy measures that regulate MNC location choice mainly in order to alleviate the problems of the regional economy which may arise due to the location and operation of MNCs in a region.

This means regional policy can be divided into two policy streams, *inducement policy* and *remedial policy*. Between these two, the emphasis of host governments has tended to be directed towards the former. In practice the characteristics of MNCs, such as the high mobility of subsidiaries across national boundaries, have restricted the feasibility of effective remedial regional policy. As a result, the relationship between regional policy and MNC location has become largely understood in terms of the government initiatives to induce overseas investment, especially into particular regions, and the location of MNCs in response to these incentives. The relationship will be discussed in detail in section three of this chapter. After that, an analysis of the locational behaviour of Japanese MNCs in association with regional policy will follow. First of all, regional policy in the two countries is described in the next section.

4.2   Regional Policy in the UK and Korea

4.2.1   Regional policy in the UK

4.2.1.1   Concept

The existence of a complex mix of problems such as high unemployment, industrial obsolescence, low income levels and high out-migration in several regions mainly in the northern part of the British isles, which has often been called the 'north-south divide', has long been an important matter of concern for the British government; and this is the basis on which British regional policy has been continued over the last half century.

The aims of British regional policy are various, and often confusing. In general, it is accepted that regional policy aims include that of:

" ... bringing the supply and demand for labour in the [AAs] more closely into balance [and, hence,] ... helping the [AAs] move towards self-sustaining growth" (Regional Studies Association [RSA],1983,p.2).

For a long time, regional policy has been justified on the basis of social and political considerations. In other words, the issue of a more equitable distribution of resources and wealth between regions have been central to the discussion of regional policy. In addition, the concern has been expanded to include economic issues such as the under-utilization of infrastructure and the contribution of under-employed resources to national economic growth (ibid,pp.2-3; Smith,1989,p.81)[2].

For this purpose, industrial relocation became an immediate objective of regional policy. This goal has been pursued mainly through the combination of the regulatory control (IDC) and conducive financial assistance, or both 'stick' and 'carrot'.

4.2.1.2 Regional policy before the present government

Regional policy in the UK (apart from the Labour Transference Scheme of 1928) began with the Special Areas Act 1934 which designated four Special Areas. The areas were extended and transformed into Development Areas (DAs) by the Distribution of Industry Act 1945. This marked the beginning of an active phase of regional policy associated with regeneration at the end of the war. Regional policy in its early days placed more emphasis on the social aspect of unemployment than its economic effect, and this tradition still continues (Parsons,1988,p.7)[3].

In the 1950s, at a time of prosperity in the national economy, the regional problem was not a significant concern of either government or people. Regional policy continued without any substantial change. However, the 1960s was a period of transition for regional policy. In particular, between 1964 and 1970, the Labour government implemented a group of powerful policies to disperse factories and their employment to aid the development areas (DAs). During the period, the IDC control was tightened and financial assistance to the enlarged designated areas was greatly increased. In particular, the introduction of the Regional Employment Premium (REP) and the creation of Special Development Areas (SDAs) within DAs (1967) and Intermediate Areas (IAs) by the Local Employment Act 1970 were the most notable results of the strengthened regional policy at the time[4].

However, the 1970s was a period of uncertainty for regional policy. This was mainly caused by the changing economic situation, especially the growing national unemployment, and Conservative government policy. The Conservative government (1970-1974) loosened many implementing policies with the relaxation of the IDC control and the intended suspension of REP and of investment grants. The government put more emphasis on discretionary aid and on infrastructure spending instead of grants to firms. The participation of the UK in the EEC in this period was another important event having a substantial implication for British regional policy thereafter (Hansen et al.,1990,p.106).

Restored to power in 1974, the Labour government resumed its earlier effort to strengthen regional policy such as the continuation of REP, the tightening of the IDC control and the dispersion of government offices from London. However, the mounting recession during 1974-1978 made the government retreat once again on grounds of cost including the reduction, delay in payment and, finally, abolition of REP (McCallum,1979,ch.1).

4.2.1.3 The changing context of regional policy

Since the mid-1970s the context of regional policy has changed dramatically. The main causes of this change can be listed as follows (RSA,1983,pp.53-57; Damesick, 1987a, pp.7-11; Smith,1989, pp.98-102):

1) The declining economic situation resulted in a switch of government attention from regional problems towards national problems such as sluggish growth, high inflation and rising unemployment. In particular, the recession in the 1980s, which resulted in a high level of unemployment everywhere in the country, challenged the relevance of the aim of regional balance in employment[5]. In addition, regional policy was weakened by the changes in industrial investment activity (an increase in the capital intensity of industry), by the rationalization of production and by the switch from manufacturing (the main focus of regional policy) to services.

2) In this worsening economic situation, it became difficult to find enough migrant firms, especially in manufacturing, to support regional policy of the old kind. In consequence, the concern of the central government and local authorities began to be directed more towards the promotion and encouragement of indigenous firms in situ especially in the AAs.

3) There developed a new pattern of spatial economic inequality. Unlike in previous periods, unemployment began to increase in most regions including formerly prosperous regions such as West Midlands and North West while it decreased in parts of AAs where, for example, oil development was located. Moreover, the inner city problem emerged as a major subject of policy concern in particular regions. This resulted in innovations in industrial development policy; namely the introduction of Enterprise Zones (EZs) and Urban Development Corporations (UDCs) (Parsons,1988,pp.195-197; Hall,1991,p.68).

4) There was also an increase in the influence of international market forces on the British economy. A large part of the regional problems of the 1970s was caused by decisions of MNCs at the international level. It became apparent that this factor demanded the development of a different kind of approach to regional problems. In addition, the policy of the European Community, which is equipped with European Regional Development Fund (ERDF) and is pursuing balanced development between regions in member countries, has influenced, and in some respect restricted, the perspective and measures of British regional policy (Cheshire et al.,1991, pp.291-295).

5) The policy of the Conservative government was also significant in reducing the

87

strength and scope of regional policy. A series of policies by the Conservative government have strengthened central control at the expense of regional policy and regional politics (Gordon,1990,p.435). On the other hand, the lack of financial resources available to government as whole was a significant obstacle to continuing the concentrated investment in some designated AAs. This was chiefly caused by the decline in the UK economy and the Conservative government's policy which emphasized expenditure cuts in the public sector.

In these circumstances, traditional regional policy has come under severe criticism, and thus has met revision. In particular, the insufficient employment effects of subsidies, the concentration of policy efforts on the manufacturing sector, the failure in developing the AAs into self-reliant regional economies and the lack of a regional point of view in drafting and implementing policy by the central government have been the major targets of a barrage of criticism (Green and Clough,1982,pp.87-92; Parsons, 1988,p.210; Martin,1989,p.50). The criticism is expressed even as follows:

" ... regional policy carried undesirable connotations of excessive state intervention and subsidies to preserve inefficiency and overmanning which, far from helping the regions, actually inhibited their development" (Smith,1989, p.95).

4.2.1.4   Regional policy under the Conservative government

Thus, there has been a substantial change in the context of regional policy since the coming into power of the Conservative government in 1979. In particular, the declining economic situation in the midst of the worldwide structural change has diverted the focus of government policy from regional problems both to the national economy and to the urban one (Martin,1989, pp.52-53).

Since 1979, the regional policy system has been reformed but largely maintained in the form of Regional Development Grant (RDG) and Regional Selective Assistance (RSA) (although the former ended on 31 Mar. 1988). However, both the geographical coverage and the instruments of regional policy have experienced a series of changes, mainly towards reduction and decline:

First of all, there has been a substantial descheduling of areas qualifying for regional assistance together with the replacement, in 1984, of the previous three-tier system of assisted areas by two tiers. SDAs were abolished, leaving DAs and IAs. The total coverage of AAs, which was over 40% of the UK working population in 1979, has been reduced to 27.5% in 1982, but now is 35% with the inclusion of the West Midlands AA (Damesick,1987b,pp.57-59). Figure 4.1 portrays the AAs defined in 1984.

Fig. 4.1 Assisted Areas in the U.K.

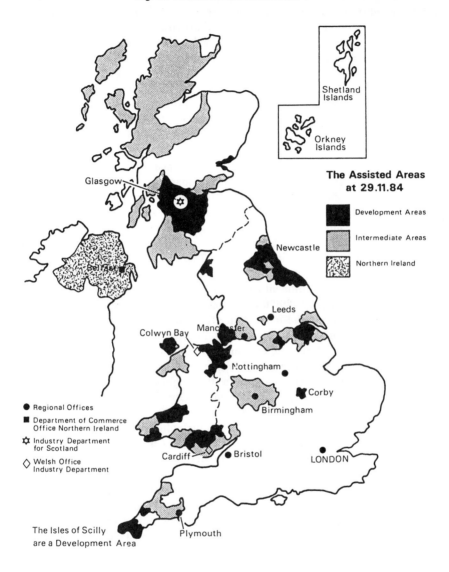

The Assisted Areas
at 29.11.84

■ Development Areas

▨ Intermediate Areas

▨ Northern Ireland

Shetland Islands

Orkney Islands

Glasgow

Newcastle

Belfast

Leeds

Colwyn Bay   Manchester

Nottingham

Corby

Birmingham

● Regional Offices

■ Department of Commerce
   Office Northern Ireland

✿ Industry Department
   for Scotland

◇ Welsh Office
   Industry Department

Cardiff   Bristol   LONDON

The Isles of Scilly
are a Development Area   Plymouth

*Source: Industrial Development Act 1982. Annual Report by the Secretaries of State
for Trade and Industry for the year ended 31st March 1985, HMSO*

Secondly, the RDG scheme was reshaped in 1984. The new RDG scheme was differentiated from the old one in three respects: 1) projects which either increased productive capacity or changed the nature of the firm's product significantly were made eligible for the assistance; 2) grants became payable to certain service industries such as advertising and software development; and 3) there was a limit of grant to 15% of capital expenditure or £ 3,000 per new job created. The mainspring of this change is attributable to the unsatisfactory job creation effect of RDG expenditure. In addition, practical difficulties in applying the RDG scheme have also been pointed out (Pettigrew and Dann,1986,pp.182-184). As a result, the emphasis of the present government's regional policy has moved to selective assistance.

And, thirdly, RSA also has been changed since 1979. According to some evidence, the expenditure under this discretionary assistance scheme has been mainly directed to the new high technology industries, especially electronics. This concentration of RSA on new high technology and expanding industry is interpreted as meaning that the emphasis of discretionary assistance is chiefly focused on changing the industrial structure towards fast-growing and large employment gaining industries (Johns,1987,pp.555-558)[6]. Together with these changes, the IDC control was suspended in 1982.

Furthermore, the government announced another reform of regional policy in 1988. Accordingly, from 1989/90 RDG was ended and the emphasis was directed towards new investment and innovation grants to small and medium sized firms in DAs (up to 500 employees). By contrast, the map of AAs, spending on regional assistance and the RSA scheme continued without any significant change except for the extension of assistance to some other areas and parts of the service sector. By introducing the above changes in the regional assistance package, the government has reduced expenditure from £ 983m in the early 1980s to £ 477m in 1988/9 (1988 prices) (Wren, 1990,p.52)[7].

Overall, regional policy as well as economic policy in the UK has experienced and is now experiencing a series of drastic changes. The main thrust of this change is attributed to the underlying conviction of the current government, in conjunction with the drastically changing national and international economy, that private activity is more efficient than public intervention in the economy. There is also a belief, despite the obstacles involved, that those without jobs at present rates of pay in regions with high unemployment especially should be more mobile and flexible in their job search. As a result, the weakened status of regional policy is expressed even as:

"the traditional tools of policy-making, such as capital subsidies to attract mobile investment, are no longer adequate to counter widening regional disparities" (Gibbs, 1989,p.1).

In this process, there has been, and certainly still is, a sharp debate between the theorists demanding the restoration of regional policy on the one hand and the arguers emphasising the relevance of the present policy which allows the priority of the national economy as a whole. However, the pendulum has obviously swung towards the latter recently[8].

Nevertheless, the desirability of balance between regions is still alive and, thus, it is more proper to find a breakthrough for regional policy by accommodating the policy to the changing national and international economic context rather than to abolish it completely[9]. At present, the maintaining of regional policy is necessitated at least by the competition with other countries in attracting inward investment as well as political considerations (Hansen et al.,1990,pp.113-114). This means that the possibility of taking advantage of inward investment became an important aim in implementing regional policy. (Therefore, the present study devotes its main part to identifying this relationship.)

4.2.1.5 The effect of government regional policy

In principle, the effectiveness of regional policy can be determined by calculating both the costs and the effects of the policy. Here, the costs of regional policy include not only public expenditure but also a number of economic costs such as the management cost of moving firms, additional transport cost, regional efficiency variations, wage inflationary pressures and the resource cost caused by the unbalanced use of infrastructure (Rees,1985,pp.473-475).

However, researchers have been interested in measuring directly the quantitative effect of regional policy on regional economic indicators and have poured their main efforts into this field[10]. And it was the regional policy *before the reform in 1984* that most researchers have focused on to measure the effectiveness. Therefore, the examination of policy effect in this study is also concentrated mainly on the pre-1984 regional policy.

Since Moore and Rhodes tried to identify the exact effect of regional policy in 1973, most researchers have depended, in implementing their work, on applying shift-share analysis to aggregate macro-statistics. And the predominant results of these researches have been to emphasize the important impact of regional policy on various aspects of the economy (Begg and MacDowall,1987, p.460), and, especially, the important role played by the IDC control (Ashcroft and McGregor,1989,p.312; Fingleton and Tyler,1990,p.443). In general, these researches have used the following three indicators for measuring the effects of regional policy; namely, employment, industrial movement and additional private investment (DTI,1983,pp.92-113; Moore et al.,1986,p.13).

1) The effects on manufacturing employment in the AAs: This impact has been the most frequently used objective of these researches. Studies included in this category can be listed as follows: Buck and Atkins (1976) using the analysis of variance technique; Moore and Rhodes (1973) and Marquand (1980) using

the conventional method; Moore et al. (1986) using the modified method of shift- share analysis; and Wren (1989b,1991) using regression analysis. Common findings of these studies can be summarized as saying that regional policy has influenced manufacturing employment in the AAs significantly. They estimated the cumulative employment effect of some twenty years of regional policy by 1981 as ranging from 250,000 to 445,000 jobs in the AAs.

2) The effects on industrial movement: In estimating this effect, there have been two approaches. The one is the micro-approach using the method of surveying firms and the other is the macro- approach applying regression analysis to time-series and cross- sectional data. While the works of House of Commons (1973), Keeble (1978) and Massey (1979a) are included in the former approach, those of Ashcroft and Taylor (1977) and Twomey and Taylor (1985) are from the latter (Armstrong and Taylor,1985,pp.290-294). As in the case of the employment effect, most research concluded that regional policy has had a substantial effect on industrial movement ranging from 500 to 900 moves in varying periods.

3) The effects on industrial investment: Inducing additional investment from the private sector is one of the most important objectives of regional policy to make self-sustaining growth possible in the AAs' economy. The studies of Rees and Miall (1979) and Padgett (1985) are included in this category. The main finding of these studies is that regional policy (especially, REP in the latter's study) has been important in increasing the level of manufacturing investment in the AAs and that the level of induced investment has had a positive relationship with the strength of regional policy.

On the other hand, regarding *the effect of current regional policy,* which is characterised as market-based and small firm- and high technology-orientated, only a small number of researches have been undertaken (Martin,1988; Hansen et al.,1990; Amin and Tomaney,1991). This time, instead of evaluating the direct effects of financial incentives, the role of which has been diminished since the late 1970s, authors have explained the effect indirectly by the resulting differences between regions of employment growth (Pattie and Johnston,1990), of small firm and service industry (Keeble et al.,1991), of high technology industry (Keeble,1989), of the defence industry (Oakey,1991), etc. Through these analyses, many of them criticize regional policy in the 1980s in that the policy has not halted the spatial inequalities between regions. In addition, a writer criticizes the 1988 reform of regional policy, in particular the abolition of RDG, saying that the revision was 'hasty and perhaps ill-informed' (Wren,1989a,pp.127-137 and 1990,p.62)[11].

Configurating the results of above researches, we are able to conclude that regional policy has had a substantial effect on the regional economy of the AAs and has played an important role in decreasing regional disparities. However, this conclusion is open to counter-argument mainly in terms either of its cost-effectiveness (in the case of traditional regional policy) or of its aggravating impact on regional balance (the policy in the 1980s)[12]. One thing that should be noted is that a large number of these researches have pointed to the diminishing effect of regional incentives, and this has had important implications both for explaining the recent change of government policy and for forecasting its direction. Recently, as the importance of the supply side of regional growth has become recognized, a region's overall 'environment' for the location of business began to be stressed rather than individual location factors (Glasson,1992, pp.507-509).

4.2.2 Regional policy in Korea

4.2.2.1 Concept

Over the last three decades, the Korean economy grew rapidly and, during the process, government policy has provided the main impetus behind this growth. This development of Korea based on industrialisation has been accompanied by drastic urbanisation. From 1960 to 1985, the rate of urbanisation, i.e. the percentage of population living in urban areas to the whole population, more than doubled from 35.8% to 73.8%. During this process of industrialisation and urbanisation, there appeared a number of problems in the Korean economy and society. Widening regional imbalance is among these problems.

Regional policy in Korea has not been formed and implemented in a consistent way under one unambiguous objective. In practice, regional policy has been understood mainly in conjunction with the decentralization of population and industry from the capital city of Seoul. In other words, the over-concentration of population and industry in Seoul and the spatial inequalities resulting from it are seen by the government to comprise the main part of the regional problem in Korea to be addressed by regional policy (Kwon, 1988,pp.106-108)[13]. Seoul is not only the capital city but also the centre of politics, administration, the economy and the culture of Korea. This appears to have been the main reason for the concentration of population and industry there[14]. The importance of Seoul city in Korea is shown in Table 4.1.

Furthermore, Seoul and adjacent cities[15] form a metropolitan region (MPR) in which a strong interaction is apparent between Seoul and the surrounding area.

This MPR, which has one third of the whole Korean population, encompasses the area within a radius of 60 km. In terms of administrative boundaries, Seoul, Kyonggi- Do and part of Kangwon-Do are included in the MPR, making its whole area 12,489 km^2 (Ministry of Construction,1981; see Figure 4.2).

The over-concentration of population and industry in the Seoul MPR has inevitably given rise to a number of problems in national and regional geography in Korea. Inequality between regions, downgrading living conditions in Seoul and

Table 4.1 Position of Seoul in Korea   (%)

	1980		1989	
	Total	Seoul	Total	Seoul
Area (km²)	99,263	605	99,263	605
	(0.6)	(0.6)		
Population(000)	37,449	8,367	40,448	9,639 [++]
	(22.3)	(23.8)		
Manufacturing	31,700	7,741	59,928	17,120 [+++]
firms	(24.5)	(28.6)		
Water supply(%)[+]	78.7	92.4	89.1	99.3
Road(km)	14,278	4,314	56,481	7,323
	(30.2)	(20.0)		
Traffic vehicles	494	201	2,660	991
(000)	(40.7)	(37.3)		

[+] The proportion of dwellings equipped with water supply system.
[++] 1985 figure [+++] 1988 figure
Source : *White Paper on the National Economy* (1986,1990); *Yearbook of Regional Statistics* (1990).

the vulnerability in terms of national defence are among those.

In order to tackle this over-concentration problem, various kinds of policy measures, such as controls, direct investment in infrastructure and tax incentives, have been mobilized. In particular, regulatory measures such as a planning control, a green belt surrounding the Seoul MPR, and tax exemptions available to emigrating industry together with large-scale investments in the infrastructure in lagging regions have been used as the main instruments.

One thing that should be noted is that, with the explicit objectives of decentralization and balanced regional development, there is an even more important task assigned to regional policy. This is the provision of the physical basis for national economic growth. The development of industrial estates in certain designated areas has been emphasized to achieve this goal. As a result, direct investment in infrastructure, including the development of industrial sites, has come to constitute a large part of the policy concern[16].

However, the problem is that this goal of national economic development often conflicts with, or even sacrifices, the nominated objective, the reduction of regional disparities, and has resulted in the increased concentration of population and industry in certain regions (Lee,1988,p.145). In short, because of the ambiguity and duality of its policy objectives, regional planning and policy in Korea has borne a kind of constraint from its earliest beginnings. As a result, the policy is unlikely to succeed in reducing regional disparities in terms of population migration and income to any great extent.

4.2.2.2   Brief history of regional policy

Fig. 4.2 Prosperous and Lagged Regions in Korea

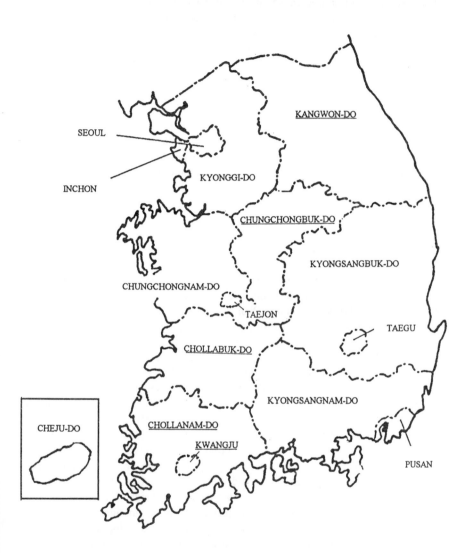

* The names of lagged regions are underlined.

Since the beginning of the 1960s, the Korean government has recognized the concentration of population in Seoul (and Pusan) as a main policy issue and has tried to find a relevant policy measure to confront it. The draft of 'the plan for restricting the population concentration in larger cities' in 1964 and the establishment of the Committee for Seoul MPR were the starting points of this kind of effort.

In 1970, the Local Industry Development Act was introduced to develop other local industrial bases elsewhere and thus to decentralize population to peripheral regions. The bulk of tax advantages have been provided for firms coming into the local industrial estates sited in these peripheral regions. The First National Comprehensive Physical Development Plan (1972-1981) was announced in 1971. Although the plan was primarily aimed at the balanced development of regions, it also emphasized the construction of bases for national economic and industrial development. The Land Use Plan was introduced by the National Land Use Management Act in 1972, and the green belt was defined in the Urban Planning Act in the same year.

The period 1976-1977 was a period of transition for regional policy in Korea. Various tax incentives were initiated to promote the development of local industrial estates and the Industry Allocation Act came into force. At the same time, in order to accelerate the dispersion of population and industry from the Seoul area, the government announced two important plans; namely the Seoul Metropolitan Population Dispersion Plan and the Banwol New Town Development Plan. In particular, the former, aiming at restricting the population of Seoul to the 7 million level until 1986, suggested a set of strong policy measures such as financial assistance, planning control, an education program, etc. Until the end of 1970s, this policy was maintained with a substantial strength.

Another important strategy introduced in the 1970s to tackle regional imbalance was the development of heavy and chemical industry (HCI) in specific areas. Numbers of factories in the field of petrochemicals, machinery and steel have been set up mainly in and around the core cities alongside the east and south coast; namely Masan, Pohang, Ulsan, Yochun and Kwangyang. The strategy has enabled these core cities to act as growth poles attracting population and linked industry against the congested Seoul and Pusan region (Auty,1990,pp.23-28).

In 1981, the Second National Comprehensive Physical Development Plan (1982-1991) was set up. The prime objective of the plan again involved the decentralization of population. For the first time, the development of growth centres and regional settlement areas in each region was included to achieve the goal (The Government of Korea,1982). The Metropolis Arrangement Planning Act 1982 followed the plan in the next year. By the legislation of the Act, the control became feasible over the service sector also concentrating in Seoul MPR. In the late 1980s, as an attempt to decentralize population from Seoul to adjacent regions and to enhance the rate of housing supply in Seoul MPR, the government launched the development of two new towns, Bundang and Ilsan, with a total size of 33 km^2.

As we have seen above, the emphasis of Korean regional policy has been heavily placed on control over the population and industry in Seoul MPR rather than on the development of lagging regions such as both Chollabuk-Do and Chollanam-Do[17]. In other words, control over the concentration of industry and population has been more accentuated than the inducement incentives to encourage mobile firms to move into some less developed regions. In this respect, it is substantially different from the British approach which emphasizes policy measures in both directions.

4.2.2.3 The effect of regional policy

So far, few research efforts, if any, have been made to quantify the effect of government regional policy in Korea. Therefore, in this study, any measuring of the effectiveness of regional policy will be made by considering the changes in several factors indirectly.

In general, regional disparity in Korea has been recognized mainly in terms of income differentials and of population movements between regions rather than in the unemployment level or the movement of industry which are the measures usually used in the UK. In particular, differentials in gross income per capita between regions have been conceived as the main source of policy concern[18].

Regional disparity expressed by gross regional product is shown in Table 4.2[19]. According to the table, regional product differentials have been reduced since 1970. The range has fallen from 234.1/71.3 in 1970 to 126.8/80.7 in 1985, with two regions in particular moving above the national average and another two leaders falling closer to it.

This may be thought of as the effect of successful regional policy since the 1970s. However, in order to reach such a conclusion, it is necessary to consider another aspect of the regional problem, population migration. Table 4.3 shows the net migration of population coming into Seoul. According to the table, the movement of population to Seoul has continued (though down in rate in the 1980s), and concentration has ever been exacerbated.[20]

Integrating these conflicting results, it becomes obvious that the reduction of regional income disparity results from the rapid population concentration, not from the growth of income level in the lagged regions[21]. In addition to regional income differentials, a number of changes can be taken into account as indicators for estimating the effectiveness of Korea's regional policy:

Firstly, as discussed earlier, control over the growth of Seoul MPR has always been the major policy concern of the Korean government. The master plan for the control, the Seoul MPR Population Dispersion Plan, and other policy initiatives seem not to have succeeded in achieving this anticipated goal. Today, the population of the Seoul MPR exceeds 10 million. The main causes of this shortcoming are: 1) the plan lacked the practical instruments to control the

97

Table 4.2   Gross regional product per capita (as % of the national average)

Province (Region)	1970	1975	1980	1985
Korea	100.0	100.0	100.0	100.0
Seoul	234.1	157.6	149.9	126.8
Pusan	138.0	117.1	105.6	106.6
Kyonggi-Do	112.5	121.6	108.3	114.7
Kangwon-Do	74.5	76.6	84.9	95.3
Chungchongbuk-Do	81.1	90.8	100.2	94.5
Chungchongnam-Do	73.9	76.6	86.7	80.7
Chollabuk-Do	71.3	77.3	84.0	81.6
Chollanam-Do	65.4	75.1	90.3	80.7
Kyongsangbuk-Do	87.3	96.4	79.9	95.3
Kyongsangnam-Do	85.7	108.1	125.5	121.1
Cheju-Do	76.5	84.8	96.6	92.9

Taegu, Inchon, Kwangju and Taejon cities are involved in Kyongsangbuk-Do, Kyonggi-Do, Chollanam-Do and Chungchongnam-Do respectively.
Source : Ministry of Home Affairs (1970-1985 estimation, Unpublished data).

Table 4.3   Net population movement to Seoul (persons per annum)

Originating Region	1971	1977	1983	1989
Total Movement to Seoul	252,689	214,377	141,831[+]	109,880[+]
Pusan	19,104	15,472	23,559	14,412
Kyonggi-Do	-54,890	-53,701	-171,504	-90,197
Kangwon-Do	25,703	26,847	25,570	21,083
Chungchongbuk-Do	29,682	32,994	25,967	15,070
Chungchongnam-Do	44,622	32,126	37,369	24,450
Chollabuk-Do	50,496	46,768	47,849	34,412
Chollanam-Do	54,165	44,537	57,728	47,335
Kyongsangbuk-Do	46,870	38,069	50,507	28,357
Kyongsangnam-Do	33,467	24,713	29,842	13,550
Cheju-Do	3,560	6,552	2,341	1,172

[+] Including others such as the immigration from foreign countries are included; 12,603 (1983), 236 (1989).
Source : Korean Research Institute for Human Settlement [KRIHS] (1982); *Yearbook of Population Movement* (1983,1989).

education field and service sector; 2) the development of other regions, especially the five designated regional growth centres, was neglected; and 3) there was a time lag between the construction of New Towns such as Banwol and the absorption in these towns of population moving from Seoul (Hwang, 1984,pp.363-365).

Secondly, the development of industrial estates has constituted an important part of regional policy. Since the 1960s, the government has developed a number of industrial sites and Free Export Zones. It is estimated that 5,000 companies have been absorbed into, and 500,000 jobs have been created by, these government built industrial sites alone without mentioning the local industrial estates (Ministry of Finance,1987). Although these activities have contributed to national economic growth and industrial development as a whole, the policy is criticized for having exacerbated the regional imbalance problem[22]. Likewise, the performance of the strategy of growth pole theory including HCI growth poles, which was introduced and implemented to alleviate regional problem, has been estimated to be marginal compared to the huge scale of the regional problem (Lee,1989, pp.160-162; Auty, 1990,pp.31-33).

Thirdly, the two National Comprehensive Physical Development Plans have been successful in providing industrial estates and infrastructure for national economic development. However, the plans have not improved, and may even have aggravated, regional imbalance by concentrating development efforts in certain regions, mainly in both Kyongsang-Dos. Recently, with recognition of this problem, special policy efforts have begun to be directed towards the development of lagging regions such as Cholla-Dos. In particular, the Kwangju Area Development Project, which was initiated in 1981 and includes a range of construction plans including the West-coast Motorway, Daebul Industrial Estate, Kwangju High-Tech Site, etc., are worth noting.

And, finally, regional policy in Korea has depended more heavily on regulatory control than financial assistance. The over-dependence on control measures, although it has reached its goal to a certain extent, inevitably brought about various side effects, which ultimately became impediments for the regional policy, like the distortion of market mechanisms, unexpected victims of regulation, etc. (Kwon,1988,pp.133-134).

In total, it seems possible to conclude that regional policy in Korea has been very successful in providing bases for national economic growth but at the expense of more balanced regional development. And this latter failure has been caused by the dual structure of regional policy objectives, as mentioned above (4.2.2.1).

4.2.3 Comparison

It is difficult to compare the contents and effects of regional policy in the UK and Korea with the same gauge. Regional policy in the two countries differs in various aspects:

1) There is a difference in policy objective. In the UK, regional policy aims to encourage industry to move into the depressed regions in order to alleviate or narrow the employment gap. In Korea, the objectives are twofold. The

one is explicitly defined as balanced regional development (limiting concentration in Seoul) and the other is the provision of a basis for national economic growth, and these two have often given rise to conflicts and competition[23].

2) The standpoint for recognizing regional problems is different. While UK regional policy starts mainly from the problems, especially unemployment, from which some declining regions are suffering, that of Korea begins with the problems confronting a prosperous region, Seoul MPR. Although intra-regional planning and the New Town overspill policy of the UK government have been introduced to confront this problem, the extent to which each government emphasizes these is significantly different between the two countries.

3) The function of implementing regional policy is more dispersed between government departments in Korea compared to the UK. For example, while regional development plans are established by the Ministry of Construction in Korea, incentives are mainly offered by the Ministry of Trade and Industry and the Ministry of Finance. Moreover, the power of the Economic Planning Board, which is in charge of national economic planning and government expenditure, often threatens the feasibility and the continuity of regional development plans[24].

4) In Korea, unlike in the UK, there is no designation of spatially widely-drawn AAs. Assistance is directed on a specific industrial estates basis.

Among the differences in the nature of regional policy above, the last one has a particular implication for the empirical analysis in this study. While there has been no significant change in the boundaries of assisted industrial estates in Korea since the latter half of the 1970s, the map of the designated AAs in the UK has experienced two major changes, in 1979-81 and 1984. In order to move forward our discussion on the locational behaviour of Japanese companies in the two countries, it is necessary to clarify the geographical boundaries of the assisted regions in both countries. The AAs of the two host countries in the 1980s can be summarised as in Table 4.4.

Overall, there is profound divergence between the regional policy in the two countries as examined so far. The fundamental reasons that lie behind this divergence are the differences in the 'socio-economic policy' and 'socio-economic philosophy' which have sustained regional policy in the two countries[25]. However, there is a common task assigned in both. This is the improvement of regional balance by incorporating the force of the world economy. This issue can largely be grasped by exploring the relationship between regional policy and the activities of MNCs.

4.3 Regional Policy and the Location of Multinational Companies

Table 4.4 Comparison of the geographical boundary of AAs

Korea	UK
1) Free Export Zone (2)	1) SDAs
. Masan . Iri	o to 1984: 13% of total working population
2) Industrial Estates (76)	o from 1984: status ended
o Government built Estates (10)	
. Changwon . Yochon, etc.	2) DAs
o Local Estates (61)	o to 1984: 9% of total working population
. Pohang . Songnam, etc.	
o Private Estates (5)	o from 1984: 15%
. Yongdungpo	
. Inchon, etc.	3) IAs
	o to 1984: 6% of total total population
	o from 1984: 20%

( ) indicates numbers of each.

So far, it has been presumed that there would be a considerable relationship between regional policy and MNC activity and this has been examined. In particular, the studies of Yannapoulos and Dunning (1976), Ashcroft and Taylor (1979), O'Farrell (1980), Young et al. (1988), etc. are important ones for identifying the relationship between UK regional policy and development, and foreign firm movement. In the case of Korea, there are few studies of the relationship between government incentives and the activity of MNCs because of various restrictions on undertaking this kind of research. Therefore, in this chapter, the impact of regional policy on foreign firm movement and the spatial results of MNC location will be discussed mainly on the basis of British experience.

4.3.1 The impact of regional policy on MNC location

With the growing recognition of the importance of foreign firms in regional development and employment, the extent of regional policy influences on foreign firm movement to the AAs in the UK has become an important matter of research concern. The question is this; 'has regional policy succeeded in attracting mobile foreign firms into AAs and, if so, to what extent?'

Theoretically, in micro-economic terms, financial and fiscal incentives as measures of regional policy should be enough to compensate for the locational disadvantages of operating in AAs if regional policy is to influence the locational decision-making of mobile firms. If incentives offered through regional policy exceed the cost differentials of depressed regions, mobile firms are thought likely to be induced to locate in the AAs.

However, in practice, the responsiveness of a firm is influenced by various factors such as either firm-specific factors or structural factors including vertical integration and scale economies. The extent to which regional policy influences the locational decision-making of a firm will be determined by the powerfulness of these other factors (Yannopoulos and Dunning, 1976,pp.393-398).

Regarding this, it has been conceived that the location choice of the MNC, either between nations or between regions, will be governed by various kinds of locational factors, and that some at least of the factors will be different from those affecting indigenous firms (Vernon,1974,pp.109-111; Law,1980,Ch.7). From this viewpoint, regional policy, being one of the important factors, is expected to have different implications for the location of MNCs than for indigenous firms. Having no simple criteria and relevant data for measuring the absolute level of influence, many researchers have tended to depend on the comparison between the level of migration of MNCs and that of indigenous firms into AAs under given government assistance.

Concerning the extent to which regional incentives influence MNC location, scholars' findings are contradictory. A group of writers contend that it is difficult to find any significant difference between the influence of regional policy on the attraction of foreign firms and that of indigenous firms (Yannopoulos and Dunning,1976; Blackbourn,1978). In particular, Blackbourn, presenting empirical evidence of the concentration of foreign-owned firms in core regions in Canada, the US, the UK, and elsewhere, asserts that regional subsidies are unlikely to have succeeded in attracting many MNC affiliates to the AAs (Blackbourn,1978,p.125). In the case of the US, from the same viewpoint, a doubt about the effectiveness of state and local incentives in attracting mobile foreign firms has been cast by O'hUallachain (1986)[26].

Another group of writers, disputing the above opinion, claim that there exists a substantial difference between them with a bias towards greater influence on foreign firms. Based on the analysis of differentials in adaptation of plans to take account of regional policy measures between MNCs and indigenous firms, Ashcroft and Ingham argue that MNCs pay more attention than indigenous firms to the available incentives when choosing the appropriate technology and location for their subsidiaries (Ashcroft and Ingham,1979,p.36). In another study of the comparative impact of regional policy on foreign and indigenous firm movement, they confirm that foreign-based firms were more strongly affected by the financial incentives available in the AAs than indigenous firms (Ashcroft and Ingham,1982,p.96). O'Farrell (1980) also concludes that MNCs had a marginally stronger tendency than indigenous firms to locate in DAs in the case of Ireland.

One writer interprets these results as showing that, because of MNCs' tendency to search thoroughly for an initial location and because of their weak local linkages, MNCs have been more responsive to regional incentives (Hamilton,1985,pp.22-24). The findings of these researchers emphasising the role of regional policy in MNC locations is reaffirmed by Young et al. by the expression that;

" ... regional policy is .... necessary because without regional aid a significant proportion of new inward investment projects could go elsewhere ..." (Young et al., 1988,p.149).

As we have seen above, a lot of research effort has been devoted to finding the significance of regional policy for causing MNC location in AAs rather than elsewhere. However, deriving any general explanation of the effect from these researches needs a great deal of caution. This is because the results of these studies seem to have been affected by the characteristics of the cases examined and the methods used in the analyses. Nonetheless, from the arguments so far, it seems possible to draw a set of conclusions about the effects of regional policy on MNC location:

Firstly, theoretically, the assertion is indisputable that, since a number of structural and organisational factors interact with each other in the locational decision-making of MNCs, it is impossible to establish a general relationship applicable to every situation (Yannopoulos and Dunning,1976,p.398).

Secondly, it is necessary to distinguish between the influence of regional incentives on the locational decision-making of MNCs in choosing a host country from that in choosing a host region within that host country. In practice, the former has tended to be more influenced by broader and more various kinds of locational considerations compared to the case of choice between regions. Also, the locational decisions made at regional level have been widely accepted as being more responsive to regional incentives than those at the national level (Dunning,1972; Ashcroft and Ingham,1982,p.86).

And, thirdly, taking into account the empirical evidence of the above research comparing influences on MNCs and on indigenous firms, it is likely to be possible to conclude that the financial incentives in a regional package as a whole are marginally more influential for the location of MNCs than for indigenous firms. Contradictory arguments against this viewpoint come mainly from theoretical considerations or from the analysis of MNC location only, and as such they are not seen to be enough to cause retreat from the former argument decisively. However, this conclusion needs to be subjected to further research effort to find out enough evidence through more sophisticated techniques of analysis.

As an indirect answer to this issue, the assertion of Mr Peter Walker, the Secretary of State for Wales in 1987, arguing that regional aid was indispensable for the attraction of foreign investment into the AAs, and the marked achievement of the Welsh economy in this direction is worth considering (Balchin,1990, pp.172-174).

4.3.2 The effect of MNC location on regional balance

Given the growing force and influence of MNCs in the world economy as described in Chapters one and three, host governments have initiated various kinds of economic and industrial policy measures either as an inducement to or a promotion of foreign MNC activities, or as a response to the impacts which MNC activities have generated in their economies. Within a host country, the issue of where and how the incoming MNCs locate has an important meaning for the geography of regions. Differences between regions in the numbers and types of incoming MNCs give rise to the inequality problem between these regions[27].

Authors usually have stuck to the question as to whether the introduction of foreign owned firms in a country will reduce or accelerate regional imbalance. And this issue is closely related to that of the effectiveness of regional policy. Faced with this question, some writers assert that MNCs have tended to concentrate in the more prosperous regions and, thus, to exacerbate regional disparity (Firn,1975,pp.407-408; Blackbourn,1978,p.126). They argue, as Howells and Charles noted, that:

> " ... successful regions [in attracting inward investment] are likely to create a strong 'shadow effect' on ... regions surrounding them" (Howells and Charles,1989,p.37).

The studies of McDermott (1977), Dicken (1976), Hamilton (1987), etc. have shown, on the contrary, the decentralisation trend of foreign investment away from the prosperous South East region. The previously mentioned DTI report (1983), based on the survey of 140 MNCs, argues that regional incentives became the most important locating factor in MNC choice in the 1970s (DTI,1983,p.94). And, as such, it was expected that more inward investment would be attracted to AAs and, thus, would contribute to mitigating the regional imbalance problem. Young et al. also stress the beneficial effects of the MNC presence in host regions, especially in AAs (Young et al.,1988,p.147).

However, it seems proper to say that the effect on the regional problem will be determined by the type and volume of the MNC investment, and that the kind of policy measure introduced to counter MNC activity will be determined on the basis of the policy maker's estimation of this effect and on whether it is beneficial or malign (Rodwin,1991,p.33). Moreover, the influence of a MNC located in a specific region on other regions through various linkages, such as component supply and subcontracting, makes the evaluation of the effect on the regional problem more complex and frustrating.

Overall, regardless of whether the effect is beneficial or malign, it is obvious that the location of a MNC in a region has a substantial impact on the regional economy (Massey, 1984,p.1) and, ultimately, regional balance. In the absence of precise estimation of the effect of MNC location, it is likely to be too early for discussion of the necessity of some policy response to counter the negative effect of MNC location.

4.3.3 Japanese MNCs and regional policy

Not much research effort has been directed at assessing the responsiveness of specifically Japanese MNCs to regional incentives and, conversely, to these MNCs' impact on regional balance in the UK. In practice, most incoming Japanese firms have been offered a large amount of financial assistance from the earliest stage of their investment decisions. As such, it is predicted that they will be highly responsive to such financial assistance offered through regional policy or other initiatives[28].

The variety of public schemes to promote inward investment prevent our efforts to examine how much Japanese MNCs have received in financial assistance and how far they are responsive to these incentives. Japanese managers usually have contact with three sources of assistance in Britain; the DTI, regional agencies and local authorities. Even if we confine our concern to financial assistance offered by central government, this financial assistance is likely to have had significant influence on the location of Japanese MNCs.

In an analysis of Japanese investment in consumer electronics, Brech and Sharp demonstrate that most Japanese companies have chosen their locations in DAs in which they are eligible for both RDG and RSA[29]. Presenting this result, they conclude that financial assistance as an instrument of regional policy was important, even though not critical, to the decision of Japanese MNCs to invest in this country (Brech and Sharp,1984,pp.69-74). Dunning also stresses the importance of regional assistance for the location of Japanese MNCs. According to his analysis, Japanese MNC affiliates were strongly concentrated in areas qualifying for regional development assistance[30]. Through his own investigation and that of the Japanese External Trade Organisation (JETRO), he draws the conclusion that Japanese companies have been particularly responsive to regional assistance(*ibid*,Ch.2)[31].

On the other hand, the impact of Japanese MNCs on the regional economy was examined by several authors in various aspects including their impact on UK suppliers, on competitors and on employees. In brief, even though some allowance should be made for the initial conflict in accommodating to the UK and for the suffering of local small firms meeting strong competitors, Japanese companies have had a significant level of positive effects on the UK regional economy either through the enhancement of the technical level of local suppliers, through the increased competitiveness of UK manufacturers after contact with the Japanese MNCs, through the provision of high quality products for customers at a lower cost and through the increased job opportunities in the located regions (Dunning,1986; Peck,1990; Sadler,1992; see also Chapter five).

Given the evidence from the above discussion, it seems possible to draw a conclusion that the location of Japanese MNCs has been closely related to regional policy. In other words, they have a strong tendency to locate in AAs to utilize the proposed incentives. In turn, they have had a significant effect on the regional economy after their arrival. These facts may be interpreted as showing that Japanese MNCs have played at least some role in alleviating regional differentials.

The implications of this conclusion for the present study are: how far have Japanese MNCs been influenced by regional assistance and other important locational factors?; what is the impetus for Japanese companies to decide location in that way?; and what is the implication of this result for the regional policy in host countries? Regarding these issues, in contrast to other studies based mainly on survey method, this study tries to find out an answer both through macro-analysis using regression and micro-analysis based on individual survey. These analyses will be proceeded within Part II and Part III.

5 Methodology

5.1 Introduction

Previous chapters have set the research questions, looked at the theory and introduced some of the evidence on Japanese MNC investment and location choice. The need now is to indicate and justify the methods being adopted in this study to answer the research questions set.

In the earlier look at industrial location theory (Chapter three), two different approaches have been identified. They are the 'neoclassical theory' and the 'behavioral location theory'[1]. While it was pointed out that the former has focused on the optimal location of firms as the central aim of complicated locational decision-making, the latter emphasizes the attempt to account for the actual pattern of changes. This approach usually involves the use of a group of hypothesis-testing techniques at either micro- or macro-level (Keeble,1976,Introduction).

However, one of the major problems with the latter approach is how to relate the actual behaviour of companies to the measurable force of individual geographical factors. In fact, measuring the influence of a large number of geographical factors on locational decision-making is hardly a simple task. Our difficulty is compounded by the fact that there has not been a sufficient amount of methodological diversification in this kind of analysis.

Fortunately, in spite of these difficulties, we can find a number of works which attempt to measure the influence of a specific factor on a target variable. Such an attempt has been implemented most notably in estimating the impact of regional policy, one of the important locational factors with which we are concerned here, on employment, investment and industrial movement (Chapter three).

In such analyses, measuring the impact of a locational factor on a selected variable has been largely implemented in one or more of the following approaches apart from questionnaire and interview surveys which seek for qualitative policy effects: firstly, calculating the effects of policy on a target variable as a residual

107

of other factors; secondly, measuring the impact of policy by means of a standardisation technique to exclude the influence of other factors (e.g. shift-share analysis); and, thirdly, modelling the impacts of policy and non-policy factors in a form of equation using scale measures of policy, dummy variables, etc. (e.g. regression analysis) (Ashcroft,1982, pp.288-294).

As indicated earlier, the present study aims to identify possible location factors and to infer their individual and collective influences on the actual location decisions of Japanese companies in the two countries. For this purpose, it is likely that the third approach is the most appropriate because it fits our chief matter of concern, identifying the effect of many possible factors, not a selected one. Therefore, from the macro-level point of view, selecting all or a wide range of the possible locational factors and measuring the significance of these factors using regression analysis is the major procedure of this study. During the process, the stepwise multiple regression technique becomes a useful method for our study, for it depicts the different influences of different variables clearly.

Depending solely on this kind of macro-level analysis, however, the researcher can fall into the trap of interpreting the locational behaviour of plants as a result of a limited group of well-known, or pre-determined, factors in the chosen location (external or pull factors) irrespective of the actual causes in the moving companies (internal or push factors). That is the reason why a micro-level analysis, questionnaire and interview survey, also needs to be carried out in this study[2]. By comparing and integrating the results of these two different kinds of, and sometimes even contradictory, approaches, this study tries to identify the important geographical factors, which dominate the locational pattern of Japanese MNCs in the chosen host countries, in the changing context of the international economic structure and the MNCs' managerial strategy.

However, before searching for important geographical factors that may influence the locational decision making of Japanese MNCs, it seems necessary to depict the broad characteristics of the locational distribution of Japanese companies in each of the two host countries. Therefore, in this study, an analysis using a group of descriptive statistics will be made before finding specific locational factors based on the regression and survey analyses. The rest of this chapter presents the methodology of these three kinds of analyses. The consequences of these analyses are discussed in the following chapters.

5.2   The Analysis of Locational Distribution Using Descriptive Statistics

The examination of a series of descriptive statistics is useful for identifying the main features of the locational distribution of Japanese MNCs. The characteristics of observed distributions can be described statistically by various forms of numerical values. Mean size, standard deviation, variance, etc. comprise the main body of this kind of analysis.   Through this analysis, the most fundamental features such as location, dispersion and skewness can be represented.

The figures obtained in this way illustrate the locational characteristics across all Japanese companies and across each sub-sector, the trend of locations in each examined area, and so on. Therefore, in the next chapter, the features of the locational distribution apparent in these figures are displayed by using graphs and tables. In particular, the emphasis is placed on the trends in locational choice by Japanese MNCs across the whole of Korea and Great Britain[3]. The spatial unit, the number of companies to be studied and their industrial fields are the same as those for the regression analysis (5.3.2).

5.3 Locational Factor Analysis through Regression Analysis

5.3.1 The structure and assumptions of regression analysis[4]

In identifying factors determining the location of manufacturing establishments, regression analysis, in particular multiple regression, has been used as one of the most robust techniques. Basically, the technique focuses on the relationships between a group of independent variables and a dependent variable which needs explaining. The relationship is usually represented as a linear equation, that is;

$$Y = f(X) = b_0 + b_1 X_1 + b_2 X_2 + \ldots + u \ldots \ldots \ldots \ldots \ldots \ldots \quad (5.1)$$

Here, X_1, X_2,.... are the independent, or explanatory, variables which affect or explain the variation in the dependent variable Y. Y is a dependent variable to be explained by the activities of the independent variables. In geographical study, employment and investment are the most frequently used dependent variables. The u value, a stochastic error term, represents a part of a dependent variable which cannot be explained by the given independent variables. The b_0, b_1, b_2,.... are coefficients.

In general (and also in this study), a linear regression analysis has a set of assumptions:

1) that there is a linear relationship between dependent and independent variables. There are methods of transforming variables so that a non-linear relationship can be transformed into a linear relationship.

2) that the independent variables do not have a complete linear relationship either with each other, or with a combination of other independent variables. Therefore, it is necessary to examine the correlation matrix to find the relationship between independent variables.

3) that the residuals are independently and normally distributed. That is:

$$E(u) = 0 \qquad \ldots \ldots \ldots \ldots \ldots \ldots \ldots \ldots \quad (5.2)$$

4) that the variance of residuals is constant. This important assumption, called homoscedasticity, means that u has the same variance for each value of X.

The lack of homoscedasticity indicates that the estimates of the regression coefficients are inefficient, if not unbiased (Clark and Hosking,1986,p.367).

$$\text{var(u)} = \sigma^2 \qquad \dots\dots\dots\dots\dots\dots \quad (5.3)$$

5) that the residuals in a regression model are uncorrelated with other variables. This means that the covariance between independent variables X and the stochastic variable u is zero. That is;

$$\text{cov(X,u)} = E[(X-E(X))(u-E(u))] = 0 \quad \dots\dots\dots\dots\dots \quad (5.4)$$

However, the problem is that it is difficult to meet a desirable situation in which all the above assumptions are fulfilled. Moreover, uncertain specification of the regression and, thus, improper estimation of certain critical variables can result from the problems of non-linearity, autocorrelation and heteroscedasticity of variables (Keeble and Hauser,1972,pp.12-14). In order to confront these difficulties, this study has taken several additional considerations or tests such as: 1) the transformation of variables to the logarithmic and exponential forms; 2) the check of intercorrelations between variables; and 3) the analysis of residuals in addition to the ordinary regression procedure.

5.3.2   The framework : Scope of the analysis

Three issues need to be clarified before identifying the locational behaviour of Japanese manufacturing companies by regression analysis; time period, areal unit and the industrial field of the companies to be studied.

5.3.2.1   Time period for analysis

Firstly, this regression analysis requires a set of data spanning a certain period of time. In particular, since this study tries to illuminate the locational preferences of Japanese companies reflected in the changes in the numbers employed by Japanese companies and in the number of such companies as well as in the absolute figures for these at a fixed time, it is necessary to determine the time span over which these changes are to be measured. In the case of change analysis in this study, the time span of dependent variables is the period between 1981 and 1990 (leaving the issue of time lag until a little later).

In addition, in order to identify the characteristics of the locational behaviour of Japanese MNCs more accurately, this study goes a step further to divide the above 10-year time span into two sub-periods and to analyze the locational features in each sub-period. The comparison and aggregation of the results identified in these divided time spans is expected to provide a more relevant portrait of the features of the overall period. The sub-periods introduced on this basis are between 1981 and 1986 (6 years) as the former sub-period and between 1987 and 1990 (4 years) as the latter sub-period. This 'divided and aggregated analysis' has been adopted throughout the study[5].

It has been decided to terminate the study period at the end of 1990. Therefore, in principle, Japanese companies arriving in Britain after that date have been excluded from this study. However, this principle, it was found, could not be maintained without exceptions. During the process of micro-level analysis, some companies, whose establishment was announced by the end of 1990, were unable to be contacted, whereas some companies announced in the first half of 1991 had already begun their activities by the end of 1990. This study, in order to keep consistency in the number of objective companies analyzed in both approaches, excludes the companies in the former case, while it includes the latter companies. The numbers in either case are very small.

On the other hand, with regard to the time span of independent variables, it is necessary to take into account the issue of time lag (Moore and Rhodes,1976,p.22; Ashcroft and Ingham,1982,p.94; Billet,1990,pp.19-20). This is based on the assumption that a certain period of time is needed to analyze the circumstances of an area and to compare these results in making a locational decision. Therefore, the data for independent variables of this study cannot simply be those of 1981 to 1990. The present analysis, supposing a two year time lag for decision making, uses the figures of 1979 to 1988 for independent variables. Therefore, the independent variables used in the analysis are basically either a total increase in, or an average figure for, each locational factor in each area across the years 1979 to 1988 in the whole period and 1979 to 1984 and 1985 to 1988 in sub-periods[6].

In general, the data which would be examined by Japanese decision makers cannot always be consistent with those of the year when decisions are made mainly due to the unevenness of publishing time between the statistical series. However, the two-year time lag just mentioned is supposed to include this time period for obtaining the data of the objective years. Therefore, in this study, each variable figure was constructed based on the statistics of the objective years which are usually published subsequently rather than those considered to be obtainable at the estimated time of decision making. If the data of a certain year is not available, the mean value between the figures of the previous year and the next year was used instead.

5.3.2.2   Spatial unit of analysis

Secondly, there is the issue of the unit of area to be studied. Here, the County in the UK and the Do in Korea are taken as the geographic units. Although the

111

standard region in the UK is another possible convenient unit for the analysis, it was found in this study to be too broad to find significantly different features between these regions. Northern Ireland was excluded from the study mainly due to the difficulty in comparing its statistical figures with the counties in Great Britain. On the other hand, the Gun in Korea (in total 238) is too small to secure relevant statistical figures. Therefore, 64 counties in the UK and 13 Do and metropolitan regions in Korea has provided the spatial bases for this analysis.

5.3.2.3 Industrial field of analysis

Thirdly, it is necessary to specify the industrial fields of the Japanese companies to be examined. Needless to say, industrial classification systems in both countries are not identical. Although statistical figures for the manufacturing sector are produced in the same manner in the UK and Korea, there seems to be a little difference in the concept. This study, for the convenience of analysis and interpretation, followed the classification and the concept of the UK system. Thus, the manufacturing sector examined in this study covers divisions 2, 3 and 4 in the 1980 Standard Industrial Classification (SIC) of the British government.

Furthermore, the Japanese subsidiaries studied in this study are limited to those in which the Japanese parent companies are believed to hold 50 percent or more of the total equity in the subsidiary. In addition to these, a few companies which are listed by IBB or JETRO as Japanese manufacturing companies operating in the host countries but which, although they have opened with activities on the fringe of manufacturing, have not yet begun their actual manufacturing activities are also included in this study on the assumption that manufacturing will occur shortly.

5.3.3   The framework : Procedure of the analysis

The regression analysis of this study is implemented in three steps. The initial step is the analysis using static variables at the fixed time of the end of each time span. The dependent variables in the static figures are matched with the independent variables representing the absolute value either of a given time or of an average over the considered time period. The consequence of this regression yields the main causes of, or the most influential factors evident in, the choice of the present locations of Japanese MNCs.

The second step is the analysis of change. The changes of dependent variables, either in the form of absolute change or percentage change during a given period of time, are regressed against a set of independent variables. This regression mainly aims to associate the increase in Japanese investments with the changes of circumstance which host countries and host regions have experienced[7]. (These first and second regression steps are used in sub-period analysis in the same way, except for the divided time span.)

And, thirdly, this study tries to regress the locational factors in the form of an integrated index which is obtained from the amalgamation of separate variables into a group of representative locational factors. This step is necessary in that a decision maker will consider all the related possible variables in estimating a locational factor rather than consider a specific representative one[8]. Therefore, constructing an integrated index for a certain locational factor by imposing a subjective weight to each locational variable is thought to bring about a meaningful outcome for this study.

The above measures are common in objectives and complementary to each other in that they all try to find the important factors that are likely to have influenced the decisions of Japanese companies in choosing a location in Britain and in Korea in the 1980s. Of course, for certain variables, it is meaningless or even impossible to express them in all three forms of figures, for example, distance to major conurbations, the number of Japanese manufacturing companies in 1980, etc. In such cases, one representative figure for each variable is included in each equation. By implementing these three steps of the analyses, the locational behaviour of Japanese companies is expected to become more explicable. In particular, the first two steps of regression in conjunction with each other are critical for deriving the regression equations which fit best for the two host countries.

Two issues should be noted in both implementing the regression and interpreting the results. In the first place, being a 'cross-sectional analysis' trying to explain the variations between regions, this analysis is subject to a lot of unexplained variation between variables[9] and has limitations in finding accurate causal relationship between variables. And, secondly, finding a set of identical statistics in two host countries is improbable. Therefore, certain locational factors in Korea have had to be represented by other indicators than those used in the British exercise.

5.3.4 The framework : Testing measures

As mentioned before, the aim of this analysis is to identify the locational factors which influence (or have a close relationship with) locational decisions and to measure their strengths. The following measures form the main framework of the present analysis to meet this objective.

Firstly, this study examines R^2 value. The coefficient of determination (R^2) in multiple regression measures the extent to which dependent variable Y can be explained by all the independent variables involved in the equation. In other words, it indicates how well a multiple regression fits the data. In stepwise regression, the R^2 value is used to see how much each independent variable accounts for the change in the dependent variable. In particular, the adjusted R^2 value, which considers the degree of freedom, provides a more precise degree of explanation than the simple R^2 value.

Secondly, the significance test is undertaken. One of the main purposes of the multiple regression is to find the most important variables that influence the result[10]. This is much more the case in something like the present study which includes all possible cases rather than in one using a random or other selection. Among measures to test the significance of each independent variable, the 't-test' is the most usual one. By calculating the t-value, it is possible to find the statistical significance of the coefficient of each variable in a multiple regression equation. Using this method, the least significant variables can be deleted from the equation.

Thirdly, this study implements the F-test. In addition to the significance test, it is necessary to examine the validity of each calculated relationship. By using the F-test, it is possible to know whether each calculated value sufficiently explains the relationship being investigated. In other words, the significance of the R^2 value can be tested by the F value[11].

Fourthly, the investigation of unexplained variation is necessary. Even after the identification of significant factors through the above measures, there can remain some unexplained variation. This should be reduced by analyzing the residuals[12] and by introducing extra variables.

In selecting significant variables and computing the explicability of the selected variables, this study depends on the stepwise method. This method chooses the important variables and excludes unimportant variables on the basis of the t-value of each variable[13]. With regard to stepwise regression, a number of warnings have been issued in that the method tends to involve a specification error (Ryu,1986,p.136). Nonetheless, the stepwise regression analysis has been widely used to search for important variables according to their significance in the regression model. After which, the relationships between dependent and independent variables identified through the above measures are to be compared between two countries.

5.3.5 Variables for this analysis

Since multiple regression analysis is represented by the relationship between variables, selecting a set of relevant dependent and independent variables is critical for the analysis.

The regression analysis for the British case began with the following possible variables in Table 5.1 at the end of this chapter. The independent variables listed in this table cover a wide range of the possible geographical factors which seem likely to have been taken into account at the time of the decision- making in the Japanese companies about the choice of a location somewhere in Britain. In other words, these variables were selected with the assumption that Japanese companies (and other companies also) investing in foreign countries do analyse these data, or at least are likely to think about the issues represented by these variables, when making location decisions.

Details as to the concept, derivation, sources and some important explanations of these variables are expounded in Appendix 1 at the end of this thesis[14]. (However, in addition to these variables, another eight variables are introduced in static and change analysis in order to examine more thoroughly the relationship between regional assistance factor and the location of Japanese companies. See 7.1.1.5.)

The selection of these variables has been undertaken in relation to the British experience. Therefore, there are some differences between these and the Korean variables and statistics. In particular, the scantiness of statistics available in Korea has been the primary reason to seek for different indicators other than those of the British case in explaining the same locational factors. The dependent and independent variables for the analysis of the Korean case are listed as the Table 5.2 at the end of this chapter. The concept and derivation of these variables are in most part similar to those of the British case. Appendix 2 shows the derivation and sources of these variables.

Using these variables, regression analysis has been implemented mainly in the following procedure: 1) all the possible geographical factors that can influence location choice are listed; 2) a correlation matrix is computed, which represents the simple correlations between dependent and independent variables; 3) independent variables which have a relatively high correlation (in this study, a correlation coefficient greater than 0.2) with the dependent variables are initially selected; 4) during these procedures, certain independent variables which have non-linear relationships with dependent variables are transformed into logarithmic or exponential form in order to make them fit the linear equation model; 5) the regression is undertaken with these selected, and in some cases transformed, variables; 6) among the significant variables chosen in this regression, one of the independent variables which have intercorrelations 0.8 or higher with other variable is excluded through the examination of the intercorrelation matrix (in this study, pairwise correlations between variables); 7) the equation of regression is constructed again using the remaining significant variables.

5.4   Locational Factor Analysis Through Survey

As another way to identify important locational factors, this study has carried out micro-level analysis through company survey. The survey in this study has depended mainly on questionnaire and supplementarily on interview. As illustrated in the previous section, the time span, the number of objective companies, etc. are the same in both the regression and survey analyses. Specifically, the following procedure has been carried out.

5.4.1   Questionnaire survey

First of all, a questionnaire form was prepared. The questionnaire consists of five major sections : 1) the profile of the firm; 2) the main reason or push factors which made the firm invest outside Japan; 3) attractive or unsatisfactory locational factors; 4) the role of host government assistance; 5) alternative locations considered. These questions were asked to find out the positive and negative geographical factors which influence the locational decisions of Japanese companies.

A copy of the questionnaire form (Appendix 3) was sent to each Japanese manufacturing company operating in the two countries. Specifically, all the companies which have been announced as being established in both countries became the objects of this survey, at least at the initial stage. Amongst those, the companies whose existence cannot be confirmed by the post office were excluded from the list of objective companies to be analyzed regardless of whether they have gone away or changed their plan to invest. About a month after the initial sending out of the questionnaire, a reminder letter was sent to those companies which had not replied until that time.

5.4.2 Interview survey

The interview survey was undertaken in order to supplement the answers to the questionnaire. As shown in Appendix 3, the questionnaire form contains a question about whether the respondent would allow the researcher to have an opportunity to visit the company and to discuss the issues more deeply. Therefore, the interviewees were the managers of those companies which were accessible to the researcher. This interview survey was carried out with another list of questions (Appendix 4), which was prepared before the visits to companies were made. The interview questions consist of five major items like the questionnaire form. However, the questions are more detailed than in the case of questionnaire. The interviews normally lasted one hour.

The responses and answers of the companies in the questionnaire and interview surveys were analyzed mainly using descriptive statistics. For this purpose, the respondents' answers were coded and cross-tabulated. These answers were analyzed, interpreted and compared based mainly on the periodical classification of arrivals, i.e. comparison between the companies that arrived before the beginning of 1987 and those that arrived thereafter. And, in some cases where necessary, the classifications of companies according to size and industrial distributions were also referred to. The results of this analysis and its comparison with those of the regression analysis are deployed in Chapter eight.

Table 5.1 Dependent and Independent Variables (British Case)[15]

===

1) dependent variables

Y_1 : the number of Japanese manufacturing companies in each county in 1990

116

Y_2 : the absolute change in the number of Japanese manufacturing companies in each county 1981-1990

Y_3 : the total numbers employed by Japanese manufacturing companies in each county in 1990

Y_4 : the absolute change in the total numbers employed by Japanese manufacturing companies in each county 1981-1990

2) independent variables relating to characteristics of the range of locations from which each Japanese company is choosing

a. labour supply in the host county
i) potential workforce available of both sexes in the host county

X_1 : total numbers in the working population of both sexes (average of 1979-1988)

X_2 : absolute change in this working population 1979-1988

X_3 : total numbers unemployed (average of 1979-1988)

X_4 : absolute change in the numbers unemployed 1979-1988

X_5 : average unemployment rate 1979-1988

X_6 : % point change in unemployment rate 1979-1988

X_7 : numbers employed in the manufacturing sector (average of 1979-1988) (employees in employment in manufacturing)

X_8 : absolute change in the numbers employed in the manufacturing sector 1979-1988

ii) labour cost in the host county
X_9 : average gross weekly male earnings (average of 1979-1988)

X_{10} : absolute change in these gross weekly earnings 1979-1988

iii) education level of the workforce in the host county
X_{11} : average percentage of pupils aged 16 staying on at school (average of 1979-1988)

X_{12} : % point change in the pupils aged 16 staying on at school 1979-1988

X_{13} : the number of institutions for further education (average of 1979-1988)

X_{14} : absolute change in the number of institutions for further education 1979-1988

iv) militancy of labour in the host county
X_{15} : number of working days lost by stoppages of work due to industrial disputes (average

of 1979-1988)

X_{16} : absolute change in the working days lost by stoppage of work due to industrial disputes 1979-1988

v) productivity of labour in the host county

X_{17} : gross value added per employee in the manufacturing sector (average of 1981-1988)

X_{18} : absolute change in gross value added per employee in the manufacturing sector 1981-1988

b. public policy in the host county
i) regional assistance in the host county

X_{19} : the proportion of the travel to work areas (TTWAs) qualifying for regional assistance (average of 1979-1988)

X_{20} : % point change in the proportion of the TTWA areas qualifying for regional assistance 1979-1988

X_{21} : the total amount of public sector investment in the enterprise zones in the area from designation to 1988

X_{22} : public expenditure for economic development and promotion per 1,000 population (average of 1979-1988)

X_{23} : absolute change in the public expenditure for economic development and promotion per 1,000 population 1979-1988

ii) local rates in the host county

X_{24} : total rate poundage (average of 1979-1988)

X_{25} : absolute change in total rate poundage 1979-1988

c. industrial land and premises in the host county

X_{26} : total stock of commercial and industrial floorspace (average of 1979-1988)

X_{27} : absolute change in the stock of commercial and industrial floorspace 1979-1988

X_{28} : rent per square foot per annum for industrial premises in 1988

d. accessibility of the host county
i) transportation in the host county

X_{29} : total foreign and domestic seaport traffic (average of 1979-1988)

X_{30} : absolute change in foreign and domestic seaport traffic 1979-1988

X_{31} : distance to the nearest major seaport[16]

118

X_{32} : total air passengers through custom airport (average of 1979-1988)

X_{33} : absolute change in total air passengers through custom airport 1979-1988

X_{34} : distance to the nearest major airport[17]

X_{35} : total length of motorways and trunk roads (average of 1979-1988)

X_{36} : absolute change in length of motorways and trunk roads 1979-1988

X_{37} : the number of railway stations in the area

ii) market accessibility in the host county
X_{38} : population of the major conurbations within the area of 100 mile radius from the county

e. linkages in the host county
i) manufacturing suppliers or subcontractors in the county
X_{39} : the number of manufacturing firms in the county (average of 1979-1988)

X_{40} : absolute change in the number of manufacturing firms in the area 1979-1988

ii) presence of Japanese companies in the host county
X_{41} : the number of Japanese manufacturing companies in the area in 1979

X_{42} : the total numbers employed in 1979 by Japanese manufacturing companies established[18]

X_{43} : total number of Japanese companies in other sectors in 1988

X_{44} : absolute change in the number of Japanese companies in other sectors 1979-1988

iii) service sector in the host county
X_{45} : percentage of employees in 1988 in the service sector including banking, finance and business services

X_{46} : % point change in the employees in the service sector including banking, finance and business services 1979-1988

f. environmental circumstances in the host county
i) the 'greenness' of the county
X_{47} : the proportion of agricultural area to total area (average of 1979-1988)

X_{48} : % point change in the proportion of agricultural area to total area 1979-1988

X_{49} : density of population (average of 1979-1988)

X_{50} : absolute change in the density of population 1979-1988

X_{51} : total national park area in the county in 1988

X_{52} : the number of public parks in the county in 1988

ii) leisure and recreation facilities in the host county

X_{53} : public expenditure per head on leisure and recreation facilities(average of (1979-1988)

X_{54} : absolute change in the public expenditure per head on leisure and recreation facilities 1979-1988

X_{55} : the number of golf courses in the area (average of 1979-1988)

iii) crime in the host county

X_{56} : reported serious crime per 1,000 population (average of 1979-1988)

X_{57} : absolute change in reported serious crime per 1,000 population 1979-1988

iv) houses for employees in the host county

X_{58} : total stock of dwellings (average of 1979-1988)

X_{59} : absolute change in the stock of dwellings 1979-1988

X_{60} : mean re-registered rent in the area (average of 1979-1988)

X_{61} : absolute change in the mean re-registered rent in the area 1979-1988

Table 5.2 Dependent and Independent Variables (Korean Case)

1) dependent variables

Y_1 : the number of Japanese manufacturing companies in each Do in 1990

Y_2 : the absolute change in the number of Japanese manufacturing companies in each Do 1981-1990

Y_3 : the investment of the Japanese manufacturing companies in each Do in 1990

Y_4 : the absolute change in the investment of Japanese manufacturing companies in each Do 1981-1990

2) independent variables

a. labour supply in the host Do
i) potential workforce available in the host Do
X_1 : total numbers in the working population of both sexes (average of 1979-1988)

X_2 : absolute change in the working population 1979-1988

X_3 : unemployment rate in each Do in 1988

X_4 : total population in the host Do (average of 1979-1988)

X_5 : absolute change in total population in the host Do 1979-1988

X_6 : net increase in population through inter-regional migration 1988

X_7 : % change in the net increase in population through inter-regional migration 1979-1988

X_8 : numbers employed in the manufacturing sector (average of 1979-1988)

X_9 : absolute change in the numbers employed in the manufacturing sector 1979-1988

ii) labour cost in the host Do
X_{10} : average wage levels in the manufacturing sector 1979-1988)

X_{11} : % change in average wage levels in the manufacturing sector 1979-1988

iii) education and skill level of the workforce in the host Do
X_{12} : average percentage of students attending colleges and universities in total population in the Do (average of 1979-1988)

X_{13} : % point change in students attending colleges and universities in total population in the Do 1979-1988

X_{14} : the number of vocational training facilities (average of 1979-1988)

X_{15} : absolute change in the number of vocational training facilities 1979-1988

iv) militancy of labour in the host Do
X_{16} : the proportion of union members in total employees in the manufacturing sector (average of 1979-1988)

X_{17} : % point change in the proportion of union members in total employees in the manufacturing sector 1979-1988

v) productivity of labour in the host Do
X_{18} : gross value added per employee in the manufacturing sector (average of 1979-1988)

X_{19} : absolute change in gross value added per employee in the manufacturing sector 1979-1988

b. public policy in the host Do
i) regional assistance in the Do
X_{20} : total government investment in industrial estates until 1988

ii) tax burden

X_{21} : local tax collected per person (average of 1979-1988)

X_{22} : % point change in the local tax collected per person 1979-1988

c. land and premises availability in the host Do
X_{23} : stock (area) of industrial estates (average of 1979-1988)

X_{24} : absolute change in the stock of industrial estates 1979-1988

X_{25} : total stock (area) of commercial and industrial floor space (average of 1979-1988)

X_{26} : absolute change in the stock of commercial and industrial floor space 1979-1988

X_{27} : average annual increase of land price (average of 1979-1988)

X_{28} : % point change in the increase of land price 1979-1988

d. accessibility of the host Do
i) transportation
X_{29} : total registered vessels for seaport traffic in each Do (average of 1979-1988)

X_{30} : absolute change in the registered vessels for seaport traffic 1979-1988

X_{31} : total air passengers through custom airports in 1988

X_{32} : total length of motorways and trunk roads in the Do (average of 1979-1988)

X_{33} : absolute change in the length of motorways and trunk roads in the Do 1979-1988

X_{34} : the number of railway stations in the Do in 1988

ii) market accessibility
X_{35} : total population of the major cities within the area of 100 mile radius

e. linkages in the host Do
i) manufacturing suppliers or subcontractors in the host Do
X_{36} : total number of manufacturing firms in the Do (average of 1979-1988)

X_{37} : absolute change in the number of manufacturing firms in the Do 1979-1988

ii) presence of Japanese companies in the host Do
X_{38} : the number of Japanese manufacturing firms in the Do at the end of 1979

X_{39} : the amount of investment of the Japanese manufacturing firms in the Do at the end of 1979

X_{40} : the number of Japanese companies in other fields in 1988

122

X_{41} : absolute change in the number of Japanese companies in other fields 1979-1988

iii) finance and business services in the host Do

X_{42} : total establishments in the fields of banking, finance and business services in the Do in 1988

X_{43} : numbers employed in the fields of banking, finance and business services in the Do in 1988

X_{44} : loans and discounts of deposit money banks in the Do (average of 1979-1988)

X_{45} : absolute change in loans and discounts of deposit money banks in the Do 1979-1988

f. environmental circumstances in the host Do

i) the 'greenness' of the Do

X_{46} : total urban park area in the Do in 1988

X_{47} : total area of national park in the Do in 1988

X_{48} : total forestry growing stock in the Do 1988

X_{49} : absolute change in total forestry growing stock in the Do 1979-1988

X_{50} : the number of golf courses in the Do in 1988

ii) housing and water supply in the host Do

X_{51} : stock of dwellings in the Do (average of 1979-1988)

X_{52} : absolute change in the stock of dwellings in the Do 1979-1988

X_{53} : ratio of dwellings per household in the Do (average of 1979-1988)

X_{54} : % point change in the ratio of dwellings per household in the Do 1979-1988

X_{55} : total houses constructed in each Do (average of 1979-1988)

X_{56} : absolute change in total houses constructed each Do 1979-1988

X_{57} : the proportion of dwellings equipped with a water supply system in the Do (average of 1979-1988)

X_{58} : % point change in the proportion of dwellings equipped with a water supply system in the Do 1979-1988

X_{59} : number of telephone facilities in the Do (average of 1979-1988)

X_{60} : absolute change in the number of telephone facilities in the Do 1979-1988

iii) crime in the host Do

X_{61} : reported serious crime per 1,000 population in the Do (average of 1979-1988)

X_{62} : absolute change in the reported serious crime per 1,000 population in the Do 1979-1988

iv) amenities in the host Do

X_{63} : the number of cultural properties in 1988[19]

X_{64} : the number of hotels and restaurants in 1988

X_{65} : numbers employed in hotels and restaurants in 1988

---

6 Empirical evidence I: The geographical distribution of Japanese multinational companies in the two host countries

According to the methodology discussed in the previous chapter, this and the following two chapters clarify the main features of the locational behaviour of Japanese manufacturing companies reflected in the empirical data. First of all, a broad picture of their locational pattern is outlined in this chapter. Based on the overall findings depicted in this chapter, the next two chapters investigate the specific geographical factors that evidently have influenced locational decision making in the Japanese companies in recent years by means of the regression analysis at macro-level and the descriptive analysis of survey results at micro-level.

6.1 The Geographical Distribution of Japanese Multinational Companies in Great Britain

6.1.1 General features

By the end of 1990, regardless of the stage reached in their operation, a total of 181 Japanese manufacturing companies were operating in Great Britain[1]. Those companies, which by that date had not decided on their location in a particular area of Britain and those where the majority of their equity is owned by non-Japanese companies, are excluded from this number and the discussion.

Among these 181, 20 subsidiaries had begun their British activities before 1981. Therefore, since the turning of 1981, 161 Japanese manufacturing companies have arrived in Great Britain and sited in a particular area. Table 6.1 portrays the spatial distribution of these Japanese manufacturing companies in terms of both numbers of companies and approximate numbers of employees across standard regions in Britain in 1990.

The South East and Wales respectively take the lion's share in terms of the numbers of the Japanese companies (SE : 19.9%; to be compared with its 24.5% of total national employment) and total employment (Wales: 28.8%) each, the ranking reflecting the larger establishments locating in Wales. The West Midlands takes the third largest share both in terms of numbers of companies and employment. After that the North and Scotland follow[2].

Table 6.1 Regional distribution of Japanese manufacturing companies in Britain in 1990[3]

Region[4]	Numbers of Companies(%)	Numbers of Employees(%)	% Share in Total National Employment
Total	181 (100)	59,123 (100)	100
S E	36 (19.9)	10,102 (17.1)	24.5
Wales	32 (17.8)	17,007 (28.8)	4.8
W M	27 (14.9)	8,713 (14.7)	13.8
North	24 (13.2)	6,545 (11.1)	5.6
Scotland	19 (10.5)	5,063 (8.6)	7.8
N W	12 (6.6)	3,071 (5.2)	12.9
E M	10 (5.5)	2,065 (3.5)	9.8
Y & H	8 (4.4)	3,020 (5.1)	9.9
S W	8 (4.4)	2,609 (4.4)	7.3
E A	5 (2.8)	928 (1.5)	3.6

Source : IBB, JETRO, AJEI.

Thus five regions out of a possible ten, namely the South East, Wales, West Midlands, North and Scotland, appear to be the most important areas for the location of Japanese manufacturing companies in this country. Indeed 76.3% of the total number of Japanese companies and 80.3% in total numbers employed by Japanese companies are located in these five main regions (compared to 56.5% of national employment in 1990, *Business Monitor* PA 1003, pp.73-81).

This broad description of the locations of Japanese manufacturing companies in Britain can be traced in more detail by examining the following aspects of the spatial distribution of these companies; the historical trend in location, the average employment size and the fields of activity of each concern.

6.1.2   The historical trend in geographical distribution

As already mentioned, the recent influx of Japanese companies into Britain has been said to be the consequence of the strengthened trade barriers of EEC

126

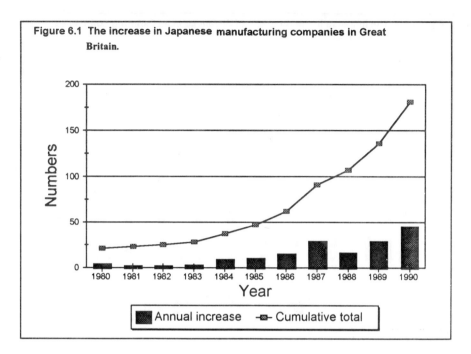

Figure 6.1 The increase in Japanese manufacturing companies in Great Britain.

Annual increase   Cumulative total

countries, the rapid rise of the value of the yen and the increase in labour costs involved in producing in Japan. In practice, the sharp increase in the number of Japanese companies operating in overseas countries including the UK recently accounts for the main historical change in geographical distribution as there have been more companies to take up locations.

The number of Japanese manufacturing companies that have come into this country year by year is shown in Figure 6.1. As has been pointed out by many authors and is evident from the figure, the inflow of Japanese companies reached a turning point in the mid-1980s. 73.5% of the companies studied here are newcomers who have come into this country in the second half of the 1980s and 65.7% specifically since 1987.

From the spatial viewpoint, the trend in the number of Japanese companies locating in each region reveals some interesting aspects. The increase in the number of Japanese companies in each region is shown in Figure 6.2. As indicated in this figure, the number of Japanese companies has grown rapidly in all the regions popular with the Japanese during the last decade. In particular, the performance of the South East, Wales and West Midlands are the most remarkable.

On the other hand, when the cumulative share of each region measured by company numbers (Figure 6.3) is analyzed according to three levels of share,

127

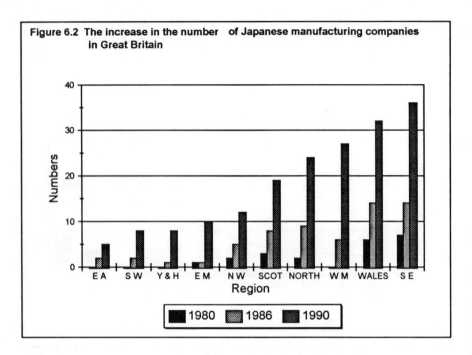

Figure 6.2 The increase in the number of Japanese manufacturing companies in Great Britain

namely high share (over 20% of total in that year), middle share (10-20%) and low share (below 10%), the figure below briefly demonstrates the relative importance of each region at each date for the location of these Japanese companies[5]. According to this figure, the South East and Wales have maintained the highest positions for a long period, whereas Scotland and the North have held the middle position without any considerable fluctuation over the last decade.

The case of the West Midlands is special in that it has enhanced its position from bottom to the middle during the last decade. This performance is striking considering the stagnating, or worsening, economic health of the West Midlands in the early 1980s. Its experience is, thus, an important finding from this analysis.

Another aspect worth mentioning is the fact that the locations chosen by Japanese manufacturing companies have become more widely dispersed since the beginning of the 1980s in proportion to the rapid increase of numbers coming into this country. In 1975, no other regions except the top five had succeeded in attracting a single Japanese company to their areas. However, by 1985, all regions have come to possess one or more Japanese companies within their boundaries. By the end of 1990, the latest arrivals amongst Japanese companies seem to be dispersing ever more widely over the regions, although most of these companies are still thought to have a strong tendency to follow the lead of existing Japanese

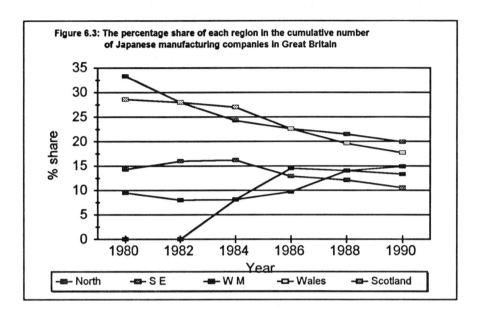

Figure 6.3: The percentage share of each region in the cumulative number of Japanese manufacturing companies in Great Britain

companies in their location choice. Consequently, no region takes the high share, namely over 20%, in the total number of Japanese companies operating in this country at the end of 1990.

6.1.3 The size distribution of Japanese manufacturing companies

The mean employment size of Japanese companies currently operating in Britain is 339 employees[5]. The employment size of 339 is relatively large compared to that of total British manufacturing companies (30 in 1990)[6] and is comparable with that of foreign companies from other countries located in Britain (US-owned 373, European-owned 240 and total other foreign-owned 333 in 1989) (*Business Monitor* PA 1002 and 1003,1989). The largest Japanese company has an employment size of 6,000 in all its branches combined obtained through recent acquisition[7] while the smallest one employs only five.

With regard to the longer term trend, it is difficult to find any persistent tendency in the employment size and growth of Japanese companies. Specifically, the current mean size of the companies established in each year shown in the Table 6.2 below can be said to follow a variable trend[8].

However, when companies are grouped by commencement in three periods of time, i.e. before the end of 1980, from 1981 to 1986 and from 1987 to 1990, a significant variation between the groups can be found. The current mean size of

129

Table 6.2   The current mean size of Japanese companies [+]

Year	Numbers of	Mean size	
	Companies	Each year	Group of years
Total	181	327	327
before 1976	7	825	
1976 - 1980	14	381	529
1981	2	777	
1982	2	637	
1983	3	471	489
1984	9	832	
1985	10	514	
1986	15	212	
1987	29	238	
1988	16	117	235
1989	29	165	
1990	45	320	

[+] Present employment size but year of establishment.

the Japanese-owned companies established in the first two periods are quite large (529 and 489) compared to the current size of those established in the latest period (235). This means either that the size of the Japanese companies coming into Britain has decreased or that the companies which arrived in the earlier years have grown consistently. Between these two possible explanations, the first seems the more likely when the recent acquisition or establishment of large companies such as ICL and Calsonic International are taken into account. Of course the latter cause, i.e. the expansion of a few large companies which arrived in the earlier periods, has also contributed significantly to this trend (West Midlands Development Agency,1990,p.52).

Turning from distribution over time to the spatial viewpoint, the mean size of Japanese manufacturing companies in each region is summarized in Table 6.3. In this table, the current average size of the Japanese companies established since 1987 in six standard regions is seen to be smaller than that of earlier arrivals in the 1980s in these regions, while in the remaining four regions the mean size in recent arrivals is higher. However, it is noteworthy that the mean size of the companies in the four most popular regions except the South East, namely the Wales, West Midlands, North and Scotland, demonstrate either a steadily or an abruptly decreasing size trend across the whole period. Particularly, the steady and rapid decline in the mean size of Japanese subsidiaries in Wales and the West Midlands is quite impressive.

This finding can be interpreted in two ways: first, that the influx of Japanese companies in recent years has comprised small and medium sized suppliers

130

following their main customers rather than large main customers themselves; or, second, that there is an emancipation from a kind of threshold unit size in investing in European countries that seems to have suited the small and medium Japanese companies along with the changes in the economic situation both in Japan and the UK.

Table 6.3 Current mean size of Japanese manufacturing companies in each region (employees)

Region	Numbers of Companies	Mean Size of the Companies Established			
		Total	- 1980	1981-1986	1987-1990
Total	181	327	529	489	235
S E	36	281	399	139	288
Wales	32	531	1,034	900	200
W M	27	323	-	617	239
North	24	273	469	536	124
Scotland	19	267	301	406	194
N W	12	256	129	200	316
E M	10	207	7	-	229
Y & H	8	377	-	100	417
S W	8	326	-	540	255
E A	5	186	-	303	108

With regard to these, the case of Wales among all the regions seems to be depicted most obviously by the former explanation. In reality, a large part of the newly arriving Japanese companies in Wales are linked to their predecessors in the region either as a component supplier or as a branch plant of an existing concern. However, as shown in Table 6.1 above, Wales' share in total employment is still very large compared to its share in company numbers, while those of most other regions are relatively small. This means that, in spite of the recent influx of small and medium size supplier companies, Wales has more large final-product-manufacturers within its area than other regions.

On the other hand, four regions, the South East, North West, East Midlands and Yorkshire & Humberside are worth considering with regard to the growth in mean size. An interesting thing is that, contrary to the Welsh case, the share in total employment of three regions among the four (except Yorkshire & Humberside) is still small compared to their share in company numbers. This is mainly caused by the fact that these regions began to succeed in attracting some large Japanese investments recently. With the clustering tendency of Japanese component suppliers around main customers, this success provides an important implication for forecasting future trends.

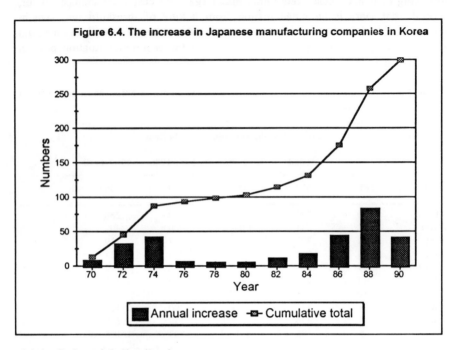

Figure 6.4. The increase in Japanese manufacturing companies in Korea

6.1.4 Industrial distribution

The operating fields of Japanese manufacturing companies in Britain can be largely divided into four main groups, plus a residual one, namely i) industrial and consumer electronics; ii) light engineering; iii) chemicals and plastics; iv) heavy machinery and vehicles; and v) others (Dunning,1986)[9]. According to this classification, the whole batch of Japanese manufacturing companies in Britain is grouped as Table 6.4.

Among the operating fields of Japanese companies in Britain, the electronics field takes by far the largest share, with nearly one half the number of companies and two thirds of the employment. Furthermore, the average size of the companies in the electronics field is much larger than the average in other fields. The overriding importance of the electronics companies in the total is one of the most important features of Japanese investment in Britain. By contrast, others take only a modest share in the number of employees in Japanese companies, while these fields take the largest proportion (45.6%) in the total manufacturing employment in this country. This small share is thought to be caused by the difficulty in investing in other countries by their own nature.

Another thing to be noted is that the companies in the field of heavy machinery and vehicles (namely, cars, car components, earth moving equipment,

132

investing in other countries by their own nature.

Another thing to be noted is that the companies in the field of heavy machinery and vehicles (namely, cars, car components, earth moving equipment, etc.) take the second position in the number of companies, although smaller in terms of the employment size of companies[11]. This can be interpreted as reflecting that the companies in this field are on the whole small component suppliers rather than large final product manufacturers. In fact, a number of car component manufacturers has arrived in this country either in tandem with or following the establishment of major car manufacturers like Nissan, Honda and Toyota[12] and the size of the latter has been overwhelmed by the former in the mean size statistics.

A modest degree of specialization in the operating fields of Japanese companies is found between regions. The shares of the major regions in each operating field is listed in Table 6.5.

The table makes clear that the Japanese electronics companies are heavily concentrated in Wales but are also quite wide spread, and those in the field of heavy machinery and vehicles are concentrated in the North. The South East is characterized by the clustering of Japanese firms in the field of chemicals and plastics.

This concentration of Japanese electronics companies in Wales has been commented on by many authors. This situation is evidence supporting the argument that Japanese companies coming into Britain have a strong tendency to follow a existing Japanese company (e.g. Sony and Matsushita) into an area when making their locational decisions[13].

Table 6.4 The operating fields of Japanese manufacturing companies in Britain

Fields	Numbers of Companies(%)	Numbers of Employees(%)	Mean size of Employment	% Share in TME[+]
Total	181 (100)	59,123 (100)	327	100
Electronics	78 (43.1)	37,038 (62.7)	475	12.3
Light engineering	10 (5.5)	3,121 (5.3)	312	8.9
Chemicals and plastics	26 (14.4)	5,390 (9.1)	207	10.5
Heavy machinery and vehicles	39 (21.5)	8,877 (15.0)	228	22.7
Others	28 (15.5)	4,697 (7.9)	168	45.6

[+] % share in total manufacturing employment in Britain (Source: *Business Monitor* PA 1003,1990).

6.1.5 Summary

By configurating the above findings, it seems possible to draw some conclusions regarding the locational distribution of Japanese manufacturing companies in Britain. To begin with, the historical trends may be noted. Japanese manufacturing investment in Britain has grown remarkably since the mid-1980s. The number of these companies in Britain increased sharply from 20 in 1980 to 62 in 1986 and to as many as 181 in 1990.

Among regions, the South East and Wales have consistently attracted the largest number of these companies out of all the regions. Although gaining Japanese companies, the South East has less than its share (relative to its employment) while Wales has five times its share of Japanese companies on the same basis (Table 6.1). These two regions have taken the key role in attracting the Japanese companies coming to Britain since the 1970s, and this trend is expected to continue for the time being, although the importance of the two regions is diminishing in recent years with the growth of other regions in attracting incoming Japanese companies. On the other hand, the increasing importance of the West Midlands as the location choice of Japanese manufacturing companies these days is worth evaluating in relation to recent changes in the government policy[14].

Table 6.5 Distribution of the operating fields of Japanese manufacturing companies between regions in Britain   (%)

Regions	Share in Total	Elec- tronics	Light Eng.	Chemi & Plastics	Heavy mach & Vehicles	Others
Total	181	78	10	26	39	28
	(100)	(100)	(100)	(100)	(100)	(100)
S E	36	13	2	10	5	6
	(19.9)	(16.7)	(20.0)	(38.5)	(12.8)	(21.4)
Wales	32	18	1	7	3	3
	(17.8)	(23.0)	(10.0)	(27.0)	(7.7)	(10.7)
W M	27	13	2	3	7	2
	(14.9)	(16.7)	(20.0)	(11.5)	(17.9)	(7.2)
North	24	6	1	3	9	5
	(13.2)	(7.7)	(10.0)	(11.5)	(23.1)	(17.9)
Scotland	19	12	1	0	3	3
	(10.5)	(15.4)	(10.0)	(0.0)	(7.7)	(10.7)
Other	43	16	3	3	12	9
regions	(23.7)	(20.5)	(30.0)	(11.5)	(30.8)	(32.1)

Secondly, in terms of employment size, the subsidiaries of Japanese companies in Britain can be said to be mainly medium sized. However, though the evidence is not produced here, their parent companies in Japan are not in the least all small or medium sized enterprises (SMEs). Therefore, the assertion about the predominance of SMEs in originating the whole Japanese overseas investment cannot be applied in the British case. Although the mean employment size of 339 per Japanese subsidiary is smaller than that of US counterparts, it is a much larger size compared to the subsidiaries of European companies in Britain or to indigenous concerns. At the regional level, Wales stands out above other regions in the magnitude of the employment size of its Japanese concerns. On the other hand, the decreasing employment size of the Japanese companies coming lately in Wales is interpreted as the arrival of small component manufacturers to supply their products to main customers already existing in the region.

And, thirdly, among various fields in the manufacturing sector, industrial and consumer electronics is the most important in terms both of the number of Japanese companies in Britain and of their total employment. The increase in the number of Japanese electronics companies and in the employment size of these companies has been sustained without any significant fluctuation despite the strong growth in other fields. The concentration of these companies in Wales forms another important feature of the locational distribution of Japanese manufacturing companies in this country, serving also to boost numbers arriving in Wales.

In consequence, it can be said that the recent influx of Japanese companies into Britain has been led by electronics companies in its industrial field and by the South East and Wales in its destination.

6.2 Locational Distribution of Japanese Multinational Companies in Korea

6.2.1 General features

Table 6.6 Regional distribution of Japanese manufacturing companies in Korea

Do	Numbers of Companies(%)	Investment ($ 000)(%)	% Share in TME [+]
Total	299 (100)	825,083 (100)	100
Seoul	77 (25.8)	130,186 (15.8)	37.7
Kyongsangnam-Do	67 (22.4)	327,199 (39.7)	9.7
Kyonggi-Do	58 (19.4)	67,092 (8.1)	17.5
Inchon	22 (7.4)	64,351 (7.8)	5.8
Pusan	18 (6.0)	41,344 (5.0)	10.0
Kyongsangbuk-Do	16 (5.4)	32,973 (4.0)	4.9
Chungchongnam-Do	16 (5.4)	16,507 (2.0)	2.9
Chollabuk-Do	9 (3.0)	7,233 (0.9)	1.9
Chollanam-Do	7 (2.3)	124,155 (15.1)	2.5
Chungchongbuk-Do	4 (1.3)	5,847 (0.7)	1.8
Kangwon-Do	3 (1.0)	7,797 (0.9)	0.7
Taegu	1 (0.3)	100 (0.0)	4.5
Cheju-Do	1 (0.3)	299 (0.0)	0.1

[+] % share in total manufacturing employment in Korea.
Source : Ministry of Finance, Korea (1990); *Yearbook of Regional Statistics* (1990).

In total, 299 Japanese subsidiaries were operating in Korea at the end of 1990. Among these, 103 companies arrived in Korea before the end of 1980, while the remaining 196 companies have arrived since 1981. The locational distribution of these Japanese subsidiaries is shown in Table 6.6. Employment data is however not available and size has to be measured in terms of investment.

The capital city, Seoul, is the most important place for the location of Japanese manufacturing companies in Korea in terms of the number of companies (25.8%). Equally, Kyongsangnam-Do, which contains Pusan, the second largest city in Korea and the nearest point to Japan (see Figure 4.2), is the most prominent in terms of investment size of Japanese companies (39.7%) and, thus, proved to be another main region in which Japanese companies concentrate. Moreover, this Do has markedly greater share in the number of Japanese companies than its share in total manufacturing employment. These two regions in aggregation had nearly a half of all the Japanese companies in Korea, and over a half of the total investment in these companies. However, they hold 47.4% of Korean economic activity (manufacturing employment) and only 27.9% of national population. Several regions have only a few Japanese companies.

This polarised situation may be the most prominent characteristic of the spatial distribution of Japanese manufacturing companies in Korea. Furthermore, if an allowance is made that Inchon and a large part of Kyonggi-Do are involved in the wider Seoul MPR, the importance of these two regions becomes even more obvious in demonstrating the polarised geographical distribution of the Japanese subsidiaries in Korea.

At the other extreme, there are the four Dos which have not succeeded in attracting over 2% of the incoming Japanese companies. The apparent distaste of Japanese companies for these regions has significant implications for this analysis in relation to regional policy. This issue will be taken up later.

6.2.2   The historical trend in the geographical distribution of Japanese companies

Historically, Korea has been one of the major destinations for the FDI of Japanese MNCs. This Japanese capital, conversely, has played a significant role in the growth of the Korean economy during the last three decades. Japanese companies continue to provide the largest share of total inward FDI in Korea. However, it seems that the influx of Japanese manufacturing companies showed a relative eclipse from the mid-1970s to 1983 and once again at the end of 1980s compared to previous years. In particular, the beginning of the 1990s witnesses another absolute decline in the number of incoming Japanese manufacturing companies into Korea. The arrival of Japanese companies in Korea in each year is shown in the Figure 6.4 below.

As shown in this figure, the diminishing or stagnating trend of incoming Japanese companies commenced in about 1975 and continued until 1983. The number of Japanese companies arriving in Korea began to rise again from 1984. It is worth noting that this fresh surge has occurred at the same time as Korean politics began to stabilize again and the Korean economy started to grow rapidly. On the other hand, the decreasing trend in the number of incoming Japanese companies from 1988 has been thought to be related to the increasing labour disputes and soaring labour costs in Korea (*Financial Times*, Nov. 27 1989 and Jun. 5 1991). It is also worth relating this to the growing outward direct investment of Korean companies these days.

When we consider the historical trend of the incoming Japanese companies by comparing the average annual arrivals of these companies divided between sub-periods, the long term trend of the Japanese inward investment into Korea can be said to follow a kind of increasing trend. However, this trend cannot be called a steady increase but a cyclical increase as seen in Figure 6.4.

The spatial distribution of these Japanese companies confirms the polarisation feature indicated in the general description above.

Figure 6.5, which follows the model of Figure 6.3 for Britain with its three levels, shows the historical change in the number of Japanese manufacturing companies in each region in Korea[15]. As seen in the figure, the dominance of the two host regions has largely continued. Only one thing, the decreasing trend in the relative importance of Kyongsangnam-Do in contrast to the Figure 6.5.

The percentage share of each region in the cumulative number of Japanese

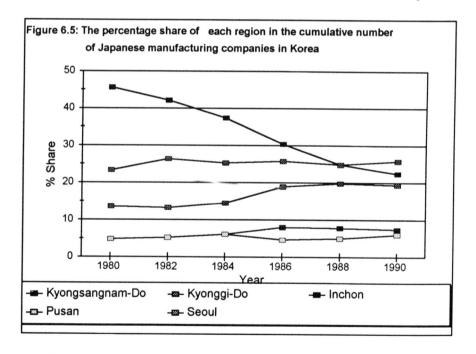

Figure 6.5: The percentage share of each region in the cumulative number of Japanese manufacturing companies in Korea

manufacturing companies in Korea increasing trend of Kyonggi-Do in the latter part of the 1980, might be mentioned as a noticeable change. However, considering the fact that the large part of Kyonggi-Do is included in the Seoul MPR, it can be said that the Japanese manufacturing companies coming into Korea have shown a continuing tendency to choose either Seoul or Kyongsangnam-Do for their sites. From this evidence, the effectiveness of Korean regional policy which has been aimed at dispersing population and industry from Seoul becomes more questionable. Furthermore, the growing share of Kyonggi-Do region, which surrounds Seoul, in the total locations of the Japanese companies, serves simply to make the concentration stronger.

6.2.3 Current investment size distribution of Japanese manufacturing companies in Korea

The current investment size distribution of Japanese subsidiaries in Korea provides a rather different picture from the already mentioned polarisation of the geographical distribution of these companies. The mean size of total Japanese subsidiaries represented by the amount of investment is $ 2.8m. This figure is comparable with the British experience, average investment of £ 5.4m (approximately $ 9.5m)[16].

Table 6.7 Current investment size distribution of Japanese manufacturing companies between regions in Korea   ($ 000s)

Region	Numbers of Companies	Total	Mean Size of the Companies Established		
			- 1980	1981-1986	1987-1990
Total	299	2,760	3,604	2,304	2,322
Seoul	77	1,691	2,017	1,345	1,673
Kyongsangnam-Do	67	4,484	6,130	2,538	1,706
Kyonggi-Do	58	1,157	1,585	1,163	912
Inchon	22	2,925	1,014	5,631	1,075
Pusan	18	2,297	284	2,385	3,277
Kyongsangbuk-Do	16	2,061	564	3,298	2,423
Chungchongnam-Do	16	1,032	582	540	6,675
Chollabuk-Do	9	804	1,319	617	672
Chollanam-Do	7	17,736	0	8,658	24,546
Other regions	9	1,560	582	320	2,137

The investment size distribution of these Japanese companies between regions is shown in Table 6.7. Differently from the case of the number of companies arriving in Korea over the period studied, the size distribution of Japanese companies is not identified with a polarisation.

In particular, the notable example is the case of Chollanam-Do (see Figure

138

4.2). The mean size of the companies located there is substantially bulky (in investment terms at least, employment may be relatively small) compared to those of other regions even though the number of companies located there are only a few. This is caused by several very large scale companies in the field of petro-chemicals placed in the region. The choice of these large companies to locate in Chollanam-Do is thought to have been influenced by the government policy to construct another large-scale industrial estate for petro-chemicals, i.e. Yochon Industrial Estate, outside Kyongsangnam-Do region[17].

Another important feature found in this table is the diminishing size of Japanese-owned companies as a whole, especially those arriving in the period of 1981-1986. In 1986, the current mean size of the companies which have been established since 1981 is less than two thirds of that of the companies established before the end of 1980. This trend, the diminishing current size of Japanese-owned companies, although the average amount of investments increased slightly in the latter part of 1980s, seems to be suggestive for understanding the worldwide managerial strategy of Japanese companies[18] as it parallels that found in Britain.

6.2.4 Industrial distribution

The operating fields of Japanese manufacturing companies, when they are divided into five groups as in the British case, are summarized in Table 6.8.

According to this table, the companies in the field of electronics again take the largest share of the total, i.e. 28.4% of total numbers of companies and 44.6% of total investment. The fields of others and heavy machinery and vehicles are found to be the second and the third in the number of companies. However, like the British case, others take an insufficient share in the number of Japanese companies compared to their share in the total number of manufacturing companies.

In terms of the number of companies, it can be said that Japanese companies operating in Korea are distributed quite evenly among industrial fields. When the share of each field in the number of companies is compared with that in the amount of investment, the magnitudes of the companies operating in the field of electronics and chemicals and plastics become outstanding. The average amount of investment of the subsidiaries in these two fields are almost the same and, after those, there is quite a gap. In spatial consideration, the regional distribution of the companies in each manufacturing field is shown in Table 6.9.

Although all the manufacturing fields can be characterized by polarisation, the proportion in Seoul of the chemicals and plastics and that of Kyongsangnam-Do in the electronics and light engineering exceed the average share of these two regions and, thus, reinforce the tendency to the polarisation of Japanese industry in Korea. On the other hand, other regions than these two show a kind of specialization to a certain extent. Inchon and Kyonggi-Do in heavy machinery and vehicles and Pusan in others can be given as examples.

139

6.2.5 Summary

The above analyses regarding the historical trend, the size distribution and the spatial distribution of operating fields furnish a broad picture of the locational behaviour of Japanese manufacturing companies in Korea.

First of all, like indigenous firms, Japanese-owned companies are characterized by the polarisation in their geographical locations. In other words, they have preferred the two most prosperous regions, Seoul and Kyongsangnam-Do (including Pusan), for most of their operating sites. This one feature dominates the overall behaviour of these companies in Korea[19].

Table 6.8 The operating fields of Japanese manufacturing companies in Korea
(%)

Fields	Numbers of Companies	Amount of Investment($ 000)	Mean Size ($ 000)	% Share in TNC[+]
Total	299 (100)	825,083 (100)	2,760	100
Electronics	85 (28.4)	367,725 (44.6)	4,326	8.7[++]
Light engineering	21 (7.0)	30,757 (3.7)	1,465	2.4
Chemicals and plastics	54 (18.1)	228,122 (27.7)	4,225	10.9
Heavy machinery and vehicles	65 (21.7)	125,684 (15.2)	1,934	21.9[++]
Others	74 (24.8)	72,795 (8.8)	984	56.3

[+] % share in total national number of manufacturing companies (Source: *Yearbook of Regional Statistics* (1990); *Korea Statistical Yearbook* (1990).
[++] Estimated numbers.

Table 6.9 Distribution of the operating fields of Japanese manufacturing companies between regions in Korea
(%)

Regions	Share in Total	Electro-nics	Light Eng.	Che & Plastics	Heavy & Vehicles	Others
Total	100	100	100	100	100	100
Seoul	25.7	20.0	23.8	33.3	27.7	25.7
Kyongsangnam-Do	22.4	30.6	38.1	16.7	18.5	16.2
Kyonggi-Do	19.4	21.2	4.8	22.2	24.6	14.9
Inchon	7.4	5.9	9.5	1.9	12.3	8.1
Pusan	6.0	1.2	4.8	5.6	6.2	12.2
Kyongsangbuk-Do	5.4	5.9	4.8	5.6	1.5	8.1
Chungchongnam-Do	5.4	5.9	4.8	5.6	7.7	1.4
Chollabuk-Do	3.0	2.4	-	-	-	9.5
Chollanam-Do	2.3	2.4	-	5.6	-	2.7
4 Other Regions	3.0	3.5	9.4	3.5	1.5	1.2

Secondly, after a pause, the influx of Japanese companies began to increase again in 1984, although the number of incoming companies began to wither again at the end of 1980s. On the other hand, the locational pattern of these companies still shows that the preference for the two prosperous regions has been maintained without any change.

Thirdly, in terms of investment scale, the Japanese subsidiaries operating in Korea can be named as SMEs. The average amount of investment hardly exceeds $ 3m. Moreover, the predominance of these small size firms has become even greater in the 1980s. However, unlike the feature of polarisation in geographical location, the size of Japanese companies located in lagging regions is much bigger than that in the prosperous regions.

And, lastly, the Japanese companies in the field of electronics form the largest group across all the manufacturing fields, leaving the next two positions to the fields of others and heavy machinery and vehicles. Although the geographical distribution of operating fields is dominated again by the above polarisation, two other regions show some success in attracting Japanese companies in certain manufacturing fields, namely Inchon and Kyonggi-Do.

6.3 Comparison between Britain and Korea

The above analyses contribute to the identification of the locational pattern of Japanese manufacturing companies in the two host countries. In fact, their locational behaviour has to be seen in the spatial context of each host country. In other words, and unsurprisingly, the locations of Japanese companies established in each host country are largely determined by the economic and geographical circumstances which are unique to the host country.

Nonetheless, it is necessary to compare the locational pattern of these companies in the one country with that in the other in order to explore the more general locational behaviour of Japanese companies and, thus, to assess the relevance to this behaviour of the host government policy concerned with inward FDI, especially that of Japanese companies. From this standpoint, here, the features in the locational choice of Japanese companies in the two host countries which were described above are compared in turn.

6.3.1 General features in locational choice of Japanese companies

In the first place, the most significant difference in the overall geographical distribution of Japanese manufacturing companies is that they are heavily concentrated in the two developed regions in Korea, while relatively scattered across the whole country in Britain. Indeed, the Japanese subsidiaries in Korea have followed the geographical pattern of Korean indigenous firms as a whole and, thus, reflect the existing polarisation of population and industry. However, in Britain, large numbers of Japanese companies have chosen sites in peripheral and

141

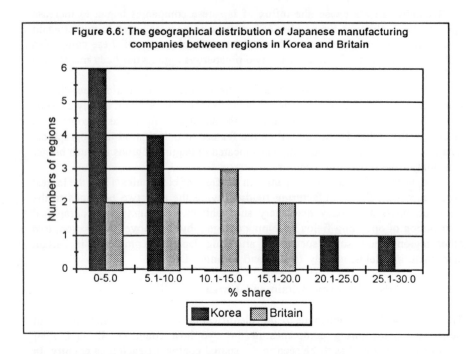

Figure 6.6: The geographical distribution of Japanese manufacturing companies between regions in Korea and Britain

non-prosperous regions such as Wales, Scotland and the North.

This difference in the pattern of locational choice can be interpreted as indicating that there is no general rule governing locational decision making at a worldwide level in Japanese companies. In other words, their locational decisions are made in such a way as to utilize the existing circumstances in host countries to the greatest extent. (However, this view needs to be complemented by more apparent and specific evidence if it is to be more persuasive. Therefore, to back up this argument, the further procedure for the investigation of geographical factors is adopted in this study by introducing the regression and survey analyses considered below.)

On the other hand, the uneven spatial distribution of Japanese companies between regions in Korea relative to that in Britain is also proved by statistical measures such as mean size, standard deviation, variance, etc. The frequency values based on the number of Japanese companies located in each region, or Do, in the two host countries are listed in Table 6.10.

By reference to these figures, the suggestion that the geographical distribution of Japanese companies in Britain is more evenly distributed between regions than in the case of Korea is confirmed again. The last two figures show the more uneven distribution of the observations in Korea than in Britain. This uneven distribution of Japanese companies in Korea relative to that in Britain becomes more evident when the distributions are drawn by histogram. The Figure 6.6 is the geographical distribution of Japanese companies in the two countries measured by the percentage share of each region of the total Japanese companies in each country.

In short, in spite of the larger number of observations, the Japanese subsidiaries in Korea show a more tilted distribution statistically and graphically than in the British case.

Table 6.10 Statistics of the geographical distribution of Japanese manufacturing companies between regions in Korea and Britain

Measures	Great Britain	Korea
Number of companies	181	299
Number of regions (Dos)	10	13
Average company numbers per region	18.1	23
Standard deviation of the regional distribution	11.09	26.43
Range	5-36	1-77

6.3.2 Historical trend

Broadly speaking, the influx of Japanese manufacturing companies into Britain can be depicted as a steadily accelerating trend, whereas the Korean case can be labelled either as in a cyclical increase or a stagnating stage.

This contrasting experience of the two countries in attracting Japanese companies provides evidence to support the shift of Japanese managers' concern from Asia to Europe and other developed countries in looking for their overseas sites as discussed in chapter four. This is at the national level.

At the regional level, on the other hand, the historical change in the geographical distribution of these Japanese companies in each host country has been different.

In brief, the Japanese companies in Britain have revealed the aforesaid tendency to choose their sites in the non-prosperous and less congested regions contrary to those in Korea which cluster in the two prosperous regions. This is an interesting dissimilarity in line with the different policy measures in the two host countries. In other words, this different pattern of geographical distribution of Japanese companies in each country is inevitably related to either the success or failure of the regional policy of the host country. This issue is mentioned further in the following chapters.

6.3.3 Ownership and geographical distribution

It has already been pointed out several times that most Japanese manufacturing companies have a strong preference for a 100% ownership of the equity of their subsidiaries or at least 100% Japanese ownership. In fact, this assertion is the exact case in Britain. Almost all the 181 subsidiaries operating at the end of 1990 are wholly owned by one or two Japanese parent companies, some as joint ventures between Japanese parents. Subsidiaries purely in the form of joint ventures with British partners form only a marginal portion. By contrast, in the Korean case, only a quarter (74) of the total subsidiaries are wholly owned by Japanese parent companies.

This difference in ownership in the two host countries can be attributed to the following aspects. Firstly, government policy in Korea until the mid-1980s promoted investment in the form of joint ventures rather than purely foreign-owned companies. Another reason is the attitude of Japanese managers who have thought that the Korean market is too unstable to form the basis for their longer-term overseas plants and, thus, have preferred the supposedly lower risk of joint venture type investment. As a result, Japanese locational choices in Korea are more likely to have been affected by the attitude of their Korean partners in a way which has no parallel in the British experience.

Under these circumstances, the locational distribution of Japanese subsidiaries in Korea has become substantially differentiated from that of similar subsidiaries in Britain.

6.3.4 The size distribution of Japanese companies in the two host countries

The difference in the size of Japanese companies in the two host countries can also be summarized by the following two points. The first is that the Japanese-owned companies in Britain are three or four times larger than those in Korea. This difference is evident from the investment size of the Japanese companies in the two countries. This feature seems to express eloquently the variation in the pattern both of overseas investment in different countries and of the worldwide management strategy of Japanese manufacturing companies.

In brief, large Japanese companies invest large amounts in far located developed countries, while small and medium sized Japanese firms tend to choose adjacent countries in Asia as their overseas sites investing relatively small amounts of capital. This gap in investment size between the companies in the two host countries is worth noting, even after allowing both for the tendency of distant subsidiaries to be larger than nearer ones and for the diminishing size of Japanese companies in Britain in the late 1980s.

This smaller, nearer size characteristic is more striking considering the fact that a large part of the products of the Japanese companies in Korea have been exported to foreign markets all over the world. Furthermore, this divergent size/distance tendency accelerated until the mid-1980s. This acceleration was seen in Korea where the size of Japanese investments has become smaller in contrast to the growing size of those in Britain. Recently, this acceleration has been slowed down by the decreasing size of Japanese investment in Britain.

Another aspect is that the size characteristic of Japanese companies is largely similar between host countries differently from the general pattern of the geographical distribution of companies in each host country. While most large Japanese companies are relatively scattered across the whole country, or are even concentrated in the less prosperous regions such as Wales and the North in Britain and Chollanam-Do in Korea, small ones tend to cluster in more prosperous regions.

This feature is worth analyzing considering the accepted tendency of Japanese companies towards choosing greenfield sites for their plants in the world generally and in Britain particularly rather than the well-industrialized areas as they have done in Korea. The result of the later regression and survey analyses in the following chapters can also be used to exemplify this finding.

6.3.5 Industrial distribution

The operating fields of Japanese companies in the two host countries can be examined through the following two points.

Firstly, in total, the dominance of electronics companies is more apparent in Britain (43.1%) than in Korea (28.4%). This means that the proportions of each manufacturing field amongst the total Japanese companies is more equally distributed industrially in the case of Korea. This can be interpreted in two ways: it can be suggested that, firstly, electronics products are more suitable to be made in distant developed countries such as Britain than in Asian countries owing to either the necessity of high technology in production or the diseconomy of the longer distance transportation; and that, secondly, this is seen as the consequence of the recent trade barriers raised against Japanese products, especially electronics products, in the developed countries including the EC. The recent influx of Japanese electronics companies into Britain seems to be more attributable to the latter case. In addition to this, the growing competitiveness of indigenous electronic companies in Korea can be listed as another reason which has resulted in this difference.

And, secondly, as to the spatial distribution of operating fields in each country, the Korean case shows another polarisation between regions following the polarisation in the overall locational distribution of Japanese companies. In other words, the operating fields of the Japanese companies in Britain are relatively evenly allocated between regions. For example, the electronics companies are concentrated in Wales, the companies in the field of heavy machinery and vehicles in the North and those in other fields in the South East and Scotland. By contrast, in Korea, the two main regions again dominate all the operating fields of the Japanese companies.

Given these findings on the geographical distribution of Japanese manufacturing companies in the two host countries, the regression and survey analyses are undertaken to identify more clearly the specific locational factors that may have helped to bring about the above features of the geographical distribution in each host country. The results of these analyses are shown in the next two chapters in turn.

7 Empirical evidence II: Factors influencing the locational choices of Japanese multinational companies – Regression results

This chapter presents the major results of the regression analysis as the empirical evidence on issues relevant to the locational choices of Japanese manufacturing companies. These are considered in turn; first, the British case, then the Korean case and finally the comparison between the two cases. The regression analysis of each country consists of static and change analysis, index analysis and sub-period analysis.

7.1 Significant Geographical Factors in Great Britain

7.1.1 Static and change analysis

In the first place, the static analysis and the change analysis using the variables listed at the end of Chapter five were implemented. In other words, given a set of explanatory variables, regressions were undertaken with the dependent variables from Y_1 to Y_4 in turn. As shown in Chapter five, the dependent variables are:

Y_1 : the number of Japanese manufacturing companies in each county in 1990 (NUM);

Y_2 : the absolute change in the number of Japanese manufacturing companies in each county 1981-1990 (ΔNUM);

Y_3 : the total numbers employed by Japanese manufacturing companies in each county in 1990 (EMP);

Y_4 : the absolute change in the total numbers employed by the Japanese manufacturing companies in each county 1981-1990 (ΔEMP).

The stepwise procedure of the regression programme allows a selection of independent variables to be made from the full list of the variables. The cut-off point used in these analyses is that the significance level of the coefficient of any additional variable (measured by t value) should be less than 0.05[1]. The results of these regressions are listed below in turn.

7.1.1.1 Static analysis about the number of Japanese manufacturing companies in 1990 (Y_1)

The regression with the number of Japanese manufacturing companies in 1990 based on the data for each county in Britain produced the following equation[2]:

$$Y_1 \text{ (NUM)} = 1.14 + 3.20\ X_{41} + 0.308\ X_{21}\text{(log)} \quad \dots\dots\dots\dots \quad (7.1)$$
$$(5.78)^{**} \qquad (3.83)^{**}$$

$$R^2 = 0.387 \qquad F = 20.87 \ \ (\ p = 0.000\ )$$

where X_{41} is the number of Japanese manufacturing companies in the area (county) in 1979;

and X_{21} is the total amount of public sector investment in the enterprise zones (EZs) from designation in the area up to 1988.

The figures in the parentheses are the t-values of each coefficient and the double asterisk means that the variable is significant at the 0.01 level. (One asterisk means it is significant at the 0.05 level and no asterisk at the 0.1 level.) The p-value is the probability of an error, or attained significance level, indicating the possibility of making an error by adopting this equation in the given significance level.

The following correlation matrix shows the relationship between these variables. There is no significantly high inter-correlation between explanatory variables.

According to the equation (7.1) and the above matrix, two explanatory variables, namely X_{41} and X_{21} are the most significant variables in explaining the spatial distribution of Japanese manufacturing companies represented by the number of companies in each county. In other words, the geographical distribution of Japanese companies was closely related, first of all, to the existence of leading (i.e. pre-located) Japanese manufacturing companies in the host county in 1979; and, second, to the investment of the public sector in EZs located in the host county.

	Y_1(NUM)	X_{41}	X_{21}(log)
Y_1(NUM)	1.000	0.514	0.285
X_{41}		1.000	-0.169
X_{21}(log)			1.000

Of these, the priority of the X_{41} variable represents the unique feature of the location of these companies as expected. This result is meaningful in that the tendency of incoming Japanese companies to follow the lead of other Japanese companies into the area is proved statistically by the involvement of variable X_{41}.

The involvement of X_{21} shows that the designation of EZs as a part of spatial policy, which was newly introduced by the Thatcher government in the early 1980s, became an important locational factor in the UK. However, interpreting this result needs great caution. This is because an EZ is only a tiny designated area in the surrounding county, which is the unit area in this analysis, and, thus, the Japanese companies coming into this country are unlikely to choose the county for the location of their plants just by the reason that the county has a small area of EZ within its boundary[3]. In fact, only nine Japanese companies have located in these EZs so far[4].

Therefore, it seems more plausible to investigate other related features or variables which are concealed in the notion of an EZ rather than to conclude plainly that the existence of an EZ in the county is one of the most important variables for the location of Japanese companies. This issue will be discussed later (7.1.1.5). Before then, the X_{21} variable involved in each equation is interpreted simply as the influence of the existence of an EZ in the county on the location decisions of Japanese companies. In aggregate, the explicability of the dependent variable Y_1 by using these variables is satisfactory. The magnitude of R^2 value, 0.387, which means that around 40% of the variation in Y_1 has been explained, can be said to be relatively high.

7.1.1.2 Change analysis based on the absolute change in the number of Japanese manufacturing companies 1981-1990 (Y_2)

In a way somewhat different from the result of the static analysis, the regression about the changes in the number of Japanese manufacturing companies during the period of 1981-1990 picked out two significant variables with the one representing the existence of leading Japanese companies being the most important. The equation constructed by these variables is:

$$Y_2 \text{ (}\Delta\text{NUM)} = -5.14 + 1.52\ X_{43}(\log) + 0.521\ X_5 \qquad \dots\dots\dots \text{ (7.2)}$$
$$(5.46)^{**} \qquad (5.02)^{**}$$

149

$$R^2 = 0.370 \quad F = 19.52 \quad (\ p = 0.000\ )$$

where X_{43} is the total number of Japanese companies in other sectors in 1988; and X_5 is average unemployment rate 1979-1988.

The double asterisk shows that these variables are significant at the 0.01 level. The inter-relationships between these variables are:

	$Y_2(\Delta NUM)$	$X_{43}(log)$	X_5
$Y_2(\Delta NUM)$	1.000	0.372	0.305
$X_{43}(log)$		1.000	-0.412
X_5			1.000

As indicated in the above equation and correlation matrix, the increase of Japanese manufacturing companies in Britain is explained by these two explanatory variables at just below 40% level. The propensity of Japanese companies for locating near their compatriot concerns was affirmed by the inclusion of X_{43}. The abundance of unemployed labour (X_5) was found, as expected, to be an important geographical factor for the location of Japanese companies in particular counties in this country. The magnitude of R^2, 0.370, is similar with the case of Y_1.

In order to enhance the explicability of the dependent variable, the step was taken of lowering the cut-off level to 0.1. The regression equation produced at this lowered cut-off level was:

$$Y_2\ (\Delta NUM) = -17.1 + 0.830\ X_5 + 2.23\ X_{43}(log) + 0.0340\ X_8$$
$$(5.96)** \qquad (6.90)** \qquad\qquad (3.88)**$$
$$+\ 1.61\ X_{39}(log) - 0.563\ X_{49}(log)\ \ldots\ldots\ (7.2.1)$$
$$(3.05)** \qquad\qquad (-1.73)$$

$$R^2 = 0.495 \quad F = 13.35 \quad (\ p = 0.000\ )$$

where X_5 is average unemployment rate 1979-1988;

X_8 is the absolute change in the numbers employed in the manufacturing sector 1979-1988;

X_{43} is the total number of Japanese companies in other sectors in 1988;

X_{39} is the number of manufacturing firms in the county;
and X_{49} is density of population.

Among these, four variables are significant at 0.01 level. The inter-relationships between these significant variables are:

150

	Y₂(ΔNUM)	X₄₃(log)	X₅	X₈	X₃₉(log)	X₄₉(log)
$Y_2(\Delta NUM)$	1.000	0.372	0.305	-0.253	0.324	0.280
$X_{43}(log)$		1.000	-0.412	-0.558	0.635	0.526
X_5			1.000	-0.412	-0.153	0.085
X_8				1.000	-0.108	-0.708
$X_{39}(log)$					1.000	0.706
$X_{49}(log)$						1.000

The opposite signs between the parameters in the equation and the correlation coefficient in the matrix of the same variables, X_8 and $X_{49}(log)$, seemed to be the result of multicollinearity among variables included. The examination of the correlation matrix between the independent variables revealed the interrelationship between X_8, $X_{43}(log)$ and $X_{39}(log)$. The presence of multicollinear-ity in the model has been explained as significantly hampering the plausibility of the regression equation (Mendenhall and Sincich, 1989,pp.234-241)[5].

The exclusion of the variable X_8 from the equation decreased the significance level of $X_{39}(log)$ and $X_{49}(log)$ and, consequently, left no other suitable equation than the equation (7.2). Therefore the previous equation (7.2), with R^2 value of 0.370, was confirmed as the suitable regression equation explaining the Y_2 variable.

7.1.1.3 Static analysis about the total numbers employed by Japanese manufacturing companies in 1990 (Y_3)

The regression for the total numbers employed by Japanese manufacturing companies in 1990 threw up a different set of significant variables; X_{42}, X_{21} and X_{16}. The relationship between variables is summarized by the following equation and correlation matrix.

$$Y_3 \text{ (EMP)} = 2580 + 1.37\ X_{42} + 102\ X_{21}(log) - 94.5\ X_{16}(sqrt) \quad (7.3)$$
$$(6.73)** \qquad (3.37)** \qquad (-2.80)**$$

$$R^2 = 0.488 \qquad F = 20.98 \ (\ p = 0.000\ )$$

where X_{16} is the absolute change in the working days lost by stoppages of work due to industrial disputes 1979-1988;

X_{21} is the total amount of public sector investment in the EZs from designation in the area to 1988;

X_{42} is the total numbers employed by Japanese manufacturing companies established before the end of 1979.

151

All these variables are significant at the 0.01 level. The correlation matrix between these variables is shown below.

	Y₃(EMP)	X₄₂	X₂₁(log)	X₁₆(sqrt)
Y_3(EMP)	1.000	0.562	0.265	-0.319
X_{42}		1.000	-0.167	0.005
X_{21}(log)			1.000	-0.204
X_{16}(sqrt)				1.000

This outcome reveals that the total employment of Japanese manufacturing companies in a county has been related to the existence of leading Japanese companies, the eligibility for spatial assistance in the form of public expenditure on EZs and the militancy of labour. This can be interpreted in such a way that the Japanese companies prefer counties which have the advantages that go with EZs, numbers of Japanese manufacturing companies already operating and attractive labour that is cooperative with management. In particular, with regard to the criteria of Japanese companies in recruiting workers, it is worth noting that the non-militancy of labour was found to be one of the most important variables for the location of Japanese manufacturing companies measured by the static employment size.

7.1.1.4 Change analysis based on the absolute change in the total numbers employed by Japanese manufacturing companies 1981-1990 (Y_4)

Through the regression about the dependent variable Y_4, the following outcome was produced:

$$Y_4 \ (\Delta EMP) = 3964 + 128 \ X_{21}(\log) - 171 \ X_{16}(\text{sqrt}) - 9.13 \ X_{15}$$
$$(3.33)^{**} \qquad (-4.09)^{**} \qquad (-1.74)$$

$$+ \ 0.807 \ X_{22} + 19.4 \ X_2 \qquad \dots \dots \dots \dots \dots \dots \ (7.4)$$
$$(3.13)^{**} \qquad (2.27)$$

$$R^2 = 0.402 \qquad F = 8.13 \ \ (\ p = 0.000 \ )$$

where X_2 is the absolute change in total numbers in the working population of both sexes 1979-1988;

X_{15} and X_{16} are the number of working days lost by stoppages of work due to industrial disputes and its absolute change 1979-1988;

X_{21} is the total amount of public sector investment in the EZs from designation in the area to 1988;

152

and X_{22} is the public expenditure for economic development and promotion per 1,000 population 1979-1988.

The three variables with double asterisks are significant at the 0.01 level. The inter-relationships between the variables are;

	$Y_4(\Delta EMP)$	$X_{21}(log)$	$X_{16}(sqrt)$	X_{15}	X_{22}	X_2
$Y_4(\Delta EMP)$	1.000	0.407	-0.388	0.259	0.421	-0.206
$X_{21}(log)$		1.000	-0.204	0.521	0.480	-0.476
$X_{16}(sqrt)$			1.000	-0.611	-0.195	0.511
X_{15}				1.000	0.398	-0.648
X_{22}					1.000	-0.582
X_2						1.000

In the cases of X_{15} and X_2, the signs in the equation are different from those in the matrix. This implies that there is a multicollinearity between the variables included in the equation. By the examination of the correlation between the variables, X_{15} and X_2 were found to be closely related to other two variables, $X_{16}(sqrt)$ and X_{22}. The exclusion of those variables which contained the problem of multicollinearity produced the following regression equation for the explanation of Y_4:

$$Y_4 (\Delta EMP) = 2715 + 91.7\ X_{21}(log) - 96.5\ X_{16}(sqrt) \dots\dots\dots (7.4.1)$$
$$(3.04)** \qquad\qquad (-2.83)**$$

$$R^2 = 0.238 \quad F = 10.85 \quad (p = 0.000)$$

Another effort to enhance the R^2 value by lowering the cut-off level to 0.1 produced a different regression equation:

$$Y_4 (\Delta EMP) = 2091 + 76.1\ X_{21}(log) - 77.9\ X_{16}(sqrt) + 0.445\ X_{22} \quad (7.4.2)$$
$$(2.01) \qquad\qquad (-2.22)* \qquad\qquad (1.79)$$

$$R^2 = 0.277 \quad F = 7.78 \quad (p = 0.000)$$

In comparison to the previous equation (7.4.1) this equation shows a slightly increased R^2 value. Even though the significance of the variables included in the equation is lowered in this new equation, i.e. only one variable is significant at the 0.05 level, the dependent variable Y_4 can best be explained by this equation.

In all, once again, the public sector investment in the EZs (X_{21}) stood out above other variables for explaining the increase in the total number of employees in Japanese manufacturing companies in each county. In combination with the importance of the economic development activities of local authorities (X_{22}), this variable can be said to prove the significance of the public policy[6]. Also the militancy of labour represented by stoppages of work due to industrial disputes (X_{16}) has influenced substantially the arrival of Japanese companies in the county area. The R^2 value, 0.277, seems to be relatively low compared to the cases from Y_1 to Y_3.

From the equations (7.3) and (7.4.2), it seems evident that public sector investment and assistance, from either central or local government, to develop the economy in certain areas and the non-militancy of labour (i.e. the relative absence of disputes) as well as the existence of leading Japanese companies were the most crucial geographical factors influencing the locational decisions of Japanese companies in this country.

7.1.1.5 Further analysis

Introduction of new variables

In order to examine in detail the relationship between the regional assistance factor with the location of Japanese companies, another variable representing the extent of regional assistance has been introduced. This is the amount of RDG paid per county during the period of 1979-1988. Therefore, two variables, the total amount of RDG paid (average of 1979-1988, X_{71}) and the absolute change in the amount of RDG paid 1979-1988 (X_{72}), were introduced in the regression[7].

These variables were included in the regression with the previous explanatory variables. The outcomes of these regressions were the same as the results of the previous regressions in the cases of Y_2 and Y_4. In other words, the variables X_{71} and X_{72} made no significant independent contribution. However, the equations of Y_1 and Y_3 were changed by the introduction of these new variables as follows.

$$Y_1 \text{ (NUM)} = 1.26 + 3.08\ X_{41} + 0.304\ X_{21}(\log) + 0.000065\ X_{72} \quad (7.5)$$
$$(5.61)^{**} \qquad (3.86)^{**} \qquad\quad (1.82)$$

$$R^2 = 0.409 \qquad F = 15.54 \quad (\,p = 0.000\,)$$

$$Y_3 \text{ (EMP)} = 2424 + 1.36\ X_{42} + 103\ X_{21}(\log) - 86.6\ X_{16}(\text{sqrt})$$
$$(6.85)^{**} \qquad (3.48)^{**} \qquad (-2.60)^{**}$$
$$+\ 0.0249\ X_{72} \qquad \dots\dots\dots\dots\dots\dots \quad (7.6)$$
$$(1.89)$$

$$R^2 = 0.509 \qquad F = 17.30 \quad (\,p = 0.000\,)$$

Here, X_{16} is the absolute change in the working days lost by stoppages of work due to industrial disputes;

X_{21} is the total amount of public sector investment in the enterprise zones from designation in the area to 1988;

X_{41} and X_{42} are the number of Japanese manufacturing companies in the area in 1979 and the total numbers employed by these companies;

and X_{72} is the absolute change in the amount of RDG paid 1979-1988.

The variables with double asterisks are significant at the 0.01 level. These equations show that regional assistance represented by the amount of RDG paid is another important variable for understanding the locational distribution of Japanese companies[8]. However, when the total amount of regional assistance in each region was used instead of the above variables (X_{73} and X_{74}) by dividing and allocating the regional level figure evenly to the counties constituting each standard region, the result produced was insignificant. This result is quite different from the outcomes above. These two apparently contradictory outcomes are very tricky to interpret.

Although it is caused by the use of aggregated data, it may be interpreted in a different and totally logical way; namely, that the Japanese companies are highly concentrated in the specific counties which are eligible for regional assistance rather than affected by the amount of grant paid in the region as a whole. This fact seems to be further evidence supporting the attractiveness of regional financial assistance to the incoming Japanese companies[9].

On the same grounds, another explanatory variable concerned with public policy that promotes private investment in certain areas was introduced; that was X_{75}, the number of New Towns, EZs, Urban Development Corporations (UDCs), Free Ports and Steel Closure Areas in each county in 1986[10]. However, the involvement of this new variable in the regression made no significant change in the selection of the variables involved, even though the correlation coefficients of this variable with the four dependent variables are relatively high (0.507, 0.490, 0.317 and 0.394 each). This implies that X_{75} has made high correlations with other variables.

On the other hand, to test the importance of accessibility through the railway and environmental circumstances more deeply, several other variables such as travel time to London by rail and the number of inter-city railway trains to London (X_{76} and X_{77})[11] and average house prices in 1988 (X_{78})[12] were included among the explanatory variables. However, these variables have brought no change in the equations above explaining the locations and the locational changes of Japanese companies.

Disaggretion of X_{21} variable

As discussed above (7.1.1.1), the equation which involves the X_{21} (the total amount of public sector investment in the EZs from designation in the area to 1988) is hard to interpret as it seems over simplistic that the locations of Japanese companies have been influenced by the designation of EZs and the public sector investment in these. Therefore, other significant variables constructing the X_{21} variable need to be revealed.

For the purpose, this study made two kinds of efforts. One was the examination of correlation coefficients between X_{21} and other explanatory variables and the other was the implementation of regression excluding the X_{21} variable. The variables which were found to have high correlation coefficients with X_{21} are listed as follows(see Table 7.1):

As seen below, it seems more reliable to infer that the gathering of Japanese companies within and around EZs resulted from the advantage of the areas reflected through abundant labour force (X_1 and X_4) and industrial premises (X_{26}), sufficient suppliers or subcontractors (X_{40}) and the existence of compatriot companies (X_{43} and X_{44}) in the area than to interpret it as the products of public assistance simply in EZs *per se*.

In other words, the relationship between the location of Japanese companies and the public investment in EZs can be said to be due to the coincidence of these two procedures resulting from similar criteria being taken by Japanese companies and the British government regarding labour, especially the unemployed, industrial premises and a bundle of manufacturing firms rather than the unilateral influence of the EZ investment on the location of Japanese companies. On the other hand, the high correlation coefficients of the last two variables (X_{43} and X_{44}) underline that Japanese companies in other sectors also, as well as manufacturing companies, tend to be influenced by these factors.

Table 7.1   The variables which have high correlation coefficient with X_{21}

Variable	Correlation coefficient with X_{21}
X_1 (total numbers in the working population of both sexes, average of 1979-1988)	0.843
X_4 (absolute change in the numbers unemployed 1979-1988)	0.816
X_{26} (total stock of commercial and industrial floorspace, average of 1979-1988)	0.827
X_{40} (absolute change in the number of manufacturing firms in the area 1979-1988)	-0.852
X_{43} and X_{44} (total number of Japanese companies in other sectors and its absolute change 1979-1988)	0.869 each

Another effort made to investigate the concealed locational factors behind EZ investment was the regression excluding the X_{21} variable. This attempt produced an interesting result. The main difference between the regression results including X_{21} and those without X_{21} can be summarised as in Table 7.2. Surprisingly enough, the elimination of the X_{21} variable from the regression resulted, without any exception, in the appearance of two main alternative variables, the existence of Japanese companies in other sectors (X_{43}) and the unemployment rate in the area (X_5), and, moderately, of government regional assistance (X_{72}).

This fact, if X_{43} is put aside, strongly suggests that the importance of EZs for the attraction of Japanese companies was, in fact, caused by other important factors hidden behind the curtain of the EZs, i.e. abundant unemployed workers in the main and regional assistance supplementarily.

Table 7.2 Important variables chosen by the regressions including and excluding X_{21}

Dependent Variables	Including X_{21} (1981-1990)	Excluding X_{21}(1981-1990)
Y1 (NUM)	X_{41}, X_{21}(log) X_{72} ($R^2 = 0.409$)	X_{41}, X_{43}(log), X_5 ($R^2 = 0.498$)
Y_2 (ΔNUM)	X_{43}(log), X_5 ($R^2 = 0.370$)	X_{43}(log), X_5, X_{72} ($R^2 = 0.403$)
Y_3 (EMP)	X_{42}, X_{21}(log) X_{16}(sqrt),X_{72} ($R^2 = 0.509$)	X_{42}, X_{43}, X_5, X_{72} ($R^2 = 0.562$)
Y_4 (ΔEMP)	X_{21}(log), X_{16}(sqrt), X_{22} ($R^2 = 0.277$)	X_{43}(log), X_5, X_{72} ($R^2 = 0.381$)

Here, X_5 is the average unemployment rate 1979-1988;

X_{16} is the absolute change in the working days lost by stoppages of work due to industrial disputes 1979-1988;

X_{21} is the total amount of public sector investment in the EZs from designation in the area to 1988;

X_{22} is public expenditure for economic development and promotion per 1,000 population (average of 1979-1988).

X_{41} and X_{42} are the number of Japanese manufacturing companies in the area in 1979 and the total numbers employed by these companies;

X_{43} is the total number of Japanese companies in other sectors in 1988;

and X_{72} is the absolute change in the amount of RDG paid 1979-1988.

Another thing to be noted is that the R^2 value in each regression was increased substantially by the exclusion of X_{21}. This can be interpreted in such a way that, by excluding X_{21}, other significant factors such as labour force available and regional assistance, whose actual influence on the location of Japanese companies were not sufficiently integrated in X_{21}, can now contribute fully and directly to the explanation of Y variables.

From these consequences, it seems possible to conclude that the appearance of EZs as an important factor for the location of Japanese companies in the regressions result can be interpreted, or translated, as the role of an abundant potential workforce and public policy.

7.1.1.6 Summary

The important explanatory variables for each dependent variable which have been found from the procedures so far can be summarized in the table below. This table helps estimating and comparing the importance of the locational factors reflected in the variables involved. By comparing these selected explanatory variables, it seems possible to draw the conclusion that the locational behaviour of Japanese companies has been highly correlated with i) the existence of leading Japanese companies, either in the manufacturing sector or in other sectors, already operating in the area; ii) the eligibility of the area for regional assistance in the form of either public investment or financial assistance; and iii) the supply of readily available labour and its non-militancy.

Table 7.3 The significant variables chosen in static and change analysis (Britain)

Locational Factors	Variables	Y_1 (NUM)	Y_2 (ΔNUM)	Y_3 (EMP)	Y_4 (ΔEMP)
Labour	X_5		0.305		
supply	X_8		-0.248		
	X_{16}(sqrt)			-0.318	-0.385
Public	X_{21}(log)	0.282		0.265	0.405
policy	X_{22}			0.399	
	X_{72}			0.206	
Linkages	X_{41}	0.522			
(leading	X_{42}			0.561	
companies)	X_{43}(log)		0.369		
Environmental circumstances					
	X_{49}(log)		0.273		

7.1.2 Index Analysis

7.1.2.1 The construction of indices

In order to examine the relative importance of each locational factor as a whole, a set of indices for every locational factor have been constructed by amalgamating the variables involved in the static and change analysis. The indices which are provided here are constructed based on the extent of the relationship of each county with the explanatory variables constituting each locational factor. In detail, the following procedure is undertaken to make an index for each locational factor:

1) Three or four of the representative explanatory variables involved in each locational factor, which have high correlation coefficients with the dependent variables, are selected. Where two explanatory variables are highly correlated with each other, one is excluded to avoid overloading the index with that aspect.

2) To obtain the relative importance of each county for a variable, a procedure of standardization is undertaken by calculating the Z-score of each county for the selected variable, thus;

$$Z_i = (X_i - m_i)/sd_i.$$

where m_i is the mean value of X_i with Y_i and sd_i is the standard deviation of the variable X_i.

3) A weight is given to the computed relative importance, i.e. Z-scores above. Here, the weight given is the correlation coefficient of each explanatory variable with a dependent variable. Therefore, if the correlation coefficient is negative, the figure of a variable given a weight appears as a negative.

4) The weighted values above are summed up to produce an integrated index for locational factor.

And then this aggregated figure is divided by the number of variables involved in the calculation of the index for each locational factor. In consequence, an integrated index for a locational factor includes standardized variables and, thus, the figure for this integrated index has a distribution with the mean value of 0. In short, an index constructed for a locational factor is;

$$X_z = 1/n \ \Sigma \ r_i*(X_i - m_i)/sd_i \qquad \ldots \ldots \ldots \ldots \ldots \ldots \ldots \quad (7.7)$$

159

where X_z refers to the index for each locational factor, r_i is the correlation coefficient of X_i with Y_i, m_i is the mean value of X_i, sd_i is the standard deviation of the variable X_i and n is the number of variables included in the calculation of the index.

Through this procedure, each county has a set of indices for the six locational factors, namely, labour supply, public policy, land and premises availability, accessibility, linkages and environmental circumstances. These indices are regressed on dependent variables again to derive the correlation coefficient (r_z) for the locational factors and to find out the most significant factors. After obtaining the r_z value by using the indices as independent variables, a comparison is made to find out the locational factor which most influences each dependent variable[13].

7.1.2.2   Selected variables for the construction of indices

Table 7.4 Variables constructing the indices of locational factors (Britain)

Locational Factors	Y_1 (NUM)	Y_2 (ΔNUM)	Y_3 (EMP)	Y_4 (ΔEMP)
Labour supply (X_a)	X_3(log),X_5 X_{13}, X_{16}	X_3(log),X_5 X_8, X_{13}	X_3(log),X_5 X_5,X_8, X_{16}(sqrt)	X_3(log), X_5, X_8, X_{16}(sqrt)
Public policy (X_b)	X_{21}(log), X_{22}, X_{71}, X_{72}	X_{21}(log), X_{22}, X_{71}, X_{72}	X_{19},X_{21}(log) X_{22}, X_{71}(sqrt)	X_{19},X_{21}(log) X_{22},X_{72}
Land and premises (X_c)	X_{26}(log), X_{28}	X_{26}(log), X_{28}(log)	X_{26}(log), X_{27}(log)	X_{26}(sqrt), X_{28}(log)
Accessibility (X_d)	X_{34}(log), X_{37}(log), X_{38}(log)	X_{34}(log), X_{37}(log), X_{38}(log)	X_{34}(log), X_{37}(log)	X_{33}(sqrt), X_{34}(log)
Linkages (X_e)	X_{39}(log), X_{41},X_{43}(log) X_{46}(log)	X_{39}(log), X_{41}, X_{43}(log)	X_{39}(log), X_{41}, X_{42} X_{43}(log)	X_{39}(sqrt), X_{43}(log)
Environmental cirmumstances (X_f)	X_{49}(log), X_{53}, X_{55}, X_{58}(log)	X_{49}(log), X_{53}, X_{55} X_{58}(log)	X_{47},X_{49}(log) X_{53}, X_{54}(sqrt)	X_{49}(sqrt), X_{53},X_{54}(log) X_{58}(log)

The above variables were selected to construct a set of   indices representing the locational factors. The criterion for selecting these variables was the degree of correlation coefficient between the dependent and independent variables. By integrating the values of these variables, a set of amalgamated indices were produced for each locational factor in each county.

The indices for the six locational factors which are constructed according to the above procedure are listed in Appendix 5. These indices can be used for

160

measuring roughly the strength or weakness of each county in each locational factor. For example, regarding the number of Japanese companies in each county, London and the West Midlands proved to be advantageous in all the six locational factors, while Lincolnshire, Dorset, etc. appeared to be disadvantageous in all the locational factors (Appendix 5.1)[14].

7.1.2.3 Results of the regression using indices

The relative importance of the indices for the explanation of dependent variables also can be represented briefly by using a correlation coefficient matrix. The following matrix shows the significance of each locational factor:

	Labour Supply X_a	Public Policy X_b	Land & Premises X_c	Accessibility X_d	Linkage X_e	Environments X_f
Y_1(NUM)	0.412	0.367	0.227	0.290	0.572	0.406
Y_2(ΔNUM)	0.408	0.396	0.233	0.288	0.480	0.391
Y_3(EMP)	0.417	0.423	0.189	0.273	0.608	0.423
Y_4(ΔEMP)	0.484	0.540	0.234	0.282	0.360	0.385

The regression equations using these indices are presented below.

$$Y_1 \text{ (NUM)} = 2.97 + 9.42 \ X_e + 10.4 \ X_b - 7.09 \ X_f \quad \cdots\cdots\cdots \quad (7.8)$$
$$(4.96)** \quad (4.17)** \quad (-2.45)*$$

$$R^2 = 0.391 \quad F = 12.33 \quad (\ p = 0.000 \ )$$

$$Y_2 \text{ (ΔNUM)} = 2.63 + 9.58 \ X_b + 6.95 \ X_e - 5.88 \ X_f \quad \cdots\cdots\cdots \quad (7.9)$$
$$(3.98)** \quad (3.73)** \quad (-1.96)$$

$$R^2 = 0.306 \quad F = 8.78 \quad (\ p = 0.000 \ )$$

$$Y_3 \text{ (EMP)} = 989 + 2822 \ X_e + 2378 \ X_b \quad \cdots\cdots\cdots\cdots \quad (7.10)$$
$$(5.56)** \quad (4.15)**$$

$$R^2 = 0.469 \quad F = 24.37 \quad (\ p = 0.000)$$

$$Y_4 \text{ (ΔEMP)} = 817 + 2724 \ X_b + 930 \ X_c \cdots\cdots\cdots\cdots \quad (7.11)$$
$$(4.53)** \quad (2.14)*$$

$$R^2 = 0.324 \quad F = 13.69 \quad (\ p = 0.000 \ )$$

161

Among these, the first two regression equations include the index for environmental circumstances (X_f) which shows the opposite signs between matrix and equations. This implies that the X_f has the likelihood of multicollinearity with other variables, in this case other indices, included in the equations. In fact, X_f was found to have close relationship with both X_b and X_e. The exclusion of X_f to confront this problem produced another set of equations as follows:

$$Y_1 \text{ (NUM)} = 2.94 + 6.51 \ X_e + 7.20 \ X_b \ \ldots\ldots\ldots\ldots\ldots\ldots \quad (7.8.1)$$
$$(4.19)** \quad (3.23)**$$

$$R^2 = 0.331 \quad F = 14.12 \quad (\ p = 0.000\ )$$

$$Y_2 \text{ (}\Delta\text{NUM)} = 2.61 + 6.95 \ X_b + 4.53 \ X_e \ \ldots\ldots\ldots\ldots\ldots\ldots \quad (7.9.1)$$
$$(3.38)** \quad (3.16)**$$

$$R^2 = 0.267 \quad F = 10.66 \quad (\ p = 0.000\ )$$

As seen in the matrix and equations, the explanatory indices which have most influence on each dependent variable were identical. This means that the measure of the extent to which the incoming Japanese companies are influenced by each locational factor is almost similar regardless of the forms of the dependent variables. The replacement of X_{21} by X_{75} in forming the index for public policy (X_b) in order to minimise the coincidence effect of X_{21} with dependent variables, however, made no difference from the above equations except the increase of R^2 value (0.355, 0.287, 0.462 and 0.330 for each Y_i). In brief, the above matrix and equations show explicitly that linkage and public policy have been the most important geographical factors behind the locational decisions of Japanese companies coming into counties in this country.

Especially, the linkage issue stood out of other factors in terms of its importance for the explanation of locations of Japanese companies. The existence of leading Japanese companies already operating in the area was central to this locational factor. The involvement of this factor in all the four analyses, from Y_1 to Y_4, as the most important factor in two equations and the second most important in the other two, is wholly due to the role of these Japanese predecessors in each area. Moreover, this factor shows the highest correlation coefficient among locational factors with every kind of dependent variable except the case of Y_4. This finding offers the statistical evidence for the argument about the tendency of Japanese companies to cluster in particular areas.

The issue of public policy took the equivalent position with linkage in importance for the locational choice of Japanese companies. This factor has been found to be the most significant in two out of the four different regressions, Y_2 and Y_4. The strength of this factor originated from the relatively similar importance of the variables involved, namely the public sector investment in EZs, the public expenditure for economic development and promotion and regional financial assistance, with the dependent variables.

In other words, for the locational choice of Japanese manufacturing companies in Britain, the efforts of the government at both central and local level have become an important contributor. This fact is reinforced by the greatest importance of this factor in the cases of Y_2 and Y_4, which are measured by the changes either in company numbers or in employment size, showing that the influence of these variables has been crucial for the increase in the number of Japanese companies and in the employment size (their growth) of these companies during the last ten years.

Among the above policy measures, the importance of the first one, the existence of EZs and the investment of the public sector in these zones, is worth noting. Although the significance of this factor in the regression analyses is considered as the coincidence between the designation of EZs and the locations of Japanese companies rather than as the influence of the former on the latter, the variable still provides a valuable indication for tracing and inferring the location decisions of Japanese companies in the changing context of regional policy in this country.

The fact that this new policy initiative appeared to be the most important policy instrument in this statistical analysis can be interpreted in two ways. The first is the timeliness of the diversification of the policy initiatives in British regional policy, when the effect of policy change is measured in terms of the attractiveness for the incoming foreign investments. In other words, the shift of the policy concern from the traditional approach, which has relied heavily on financial assistance to migrant firms coming into widely drawn assisted areas, towards the concentration of efforts to develop a list of more specific local economies can be said to have been valid at least in this regression analysis.

And the second is that the location decisions of Japanese companies in this country have been based on the accurate analysis of locational factors in order to make use of all the given circumstances including availability of labour, existence of subcontractors and even the slightest change in the context of spatial policy[15]. This implies that it is the configuration, or combination, of all the related locational factors rather than one or two extraordinary factors which decides the locations of Japanese companies. Another thing to be considered is that, in conjunction with new policy measures, government regional assistance still appeared as one of *non-negligible* locational factors for the incoming Japanese concerns.

All these findings are noteworthy in measuring the anticipated locational pattern of Japanese manufacturing companies and the future role of regional policy. On the whole, the importance of government spatial policy, including financial assistance to the incoming Japanese companies, is highlighted again by these findings. The locational behaviour in the changing context of regional policy is examined further in the chapters in Part III.

Apart from these two predominant locational factors, another important factor influencing the locational behaviour of Japanese companies was the availability of abundant labour. In other words the supply of labour has been one of the important factors behind the locational decisions of Japanese companies coming into this country. This is mainly indebted to some significant variables involved, such as the militancy of labour and unemployment rate, with the dependent variables.

Environmental circumstances were also found to have influenced substantially the location of Japanese companies. The abundance of leisure and recreation facilities and the availability of dwellings constitute the main part of this factor. This is worth considering in inferring the necessary conditions for the location decisions of Japanese managements.

In consequence, both the static and change analysis and the index analysis can be said to have provided the statistical evidence to support the presumptions about the locational pattern of Japanese companies in this country which have been claimed so often.

7.1.3 Sub-period analysis

7.1.3.1 Necessity and methods

Both the static and change analysis and the index analysis described so far were to investigate the significant factors for the location of Japanese companies using the data spanning the whole period from 1981 to 1990. In order to portray clearly the changing features of the locational pattern of these Japanese manufacturing companies, another type of regression was undertaken. This was the regression analysis on the locational decisions of Japanese companies in the two divided sub-periods, i.e. 1981-1986 and 1987-1990, as suggested in Chapter five. This sub-period analysis is necessary in that ten years is a long period for this kind of cross-section analysis and, as a result, some significant changes in the locational pattern during the whole period are apt to be over-looked. Therefore, apart from the static and change analysis and the index analysis, this study implemented regression for the two sub-periods.

The method of analysis is the same as the regression analysis of the whole period. Therefore there is no change in the dependent and independent variables listed in Chapter five. The procedure of analysis is also the same as that of the whole period. Therefore, the dependent variable Y_1 (the number of Japanese manufacturing companies in each county in 1990) is changed into those of 1986 and 1990. Likewise, the values of explanatory variables for static and change analysis are also divided into the two values for 1979-1984 and for 1985-1988[16].

Basically, most dependent and independent variables are produced in the same manner. However, there are a few exceptional figures which cannot be divided according to time period. The distance to the nearest major airport is an example.

164

In these cases the same figure is used in the two sub-periods. In the British case, the variables of X_{34}, X_{37}, X_{38}, X_{51}, X_{52} and X_{55} in the two sub-periods are constructed in this way.

7.1.3.2 Significant geographical factors in 1981-1986

The static and change analysis using the variables for 1981-1986 produced four regression equations involving a number of important geographical factors for the locations of Japanese companies as follows:

$$Y_1 \text{ (NUM)} = 0.353 + 1.46 \ X_{41} + 0.000551 \ X_{23} + 0.0295 \ X_{18} \ .. \quad (7.12)$$
$$(6.14)^{**} \quad (2.51)^* \quad (1.74)$$

$$R^2 = 0.475 \quad F = 16.95 \quad (\ p = 0.000 \ )$$

$$Y_2 \text{ (}\Delta\text{NUM)} = 0.072 + 0.000453 \ X_{22} + 0.568 \ X_{41} + 0.0968 \ X_{21}(\log). \ . \ (7.13)$$
$$(1.51) \quad (2.50)^* \quad (2.49)^*$$

$$R^2 = 0.223 \quad F = 6.07 \quad (\ p = 0.001 \ )$$

$$Y_3 \text{ (EMP)} = - 178 + 1.01 \ X_{42} + 0.483 \ X_{23} + 31.5 \ X_{18} - 2.18 \ X_{16}$$
$$(7.85)^{**} \quad (3.78)^{**} \quad (3.33)^{**} \ (-2.31)^*$$
$$+ \ 72.8 \ X_{12} \qquad \ldots\ldots\ldots\ldots\ldots\ldots\ldots \quad (7.14)$$
$$(1.71)$$

$$R^2 = 0.714 \quad F = 27.46 \quad (\ p = 0.000 \ )$$

$$Y_4 \text{ (}\Delta\text{EMP)} = 1121 + 0.481 \ X_{23} + 31.3 \ X_{18} - 200 \ X_8(\log) \ \ldots. \quad (7.15)$$
$$(3.96)^{**} \quad (3.33)^{**} \quad (-2.34)^*$$

$$R^2 = 0.415 \quad F = 13.56 \quad (\ p = 0.000 \ )$$

where X_8 is the absolute change in the numbers employed in the manufacturing sector 1979-1984;

X_{16} is the absolute change in the working days lost by stoppages of work due to industrial disputes 1979-1984;

X_{18} is the absolute change in gross value added per employee in the manufacturing sector 1981-1984;

X_{21} is the total amount of public sector investment in the EZs from designation in the area to 1984;

X_{23} is the absolute change in the public expenditure for economic development and promotion

165

per 1,000 population 1979-1984;

where X_{41} and X_{42} are the number of Japanese manufacturing companies in the area in 1979 and the total numbers employed by these companies.

There was no significantly high inter-relationship between explanatory variables and nor any sign of multicollinearity. As seen in these equations, three variables stood out among others in explaining the locational pattern of Japanese companies during 1981-1986; namely, the existence of leading compatriot companies (X_{41} and X_{42}), the public expenditure for economic development and promotion by local government (X_{22} and X_{23}) and the productivity of labour (X_{18}). The influence of X_{21}, the public expenditure in EZs, was not significant in this sub-period analysis except a little effect in the case of Y_2.[17] The explicability measured by R^2 of the location of Japanese companies using these variables was relatively low, in particular in Y_2.

7.1.3.3 Significant geographical factors in 1987-1990

As in the case of the first sub-period, the second sub-period, from 1987 to 1990, was analyzed by regression using the variables relevant to the period. The regression produced another set of equations as follows:

$$Y_1 \text{ (NUM)} = 3.21 + 1.74\ X_{41} - 2.05\ X_6(\log) + 0.0797\ X_{13} \ \ \ldots \ (7.16)$$
$$(11.78)^{**} \quad (-4.37)^{**} \quad\quad (3.13)^{**}$$

$$R^2 = 0.779 \quad F = 74.75 \quad (\ p = 0.000\ )$$

$$Y_2 \text{ (}\Delta\text{NUM)} = 3.21 + 0.744\ X_{41} - 2.05\ X_6(\log) + 0.0797\ X_{13} \ \ldots \ (7.17)$$
$$(5.03)^{**} \quad (-4.37)^{**} \quad\quad (3.13)^{**}$$

$$R^2 = 0.526 \quad F = 24.33 \quad (\ p = 0.000\ )$$

$$Y_3 \text{ (EMP)} = 594 + 1.10\ X_{42} - 490\ X_6(\log) + 248\ X_{43}(\log) + 0.236\ X_{23}. \ .(7.18)$$
$$(16.18)^{**} \quad (-2.86)^{**} \quad (4.29)^{**} \quad (2.94)^{**}$$

$$R^2 = 0.865 \quad F = 86.19 \quad (\ p = 0.000\ )$$

$$Y_4 \text{ (}\Delta\text{EMP)} = 821 - 625\ X_6(\log) - 143\ X_{14} + 193\ X_{43}(\log) + 0.160\ X_{23}..(7.19)$$
$$(-3.90)^{**} \quad (-2.90)^{**} \quad (3.32)^{**} \quad\quad (1.97)$$

$$R^2 = 0.466 \quad F = 12.58 \quad (\ p = 0.000\ )$$

where X_6 is % point change in unemployment rate 1985-1988;

X_{13} and X_{14} are the number of institutions for further education and its absolute change 1985-1988;

X_{23} is the absolute change in the public expenditure for economic development and promotion per 1,000 population 1985-1988.

X_{41} and X_{42} are the number of Japanese manufacturing companies in the area in 1984 and the total numbers employed by these companies;

and X_{43} is the total number of Japanese companies in other sectors 1988;

The asterisks show the significance of the variables at each level (two at 0.01, one at 0.05 and none at 0.1 level). There was no significantly high correlation coefficients between independent variables, nor any sign of multicollinearity. And the influence of X_{21} variable was minimal also in this second sub-period analysis[18].

Three important variables played a dominant role in the locational decisions of incoming Japanese companies in this sub-period. These variables are: the existence of leading Japanese companies in the host area (X_{41}-X_{43}), public expenditure for economic development and promotion (X_{23}) and the change in unemployment rate (X_6) with a negative relationship. One thing to be noted is that, in this second sub-period, the number of institutions for further education (X_{13} and X_{14}) was found to be one of the most influential location factors. This is an interesting finding implying that the concern of Japanese companies began to be directed to the skill level of the workforce.

The explicability of dependent variables using these key explanatory variables is substantially high. This means that the influence of these limited number of variables on the location decisions of Japanese companies arriving in the late 1980s became more crucial.

7.1.3.4 Comparison between the periods

The explanatory variables which were found to be significant in explaining the locational decisions of Japanese companies in the whole period and two sub-periods can be gathered into the Table 7.5 below. Comparing the important explanatory variables between the whole and the two sub-periods, we can identify some distinguishing features in the locations of Japanese companies.

Firstly, in the early 1980s, the locational decisions of incoming Japanese companies were mainly determined by the presence of leading Japanese companies, the promotional activities of local government and the productivity of labour. Differently from the role of the leading Japanese companies, which has already been expected, the influence of local government activities as an important motivator is worth noting.

Table 7.5 The significant explanatory variables for the locational decisions of Japanese manufacturing companies in each period (Britain)

Dependent Variables	Whole Period (1981-1990)	1st Sub-period (1981-1986)	2nd Sub-period (1987-1990)
Y_1 (NUM)	X_{41}, X_{21}(log) X_{72} ($R^2 = 0.409$)	X_{41}, X_{23}, X_{18} ($R^2 = 0.475$)	X_{41}, X_6(log) X_{13} ($R^2 = 0.779$)
Y_2 (ΔNUM)	X_{43}(log), X_5 ($R^2 = 0.370$)	X_{22}, X_{41}, X_{21}(log) ($R^2 = 0.223$)	X_{41}, X_6(log) X_{13} ($R^2 = 0.526$)
Y_3 (EMP)	X_{42}, X_{21}(log) X_{16}(sqrt), X_{72} ($R^2 = 0.509$)	X_{42}, X_{23}, X_{18}, X_{16}, X_{12} ($R^2 = 0.714$)	X_{42}, X_6(log) X_{43}(log), X_{23} ($R^2 = 0.865$)
Y_4 (ΔEMP)	X_{21}(log), X_{16}(sqrt), X_{22} ($R^2 = 0.277$)	X_{23}, X_{18}, X_8(log) ($R^2 = 0.415$)	X_6(log), X_{14} X_{43}(log), X_{23} ($R^2 = 0.466$)

However, considering the fact that the increased activities of local government in the field of economic and industrial development guarantee better circumstances both for the location of migrant firms and for the management of existing firms, this factor deserves to be emphasized in explaining the location decisions of Japanese companies. The appearance of labour productivity as another significant variable was also expected, even though the enthusiasm of Japanese companies for non-militant labour has long been acclaimed as more important than other variables constituting the labour factor.

Secondly, in the second sub-period in the 1980s, in which the massive influx of Japanese investments in this country began, a quite similar set of variables were selected once again as important geographical factors determining the locations of Japanese companies. The variables are: the existence of Japanese companies; the public expenditure for economic development and promotion; and the distaste for the areas with high unemployment rates[19]. Among these, the last variable seems to be odd considering the general presumption that a high unemployment rate means the availability of abundant labour and, thus, becomes a favourable condition for the location of migrant firms. This is much more so, given the importance of abundant unemployed workers for the location of Japanese companies in the whole period, which was revealed by the exclusion of X_{21} variable (7.1.1.5).

One possible explanation for this is that Japanese managements began to think of the labour in these areas as being either prone to be militant or less reliable compared to labour elsewhere, especially in terms of its skilfulness. In fact, at a time when unemployment is falling, there is a tendency for the longer term unemployed to be assumed to be less skilled, older and with less potential (Armstrong and Taylor,1988,p.8). This explanation is strongly supported further by the inclusion of variables regarding the skill level of the workforce in this period. As a whole, the shift of emphasis from higher unemployment rate and higher productivity to lower unemployment rate and higher skill level seems to be an interesting finding regarding the labour supply factor in this sub-period analysis of the locational decisions of Japanese companies.

And, thirdly, differently from the regression results of the two sub-periods, that of the whole period presented a group of diversified and sporadic independent variables to be important for the location of Japanese companies. Nonetheless the importance of the existing Japanese companies, public policy and labour factor continued. One thing to be remembered is that, in the whole period, the public investment in EZs (X_{21}) was proved to be more important than public expenditure for economic development and promotion (X_{22} and X_{23}) which was found to be a key policy measure in sub-period analysis. However, as mentioned above (7.1.1.5), this should be taken as representing the role of an abundant labour force and government financial policy rather than the direct effect of EZs themselves.

Another point worth mentioning is that, differently from the sub-period regression results, the non-militancy of labour (X_{16}) and the abundant workforce available (X_5), which were concealed in the X_{21} variable, were picked out as the most important two among the variables constituting the labour factor. This difference between the regression result of the whole period and that of the sub-periods can be interpreted in such a way that the influence of these two variables (X_{16} and X_5) has been relatively substantial for a long time, even though these variables have not been outstanding in a specific period of time.

Consequently, the importance of the three locational factors, namely the presence of leading Japanese companies, public policy and the availability of reliable labour has been reaffirmed in this sub-period analysis, even though non-negligible changes in the important variables constituting these factors are involved.

7.2 Significant Geographical Factors in Korea

7.2.1 Static and change analysis

As in the British case, the static analysis and the change analysis were undertaken initially about the number of Japanese companies and their investment size in Korea. The dependent variables for these analyses are:

Y_1 : the number of Japanese manufacturing companies in each Do in 1990 (NUM);

Y_2 : the absolute change in the number of Japanese manufacturing companies in each Do 1981-1990 (ΔNUM);

Y_3 : the investment of the Japanese manufacturing companies in each Do in 1990 (EMP);

Y_4 : the absolute change in the investment of the Japanese companies in each Do 1981-1990 (ΔEMP).

The outcomes of these regressions are presented below in turn.

7.2.1.1 Static analysis about the number of Japanese manufacturing companies in 1990 (Y_1)

In the first place, the result of the static analysis about the number of Japanese companies can be summarized as the following equation:

$$Y_1 \text{ (NUM)} = -12.3 + 8.47\ X_{38}(\text{sqrt}) + 0.00812\ X_{26} \ \ldots\ldots\ldots \quad (7.20)$$
$$(7.94)** \qquad\qquad (6.47)**$$

$$R^2 = 0.966 \qquad F = 170.58 \quad (\,p = 0.000\,)$$

where, X_{38} is the number of Japanese manufacturing firms in the Do at the end of 1979

and X_{26} is the absolute change in the stock of commercial and industrial floor space 1979-1988.

The two explanatory variables are significant at the 0.01 level (double asterisk). The correlation matrix below shows no significantly high correlation between the independent variables.

	Y_1(NUM)	X_{38}(sqrt)	X_{26}
Y_1(NUM)	1.000	0.923	0.890
X_{38}(sqrt)		1.000	0.695
X_{26}			1.000

Therefore, from the result of this regression, the location of Japanese manufacturing companies in Korea was found to be influenced by the presence of the pre-located Japanese companies (X_{38}) and the availability of commercial and industrial premises (X_{26}). The degree of explanation of these variables, 0.966, is extremely high in this kind of analysis. This high correlation coefficient and R^2 value seems mainly due to the broadness of spatial boundary studied, i.e. Do level[20].

7.2.1.2 Change analysis based on the absolute change in the number of Japanese manufacturing companies (Y_2)

The regression about the change in the number of Japanese companies produced the following equation for the explanation of the given condition:

$$Y_2 \ (\Delta NUM) = -3.65 + 0.00997 \ X_{26} \ \ldots\ldots\ldots\ldots\ldots\ldots \quad (7.21)$$
$$(11.86)^*$$

$$R^2 = 0.921 \qquad F = 140.58 \quad (\ p = 0.000\ )$$

This time, the absolute change in the stock of commercial and industrial floor space 1979-1988 appeared to be the most influential factor for the locational decisions of Japanese companies in Korea. Since regional policy in Korea has laid an emphasis on the development and provision of industrial land and premises (see 4.2.2.3), this regression result comes partly from the public policy factor.

In this change analysis, as in the static analysis, the extent of explanation by this independent variable is notably high. The remarkably high correlation coefficient of variable X_{26} and, thus, the high R^2 value can be attributed to the limitation which this kind of analysis bears. So to speak, under the circumstances where the changes of both dependent and independent variables occur simultaneously, explanatory variables tend to have a high correlation coefficient against dependent variables.

As a result, one or two variables with extremely high correlation coefficients play an important part during the regression process. This inevitably results in the exclusion of other important variables from the regression equation. In fact, the dependent variables Y_1 and Y_2 show substantially high correlation coefficient of over 0.8 in 13 and 16 cases out of total 65 respectively. To confront this problem, an attempt was made by lowering the significance level, which is discussed at the end of this section.

7.2.1.3 Static analysis about the investment of Japanese manufacturing companies in Korea in 1990 (Y_3)

The static regression about the investment of Japanese concerns in Korea also took a set of explanatory variables as significant causes for the explanation of the situation.

$$Y_3 = -1135408 + 5165 \ X_{38} + 201426 \ X_{11}(log) + 37.6 \ X_{29}(sqrt)$$
$$(11.86)^{**} \qquad (5.37)^{**} \qquad (3.75)^{**}$$
$$+ 175717 \ X_{10}(log) \qquad \ldots\ldots\ldots\ldots\ldots\ldots \quad (7.22)$$
$$(3.19)$$
$$R^2 = 0.961 \qquad F = 75.52 \quad (\ p = 0.000\ )$$

where, X_{10} and X_{11} are the wage level in the manufacturing sector and its absolute change 1979-1988;

X_{29} is the total registered vessels for seaport traffic in each Do;

and X_{38} is the number of Japanese manufacturing firms in the Do (average of 1979-1988).

The three variables with two asterisks are significant at the 0.01 level, while the remaining one with no asterisk is at the 0.1 level. The inter-relationships between these selected variables are shown in the following correlation matrix.

	Y_3(EMP)	X_{38}	X_{11}(log)	X_{29}(sqrt)	X_{10}(log)
Y_3(EMP)	1.000	0.917	0.286	0.463	0.313
X_{38}		1.000	0.016	0.379	0.226
X_{11}(log)			1.000	-0.118	-0.032
X_{29}(sqrt)				1.000	-0.202
X_{10}(log)					1.000

Once again, the role of the existing Japanese companies in each Do (X_{38}) was found to be crucial for the incoming compatriot concerns in deciding their locations, especially when it was measured by the investment size of these companies. Surprisingly enough, the two variables concerned with the wage level of the labour force (X_{10} and X_{11}) turned out to be the important geographical factors for the incoming Japanese companies, especially with positive signs. This seems to be another indicator of the concentration tendency of Japanese companies in the two developed regions in Korea where large numbers of skilled workers, even though their wage level is high, are available.

Like the cases of Y_1 and Y_2, the proportion of the whole dependent variable covered by these variables was substantially high. This is mainly due to the influence of the first explanatory variable in the equation (X_{38}), with the correlation coefficient over 0.9.

7.2.1.4 Change analysis based on the absolute change in the investment of Japanese manufacturing companies in Korea 1981-1990 (Y_4)

The regression with the change in the investment of Japanese manufacturing companies (Y_4) as dependent variable presented the following equation (7.23):

$$Y_4 \ (\Delta EMP) = -290380 + 30680 \ X_{46}(\log) \quad \ldots \ldots \ldots \ldots \ldots \ldots \quad (7.23)$$
$$(2.58)^*$$

$$R^2 = 0.321 \qquad F = 6.67 \ (\ p = 0.025)$$

Strangely enough, the total urban park area in the Do in 1988 (X_{46}) was found

172

to be the only important variable among all the explanatory variables with the significance at 0.05 level.

However, when we take into account the fact that the statistics for the area of urban parks imply the extent of urbanization in Korea, this regression result can be said to be further evidence showing the preference of Japanese companies for developed and urbanized areas in deciding their locations. The high p-value (0.025) and low R^2 value show the insufficient explicabilty of dependent variable Y_4 using one explanatory variable. Therefore, like Y_1 and Y_2, another effort was made in order to enhance the significance of the equation as described below.

7.2.1.5 Further analysis

To search for other significant variables to explain the dependent variables Y_1, Y_2 and Y_4, further regressions were implemented with lowered significance level, 0.1. The following equations are the outcomes of these regressions.

Regression of Y_1

In the first place, the result of the static analysis (Y_1) with lowered significance level can be summarized as follows:

$$Y_1 = - 18.6 + 10.5\ X_{38}(sqrt) + 0.00700\ X_{26} - 0.213\ X_{23}(sqrt)$$
$$(11.87)** \qquad (7.84)** \qquad (-3.83)**$$
$$+ 7.32\ X_{15}(log) \qquad \dots\dots\dots\dots\dots\dots \qquad (7.24)$$
$$(2.85)*$$

$$R^2 = 0.985 \quad F = 197.67 \quad (\ p = 0.000\ )$$

where, X_{15} is the absolute change in the number of training facilities 1979-1988[21];

X_{23} is the stock of industrial estates;

X_{26} is the absolute change in the stock of commercial and industrial floor space 1979-1988;

and X_{38} is the number of Japanese manufacturing firms in the Do at the end of 1979.

Three variables except $X_{15}(log)$ are significant at the 0.01 level. The inter-relationships between the variables in the equation are:

As shown below, two more explanatory variables, $X_{23}(sqrt)$ and $X_{15}(log)$, were newly involved in the equation. However, the $X_{23}(sqrt)$ has the opposite signs in equation and matrix. The examination of the first order correlation coefficients of this variable with other independent variables included in the equation showed that this variable is in a multicollinearity with the variables of $X_{38}(sqrt)$ and $X_{15}(log)$. The exclusion of this variable lowered the significance of other variables and, in the end, resulted in the same equation with that of (7.20).

	Y_1(NUM)	X_{38}(sqrt)	X_{26}	X_{23}(sqrt)	X_{15}(log)
Y_1(NUM)	1.000	0.923	0.890	0.413	0.322
X_{38}(sqrt)		1.000	0.695	0.560	0.303
X_{26}			1.000	0.330	0.316
X_{23}(sqrt)				1.000	0.765
X_{15}(log)					1.000

Therefore, from this regression result, it can be said that the location of Japanese manufacturing companies in Korea had a close relationship with the existence of other Japanese manufacturing companies (X_{38}) and the availability of industrial land and premises (X_{26}).

Regression of Y_2

The regression about the dependent variable Y_2 with the lowered significance level resulted in the following equation which is quite different from the previous equation (7.21):

$$Y_2 \ (\Delta NUM) = - \ 11.8 + 22.0 \ X_5 + 0.298 \ X_{53} - 0.0137 \ X_{47} + 0.120 \ X_{28}$$
$$(13.52)^{**} \quad (3.30)^* \quad (-4.18)^{**} \quad (4.03)^{**}$$

$$+ \ 0.0214 \ X_{63} - 0.00214 \ X_{31} \quad \ldots\ldots\ldots\ldots\ldots\ldots \quad (7.25)$$
$$(4.45)^{**} \quad (-3.39)^*$$
$$R^2 = 0.986 \quad F = 144.27 \quad (\ p = 0.000\ )$$

where, X_5 is the absolute change in total population in the host Do 1979-1988; X_{28} is % point change increase in land prices 1979-1988;

X_{31} is the total air passengers through custom airports in 1988;

X_{47} is the total area of national parks in the Do;

X_{53} is ratio of dwellings per household in the Do;

and X_{63} is the number of cultural properties in 1988.

The following matrix portrays the inter-correlation between these variables.

174

	$Y_2(\Delta NUM)$	X_5	X_{53}	X_{47}	X_{28}	X_{63}	X_{31}
$Y_2(\Delta NUM)$	1.000	0.936	-0.391	-0.449	0.378	0.607	0.375
X_5		1.000	-0.634	-0.581	0.160	0.439	0.502
X_{53}			1.000	0.797	0.304	0.095	-0.475
X_{47}				1.000	0.264	0.142	-0.401
X_{28}					1.000	0.355	0.082
X_{63}						1.000	0.329
X_{31}							1.000

Once again two variables included in the equation have opposite signs between equation and matrix. The re-adjustment of the equation by excluding the variables presented a different regression equation as follows:

$$Y_2 \ (\Delta NUM) = 4.02 + 20.6 \ X_5 + 0.131 \ X_{28} + 0.0172 \ X_{63} \ \ldots \ldots \ (7.25.1)$$
$$(10.19)** \quad (2.33)* \quad (2.07)$$

$$R^2 = 0.936 \quad F = 59.45 \quad (\ p = 0.000 \ )$$

This time the population change in the Do was found to be the most influential factor for the locational decisions of Japanese companies in Korea (with the significance at the 0.01 level). In other words the newly coming Japanese companies have placed their plants in the Do which gained population more rapidly than others. Except for this variable, the contribution of other variables included in the equation for the explanation of dependent variable can be said to be marginal.

Regression of Y_4

On the same basis, the increased cut-off level of 0.1 was applied to Y_4 as well, R^2 of which was the lowest in four. This loosened cut-off level permitted five additional explanatory variables to enter the equation and heightened R^2 value significantly as follows:

$$Y_4 \ (\Delta EMP) = - \ 73696 + 44609 \ X_{46}(\log) + 4843 \ X_{30}(\log) + 413170 \ X_7$$
$$(4.54)** \qquad (3.91)** \qquad (2.54)*$$

$$+ \ 413 \ X_{56}(\text{sqrt}) - 4271 \ X_{39}(\log) - 9396 \ X_9(\log) \ \ldots \ldots \ldots \ (7.26)$$
$$(3.99)** \qquad (-3.46)* \qquad (-2.08)$$

$$R^2 = 0.834 \quad F = 11.05 \quad (\ p = 0.005 \ )$$

where, X_7 is the % change in the net increase in population through inter-regional migration 1979-1988;

175

X_9 is the absolute change in the numbers employed in the manufacturing sector 1979-1988;

X_{30} is the absolute change in the registered vessels for seaport traffic 1979-1988;

X_{39} is the amount of investment of Japanese manufacturing companies in the Do at the end of 1979;

X_{46} is the total urban park area in the Do in 1988;

and X_{56} is absolute change in the total houses constructed in each Do 1979-1988.

The following matrix briefly depicts the relationship between these variables.

	$Y_4(\Delta EMP)$	$X_{46}(\log)$	$X_{30}(\log)$	X_7	$X_{56}(\text{sqrt})$	$X_{39}(\log)$	$X_9(\log)$
$Y_4(\Delta EMP)$	1.000	0.614	0.454	0.464	0.418	0.220	0.380
$X_{46}(\log)$		1.000	0.130	0.312	0.159	0.491	0.668
$X_{30}(\log)$			1.000	-0.083	0.276	0.275	0.440
X_7				1.000	-0.054	0.179	-0.048
$X_{56}(\text{sqrt})$					1.000	0.521	0.368
$X_{39}(\log)$						1.000	0.433
$X_9(\log)$							1.000

There is no very high correlation between independent variables, even though some moderately high ones are seen in this context. Once again, the above equation and matrix demonstrate the problem of multicollinearity between the variables included. The exclusion of those variables which bear the problem of multicollinearity resulted in the same consequence with the equation of (7.23). In other words, only the urban park area (X_{46}) explained the dependent variable Y_4 (ΔEMP). As described above (7.2.1.4), this can be said to be an outcome produced by the Japanese companies' preference for locating in developed areas in Korea.

7.2.1.6 Summary

The significant explanatory variables which were proved to be important for dependent variables from Y_1 to Y_4 in this static and change analysis, can be summarized as in Table 7.6. From this table, it seems evident the forces determining the locations of Japanese companies are derived quite evenly from geographical factors except in the case of public policy. This is very difficult to interpret.

However, considering the polarisation in the geography of Korea, which has resulted in the concentration of all the advantageous geographical factors in and around the two prosperous regions, this can be interpreted in such a way that the dependent and independent variables have shown similar trends and, thus, that there is no specific variable, or locational factor, which can explain best the

176

pattern of dependent variables.

Table 7.6 The significant variables chosen in static and change analysis (Korea)

Locational Factors	Variables	Y_1 (NUM)	Y_2 (ΔNUM)	Y_3 (EMP)	Y_4 (ΔEMP)
Labour	X_5		0.936		
Supply	X_{10}(log)			0.313	
	X_{11}(log)			0.286	
Land and	X_{26}	0.890			
Premises	X_{28}		0.378		
Accessibility	X_{29}(sqrt)		0.463		
Linkages	X_{38}		0.917		
	X_{38}(sqrt)	0.923			
Environmental	X_{46}(log)				0.614
Circumstances	X_{63}		0.607		

Nevertheless, two geographical factors, namely labour supply and linkages, especially the presence of Japanese companies, stand out among others in terms of high correlation coefficients with dependent variables. This means that these two variables have played a relatively important role in the location of Japanese companies in Korea, although not an absolutely important one.

The failure of public policy to appear in the above table is striking. Even though the factor of land and premises availability is closely connected to public policy, the result of the regression here reaffirmed the fact that the spatial policy initiatives in Korea have been insufficient and, naturally, that the effect of regional policy has been disappointing. The fact that even foreign concerns have concentrated in the prosperous regions demonstrates clearly the present status of regional policy in Korea.

In short, the location choices of Japanese subsidiaries can be said to have been influenced predominantly by the present situation of Korean geography and, to a less extent, by the existence of Japanese companies already operating in the Do, the abundance of labour force in the area and the availability of land and premises in which to locate.

7.2.2 Index Analysis

7.2.2.1 The construction of index

177

The method of constructing the index for each locational factor is exactly the same as in the British case (i.e. equation 7.7). In other words,

$$X_z = 1/n \; \Sigma \; r_i * (X_i - m_i)/sd_i$$

Table 7.7 Variables selected for the construction of indices (Korea)

Locational Factors	Y_1 (NUM)	Y_2 (ΔNUM)	Y_3 (EMP)	Y_4 (ΔEMP)
Labour Supply(X_a)	X_6, X_9(sqrt) X_{13}(log), X_{14}	X_2, X_6 X_9(sqrt) X_{17}	X_{12}(log), X_{13}(log), X_{14}(sqrt), X_{17}	X_4(sqrt), X_7, X_{11}, X_{13}(log)
Public Policy(X_b)	X_{20}, X_{22}	X_{20}, X_{22}	X_{20}(sqrt) X_{22}(sqrt)	X_{20}(log), X_{21}
Land and Premises Availability (X_c)	X_{23}(sqrt), X_{24}, X_{26}, X_{28}	X_{23}(log), X_{24}, X_{26} X_{28}	X_{24}, X_{25}(log) X_{27}(log), X_{28}	X_{23}(log), X_{24}(sqrt), X_{26}(log), X_{28}
Accessibility(X_d)	X_{30}, X_{31}, X_{34}(sqrt), X_{35}(sqrt)	X_{29}(log), X_{31}, X_{34}(log), X_{35}	X_{30}, X_{31}(log) X_{33}, X_{34}(log)	X_{29}(log), X_{30}(log), X_{31}(sqrt), X_{34}(log)
Linkages (X_e)	X_{37}, X_{38}(sqrt), X_{40}, X_{45}(log)	X_{37}, X_{38}(log), X_{40}, X_{45}(log)	X_{37}(log), X_{38}, X_{40}(log), X_{45}(log)	X_{38}(log), X_{40}, X_{41}, X_{45}(log)
Environmental Circumstances(X_f)	X_{46}, X_{52}(log) X_{58}(log) X_{63}	X_{50}, X_{51} X_{55}, X_{56}	X_{46}(sqrt), X_{55}(log), X_{58},	X_{51}, X_{56}(sqrt), X_{58}(log), X_{62}(log)

X_{60}(log)

	Labour Supply X_a	Public Policy X_b	Land & Premises X_c	Accessibility X_d	Linkage X_e	Environmental Circumstances X_f
Y_1	0.906	0.854	0.872	0.727	0.912	0.869
Y_2	0.898	0.864	0.847	0.687	0.908	0.952
Y_3	0.801	0.526	0.904	0.829	0.776	0.875
Y_4	0.723	0.456	0.569	0.606	0.465	0.712

The explanatory variables which were chosen to be involved to construct the indices are listed in Table 7.7.

The indices constructed using these variables are listed in Appendix 6. The correlation coefficients between indices of locational factors and dependent variables can be summarized in the matrix below.

7.2.2.2 Results of the regressions using indices

The regressions using the indices produced the following equations:

$$Y_1 \text{ (NUM)} = 23.0 + 28.4 \ X_e + 28.5 \ X_c + 32.3 \ X_b \quad \ldots \ldots \ldots \quad (7.27)$$
$$(4.79)^{**} \quad (4.49)^* \quad (3.37)$$

$$R^2 = 0.926 \quad F = 51.21 \quad (\ p = 0.000 \ )$$

$$Y_2 \text{ (}\Delta\text{NUM)} = 15.1 + 17.5 \ X_f + 7.83 \ X_e + 13.8 \ X_d \quad \ldots \ldots \ldots \quad (7.28)$$
$$(3.32)^{**} \quad (2.09) \quad (2.02)$$

$$R^2 = 0.935 \quad F = 58.08 \quad (\ p = 0.000 \ )$$

$$Y_3 \text{ (EMP)} = 63463 + 136825 \ X_d + 83307 \ X_f + 67546 \ X_a \quad \ldots \quad (7.29)$$
$$(1.92) \quad (2.48)^* \quad (1.92)$$

$$R^2 = 0.853 \quad F = 24.25 \quad (\ p = 0.000 \ )$$

$$Y_4 \text{ (}\Delta\text{EMP)} = 34922 + 56804 \ X_a \quad \ldots \ldots \ldots \ldots \ldots \quad (7.30)$$
$$(3.47)^*$$

$$R^2 = 0.479 \quad F = 12.01 \quad (\ p = 0.005 \ )$$

As depicted in the previous section (7.2.1.6), the influences of geographical factors on the locations of Japanese companies are relatively even as a consequence of the overriding force in Korean geography, i.e. the concentration of all the geographical factors in favour of the two prosperous regions. The above equations also show the almost equivalent figures between locational factors. It is seldom an easy task to distinguish the particularly influential factors among the six. In a rough measure, two factors stand out from the others by their high correlation coefficients with dependent variables; namely, labour supply and environmental circumstances.

It is quite surprising that X_f, environmental circumstances, appeared as one of the most important locational factors surpassing land and premises and the linkage issue in explaining the locational decisions of Japanese companies in Korea. However, as mentioned already, this high correlation coefficient of X_f has to be interpreted in such a way that, by the overwhelming forces of concentration in Korea, most variables constituting this factor also have high correlation coefficients and that, naturally, enhances the overall correlation coefficient of this factor with dependent variables.

Another important locational factor was, as expected, labour supply. In particular, the availability of competent labour with higher wage levels and skilfulness was found to be a crucial factor in the location choice of Japanese companies. Other issues concerned with labour supply such as the militancy of labour and productivity, etc. have shown only a minor influence. This seems to be caused by unique features of the labour market in Korea, for instance, the high mobility of the labour force, government control over labour disputes, etc.

Linkage issues took the next position in importance for the location choice of Japanese companies. Among the variables constituting the linkage factor, the existence of leading Japanese companies in the Do was found to be the most important. The contribution of the number of indigenous manufacturing firms was found to be minimal.

Apart from these factors, land and premises availability represented by the stock of commercial and industrial floor space has been proved to be another influential locational factor for the newly arriving Japanese companies. However, as discussed above, this factor can be said to involve, implicitly, another important locational factor, government assistance to industry, because regional policy in Korea has long been concerned with the development and provision of industrial estates. Japanese companies, not being eligible for comprehensive government assistance under the name of regional policy as in Britain, have shown a strong preference for the designated industrial estates, where some advantages like tax reductions are available, and, hence, the high correlation coefficients of this locational factor. This issue, the response of Japanese companies to the host government spatial policy, is further examined in the following chapters.

In aggregate, it seems possible to draw the conclusion that the findings of static and change analysis in the previous section was affirmed again. In other words, the locational behaviour of Japanese companies in Korea has been largely determined by the overall tendency in Korean geography, which is characterised by the over-concentration in the prosperous regions, and moderately by the previous existence of leading Japanese manufacturing companies in the area, the abundance of skilled labour and the availability of industrial land and premises.

7.2.3 Sub-period Analysis

Like the British case, another regression for sub-period analysis was implemented to find out any particular change in the pattern of locational choices of Japanese companies and, therefore, in the locational factors influencing them. The method taken here was exactly the same with that in the British case (7.1.3).

7.2.3.1 Significant locational factors in 1981-1986

Four regression equations were produced by the static and change analysis using the variables in the period of 1981-1986. The equations are:

$$Y_1 \text{ (NUM)} = -8.26 + 8.74 \ X_{38}(\text{sqrt}) + 0.000095 \ X_7 \quad \ldots \ldots \quad (7.31)$$
$$\phantom{Y_1 \text{ (NUM)} = -8.26 + } (24.23)^{**} \qquad (5.69)^{**}$$

$$R^2 = 0.987 \quad F = 452.05 \quad (\ p = 0.000\ )$$

$$Y_2 \text{ (}\Delta\text{NUM)} = -2.17 + 5.33 \ X_5 + 0.190 \ X_{15} + 0.000238 \ X_{56}$$
$$\phantom{Y_2 \text{ (}\Delta\text{NUM)} = -2.17 + } (3.00)^* \quad (3.47)^{**} \quad (4.98)^{**}$$
$$+ 1.55 \ X_4 \qquad \ldots \ldots \ldots \ldots \ldots \quad (7.32)$$
$$(4.37)^*$$
$$R^2 = 0.983 \quad F = 171.03 \quad (\ p = 0.000\ )$$

$$Y_3 \text{ (EMP)} = 12161 + 1.02 \ X_{39} \qquad \ldots \ldots \ldots \ldots \quad (7.33)$$
$$\phantom{Y_3 \text{ (EMP)} = 12161 + } (17.56)^{**}$$

$$R^2 = 0.962 \quad F = 308.28 \quad (\ p = 0.000\ )$$

$$Y_4 \text{ (}\Delta\text{EMP)} = -393822 + 2.49 \ X_{21} + 43581 \ X_{18}(\text{log}) - 9175 \ X_{44}(\text{log})$$
$$\phantom{Y_4 \text{ (}\Delta\text{EMP)} = -393822 + } (7.58)^{**} \quad (7.43)^{**} \qquad (-3.88)^{**}$$
$$+ 3137 \ X_{52}(\text{log}) - 564 \ X_{17} \ldots \ldots \ldots \ldots \quad (7.34)$$
$$(3.28)^* \qquad (-2.03)$$

$$R^2 = 0.885 \quad F = 19.44 \quad (\ p = 0.001\ )$$

where X_4 and X_5 are the total population in the host Do and its absolute change 1979-1984;

X_7 is the % change in the net increase in population through inter-regional migration 1979-1984;

X_{15} is the absolute change in the number of vocational training facilities 1979-1984;

X_{17} is the % point change in the proportion of union members in total employees in the manufacturing sector 1979-1984;

X_{21} is the local tax collected per person;

X_{18} is the gross value added per employee in the manufacturing sector;

X_{38} and X_{39} are the number of Japanese manufacturing companies in the area in 1979 and the investment size of these companies;

X_{44} is the loans and discounts of deposit money banks in the Do;

X_{52} is the absolute change in the stock of dwellings in the Do;

and X_{56} is the absolute change in total houses constructed in each Do 1979-1984.

The double asterisk shows the significance of the variables at the 0.01 level, one asterisk at the 0.05 level and none at the 0.1 level. In the case of the equation (7.30) two independent variables, X_{44}(log) and X_{17}, were found to have opposite signs in comparison to the correlation coefficient with Y_4. The exclusion of these variables brought about a new regression equation for the explanation of Y_4:

$$Y_4 \ (\Delta EMP) = - \ 295076 + 1.43 \ X_{21} + 30755 \ X_{18}(log) \quad \ldots \ldots \quad (7.34.1)$$
$$(4.40)** \qquad (3.25)**$$

$$R^2 = 0.611 \quad F = 10.44 \quad (p = 0.004)$$

From the above equations, we can find the two most important factors; namely, the existence of leading Japanese companies (X_{38} and X_{39}) and the availability of potential labour represented by the increase in population (X_4, X_5 and X_7). These factors explained most of three dependent variables out of four. On the other hand, the change in the investment size of the Japanese companies in this period (Y_4) was determined by various reasons led by average tax rates and productivity of labour.

Therefore, it seems possible to summarize that the Japanese companies that arrived during 1981-1986 were largely influenced by two significant factors, the existence of leading Japanese companies and the availability of potential labour. Once again, the explicability of the dependent variables using these variables are extremely high due to the afore-mentioned causes.

7.2.3.2 Significant locational factors in 1987-1990

In the same way with the above regressions for the first sub-period, another set of regressions were implemented for the second sub-period, 1987-1990. A different set of equations were produced by the regressions as follows:

$$Y_1 \ (NUM) = - \ 39.0 + 1.26 \ X_{38} + 4.71 \ X_{43}(log) \quad \ldots \ldots \ldots \quad (7.35)$$
$$(13.30)** \qquad (2.79)*$$

$$R^2 = 0.968 \quad F = 181.00 \quad (p = 0.000)$$

$$Y_2 \ (\Delta NUM) = - \ 0.95 + 0.00707 \ X_{25} \quad \ldots \ldots \ldots \ldots \ldots \quad (7.36)$$
$$(10.03)**$$

$$R^2 = 0.893 \quad F = 100.67 \quad (\ p = 0.000\ )$$

$$Y_3\ (EMP) = -\ 252443 + 1.02\ X_{39} + 4329\ X_{51}(sqrt) - 3.06\ X_{22}$$
$$(13.73)^{**} \quad (3.16)^* \quad\quad (-2.51)^*$$
$$+\ 54766\ X_{11}(log) + 54767\ X_5(log) \quad\ldots\ldots\ldots\ldots \quad (7.37)$$
$$(2.01) \quad\quad\quad (1.71)$$

$$R^2 = 0.969 \quad F = 74.88 \quad (\ p = 0.000\ )$$

$$Y_4\ (\Delta EMP) = 91711 + 96.0\ X_8 - 14008\ X_{37}(log) + 1543\ X_{40}\ \ldots\ (7.38)$$
$$(9.86)^{**} \quad (-18.84)^{**} \quad (3.47)^{**}$$

$$R^2 = 0.969 \quad F = 124.14 \quad (\ p = 0.000\ )$$

where X_5 is the absolute change in total population in the host Do 1985-1988;

X_8 is the numbers employed in the manufacturing sector;

X_{11} is the absolute change in average wage levels in the manufacturing sector 1985-1988;

X_{22} is the absolute change in the local tax collected per person 1985-1988;

X_{25} is the total stock of commercial and industrial floor space;

X_{37} is the absolute change in the number of manufacturing firms in the Do 1985-1988;

X_{38} and X_{39} are the number of Japanese manufacturing companies in the area in 1984 and the investment size of these companies;

X_{40} is the number of Japanese companies in other fields in 1988;

X_{43} is the total numbers employed in the fields of banking; finance and business services in the Do in 1988;

and X_{51} is stock of dwellings.

Among these, the equation of (7.37) was found to involve the variable, X_{22}, showing opposite signs. The re-adjustment of the equation not to involve this problem produced a new equation as follows:

$$Y_3\ (EMP) = -\ 351150 + 0.928\ X_{39} + 2570\ X_{51}(sqrt)$$
$$(12.06)^{**} \quad (2.09)$$
$$+\ 64844\ X_{11}(log) \quad\quad\quad \ldots\ldots\ldots\ldots\ldots\ldots \quad (7.37.1)$$
$$(2.05)$$

$$R^2 = 0.953 \quad F = 81.42 \quad (\ p = 0.000\ )$$

Once again the existence of Japanese companies in the area (X_{39}, X_{40} and X_{41}) has proved to be the most important variable for the location choices of Japanese companies arriving in this period. On the other hand, the influence of the labour supply factor was diminished compared to the previous sub-period. This factor was influential only in the analysis of Y_4. Instead, other variables relevant to the circumstances needed for the establishment of these companies including the stock of dwellings, industrial floor space and tax rates became important at the expense of the labour factor. This seems to be an important change revealed in this sub-period analysis.

The negative relationship of X_{37} variable, the absolute change in the number of manufacturing firms, can be said to be a result of the location of huge, capital-intensive companies outside prosperous regions in this period. In other words, those companies, which need big estates with a low density of population around their factories, have tended to locate far from the over-crowded prosperous regions. As a whole, R^2 values were once again very high like those of the whole period and previous sub-period.

7.2.3.3 Comparison between the periods

The important variables found for the explanation of the location of Japanese companies in Korea in the whole- and two sub-periods can be summarized as in the following Table 7.8.

Table 7.8 The significant explanatory variables for the locational decisions of Japanese manufacturing companies in each period (Korea)

Dependent Variables	Whole Period (1981-1990)	1st Sub-period (1981-1986)	2nd Sub-period (1987-1990)
Y_1 (NUM)	X_{38}(sqrt), X_{26} ($R^2 = 0.966$)	X_{38}(sqrt), X_7 ($R^2 = 0.987$)	X_{38}, X_{43}(log) ($R^2 = 0.968$)
Y_2 (ΔNUM)	X_5, X_{28}, X_{63} ($R^2 = 0.936$)	X_5,X_{15}, X_{56}, X_4 ($R^2 = 0.983$)	X_{25} ($R^2 = 0.893$)
Y_3 (EMP)	X_{38}, X_{11}(log) X_{29}(sqrt), X_{10}(log) ($R^2 = 0.961$)	X_{39} ($R^2 = 0.962$)	X_{39},X_{51}(sqrt) X_{11}(log) ($R^2 = 0.953$)
Y_4 (ΔEMP)	X_{46}(log), ($R^2 = 0.321$)	X_{21}, X_{18}(log) ($R^2 = 0.611$)	X_8,X_{37}(log), X_{40} ($R^2 = 0.969$)

The comparison between the significant variables in each period, which were derived from each regression analysis, exhibits some interesting features.

Firstly, the variables relating to the presence of Japanese companies in the area (X_{38}, X_{39} and X_{40}) played a crucial role in the explanation of the dependent variables. This is much more the case in the static regression analysis (Y_1 and Y_3). The consistent influence of these variables in the overall periods may be indicated as the cause of this significant role of the presence of Japanese predecessors in the static analyses.

Secondly, when the number of Japanese companies and the investment size of these companies are considered in terms of changes (Y_2 and Y_4), the variables explaining the dependent variables tend to be diversified without any prominent role for one or two variables. This can be interpreted as the diversification of influential locational factors for the Japanese companies coming recently.

And, thirdly, as a whole, it may be said that the factors determining the location of Japanese companies in Korea are similar between the two sub-periods. Apart from the existence of compatriot concerns, labour supply and environmental circumstances are found to have influenced moderately the location of these companies in both sub-periods.

Consequently, in the Korean case, the importance of the existence of leading Japanese companies has been confirmed once again as well as the minimal influence of public policy.

7.3 Comparison between the Regression Results of the Two Host Countries

From the regression results presented so far, the locational pattern of Japanese manufacturing companies in the two host countries seems to come within sight. In particular, the question of which locational factor most influences the decisions of Japanese concerns in choosing their sites can be answered to a certain extent.

By reference to the above regression results, it seems possible to compare the most significant locational factors in each country, although the comparability of these two in a complete and plain measure is unlikely. Furthermore, the correlation coefficients between variables in the Korean case are much higher than in British case due to the over-concentration of industry and population in the two developed areas[22].

Nevertheless, the attempt is necessary in order that the relative importance of independent variables in each host country can be cleared through the procedure. Here, a comparison is made briefly in terms of similarities and differences between the locational patterns of Japanese companies in the two host countries manifested in the regression results.

7.3.1 Similarities

Similarities in the locational behaviour of Japanese companies in the two host countries revealed in the regression analyses can be summarized in the following aspects.

Firstly, two locational factors among all the others, namely the previous existence of Japanese companies in the area and the supply of labour have played key roles in the locational choice of Japanese companies in both countries. In particular, the predominant importance of leading Japanese companies in both countries is quite impressive.

And, secondly, the locational choice of these companies in the two host countries is similar in that they have been influenced very little by accessibility. Nonetheless, the influence of infrastructure such as airports and seaports in Korea to some extent is worth noting since these facilities have not been as fully developed in each region in Korea as in Britain.

7.3.2 Differences

In parallel with the similarities presented above, the locational features of Japanese companies in the two countries contain some issues which differentiate one host country from the other.

First of all, public policy has played a notably different role in the two countries. In Britain, public policy with its diversified forms has played a crucial role in the location of Japanese companies. In particular, the role of the activities of local authorities and the newly introduced government initiatives including EZs and UDCs were proved to be successful in attracting those Japanese companies. However, the role of the public policy in Korea has been marginal in terms of both its efforts and its effect. Even though the provision of land and premises has been an important policy measure in Korea, it seems to be more accurate to say that the overall performance of public policy has been unsuccessful. Furthermore, the lack of the same financial scale as the case of Britain seem to have aggravated the poor performance of the Korean regional policy. This difference in the two host countries reflects the high responsiveness of Japanese companies to the geographical context as well as to the regional policy of host governments when investing in other countries.

Secondly, in the labour supply factor, the specific variables which are found to be important in the two countries are different. In Britain, the non-militancy of labour can be said to be the most influential one among the variables comprising the labour supply factor, whereas the abundance of skilled labour seems to be the most important in Korea. One thing to be cautious about regarding this is that the gap in expectations of Japanese companies with regard to labour between these two host countries began to narrow. This development is more evident in the British case. As shown in the sub-period analysis of British experience (7.1.3.4), the emphasis of Japanese companies has moved from low-militant and readily available potential labour to high skilled labour and, thus, the difference between the two countries has narrowed[23].

And, thirdly, Japanese companies in Britain have tended to take into consideration a wider range of locational factors when they choose their sites than those in Korea. In other words, the Japanese companies in Korea were more subject to certain specific locational factors. This seems to be due to the fact that the locational pattern of Japanese companies in Korea has been largely determined by the strong force that Korean development has imposed, that is the polarisation of population and industry. As a result, the regression equations in the case of Korea revealed an exceptional example which selects only one variable to be important to explain the variation of dependent variables.

In consequence, although the locational behaviour of Japanese companies in the host countries has been determined in the main by linkages represented by the existence of previously located Japanese companies and labour supply, there exist some considerable differences in the influences of factors between the two mainly due to the geographical context that each country presents.

In particular, government spatial policy was proved to be one of the most important factors which provides different implications for the locational decisions of incoming Japanese companies in the two countries. The more detailed picture of the relationship between government policy and the location of Japanese subsidiaries is discussed in Chapters nine and ten. These chapters go on to consider the implications for future policy of the past performance of policy in influencing Japanese location decisions. Before that, the next chapter examines other empirical evidence from survey results, mainly using descriptive statistics.

8 Empirical evidence III: Factors influencing the locational choices of Japanese multinational companies – Survey results

The previous chapter portrayed the main results of the regression analysis as the macro-level empirical evidence, which was related to the locational choices of Japanese companies. As another source of empirical evidence to explore the locational behaviour of these Japanese companies in the changing context of regional policy, this chapter undertakes the micro-level analysis, the examination of survey answers.

As expounded in Chapter five, a questionnaire survey was conducted amongst all the Japanese MNCs operating in the two host countries. In addition, an interview survey was carried out partially with those which allowed access to the researcher among all the Japanese companies operating in Britain. As with the case of the regression results in the previous chapter, these survey results are considered in turn; first the British case, second the Korean case and, lastly, the comparison between the British and the Korean cases.

8.1 Significant Locational Factors in Great Britain

8.1.1 Profiles of the companies surveyed

The total number of the companies, more strictly speaking plants, which were identified by the publications of IBB and AJEI and confirmed by the deliveries of the questionnaire was 181[1]. Among these, 62 companies replied to the questionnaire with useful answers. Therefore the ratio of useful replies to the total number of companies was 34.3 %. Another 25 companies returned the questionnaire without answering by reason of either company policy or the absence of the person to answer or even the work burden of this kind of questionnaire. One company which answered the questionnaire was proved later to be located in Northern Ireland and was, therefore, excluded from this analysis. The remaining 94 companies showed no response at all.

In order to examine the representativeness of the companies which replied to the questionnaire compared to the total Japanese companies, the χ^2 test of goodness-of-fit was undertaken using the data of size, industrial fields and geographical distribution. The results of this test (χ^2 values) are 0.544 (degree of freedom = 1), 1.203 (df = 4) and 2.865 (df = 9) respectively showing that the respondent companies (the sample) are not significantly different from all the Japanese companies in Britain (population).

Among the 62 companies which replied, 21 companies (33.9% of the total) were established by the end of 1986, while 41 companies (66.1%) started their operation after that time. In terms of size, 41 companies (66.1%) were found to be small or medium-sized enterprises (SMEs) with employment size below 200 in comparison to 24 companies (33.9%) with a larger size of over 200. The proportion of the SMEs and that of large companies in each sub-period is shown in Table 8.1. Not surprisingly, more of the large were established before 1987 than their share of the total indicated.

Table 8.1 The size and establishment year of companies surveyed by questionnaire (Britain)   (%)

Size	Total	Before 1987	After 1986
Total	62(100)	21(33.9)	41(66.1)
Large companies	21(100)	9(42.9)	12(51.1)
SMEs	41(100)	12(29.3)	29(70.7)

With regard to the industrial fields of the respondent companies, Table 8.2 demonstrates the distribution of the companies by industry and by establishment year. Electronics companies predominated in both time periods and the industrial mix remained broadly unchanged.

Likewise, the locations of these companies can be summarised as in Table 8.3. This shows a marked change in chosen locations pre and post 1987. The sharp growth in the number of Japanese companies in the West Midlands region is remarkable in this table.

In addition, 20 companies among the above 62 have been interviewed. The profile of the 20 companies interviewed is listed in the Table 8.4. As seen in this table, those companies which arrived recently (75%), which have an employment size below 200 (SME, 65%) and which are operating in the field of electronics

189

(40%) respectively, constitute the major part among the companies interviewed. And the locations of these companies are dispersed all over the country. The position or status of interviewees in these companies and their origins are summarised in Table 8.5.

Table 8.2 The industrial distribution of companies surveyed by questionnaire (Britain) (%)

Industrial Fields	Total	Before 1987	After 1986
Total	62(100)	21(100)	41(100)[+]
Electronics	28(45.2)	10(47.6)	18(43.9)
Chemicals & plastics	12(19.4)	5(23.8)	7(17.1)
Heavy machinery & vehicles	10(16.1)	3(14.3)	7(17.1)
Light engineering	4(6.4)	2(9.5)	2(4.9)
Others	8(12.9)	1(4.8)	7(17.1)

[+] Due to rounding errors, the sum of this column is not exactly 100.

Table 8.3 The locations of the companies surveyed by questionnaire (Britain) (%)

Region	Total	Before 1987	After 1986
Total	62(100)	21(100)[+]	41(100)
Wales	15(24.2)	6(28.6)	9(22.0)
South East	13(21.0)	7(33.3)	6(14.6)
West Midlands	11(17.8)	1(4.8)	10(24.4)
Scotland	7(11.3)	2(9.5)	5(12.2)
North	4(6.5)	1(4.8)	3(7.3)
Yorkshire & Humberside	3(4.8)	0(0.0)	3(7.3)
South West	3(4.8)	1(4.8)	2(4.9)
North West	3(4.8)	1(4.8)	2(4.9)
East Midlands	2(3.2)	1(4.8)	1(2.4)
East Anglia	1(1.6)	1(4.8)	0(0.0)

[+] Due to rounding errors, the sum of this column is not exactly 100.

Apart from these interviews, another interview was undertaken with an official of Telford Development Corporation[2], which played a central role in attracting Japanese companies to the Telford area. This interview was to hear about the experience of Telford's promotional activity and the causes of the locational decisions of Japanese companies from a different standpoint.

Table 8.4 The profile of the companies interviewed

Name	Start	Employment	Industry[+]	Location
(Before 1987)				
COMPANY A	72	250	Lig	N W
COMPANY B	77	230	Lig	Scotland
COMPANY C	79	20	Che	S E
COMPANY D	84	400	Ele	W M
COMPANY E	86	5	Mac	E A
(After 1986)				
COMPANY F	87	414	Ele	Scotland
COMPANY G	87	177	Oth	Wales
COMPANY H	87	120	Che	Wales
COMPANY I	87	39	Mac	Scotland
COMPANY J	88	80	Mac	W M
COMPANY K	88	40	Che	W M
COMPANY L	88	40	Che	S E
COMPANY M	89	100	Ele	S E
COMPANY N	89	100	Ele	Scotland
COMPANY O	89	72	Che	Wales
COMPANY P	89	50	Mac	W M
COMPANY Q	90	1000	Ele	S E
COMPANY R	90	400	Ele	S E
COMPANY S	90	200	Ele	E M
COMPANY T	90	9	Mac	N W

([+]) Ele: Electronics, Lig: Light Engineering, Che: Chemicals and Plastics, Mac: Heavy Machinery and Vehicles, Oth: Others.

Table 8.5 Position and origin of the interviewees

Position or Status	Total	Origin	
		British	Japanese
Total	20	10	10
Chief Executive (Managing Director)	8	5	3
Middle Management	10	4	6
Lower Management	2	1	1

8.1.2　Findings of the survey

The responses of the 62 managers to the questionnaire and interview surveys can be analyzed in various ways. This study divides the questions and responses, according to the groupings in the questionnaire, into five groups and carries out analysis: namely, the main market for the company; the push factor in Japan; the attractive or unsatisfactory locational factors; the role of the host government; and the alternative locations considered. These analyses and findings are based mainly on the questionnaire answers and supplemented by the answers in the interviews.

8.1.2.1 Main market for the companies

Managers were asked about the main market for the products of their firms. In answer, managers indicated the main manufacturers in this or an adjacent country as their prime market. Specifically, the responses of the managers are as follows.

Table 8.6 Main markets of the companies surveyed (Britain) (%)

Markets	Total	Established Before 1987	Established After 1986
Total	75(100)[+]	28(100)	47(100)
Main manufacturers in this or adjacent country	32(42.7)	8(28.6)	24(51.1)
Foreign consumer market	20(26.7)	9(32.1)	11(23.4)
Local consumer market	18(24.0)	8(28.6)	10(21.3)
Others	5(6.6)	3(10.7)	2(4.2)

[+] Thirteen companies picked out two kinds of markets as their main markets.

Among the total, 42.7% of companies indicated the main manufacturers in this and adjacent countries as their main market. In particular, for those companies which have arrived in this country since 1987, this market is more crucial (51.1%) than for those who arrived earlier (28.6%). This indicates that the majority of Japanese companies operating in this country, especially those arriving recently, supply intermediate goods to other manufacturers rather than finished goods direct to consumers. This can be said to be related closely to the recent arrival of many component manufacturers following their main customers.

The response of 'others' has been made by firms with particular types of products and markets such as the information technology systems sold worldwide and the packaging materials used by distributors.

8.1.2.2 Push factors in Japan

Regarding the main reason which made these firms invest outside Japan, or push factors in Japan, managers of the Japanese companies operating in this country picked out trade barriers of other countries as the prime reason for their overseas investment. Table 8.7 depicts the relative importance of each reason for the investment of these companies outside Japan.

The reason 'trade barriers of other countries' took the predominant position in providing understanding of the motive of the outward movement of Japanese companies. This reason was indicated to be most important by the Japanese companies regardless of the difference in their arrival date. Two other reasons, i.e. the high rate of the yen and the lack of big markets in Japan, took the second and third positions as expected.

Table 8.7 Push factors in Japan resulting in overseas investment (Britain)

Reasons	Total	Importance		
	Rating	1st	2nd	3rd
Trade barriers of other countries	60	12	8	8
High rate of the yen	29	1	10	6
Lack of big markets in Japan	27	4	4	7
High wage level compared to other countries	14	2	2	4
High land price in Japan	11	0	4	3
Labour shortage in Japan	8	0	2	4
Others	64	11	0	31

Ratings are computed by a four-point scale : the first most important reason = 3; the second most important reason = 2; the third and other important reasons =1; not important = 0.

The content of the responses ticked in 'others' is interesting. In fact it was found through the examination of responses that three different answers were concealed in this item. The first is the globalisation strategy of the companies. Although this is thought to be similar to the trade barriers of other countries, the meaning of 'globalisation' is more positive than the 'circumvention of trade barriers'. In other words, these Japanese companies have laid a greater emphasis on the long-term strategy of globalisation positively over the passive reaction simply to avoid the trade barriers of other countries. Out of the total of 42 which stated 'others', fifteen companies pointed out that this reason was important for their outward investment and, among those, seven respondents expressed it as the most important. This is a meaningful finding in that this fact exhibits vividly the overall strategy of Japanese MNCs.

Another important reason was the expansion of their market into Europe. This reason can be said to be related closely to another of the listed items, the 'lack of a big market in Japan'. Nevertheless, it is interesting to find that the market potential of Europe, which is about to be closed to other countries with the agreement of the single European market, stimulated the Japanese companies to invest inside Europe. Fifteen companies assessed this reason to be important as a cause of their overseas investment.

'To supply its products to customers,' or 'the request from the customers', was found to be another important reason which caused the outward movement of Japanese companies. Ten companies listed this reason as one of the main forces which made their companies come out of their own territory. This reason, so called linkages, took the central position for component manufacturers. A manager remarked during the interview:

> "Please note, in case of component manufacturers [for TV, office automation or car industries], such as this company, they invest in accordance with investment of customers [TV makers, etc.] in foreign countries" (The manager in company H).

When the 'market expansion' and the 'lack of big markets in Japan' are regarded as identical, i.e. market acquisition, this factor shows up as the most important push factor for the Japanese companies. From this finding, it seems possible to infer that the massive movement of Japanese companies, which have long desired to be internationalised or globalised, has been triggered by the trade barriers of other countries, especially those countries in Europe. Such factors as high wage levels, high land prices and labour shortages in Japan (cost-factors contrary to market-factors above) were found to have had no significant influence on the overseas investment of these companies.

On the other hand, apart from these factors, a question was put to all the interviewees whether there had been any assistance from the Japanese government in deciding investment in overseas countries. However, all the managers of Japanese companies interviewed denied any assistance from their own government.

8.1.2.3 Attractive or unsatisfactory locational factors

Attractive locational factors

In an attempt to find out the influential locational factors in the host country, or pull factors, for the location decisions of Japanese companies, the managers were requested to choose the important factors in order of importance in the list given of locational factors. The response of the managers is fully depicted in Table 8.8.

One thing which should be expounded first regarding the factors is that locational factors at a national level between countries and those at a regional level within a country are intermingled in this question. In particular, the factors of 'single market in Europe in 1992' and 'familiar language' represent more the features of a country compared to other countries than a region compared to other regions in the same country.

Nevertheless, these factors were included in this question on the ground that the other locational factors also can be applicable at both levels to a certain extent and, thus, can be used in comparing one region with the regions in other countries as well as those in the same country[3].

Among all the locational factors, the closeness to a big market took the largest share. The top position of this factor, together with the fifth rank of the '1992 single European market', proves once again the importance of the market factor for the Japanese companies coming into this country. A manager noted the importance of the market factor saying that:

Table 8.8 Important locational factors for the Japanese companies surveyed (Britain) (%)

Locational	Ratings of the companies		
Factors	Total	Before 1987	After 1986
Total Rating	308(100)[+]	93(100)	215(100)
Closeness to a big market	55(17.9)	17(18.3)	38(17.7)
Familiar language	36(11.7)	13(14.0)	23(10.7)
Sufficient industrial land and premises	34(11.0)	10(10.7)	24(11.1)
Regional assistance from government and local authority	33(10.7)	14(15.0)	19(8.8)
Single market in Europe in 1992	28(9.1)	8(8.6)	20(9.3)
Convenient transport	24(7.8)	11(11.8)	13(6.0)
Presence of Japanese companies in the area	22(7.1)	2(2.1)	20(9.3)
Abundant workforce available	19(6.2)	8(8.6)	11(5.1)
Promotional activities of local authorities	13(4.2)	1(1.1)	12(5.6)
Existence of manufacturing suppliers or subcontractors	12(3.9)	0(0.0)	12(5.6)
High productivity of labour	9(2.9)	4(4.3)	5(2.3)
Low wage level	7(2.3)	1(1.1)	6(2.8)
Low militancy of labour	2(0.7)	1(1.1)	1(0.5)
The 'greenness' or amenity of the area	2(0.7)	1(1.1)	1(0.5)
Low rate of crime	1(0.3)	0(0.0)	1(0.5)
Abundant houses for employees in the area	1(0.3)	1(1.1)	0(0.0)
Abundant leisure and recreation facilities	0(0.0)	0(0.0)	0(0.0)
Others	10(3.2)	1(1.1)	9(4.2)

Ratings are computed by a four-point scale : the first most important factor = 3; the second most important factor = 2; the third and other important factors = 1; not important factor = 0.
[+] Respondents mentioned more than one satisfactory factor.

" At first, the demand of our products was concentrated in the southern part of England. So this site was not bad. Recently, with the increase of demand in the northern part of England and Scotland, a more convenient place for delivery is necessary. Therefore, if we choose the site once again, the central part of England is fascinating" (The manager in company A).

This finding has a consistency with those in the previous sections. In short, the locational pattern of these Japanese companies, moving out from Japan in order to access the big European market and, moreover, deciding location nearby a big market within the European market, shows a kind of consistency with their managerial strategy in developed countries. For component suppliers, this market may be reached via their manufacturing customers.

The factor of familiar language indicates the reason for the priority of the UK among all the European countries competing for the attraction of Japanese companies. By ranking this factor high in the list, Japanese companies demonstrated a unique feature that, for Japanese companies, a familiar language is more important than other locational factors including reliable labour, government assistance, good environment, etc. This may be interpreted in such a way that the regions in the UK can be more favourable than their counterparts in other countries even though there exist some disadvantageous factors in these regions.

The appearance of the 'sufficient industrial land and premises' factor high in the list is worth noting. This is, firstly, because the Japanese companies are generally thought to prefer starting-up in green field sites to taking over premises or a concern in an existing industrial area and, secondly, because there seems to be no difference between regions, since most host countries have made efforts to provide available land and premises in order to attract these companies into their territory. The high ranking of this factor tells us that this basic factor for the location of manufacturing companies is a necessary condition for the attraction of Japanese companies and provides a significant indication for the direction of regional policy. In fact, during an interview, a manager emphasised the importance of this factor saying that:

" The Welsh Development Agency (WDA) provided everything necessary for the opening of this firm including this land and building [on a rental basis]. Without the provision of land and building, the decision making in my company to locate here would need a longer period of time" (The manager in company G).

A relatively high, sixth, rank of the 'convenient transport' factor should also

196

be understood in the same context.

Regional assistance from the government and local authorities also played an important role in the location decisions of Japanese companies. Of course this factor not only includes financial assistance from central government in the form of RDG or RSA but also the assistance from local authorities including rate reduction. If the 'promotional activities of local authorities' are included in a wider concept of regional policy, the role of government regional policy becomes one of the crucial factors in attracting foreign investment, in particular, as far as Japanese companies are concerned. The continuous performance of this factor in attracting foreign investment provides a rationale to carry on government regional policy, albeit in a more diversified and modified form[4].

Two locational factors related to linkages, the presence of Japanese companies in the area and the existence of manufacturing suppliers or subcontractors, are worth considering in that the importance of these factors for the managers of Japanese companies has been growing markedly. The share of these factors in the total rating increased from 2.1% and 0% among the companies arriving before the beginning of 1987 to 9.3% and 5.6% respectively among those arriving after that time. The steeply growing importance of these factors implies both the increased arrival of Japanese component suppliers near their main customers and the increased recognition of the Japanese managers of the importance of local sourcing or local content, especially in the latter part of 1980s. This finding is meaningful in that it has a consistency with the results of Chapter six and Chapter seven showing the increased arrival of component manufacturers following the large finished goods manufacturers. Consequently, a linkage issue can be said to be one of the important locational factors for the incoming Japanese companies and its importance is growing.

Among the features related to the 'labour supply' factor, an abundant workforce available took the first place. This is rather contradictory in the light of the previous finding in the regression that a high unemployment rate in the area has not always guaranteed the choices of these companies, especially when it is measured by the change in unemployment[5]. However, it seems more plausible to interpret the reply of Japanese managers as the 'abundant [reliable or skilful] workforce available'. The next high position of 'the productivity of labour' after the abundant workforce can be regarded as supporting evidence for this argument. The last position of the militancy of labour is quite interesting. This means that the problem of stoppages of work due to industrial disputes, or militant activities among the workforce, has retreated already in this country and is no longer a significant obstacle to the location of foreign companies. An interesting revelation during the interviews is that the gathering of Japanese companies in specific areas has begun to cause a shortage in the workforce available in these areas and to become an unhappy factor among them. As a manager argued:

"The most important locational factors have been the existence of Japanese community and the availability of labour. Milton Keynes and Telford have been advantageous especially in the former respect. However, with the growing number of foreign companies in these areas, now the time has come to shift the emphasis toward the latter. It's the problem of choice" (The manager in company L).

This argument was agreed by the staff in the Telford Development Corporation and the managing director in a company located in Telford.

Table 8.9 Unsatisfactory locational factors for the Japanese companies surveyed (Britain)   (%)

Locational	Responses of Japanese companies		
Factors	Total	Before 1987	After 1986
Total Responses	152(100)[+]	46(100)[++]	106(100)
Lack of manufacturing suppliers or subcontractors	16(10.5)	6(13.0)	10(9.4)
High wage level	15(9.9)	6(13.0)	9(8.5)
High rate of crime	15(9.9)	4(8.7)	11(10.4)
Insufficient leisure and recreation facilities	14(9.2)	4(8.7)	10(9.4)
Low productivity of labour	12(7.9)	3(6.5)	9(8.5)
Remoteness from a big market	11(7.2)	2(4.3)	9(8.5)
Lack of regional assistance	8(5.3)	3(6.5)	5(4.7)
Inconvenient transport	8(5.3)	3(6.5)	5(4.7)
Unfamiliar language	8(5.3)	2(4.3)	6(5.7)
Non-existence of Japanese companies in the area	7(4.6)	2(4.3)	5(4.7)
Lack of workforce available	7(4.6)	1(2.2)	6(5.7)
Insufficient houses for employees in the area	7(4.6)	3(6.5)	4(3.8)
High militancy of labour	6(3.9)	1(2.2)	5(4.7)
Lack of 'greenness' or amenity of the area	6(3.9)	2(4.3)	4(3.8)
Insufficient industrial land and premises	4(2.6)	0(0.0)	4(3.8)
Lack of promotional activities of local authorities	3(2.0)	2(4.3)	1(0.9)
Single market in Europe in 1992	2(1.3)	1(2.2)	1(0.9)
Others	3(2.0)	1(2.2)	2(1.9)

[+] Respondents mentioned more than one unsatisfactory factor.
[++] Due to rounding errors, the actual sum of this column is 99.7.

The marginal importance of environmental circumstances seems to be strange considering the preference of Japanese companies for greenfield sites or beautiful scenery relative to built-up areas. However, the minor role of this factor was confirmed by Japanese managers during the interview survey. As a manager asserted:

"Compared to the central factors such as market or labour supply, this factor including amenities, recreation facilities, etc. is not important at all" (The manager of company M).

From the above results, it can be concluded that the Japanese companies coming into this country have been influenced by the closeness to big markets, industrial land and premises, government regional assistance and the linkages in terms of the presence of compatriot companies and suppliers.

Unsatisfactory locational factors

Along with the attractive locational factors, which influence the firms positively to locate in a certain area, unsatisfactory locational factors, which were found to be unfavourable to firms in the chosen areas, were also examined. The replies of the managers are listed in Table 8.9.

As a rough measure, this table can be said to be a reversal of Table 8.8. The items which had high ranks in the Table 8.8, such as sufficient industrial land and premises, abundant workforce available, etc., took this time a relatively low rank. In contrast, the low ranked items in the previous table including a low wage level, low rate of crime, leisure and recreation facilities, etc. appeared to be substantial here.

This seems to be a natural consequence of the location decisions of the Japanese companies which gave priorities to some locational factors among others as discussed above. In other words, these Japanese companies surveyed can be said to have determined their locations under a concrete criterion. The fact that the lack of manufacturing suppliers or subcontractors took the first place among all the unsatisfactory locational factors proves once again the importance of the linkage factor for the incoming Japanese companies and is consistent with the regression result which listed the linkages, especially the presence of leading Japanese companies, as one of the most important locational factors ahead of labour supply, accessibility, etc.

The relatively high rank of two factors, far from a big market and lack of regional assistance, are interesting because these factors also took very high positions in the former table. This may be interpreted in such a way that the demand for these factors were not fulfilled sufficiently in spite of the emphasis of Japanese managements on these factors. Once again the importance of these factors was confirmed in the responses to this question.

8.1.2.4 The role of the host government

Regarding the role of host government assistance, the managers were asked to answer the following questions: namely, to what extent did government assistance influence the location choice of the firm; and what kind of assistance was this?

The influence of government assistance

The responses of the managers to this question appear in Table 8.10. As shown in this table, the experience of the Japanese companies illustrates the fact that the influence of government assistance on the location choice of Japanese companies has been 'relatively substantial', if not crucial or essential.

Table 8.10 The influence of government assistance on the location decisions of Japanese companies (Britain)   (%)

Influence	Total	Japanese companies arrived	
		Before 1987	After 1986
Total	62(100)	21(100)	41(100)
Very substantial	4(6.5)	2(9.5)	2(4.9)
Substantial	14(22.6)	5(23.8)	9(22.0)
Moderate	15(24.2)	4(19.0)	11(26.8)
Minimal	26(41.9)	10(47.6)	16(39.0)
No answer	3(4.8)	0(0.0)	3(7.3)

46.8% of the respondents expressed the view that government assistance influenced their decision substantially or moderately. Including the companies which referred to the very substantial influence of the assistance, over half of the Japanese companies which arrived in Britain were influenced more or less by the government assistance. The extent of the influence was almost similar between the January 23, 1994Japanese companies which arrived before 1987 and those since 1987.

The breakdown of the replies according to the regional distribution of these companies provides an interesting finding Table 8.11. This table eloquently demonstrates the difference in responses between the Japanese companies located in the regions with a broad assisted area (AA) eligible for government financial assistance and those in other regions with a small or no AA.

Japanese companies located in the North, North West, Wales and Scotland regions indicated the substantial influence of the government assistance on their location choices, while those in East Midlands, East Anglia, South East and South West expressed the marginal influence.

200

Table 8.11 The influence of government assistance on the location decisions of Japanese companies by region (Britain)(%)

Regions	Total	Extent of influence				
		Very substantial	Substantial	Moderate	Minimal	No answer
Total	62(100)	4(6.5)	14(22.6)	15(24.2)	26(41.9)	3(4.8)
Wales	15(100)	3(20.0)	3(20.0)	4(26.7)	5(33.3)	0(0.0)
South East	13(100)	0(0.0)	2(15.4)	1(7.7)	9(69.2)	1(7.7)
West Midlands	11(100)⁺	0(0.0)	2(18.2)	4(36.4)	4(36.4)	1(9.1)
Scotland	7(100)⁺	0(0.0)	3(42.9)	3(42.9)	1(14.3)	0(0.0)
North	4(100)	0(0.0)	2(50.0)	2(50.0)	0(0.0)	0(0.0)
Yorkshire & Humberside	3(100)	1(33.3)	0(0.0)	0(0.0)	2(66.7)	0(0.0)
South West	3(100)	0(0.0)	1(33.3)	0(0.0)	2(66.7)	0(0.0)
North West	3(100)⁺	0(0.0)	1(33.3)	1(33.3)	0(0.0)	1(33.3)
East Midlands	2(100)	0(0.0)	0(0.0)	0(0.0)	2(100)	0(0.0)
East Anglia	1(100)	0(0.0)	0(0.0)	0(0.0)	1(100)	0(0.0)

⁺ Due to rounding errors, the sum of figures in each row is not exactly 100.

The managers in Wales and Scotland gave good marks to government assistance compared to those in other regions. This looks likely to provide a clue to understanding the success of these regions in attracting Japanese investments into their territory. In particular, the fact that a fifth of Japanese managers in Wales assessed the role of government to be *very substantial* indicates directly the effect of the activities of government and local authorities, in particular those of the WDA.

Table 8.12 The measures of assistance provided by the host government (Britain) (%)

Assistance	Total	Japanese companies arrived	
		Before 1987	Since 1987
Total	108(100)	36(100)	72(100)
Financial aid	33(30.6)	11(30.6)	22(30.6)
Advice	28(25.9)	10(27.8)	18(25.0)
Land and premises	22(20.4)	7(19.4)	15(20.8)
Speed of decision	13(12.0)	6(16.7)	7(9.7)
Planning permission	10(9.3)	2(5.6)	8(11.1)
Other	2(1.8)	0(0.0)	2(2.8)

More than one response possible.

201

The managers in the Japanese companies were requested to list all the measures of government assistance which they received. The measures of assistance listed in the questionnaire were six; namely, financial aid, provision of land and premises, advice, planning permission, speed of decision and other. The responses of managers are summarised in Table 8.12.

This table shows that financial aid, advice and the provision of land and premises have been central among the policy measures offered by the British government. These three measures, in aggregate, took over three quarters of total policy measures which are thought to be significant for the managers of Japanese companies. Among the three, financial aid took the first position and showed no change in its importance during the last ten years. This proves the unremitting significance of financial assistance in attracting foreign investments into targeted areas.

The comparison of the policy measures which were emphasised by the Japanese companies in each region seems to reveal the geographical context of each region and to provide an interesting implication for the assessment of spatial policy. The following Table 8.13 shows this comparison.

Each region has its own characteristics in providing assistance to the Japanese companies coming into the region. The West Midlands is found to be strong in providing other assistance, planning permission and speed of decision, suggesting that the efforts, or efficiency, of government or local authority officials (probably in the case of the West Midlands often the West Midlands Development Agency) can be a good policy measure to induce foreign investments into a certain area.

Table 8.13 Important measures of government assistance in each region (Britain) (%)

Region	Total	Financial aid	Advice	Land and premises	Other
Total	108(100)	33(30.6)	28(25.9)	22(20.4)	25(23.1)
Wales	37(100)	11(29.8)	10(27.0)	7(18.9)	9(24.3)
W Midlands	24(100)	6(25.0)	6(25.0)	4(16.7)	8(33.3)
Scotland	15(100)	7(46.7)	4(26.7)	3(20.0)	1(6.6)
North	11(100)	4(36.3)	2(18.2)	3(27.3)	2(18.2)
S East	7(100)	1(14.3)	4(57.1)	1(14.3)	1(14.3)
Other regions	14(100)	4(28.6)	2(14.2)	4(28.6)	4(28.6)

⁺ Respondents mentioned more than one measures.

It is interesting to compare two regions which are in different situations; Scotland and the South East. While financial aid takes the largest share in

Scotland, advice has played a pivotal role for the South East in assisting Japanese companies. Without doubt, this is a product of the different geographical context in which the two regions are situated. On the same basis, the assessments of regional assistance by Japanese companies showed a contradiction according to the context in which each company is situated. A company manager assessed regional policy by saying that:

"In general, the most important factors for the location of Japanese companies are: firstly, financial aid from the British government; secondly, language; and, thirdly, the access to EC market" (The manager in company E).

The manager in company B, which is located in Scotland, also asserted similarly this opinion. In contrast, a manager in a different situation claimed that:

"These days, few Japanese companies are attracted by regional policy or financial assistance" (The manager in company L).

On the other hand, Wales is impressive in that all the policy measures are utilised harmoniously. This seems to be the driving force of Wales in attracting foreign investment in its territory.

In order to examine the relationship between the measures of government assistance given to Japanese companies and the assessment of the benefited companies about the significance of government assistance, the following table is constructed. This table gives the means of detecting the necessary condition of government assistance for Japanese companies.

Table 8.14 Relationship between the measures of government assistance and their influence on the location of Japanese companies   (%)[+]

Influence of assistance	Total companies	Financial aid	Advice	Land and premises	Other[++]
Total	62(100)	33(53.2)	28(45.2)	22(35.5)	25(40.3)
Very substantial	4(100)	4(100)	2(50.0)	3(75.0)	4(100)
Substantial	14(100)	13(92.9)	9(64.3)	9(64.3)	7(50.0)
Moderate	15(100)	11(73.3)	9(60.0)	6(40.0)	7(46.7)
Minimal	26(100)	5(19.2)	8(30.8)	4(15.4)	7(26.9)
No answer	3	-	-	-	-

[+] The proportion of the companies which received each assistance to the number of companies which assessed the influence of government assistance at that level (% across).   [++] Includes planning permission, speed of decision and others.

In general, the extent of influence of government assistance on the location of Japanese companies is lowered in proportion to the decrease of the companies which *received* each assistance (except in the case of advice). One thing worth noting is the role of financial aid. All the companies which expressed the influence of government assistance as 'very substantial' and all but one among those which assessed it as 'substantial' received financial aid from the British government. This seems to be the evidence illustrating the fact that financial aid is a necessary, if not a sufficient, condition to affect the location decision of Japanese companies coming into this country.

8.1.2.5 Alternative locations

In order to explore competitive locations, the managers were asked to tick all the alternative areas both in the world and in this country which were considered before choosing the present site. The responses of the managers are analyzed, firstly, with regard to the alternative locations in the world and, then, the alternative locations in this country.

Alternative locations in the world

First of all, managers were requested to show all the countries which they considered as alternatives to the present location in Britain. The answers of the managers are summarised in Table 8.15.

As seen here, European countries took the lion's share in the total alternative locations in the world. About 60% of the companies searched for their alternatives in other European countries. When the companies which looked for their alternative sites in the US are added to this number, around two thirds of Japanese companies considered other developed countries rather than developing countries as the alternative countries in which to invest.

Developing countries provided merely 15.5% of the total alternative locations. In short, the consideration of alternative locations tended to be limited to those in developed countries rather than to include all those in developed and developing countries. This is a meaningful finding in that it can be a clue to trace the global strategy of Japanese companies which regulates their foreign investment or that part of it that ends up in Britain.

The circumstances of the companies which ticked 'none' also can be interpreted in this context. These answers mean that Britain was chosen as their destination from the beginning. In other words, the destination of a large part of Japanese investment has been determined at an earlier stage rather than after comparing the cost-benefits of all the alternative sites in the world. Among the alternative countries, Germany, Spain, France and the US proved to be important in developed countries, while Singapore stood out amongst the developing countries. Regarding the factors which made the Japanese companies reject the considered alternative locations in other countries, the managers responded as in Table 8.16.

The problem of unfamiliar language was pointed out as crucial in preventing

Japanese companies from choosing alternative locations in other countries. As indicated so many times by authors, English is the second language for Japanese people and, thus, Britain and the US have been the principal destinations for Japanese MNCs.

Table 8.15 Alternative countries considered in the world to Britain (%)

Continent Countries Numbers		Continent Countries Numbers	
Total	103(100)		
Europe (total)	59(57.3)	Asia (total)	14(13.6)
Germany	19(18.4)	Singapore	5(4.9)
Spain	15(14.6)	Taiwan	3(2.9)
France	14(13.6)	Malaysia	3(2.9)
Eire	4(3.9)	Korea	2(1.9)
Italy	2(1.9)	Hong Kong	0(0.0)
Others	5(4.9)	Others	1(1.0)
America(total)	10(9.7)	Other	
US	8(7.8)	Continents	1(1.0)
Mexico	2(2.9)		
Others	0(0.0)	None	19(18.4)

* Respondents mentioned more than one alternative countries.

The second position was taken by high wage levels. This factor is thought to be chosen by the companies which rejected other developed countries rather than developing countries[6]. Including this, the factors related to labour supply, such as lack of workforce availability and labour productivity obtained substantially high rankings in this list. This finding supports the previous argument that, for Japanese companies, British workers are favoured compared to the workers in other developed countries (8.2.2.3). As a manager commented:
" In total, the [overall] level of labour force [in this country] can be said to be the best in Europe" (The manager in company C).

The importance of the market factor for Japanese overseas investment was affirmed once again by the inclusion of the factor 'far from big market'. This factor is thought to have been indicated by those companies which had rejected alternative locations in developing countries.

The cross-tabulation between the rejected countries and the factors which caused the rejection is expected to show the disadvantageous factors in the alternative countries rejected. Table 8.17 illuminates this relationship. Since the questionnaire asked these two issues separately, the table below reveals only the

205

indirect, or rough, relationship between the two rather than describing directly the exact reason why the companies rejected the alternative countries.

Table 8.16 The important factors which caused the rejection of alternative locations in other countries (Britain)   (%)

Factors	Numbers
Total	122 (100)
Unfamiliar language	28 (22.9)
High wage level	13 (10.7)
Far from big market	13 (10.7)
Lack of workforce available	10 (8.2)
Low productivity of labour	8 (6.5)
Insufficient industrial land and premises	8 (6.5)
Inconvenient transport	6 (4.9)
Lack of manufacturing suppliers or subcontractors	6 (4.9)
High rate of crime	5 (4.1)
Lack of regional assistance	4 (3.3)
Lack of promotional activities of local authorities	4 (3.3)
Non-existence of Japanese companies in the area	3 (2.5)
Others	14 (11.5)

[+] Respondents mentioned more than one factor.

In the case of Germany, the unfamiliar language and the high wage level were given as the most significant obstacles to locating there, while the high wage level and the lack of workforce availability were found to be the deterrent to placing their subsidiaries in France. The case of the US is worth noting. It was revealed in this indirect comparison between alternative countries and unfavourable factors that Japanese managers have felt that the low productivity of labour in the US was a serious problem. This finding has implications for judging the recent disputes between the US and Japan surrounding the productivity of US workers[7].

As expected, developed countries have problems of high wage levels and insufficient industrial land and premises, whilst developing countries are suffering from the factors of being far from big markets and having low productivity of labour. The language problem has been a difficult issue in common for both developed and developing countries.

Alternative locations in the UK

Similarly to the case of alternative locations in the world, a request was given to managers to indicate all the regions in the UK which they considered before deciding on the present location. The following table is the summary of the responses of managers. As shown here, the regions which have taken large shares of the total Japanese companies in this country, i.e. Wales, Scotland and the West

Table 8.17 Relationship between the rejected alternative locations and unfavoured locational factors* (%)

Country	Total	Language	Wage	Market	Workforce	Land	Productivity
Total	142(100)+	50(35.2)	23(16.2)	21(14.8)	18(12.7)	17(12.0)	13(9.2)
Germany	36(100)+	14(38.9)	7(19.4)	5(13.9)	3(8.3)	4(11.1)	3(8.3)
Spain	26(100)	10(38.5)	4(15.4)	4(15.4)	3(11.5)	3(11.5)	2(7.7)
France	19(100)+	6(31.6)	4(21.1)	1(5.3)	4(21.1)	3(15.8)	1(5.3)
Eire	7(100)	4(57.1)	2(28.6)	0(0.0)	0(0.0)	1(14.3)	0(0.0)
Italy	7(100)+	2(28.6)	1(14.3)	0(0.0)	2(28.6)	2(14.3)	0(0.0)
Other Europe	13(100)+	3(23.1)	3(23.1)	2(15.4)	1(7.7)	3(23.1)	1(7.7)
US	13(100)+	4(30.8)	1(7.7)	4(30.8)	1(7.7)	0(0.0)	3(23.1)
Singapore	9(100)+	3(33.3)	1(11.1)	1(11.1)	1(11.1)	1(11.1)	2(22.2)
Taiwan	6(100)	2(33.3)	0(0.0)	2(33.3)	1(16.7)	0(0.0)	1(16.7)
Korea	3(100)+	1(33.3)	0(0.0)	1(33.3)	1(33.3)	0(0.0)	0(0.0)
Malaysia	3(100)+	1(33.3)	0(0.0)	1(33.3)	1(33.3)	0(0.0)	0(0.0)

(Note)　. Language : unfamiliar language
　　　　. Wage : high wage levels
　　　　. Market : far from big market
　　　　. Workforce : lack of workforce availability
　　　　. Productivity : low productivity of labour
　　　　. Land : insufficient industrial land and premises
+ By rounding errors, the sums of these columns are not exactly 100.
* Other minor factors except these six important locational factors included in these table are ignored from the consideration.

Midlands, also took greater portions than others in alternative locations. Around 40% of companies once considered these three regions as their alternative locations.

Two things seem to be strange. The one is the minor share in the total alternative locations of the South East, which is the region most crowded with newly arriving Japanese companies. The other is the big number which answered 'none'.

The first one can be interpreted as a result of either that the South East has a specific locational factor, whether it is attractive or unfavourable, which influences crucially the location decisions of Japanese companies at the initial stage. Thus, companies seldom compare the South East with other regions until the later stage of decisions, or Japanese companies, after comparing all the regions, tend to direct their move finally to the South East region.

Table 8.18 Alternative areas considered in the UK   (%)

Regions	Numbers
Total	82(100)
Wales	13(15.8)
West Midlands	10(12.2)
Scotland	9(11.0)
North	7(8.5)
North West	5(6.1)
South West	4(4.9)
East Midlands	4(4.9)
Yorkshire & Humberside	4(4.9)
South East	3(3.7)
Northern Ireland	2(2.4)
East Anglia	1(1.2)
None	20(24.4)

Respondents mentioned more than one region.

Table 8.19 The important factors which caused the rejection of alternative areas in the UK   (%)

Unfavourable factors	Number of responses
Total	81 (100)
Inconvenient transport	13 (16.1)
Lack of workforce available	9 (11.1)
Insufficient industrial land and premises	8 (9.9)
Far from big market	8 (9.9)
High wage level	6 (7.4)
Lack of manufacturing suppliers or subcontractors	6 (7.4)
Lack of regional assistance	5 (6.2)
High militancy of labour	4 (4.9)
High rate of crime	4 (4.9)
Other	18 (22.2)

Respondents mentioned more than one factor.

The second issue, no consideration of other regions for their locations, seems to be related to a certain extent with the first issue and can be interpreted in various ways. However, the initial contact with specific local authorities together with the special advantage of the present location is likely to be the most possible reason for this. (The following analyses are expected to provide an answer on this issue.)

The locational factors in alternative areas which were unfavourable to Japanese companies are listed in Table 8.19. Surprisingly enough, in the UK, where the road network is well constructed, inconvenient transport took the largest share among the unfavourable factors deterring location in alternative areas.

This finding needs to be taken cautiously in judging the locational circumstances in this country. In other words, although each country has its own under-developed areas in terms of infrastructure, each region in the UK can be said to have well-constructed transportation facilities compared to other countries. Therefore, it is more likely that the problem is traffic congestion or other related issues rather than simply under-development of communications.

The other category among the factors listed above seems to reflect similar considerations with those which were pointed out as the significant factors in choosing the present sites mentioned above (8.2.2.3). The relatively small share of the market factor is thought to be caused by the fact that the market which the Japanese companies coming into this country are aiming for is the European market rather than UK local market and, thus, most regions in this country are almost the same in terms of remoteness from or closeness to the big market, i.e. the European market.

As in the case of the worldwide alternative locations, the cross-tabulation between the rejected areas and the factors which caused the rejection is expected to reveal the unfavourable factors of alternative areas in this country, albeit a rough measure. Table 8.20 shows this relationship.

To extract significant features from this table seems to be a difficult task, for the answers of managers are distributed almost evenly between regions and between locational factors. However, by reference to the slight differences in the number of answers, the distinction between regions in terms of unfavourable locational factors seems to be possible.

First of all, Wales, Scotland and the West Midlands stood out from others in the factor of inconvenient transport. Among these, the case of West Midlands seems to follow the example of the previous interpretation, i.e. that the problem is congestion rather than under-development of the communications system. Regarding the case of Wales, especially those areas in the far western and northern part, the table can be used as evidence showing the insufficient accessibility of Wales through the existing facilities including the M4. On the other hand, the unsatisfactory transportation facilities in Scotland seems to be affirmed along the line of remoteness from the European and South East markets. This transportation problem seems to be compounded by Japanese preference for using the seaports in the South East rather than those in Scotland for exporting their products to Europe. Among the four Japanese companies interviewed which are located in Scotland, no company was found to use the seaports in Scotland. Instead, Southampton, Dover and Felixstowe were listed as the main gates for exporting the products and for importing raw materials of these companies.

Another thing worth mentioning is the higher rank of Wales and the West Midlands with regard to the market factor disadvantage. Although the Welsh case is understandable because of its location in the far west, the inclusion of the West Midlands seems to be strange. One possible explanation may be that, apart from distance from ports, the traffic congestion in the West Midlands region makes the Japanese managers consider the region to be difficult of access and, thus, far from the main market.

On the other hand, the managers were asked whether any alternative site in the same region as the present location was considered and the reason for rejecting that location. On this question, only two managers indicated that their companies considered alternative sites near the present location. Traffic congestion, lack of suitable premises and, slightly, remoteness from an airport and motorway network were pointed out as the main causes of rejection.

Table 8.20 Relationship between the rejected areas and unfavoured locational factors (Britain)*   (%)

Region	Total	Transport	Land	Market	Workforce	Subcontractors	Wage
Total[+]	82(100)	23(28.0)	15(18.3)	14(17.1)	11(13.4)	11(13.4)	8(9.8)
Wales	20(100)	8(40.0)	2(10.0)	4(20.0)	3(15.0)	2(10.0)	1(5.0)
Scotland	12(100)	4(33.3)	2(16.7)	1(8.3)	2(16.7)	2(16.7)	1(8.3)
W Mids	10(100)	3(30.0)	1(10.0)	3(30.0)	0(0.0)	2(20.0)	1(10.0)
N Ireland	9(100)[+]	2(22.2)	2(22.2)	0(0.0)	2(22.2)	1(11.1)	2(22.2)
S West	8(100)	2(25.0)	2(25.0)	1(12.5)	2(25.0)	0(0.0)	1(12.5)
North	8(100)	2(25.0)	2(25.0)	1(12.5)	1(12.5)	2(25.0)	0(0.0)
E Mids	7(100)[+]	1(14.3)	1(14.3)	2(28.6)	1(14.3)	1(14.3)	1(14.3)
Y & H	5(100)	0(0.0)	2(40.0)	1(20.0)	0(0.0)	1(20.0)	1(20.0)
E Anglia	1(100)	1(100)	0(0.0)	0(0.0)	0(0.0)	0(0.0)	0(0.0)
S East	1(100)	0(0.0)	0(0.0)	1(100)	0(0.0)	0(0.0)	0(0.0)
N West	1(100)	0(0.0)	1(100)	0(0.0)	0(0.0)	0(0.0)	0(0.0)

(Note) . Transport : inconvenient transport
    . Land : insufficient industrial land and premises
    . Market : far from big market
    . Workforce : lack of workforce availability
    . Subcontractors : lack of manufacturing suppliers or subcontractors
    . Wage : high wage levels
[+] By rounding errors, the sum of each columns is not always 100.
* Other minor factors except these six important locational factors included in these table are ignored from the consideration.

Overall, since the geographical circumstances of British regions are largely similar, to find distinguishably disadvantageous factors in individual regions seems to be difficult.

8.1.3 Summary of the findings

From the findings above about the important geographical factors underlying the location decisions of Japanese manufacturing companies in Britain, even though demonstrated sporadically, it seems possible to clarify some noticeable features of the locational pattern of these companies.

First of all, the market factor is central among the locational factors which influence the location decisions of these Japanese companies. The market factor, encompassing the closeness to a big market, the single market in Europe in 1992 and the trade barriers of other countries, took the first position both in terms of push factors in Japan and pull factors in the UK. However, the importance of the market factor was portrayed insufficiently in the regression analysis in the previous chapter. This seems to be caused by the fact that the regression data, which were collected to show the features of each region in this country, were unsuitable to represent properly the market factor, especially the big European market.

Another thing to be noted with the market factor is that the strategy of 'globalisation' was affirmed not only by inference from the analysis of questionnaire answers but also by the direct comment of managers during the interviews. In other words, the establishment of Japanese subsidiaries in this country is based, firstly, on the globalisation strategy of Japanese companies aiming to establish bridgeheads all over the world and, secondly, on the attraction of the magnitude of the European market.

Secondly, with regard to the investment decisions involving alternative countries, the Japanese companies investing in this country tended to decide their destination at an earlier stage of the location decision. In other words, the destination of an investment was determined from the beginning in order to capture a targeted market. Therefore, the comparison between alternative countries were made predominantly between the neighbouring developed countries, especially those in the UK, Germany and France, rather than between Asian developing countries and European developed countries. Of course, this is thought to be the natural consequence of the basic strategy of globalisation. Along with the above finding, this fact provides a significant contribution to understanding the managerial strategy of Japanese companies and the location decisions of these companies on a global scale, which was hard to grasp in the macro-level regression analysis discussed in the previous chapter.

Thirdly, among markets, the main manufacturers in this or adjacent countries were found to be the main market of Japanese companies operating in this country (with these, in turn, interested in the European market). In particular, for those companies which arrived after 1986, this market was more important than for those which arrived early in the 1980s. This is related closely to the massive arrival of Japanese component manufacturers to locate around their big main customers which had begun their operations already.

Fourthly, with regard to attractive locational factors, the market factor mentioned above was indicated as the most important location factors followed by familiar language, sufficient industrial land and premises, regional assistance from the government, convenient transport and the presence of Japanese companies in the area. On the other hand, concerning the unsatisfactory locational factors of the present locations and other alternative locations, lack of manufacturing suppliers or subcontractors, high wage levels, inconvenient transport and lack of workforce availability, etc. were listed as the significant locational factors which restrict the investment of Japanese companies in certain regions. One thing to be noted is that the importance of the basic conditions for the location of manufacturing companies such as industrial land and premises and a convenient transport system is still substantial in developed countries like the UK.

And, fifthly, the importance of financial assistance is still non-negligible for foreign companies. Most companies which assess the assistance of the British government as being 'very substantial' or 'substantial' were found to have received financial assistance from the British government. The high satisfaction level of the companies located in Scotland and Wales implicitly illustrates the significance of government assistance, in particular financial aid. In the meantime, it was found that the positive activity of local authorities including advice, planning permission and speed of decision can be influential for the foreign companies as well as financial aid.

Overall, from these findings, it seems possible to argue that, at the worldwide level, Japanese MNCs planning to invest in overseas countries tend to decide the location of subsidiaries under the aim of attacking a targeted market with quick delivery and better services in accordance with the framework of a global strategy and that, at the regional level, the location decisions of these companies have been made after considering various geographical factors including industrial land and premises, labour, linkages, accessibility and government assistance.

8.2 Significant Geographical Factors in Korea

As in the British case, a questionnaire survey was undertaken amongst the Japanese companies operating in Korea. The survey method was the same in the two countries and, thus, the same kind of questionnaire forms was prepared. However, an interview survey was not implemented in Korea mainly due to the problem of distance. This section portrays, firstly, the profile of the companies surveyed and, secondly, the analysis of survey results, i.e. the main market for the company; the push factor in Japan; attractive or unsatisfactory locational factors; the role of the host government; and the alternative locations considered. The codification and cross-tabulation of the answers of respondents to the questionnaire and the analysis and interpretation of these answers are made mainly according to arrival date, pre- and post- January 1987, as with the British case.

8.2.1 Profiles of the companies surveyed

The total number of the Japanese companies operating in Korea, which were identified by the publications of the Ministry of Finance and confirmed by the deliveries of the questionnaire, was 299. Out of this total, 106 companies replied to the questionnaire with useful answers and, thus, the ratio of useful replies to the total number of companies was 35.5%. Fifty one companies returned the questionnaire without response mainly due to the absence of the appropriate person to answer, i.e. the Japanese managers. The remaining 142 companies sent no reply. Apart from these, another 5 companies replied to the questionnaire. However, the responses of these companies were excluded from this analysis, since the share of Japanese parent companies in the total capital of these companies was found to be below 50%.

As in the British case, the χ^2 test was undertaken. The χ^2 values derived are 0.877 (df = 1), 3.587 (df = 4) and 6.925 (df = 9) respectively for the size, industrial fields and geographical location of the companies that replied.

Among the 106 companies which responded, 71 companies, or 67.0% of the total, were established before the beginning of 1987 while the remaining 35 companies, or 33.0%, arrived thereafter (a different balance than in Britain, above 8.1.1). With regard to the size of these companies, 71 companies (67.0%) can be thought to be SMEs with an investment size of less than $ 2m, while the remaining 35 companies (33.0%) have a larger investment size of over $ 2m[8]. The composition of SMEs and large companies in each sub-period can be summarised as follows.

Table 8.21 The size and established year of companies surveyed by questionnaire (Korea)   (%)

Size	Total	Before 1987	After 1986
Total	106(100)	71(67.0)	35(33.0)
Large companies	35(100)	24(68.6)	11(31.4)
SMEs	71(100)	47(66.2)	24(33.8)

In contrast to the British case, more of both the large and the small companies were established before 1987. With regard to industrial mix, the companies in the field of electronics took the largest share (35.9%) as in the British case. But this share was biased towards the pre-1987 arrivals. Table 8.22 shows the industrial

213

distribution of the companies in each sub-period.

Table 8.22 The industrial distribution of companies surveyed by questionnaire
(Korea)   (%)

Industrial Fields	Total	Before 1987	After 1986
Total	106(100)	71(100)	35(100)
Electronics	38(35.9)	28(39.4)	10(28.6)
Chemicals & plastics	24(22.6)	18(25.3)	6(17.1)
Heavy machinery & vehicles	18(17.0)	8(11.3)	10(28.6)
Light engineering	8(7.5)	7(9.9)	1(2.8)
Others	18(17.0)	10(14.1)	8(22.9)

Table 8.23 The locations of the companies surveyed by questionnaire (Korea)
(%)

Region	Total	Before 1987	After 1986
Total	106(100)	71(100)	35(100)
Kyongsangnam-Do	29(27.4)	26(36.6)	3(8.6)
Seoul	28(26.4)	18(25.4)	10(28.6)
Kyonggi-Do	13(12.3)	10(14.1)	3(8.6)
Kyongsangbuk-Do	10(9.4)	6(8.5)	4(11.4)
Inchon	6(5.7)	3(4.2)	3(8.6)
Chungchongnam-Do	9(8.5)	3(4.2)	6(17.1)
Chollanam-Do	4(3.8)	1(1.4)	3(8.6)
Chollabuk-Do	3(2.8)	2(2.8)	1(2.8)
Pusan	3(2.8)	1(1.4)	2(5.7)
Kangwon-Do	1(0.9)	1(1.4)	0(0.0)

Taegu, Kangwon-Do, Chungchongbuk-Do and Cheju-Do had no respondent.

Similarly to the overall geographical distribution of Japanese companies in
Korea, the distribution of those companies which responded to the questionnaire
showed the tendency of centralisation in Seoul and Kyongsangnam-Do especially
pre-1987. Table 8.23 demonstrates the geographical distribution of the respondents.

8.2.2 Findings of the Survey

As in the British case, the responses of the managers of the Japanese companies in Korea are analyzed and expounded according to the five groups of questions: namely, the main market for the company; the push factors in Japan; the attractive or unsatisfactory locational factors; the role of the host government; and the alternative locations considered.

8.2.2.1 Main market for the companies

Given the question about the main market for the products of their firms, the managers indicated the local consumer market as the first key market and the foreign consumer market as the second. The following table shows the importance of each market for the Japanese companies operating in Korea.

Among the companies which responded to the question, 36.2% of the companies (far more than in the British survey) pointed to the local consumer market as the main market for their products. This is an odd result in comparison with the presumption that most Asian countries including Korea have been used as a kind of platform for Japanese companies to manufacture products in a lower cost location and then to sell the products in developed countries.

This result might be interpreted in such a way that most of the Japanese companies that have invested in Korea are the manufacturers of consumer products rather than component suppliers, differently from the case in Britain. In other words, Japanese companies in Korea were established mainly to capture the growing Korean market as well as the world consumer market.

Table 8.24 Main markets of the companies surveyed (Korea)　　　　　(%)

| Markets | Total | Established | |
		Before 1987	After 1986
Total	127(100)*	86(100)	41(100)
Local consumer market	46(36.2)	31(36.0)	15(36.6)
Main manufacturers in this or adjacent country	41(32.3)	27(31.4)	14(34.2)
Foreign consumer market	39(30.7)	28(32.6)	11(26.8)
Others	1(0.8)	0(0.0)	1(2.4)

Twenty one companies picked out two kinds of markets as their main markets.

Although this finding can plainly be interpreted like this, the actual cause of this result is difficult to identify clearly. In addition, our difficulty is compounded by the almost similar shares of the three main markets. However, one thing which should be emphasised here is that the Japanese companies established in Korea are mainly consumer goods producers and the local market in Korea is one of the main targets for these companies. The lack of large scale manufacturers such as

215

Toyota, Nissan, Sony, Matshushita, Hitachi, JVC, etc. and, therefore, the scarcity of Japanese component manufacturers supplying to these main customers in Korea, seems to be a noteworthy characteristic of the investment of Japanese manufacturers in Korea and, as a result, to be a cause of this result.

Another matter worth mentioning, which has to do with the above issue, is that the share of the foreign market is diminishing among the companies which arrived after 1986 contrary to the growing importance of the local consumer market and of supply to the main manufacturers in Korea and adjacent countries. This is thought to be closely related to the expansion of Japanese FDI into developed countries from the previous destinations in Asian developing countries. In other words, the traditional FDI pattern, which was characterised by the establishment of subsidiaries in low-cost Asian countries and the export of the products of these subsidiaries to developed countries, has been changed into one of direct investment in developed countries for various reasons, especially as part of the fore-mentioned global strategy, and this changed pattern is reflected in this questionnaire result.

8.2.2.2 Push factors in Japan

Regarding the push factors in Japan which made Japanese firms invest outside their own territory, the factors related to labour were found to be the most important for those companies in Korea. The table below portrays the relative importance of each push factor.

Table 8.25 Push factors in Japan resulting in overseas investment in Korea

Reasons	Total	Importance		
	Rating	1st	2nd	3rd
Labour shortage in Japan	160	23	36	19
High wage level compared to other countries	150	28	25	16
High rate of the yen	69	11	5	26
Lack of big markets in Japan	52	7	7	17
Trade barriers of other countries	34	3	5	15
Other	58	11	1	23

Ratings are computed by a four-point scale : the first important reason = 3; the second important reason = 2; the third   and other important reason =1; not important = 0.

Two factors related to labour supply, i.e. labour shortage and high wage levels in Japan, took the largest share, around 60%, in the total rating of these push factors. This finding seems to be along the lines of the long standing argument that Japanese companies invest in Asian countries to make maximum use of low-cost labour in these countries.

If the result of the previous analysis of the main market for these Japanese companies is incorporated, the prominence of the labour factor among the push factors can be interpreted in such a way that Japanese companies, which had exported their consumer products to Korea and other countries, began to confront the obstacles of the shortage of labour and high wage levels in Japan and, thus, there was no way but to invest in Korea in order to maintain their market share.

Other reasons, namely the high rate of the yen, the lack of big markets in Japan and the trade barriers of other countries, each took only a small share. In particular, the fact that the trade barriers of other countries, which took the first position for the Japanese companies operating in the UK, took only minimal share among the push factors here obviously demonstrates the different position of these two host countries for Japanese MNCs.

The responses 'other' also contain very singular features which are unique in this Korean case. The factors which comprise the 'other' category are: access to the Korean market (12 companies), a special relationship of the manager with Korea (8), globalisation (7), a relatively lower investment cost (5), availability of sound subcontractors (5) and the supply of products to customers (3). Here, the importance of the Korean market and the globalisation strategy were emphasised once again. The special relationship of the manager with Korea means that the manager is of Korean origin. Including this factor, a lot of historical factors are intermingled in the investment decisions of Japanese companies prohibiting a simplistic interpretation of the investment patterns of Japanese companies in Korea.

8.2.2.3 Attractive or unsatisfactory locational factors

Attractive locational factors

Regarding the influential locational factors, or pull factors, for the location decisions of Japanese companies in Korea, managers chose a group of important factors in order of importance. Table 8.26 shows the result.

Once again, among all the locational factors, the factors related to the availability of abundant labour took the largest share. In line with the previous finding regarding the push factors in Japan, the leading position of these factors affirms the overriding importance of favourable labour to the Japanese companies investing in Korea. At the same time, a sort of similarity can be found between this finding and those of the previous chapter (7.2.1.6 and 7.2.2.2), even though not exactly identical.

In short, the Japanese companies coming into Korea are largely attracted by the abundance of highly skilled labour. Furthermore, other labour factors, i.e. high productivity and low-militancy of labour, also acquired relatively high rankings fortifying the prominence of labour supply for the location of these companies. One thing that should be noted in the questionnaire replies is the minimal role of the presence of Japanese companies in attracting the newly coming compatriot companies. In the regression analysis in Chapter seven, the variables involved in this factor consistently took an important position in explaining the locational pattern of Japanese companies.

Table 8.26 Important locational factors for the Japanese companies surveyed (Korea) (%)

Locational	Ratings of the companies		
Factors	Total	Before 1987	After 1986
Total Rating	568(100)	404(100)	164(100)
Abundant workforce available	133(23.4)	106(26.2)	27(16.5)
Low wage level	102(18.0)	84(20.8)	18(11.0)
Sufficient industrial land and premises	92(16.2)	65(16.1)	27(16.5)
Convenient transport	53(9.3)	32(7.9)	21(12.8)
High productivity of labour	32(5.6)	27(6.7)	5(3.0)
Closeness to a big market	23(4.0)	14(3.5)	9(5.5)
Existence of manufacturing suppliers or subcontractors	21(3.7)	14(3.5)	7(4.2)
Presence of Japanese companies in the area	20(3.5)	14(3.5)	6(3.7)
Low militancy of labour	19(3.4)	13(3.2)	6(3.7)
Promotional activities of local authorities	19(3.4)	9(2.2)	10(6.1)
Regional assistance from gov't and local authority	17(3.0)	14(3.5)	3(1.8)
The 'greenness' or amenity of the area	12(2.1)	3(0.7)	9(5.5)
Familiar language	3(0.5)	2(0.5)	1(0.6)
Low rate of crime	1(0.2)	0(0.0)	1(0.6)
Abundant houses for employees in the area	1(0.2)	0(0.0)	1(0.6)
Abundant leisure and recreation facilities	0(0.0)	0(0.0)	0(0.0)
Others	20(3.5)	7(1.7)	13(7.9)

Ratings are computed by a four-point scale : the first most important factor = 3; the second most important factor = 2; the third and other important factors = 1; not important factor = 0.

The very substantial importance of this factor in the regression analysis, contrary to the poor rating of the factor in this survey analysis, seems to be a concomitance, instead of being an influencing force, on the locations of Japanese companies. In other words, most Japanese companies have long been attracted by the existence of abundant labour and this concentration of the Japanese companies in specific areas brought about a high correlation coefficient between the newly coming Japanese companies and the presence of their predecessors[9].

The low assessment of Japanese managers of the influence of environmental circumstances contrary to the regression result also should be taken in the same way. In short, this micro-level analysis reveals obviously the importance of the labour factor for the location choices of Japanese companies among all the locational factors which are intertwined under the same roof of Korean geography, which is characterised by the attraction of all the favourable factors coincident in specific areas.

The 'sufficient industrial land and premises' took the highest position after the labour factor. As expounded in Chapter four, the policy measure behind regional policy in Korea has been concentrated on the development of industrial estates. In this regard, the emphasis of Japanese managers on this factor might be considered as a proof of the success of regional policy. However, there are some problems in interpreting the result in this way. The lack of Japanese companies in other industrial estates developed in non-prosperous regions explains the situation point-blank (see 10.1.3.2). Therefore, this finding gives a significant implication for assessing the effect and future direction of regional policy in Korea. On the other hand, government regional assistance and the promotional activities of local authorities were found to play a minor role in the location decisions of Japanese companies. These issues will be dealt with in more detail in the following chapters.

The next rank of the 'convenient transport' factor after 'industrial land and premises' provides another indication of the direction of regional policy in developing countries like Korea, where infrastructure has not yet been fully constructed[10]. Apart from these factors, abundance of suppliers or subcontractors and closeness to a big market proved to be relatively important locational factors.

When the importance of each factor is compared between the two groups of companies with different times of arrival, i.e. a group of companies which arrived before 1987 and the other group arrived after that time, a significant change is recognized. The most significant change seems to be the decreasing importance of the labour factor among the companies which arrived recently compared to their predecessors. For instance, from 26.2% and 20.8% to 16.5% and 11.0% respectively in the case of the first two factors. On the other hand, the importance of transport and the 'greenness' of the area has been increased remarkably. This seems to be a reflection of the changing circumstances in Korea for the Japanese investments; namely, the increasing militancy of labour, growing wage level, the deteriorating environmental circumstances in Korea, etc.

From these findings, it seems possible to conclude that the Japanese companies investing in Korea have been influenced primarily by the abundance of low-cost labour, even though the significance of this factor is diminishing, and complementarily by the availability of industrial land and premises and convenient transport.

Table 8.27 Unsatisfactory locational factors for the Japanese companies surveyed (Korea) (%)

Locational	Responses of Japanese companies		
Factors	Total	Before 1987	Since 1987
Total Responses	260(100)	152(100)	108(100)
Inconvenient transport	35(13.5)	18(11.9)	17(15.7)
Lack of workforce available	29(11.1)	12(7.9)	17(15.7)
High militancy of labour	22(8.5)	6(3.9)	16(14.8)
Insufficient leisure and recreation facilities	20(7.7)	11(7.2)	9(8.3)
Lack of manufacturing suppliers or subcontractors	18(6.9)	9(5.9)	9(8.3)
Lack of regional assistance	18(6.9)	15(9.9)	3(2.8)
High wage level	17(6.5)	5(3.3)	12(11.1)
Low productivity of labour	17(6.5)	7(4.6)	10(9.3)
Remoteness from a big market	16(6.2)	13(8.6)	3(2.8)
Insufficient houses for employees in the area	16(6.2)	16(10.5)	0(0.0)
The lack of 'greenness' or amenity of the area	15(5.8)	12(7.9)	3(2.8)
High rate of crime	10(3.8)	10(6.6)	0(0.0)
Unfamiliar language	9(3.5)	5(3.3)	4(3.7)
Insufficient industrial land and premises	8(3.1)	6(3.9)	2(1.9)
Non-existence of Japanese companies in the area	4(1.5)	4(2.6)	0(0.0)
Lack of promotional activities of local authorities	2(0.8)	1(0.7)	1(0.9)
Others	4(1.5)	2(1.3)	2(1.9)

Respondents mentioned more than one unsatisfactory factor.

Unsatisfactory locational factors

The examination of unsatisfactory factors in the chosen location for the Japanese companies provides another singular picture of the location decisions of Japanese companies in Korea (Table 8.27). As is the case in the UK, this list of unsatisfactory locational factors can be said to be the reverse of the list of attractive locational factors in a rough measure.

The first position in this table was taken by inconvenient transport in spite of the emphasis of Japanese companies on this factor. The appearance of this factor as the most unsatisfactory factor is thought to be caused by both the traffic congestion in the two developed areas and the insufficient facilities in other areas. The most interesting point, which has to do with the findings of the previous table, is that the factors relating to labour supply still took high rankings in this table as unsatisfactory factors.

However, this time, the complaints of the Japanese companies were mainly about the high militancy of labour, high wage levels and low productivity of labour which were not accentuated in the list of attractive factors. The case of 'lack of workforce available', which also took a high position among the attractive factors, is interesting. This seems to be a result of the diminishing preference of Japanese companies for this factor, especially among those which arrived in the latter part of 1980s. In short, with the decrease in the importance of this factor in attractiveness, the complaints about the labour factor grew.

On the same ground the less significant factors in the previous table such as 'leisure and recreation facilities' and 'regional assistance' turned out to be significant this time. Overall, the importance of labour supply and infrastructure for the locations of Japanese companies was sustained in the examination of unsatisfactory factors at the present locations.

8.2.2.4 The role of the host government

In answer to the two questions to assess the role of host government assistance, namely to what extent government assistance influenced the location choice of the firms; and what kind of assistance that was, managers replied as follows.

The influence of government assistance

Firstly, the following table shows the extent to which government assistance influenced managers' location decisions.It is surprising that 20 companies, or 18.9%, among the total respondents answered that the influence of government assistance was very substantial. Furthermore, over 30% of the managers in the Japanese companies who responded to the questionnaire were found to be satisfied with government assistance 'substantially' or 'very substantially'.

The overall level of satisfaction with government assistance in Korea was almost equivalent to that in the UK. This is a rather contradictory outcome against the regression results in the previous chapter. This issue is another that is quite tricky to interpret. The following point needs to be taken into account simultaneously in order to interpret this finding.

This is that there is a significant gap in the extent of the influence between the

Japanese companies which arrived before 1987 and those since 1987. The satisfaction of Japanese companies with government assistance decreased remarkably among the companies which arrived recently compared to those that arrived earlier. In other words, the influence of government assistance was substantial only to those which arrived in Korea in the earlier days of foreign investment.

Table 8.28 The influence of government assistance in the location decisions of Japanese companies (Korea)   (%)

| Influence | Total | Japanese companies arrived | |
		Before 1987	After 1986
Total	106(100)	71(100)	35(100)
Very substantial	20(18.9)	18(25.4)	2(5.7)
Substantial	12(11.3)	10(14.1)	2(5.7)
Moderate	22(20.8)	15(21.1)	7(20.0)
Minimal	44(41.5)	24(33.8)	20(57.2)
No answer	8(7.5)	4(5.6)	4(11.4)

In fact, regional policy in Korea, which depends heavily on the development of industrial estates, was substantial in the 1960s and 1970s. At that time the national economic development policy was at its strongest stage, with the provision of industrial land in free ports or industrial complexes, which are located mainly in two prosperous regions, and with tax cuts to those companies opening in these areas (see 4.2.2). However, this regional policy, strictly speaking a part of economic development policy, stimulated the concentration of population and industry in these specific regions. Confronting the many problems caused by the growing concentration, the Korean government began to introduce new policy initiatives aimed at the dispersal of population and industry, i.e. actual regional policy. However, as has been discussed so far, the effect of this actual regional policy can be said to be questionable.

Therefore, it seems to be more valid to interpret the strange survey result above as a reflection or consequence of the changing context of regional policy in Korea rather than purely as the effectiveness of regional policy. In short, the responses of the managers reveal most vividly the historical context of regional policy in Korea. The classification of the responses according to the regional distribution of these companies (Table 8.29) provides an additional source of evidence supporting the argument just presented.

As clearly demonstrated in this table, most companies which assessed the role of government assistance as satisfactory are located in the two prosperous areas, i.e. Kyongsangnam-Do and Seoul. Among the 32 companies which described the role as 'substantial' or 'very substantial', 23 companies, or 71.9%, have their plants in the two prosperous areas. Conversely, 27 (55.1%) out of 49 companies which are located outside these two areas, or non-prosperous regions, assessed the role of government assistance as minimal.

From this and the previous tables, it seems possible to conclude that the effect of regional policy in Korea is the reverse of that of British regional policy, and certainly of that of other countries, which emphasise the balanced development and distribution of wealth between regions. This might be claimed as both the cause and the result of the changed direction of regional policy in Korea.

Table 8.29 The influence of government assistance on the location decisions of Japanese companies by Do* (Korea)   (%)

Region	Total	Extent of influence				
		Very substantial	Substantial	Moderate	Minimal	No answer
Total	106(100)	20(18.9)	12(11.3)	22(20.8)	44(41.5)	8(7.5)
Kyongsang nam-Do	29(100)	13(44.8)	4(13.8)	6(20.7)	6(20.7)	0(0.0)
Seoul	28(100)	3(10.7)	3(10.7)	6(21.4)	11(39.3)	5(17.9)
Kyonggi-Do	13(100)	1(7.7)	0(0.0)	4(30.8)	7(53.8)	1(7.7)
Kyongsangbuk-Do	10(100)	2(20.0)	2(20.0)	2(20.0)	4(40.0)	0(0.0)
Chungchongnam-Do	9(100)+	0(0.0)	0(0.0)	2(22.2)	6(66.7)	1(11.1)
Inchon	6(100)	0(0.0)	1(16.7)	2(33.3)	3(50.0)	0(0.0)
Chollanam-Do	4(100)	0(0.0)	1(25.0)	0(0.0)	3(75.0)	0(0.0)
Pusan	3(100)	1(33.3)	0(0.0)	0(0.0)	2(66.7)	0(0.0)
Chollabuk-Do	3(100)	0(0.0)	1(33.3)	0(0.0)	1(33.3)	1(33.3)
Kangwon-Do	1(100)	0(0.0)	0(0.0)	0(0.0)	1(100)	0(0.0)

+ By rounding errors, the sum of figures in each row is not exactly 100.
* There was no respondent in Taegu, Chungchongbuk-Do and Cheju-Do.

Measures of government assistance

Regarding the government assistance measures given to the Japanese companies, the responses of managers can be summarised as in Table 8.30. In this table, advice, the provision of land and premises and speed of decision provided the major policy measures given to the Japanese companies. Nearly three quarters of total policy measures indicated by the managers of Japanese companies are one of these three measures.

Among the three, advice appeared to be the most important for the Japanese companies, surpassing the provision of industrial land and premises. This implies that the latter has not been a crucial factor for the location of Japanese companies

223

in spite of the emphasis put on it by the Korean government for so long.

On the other hand, as expected, financial aid took the last position, for there is no comprehensive financial aid program in Korea in contrast to the UK. However, considering the fact that many of those measures categorised as 'other' (15 cases out of 17) were found to be the benefit of the tax cuts on government-provided industrial estates, financial aid has a substantial potential as an important policy measure.

Table 8.30 The measures of assistance provided by the host government (Korea)
(%)

Assistance	Total	Japanese companies arrived	
		Before 1987	After 1986
Total	121(100)	90(100)	31(100)
Advice	39(32.2)	28(31.1)	11(35.5)
Land and premises	31(25.6)	27(30.0)	4(12.9)
Speed of decision	19(15.7)	12(13.3)	7(22.6)
Planning permission	8(6.6)	6(6.7)	2(6.4)
Financial aid	7(5.8)	6(6.7)	1(3.2)
Other	17(14.1)	11(12.2)	6(19.4)

Respondents mentioned more than one measure.

Table 8.31 Important measures of government assistance in each area (Korea)
(%)

Do	Total	Advice	Land & premises	Speed of decision	Other[+]
Total	121(100)	39(32.2)	31(25.6)	19(15.7)	32(26.5)
Kyongsangnam-Do	42(100)	8(19.0)	19(45.2)	7(16.7)	8(19.1)
Seoul	30(100)	13(43.3)	5(16.7)	3(10.0)	9(30.0)
Kyongsangbuk-Do	12(100)	5(41.7)	1(8.3)	1(8.3)	5(41.7)
Kyonggi-Do	11(100)	4(36.4)	1(9.1)	5(45.4)	1(9.1)
Chungchongnam-Do	9(100)	2(22.2)	1(11.1)	0(0.0)	6(66.7)
Others	17(100)	7(41.2)	4(23.5)	3(17.6)	3(17.7)

[+] Includes planning permission, financial aid and other.
Respondents mentioned more than one measure.

The comparison of the policy measures which were indicated as being important by managers in each region fortifies the findings and arguments so far. This comparison is made in the following table.

As was expected, Kyongsangnam-Do stood out from others in terms of dependency on the provision of industrial land and premises. Advice is found to have been effective in other areas than Kyongsangnam-Do. On the other hand, Kyonggi-Do is impressive in its prominence in the speed of decision. In order to examine the effective measures of government assistance through the expression of the managers in Japanese companies Table 8.32 was constructed.

Among the companies which assessed the role of government policy as 'very substantial', 75% of companies received the benefit of land and premises. In the case of other policy measures, the ratio was not so high. This means that the provision of industrial land and premises has been an influential policy measure which satisfies Japanese companies. Unfortunately, however, the overall effect of this main policy measure cannot be said to be sufficient and obvious, especially when this ratio is compared with that of financial aid in the British case portrayed in Table 8.14[11].

Table 8.32 Relationship between the measures of government assistance and its influence on the location of Japanese companies (Korea)   (%)*

Influence of assistance	Total companies	Advice	Land and premises	Speed of decision	Other[+]
Total	106(100)	39(36.8)	31(29.2)	19(17.9)	32(30.2)
Very substantial	20(100)	8(40.0)	15(75.0)	5(25.0)	11(55.0)
Substantial	12(100)	5(41.7)	5(41.7)	4(33.3)	4(33.3)
Moderate	22(100)	8(36.4)	7(31.8)	3(13.6)	6(27.3)
Minimal	44(100)	17(38.6)	4(9.1)	7(15.9)	11(25.0)
No answer	8	-	-	-	-

[+] Includes planning permission, financial aid and other.
* The ratio of the companies which received each assistance to the number of companies which assessed the influence of government assistance at different levels.

In other words, this measure cannot be said to be critical in affecting the location decisions of Japanese companies, even though it still remains more influential than other measures. In this regard, a different kind of policy initiative, or diversification, is necessitated to achieve the goal of regional policy in Korea. This issue will be further discussed in the following chapters.

8.2.2.5 Alternative locations

As in the British case, the responses of managers about the alternative locations which were considered before deciding on the present location are analyzed in order of, firstly, the alternative locations in the world and, secondly, those in Korea.

Regarding the question asking about the alternative countries in the world that were considered, the managers answered as shown in Table 8.33. Other Asian countries provided the largest share of alternative locations, over 60%, of all those alternative locations considered all over the world. This is obviously a parallel situation with the case of the Japanese companies investing in the UK, which looked for alternative locations in the neighbouring European countries. This finding affirms the previous argument that the consideration of alternative locations is limited to either the neighbouring developed or developing, countries rather than comparing all the alternative locations in developed *and* developing countries.

Table 8.33 Alternative countries considered in the world to Korea   (%)

Continent Countries Numbers		Continent Countries Numbers	
Total	209(100)		
Asia (total)	129(61.7)	Europe	15(7.2)
Taiwan	19(17.2)	Germany	4(2.0)
Thailand	32(15.3)	UK	3(1.4)
Malaysia	31(14.8)	Spain	3(1.4)
Singapore	16(7.7)	Italy	2(1.0)
Hong Kong	5(2.4)	France	0(0.0)
Others	9(4.3)	Others	1(1.0)
America(total)	36(17.2)	Other	
US	16(7.7)	Continents	1(0.5)
Brazil	7(3.3)		
Mexico	6(2.8)		
Canada	5(2.4)		
Argentina	2(1.0)		
Others	0(0.0)	None	28(13.4)

* Respondents mentioned more than one alternative countries.

If Brazil, Mexico and Argentina are included in the category of developing countries, the share of developing countries among the total alternative locations reaches to around 70%. In contrast, the share of developed countries is no more than 17.3% of the total. As argued above, this seems to be a tangible consequence resulting from the global strategy of Japanese companies in deciding their foreign investment.

Furthermore, if the responses of the companies which chose 'none' (i.e.

considered no alternative locations) are interpreted in the same way, it seems to be more clear that, from the beginning, Korea was destined to be the base of manufacturing plants in developing countries as much as the UK was in developed countries. In this context it seems certain that no comparison between Korea and developed countries such as UK, Germany and France is needed as part of a location decision.

Among developing countries, Taiwan, Thailand and Malaysia took the highest positions, while the US proved to be an important alternative among developed countries. Then, what were the main causes which brought about the rejection of these alternative locations in other countries by the Japanese companies? The following table answers this.

The issues related to labour supply were found to play the central role for Japanese companies in discarding alternative locations in other countries. Over 40% of Japanese companies rejected other countries mainly due to unsatisfactory aspects of the labour force in these countries. The fact that the issues of productivity of labour and availability of workforce took the highest two ranks reveals the core factors for Japanese companies in choosing locations in developing countries. Once again, this survey result proved the crucial importance of the labour factor for Japanese companies in placing their subsidiaries in Korea.

The importance of industrial land and premises for the location of Japanese companies was also affirmed in this table. Apart from these, the language problem influenced the location decisions of Japanese companies. This seems to be caused by the existence of a large number of Koreans who can command the Japanese language and vice versa. This is another factor which shows the historical relationship between the two countries as discussed in the previous section (8.3.2.2).

The cross-tabulation between the rejected alternative countries and the causes of rejection in order to examine roughly the disadvantageous factors of alternative countries is summarised in Table 8.35. In the case of Malaysia, low productivity of labour and lack of workforce availability were indicated as the main reasons for the rejection of this country, while Thailand and Taiwan were found to have evenly distributed problems with each factor. Other countries, regardless of whether they are developed or developing, are common in possessing, as a cause of rejection, factors related to labour supply. This fact supports the findings in the regression analysis in the previous chapter, i.e. the abundance of highly skilled labour as the main locational factor for Japanese companies in Korea.

A kind of differentiation is made between developing countries and developed countries in the causes of rejection. While, in developing countries, problems are distributed evenly among factors, the problems of developed countries are heavily concentrated on productivity of labour, high wage levels and industrial land and premises availability.

This can be interpreted in such a way that Japanese companies coming into Korea decide initially whether they are going to make a base directly in a targeted

227

market (developed countries) or to exploit low cost labour and export to the market countries (developing countries) and then, at the next stage, compare all the related circumstances for the location of their plants, i.e language, infrastructure, labour, etc.

Table 8.34 The important factors which caused the rejection of alternative locations in other countries (Korea)   (%)

Factors	Numbers
Total	161 (100)
Low productivity of labour	31 (19.3)
Lack of workforce available	19 (11.8)
Insufficient industrial land and premises	16 (9.9)
High wage level	15 (9.3)
Unfamiliar language	13 (8.1)
Inconvenient transport	11 (6.8)
Far from big market	10 (6.2)
Lack of manufacturing suppliers or subcontractors	9 (5.6)
Lack of regional assistance	9 (5.6)
High rate of crime	6 (3.7)
Lack of promotional activities of local authorities	4 (2.5)
Lack of 'greenness' or amenities in the area	4 (2.5)
Others	14 (8.7)

Respondents mentioned more than one factor.

In short, the characteristics of the locational decision pattern of Japanese companies among various countries, i.e. the choice between market and labour at the first stage and then between individual location factors at the next, seems to be confirmed in this table once again.

Alternative locations in Korea

The managers were asked about alternative areas in Korea which were considered before choosing the present site and the results are summarised in the following table. Similarly to the British case, the Dos which provided larger proportions of the alternative locations than others are those prosperous areas which already have attracted many Japanese companies to their areas, e.g. Seoul, Kyongsangnam-Do and Kyonggi-Do. The proportion of these three areas reaches to around a half of the total alternative locations considered and discarded.

In particular, the popularity of Kyonggi-Do area is worth considering. As discussed in Chapter four, a large part of Kyonggi-Do region is included in the Seoul metropolitan region (MPR) and, thus, many Japanese companies have sought for their sites here to enjoy the advantages of this region such as its

Table 8.35 Relationship between the rejected alternative countries and unfavourable locational factors (Korea)*   (%)

Countries	Total	Productivity	Workforce	Wage	Land	Language	Transport
Total	230(100)⁺	72(31.3)	40(17.4)	40(17.4)	39(17.0)	20(8.7)	19(8.3)
Malaysia	50(100)	17(34.0)	9(18.0)	8(16.0)	6(12.0)	6(12.0)	4(8.0)
Thailand	44(100)⁺	13(29.5)	7(15.9)	5(11.4)	7(15.9)	6(13.6)	6(13.6)
Taiwan	47(100)⁺	11(23.4)	10(21.3)	8(17.0)	9(19.1)	4(8.5)	5(10.6)
Singapore	22(100)⁺	7(31.8)	5(22.7)	5(22.7)	3(13.6)	1(4.5)	1(4.5)
Hong Kong	6(100)	1(16.7)	2(33.3)	1(16.7)	2(33.3)	0(0.0)	0(0.0)
Other Asia	7(100)	4(57.1)	0(0.0)	1(14.3)	1(14.3)	0(0.0)	1(14.3)
Mexico	12(100)	2(16.7)	4(33.3)	3(25.0)	3(25.0)	0(0.0)	0(0.0)
Brazil	9(100)⁺	4(44.4)	2(22.2)	2(22.2)	1(11.1)	0(0.0)	0(0.0)
US	17(100)⁺	5(29.4)	1(5.9)	3(17.6)	4(23.5)	3(17.6)	1(5.9)
Germany	5(100)	3(60.0)	0(0.0)	1(20.0)	1(20.0)	0(0.0)	0(0.0)
UK	6(100)⁺	3(50.0)	0(0.0)	1(16.7)	1(16.7)	0(0.0)	1(16.7)
Spain	5(100)	2(40.0)	0(0.0)	2(40.0)	1(20.0)	0(0.0)	0(0.0)

(Note) . Productivity : low productivity of labour
        . Workforce : lack of workforce availability
        . Wage : high wage levels
        . Land : insufficient industrial land and premises
        . Transport : inconvenient transport
        . Language : unfamiliar language
⁺ By rounding errors, the sums of these columns are not exactly 100.
* Other minor factors except these six important locational factors included in these table are ignored from the consideration.

proximity to a big market, convenient transportation, etc.

However, this area is already congested with newly arriving population and industry from non-prosperous regions. To confront the problem of over-concentration in Seoul and this region the Korean government is strengthening the control to restrict the establishment of new factories in Kyonggi-Do as well as in Seoul. Therefore, the highest position of the two regions, Kyonggi-Do and Seoul, in the list of alternative locations which were not taken, is thought to be due to the expansion of the existing problems in Korean geography.

In brief, the traditional concentration problem in Korean geography is exhibited once again in this table. On the other hand, the main unsatisfactory factors in alternative areas are manifested in Table 8.37. This table is almost similar to the Table 8.26, which lists the attractive factors in the present locations. This means that the rejection of alternative areas and the choice of the present location have been made under the same criterion centring on industrial land and premises, transportation and a favourable labour force.

One thing to be noted is that this table is also similar to Table 8.19, which represents the unfavourable factors in alternative regions in the UK. This implies that there is a kind of necessary condition for a region in the UK and in Korea alike in order not to be rejected as a location by Japanese companies. This is an interesting finding to help infer the forces by which the locational decisions of Japanese companies is accrued at the regional level.

The cross-tabulation between the rejected areas and the causes of the rejection is made in order to examine roughly the unfavourable factors of alternative areas as shown in Table 8.38. Each region has its own proportion of each unsatisfactory locational factors, and it is possible to compare different problems in different regions.

In this table, Kyonggi-Do and Inchon are found to have suffered most significantly from the lack of industrial land and premises. As mentioned above, Kyonggi-Do and Inchon are largely included in the Seoul MPR and share the problem of over-concentration of industry and population with Seoul. Kyonggi-Do is also experiencing the problem of high militancy of labour.

Table 8.36 Alternative areas considered in Korea (%)

Dos	Numbers
Total	178(100)
Kyonggi-Do	36(20.2)
Seoul	27(15.2)
Kyongsangnam-Do	26(14.6)
Chungchongnam-Do	14(7.9)
Inchon	13(7.3)
Pusan	12(6.7)
Kyongsangbuk-Do	12(6.7)
Taegu	8(4.5)
Chollanam-Do	7(4.0)
Kangwon-Do	3(1.7)
Chollabuk-Do	3(1.7)
Chungchongbuk-Do	2(1.1)
Cheju-Do	0(0.0)
None	15(8.4)

Respondents mentioned more than one alternative areas.

Seoul and Kyongsangnam-Do, the two prosperous areas, are alike in experiencing high wage levels and high militancy of labour. This seems to be natural considering the highly concentrated industry and population in these areas. Pusan is rejected mainly for high wage levels, while Chungchongnam-Do is rejected for its low productivity of labour.

Table 8.37 The important factors which caused the rejection of alternative areas in Korea   (%)

Unfavourable factors	Number of responses
Total	136 (100)
Insufficient industrial land and premises	28 (20.6)
Inconvenient transport	18 (13.2)
Lack of workforce available	18 (13.2)
High wage level	10 (7.4)
Low productivity of labour	9 (6.6)
High militancy of labour	7 (5.1)
Insufficient houses for workers	6 (4.4)
Lack of regional assistance	6 (4.4)
Lack of promotional activities of local authorities	5 (3.7)
Lack of 'greenness' and amenities in the area	5 (3.7)
Far from big market	5 (3.7)
Other	19 (14.0)

Respondents mentioned more than one factor.

Overall, it is striking to find that Japanese companies, which are located outside the two prosperous regions, also have been looking for their alternative locations within prosperous areas following their compatriot companies.

8.2.3 Summary of the findings

Various aspects have been found from the examination of locational patterns and causes already. Through these findings, the main features of the locational behaviour of Japanese companies in Korea can be summarised as follows.

First of all, the main market for the Japanese companies operating in Korea is the consumer market in Korea and in overseas countries rather than main manufacturers. And the importance of the Korean market is growing in the latter part of 1980s compared to the earlier years. This is thought to be closely related to the lack of large scale manufacturers to which small component manufacturers can supply their products. In brief, the Japanese companies in Korea are mainly small manufacturers producing final consumer goods.

Table 8.38 Relationship between the rejected areas and unfavoured locational factors (Korea)*   (%)

Dos	Total	Land	Transport	Workforce	Productivity	Wage	Militancy
Total	183(100)	57(31.1)	40(21.9)	37(20.2)	21(11.5)	18(9.8)	10(5.5)
Kyonggi-Do	43(100)	14(32.6)	8(18.6)	9(20.9)	5(11.6)	4(9.3)	3(7.3)
Seoul	32(100)[+]	9(28.1)	6(18.8)	7(21.9)	4(12.5)	4(12.5)	2(6.3)
Kyongsangnam-Do	28(100)	8(28.6)	5(17.9)	6(21.4)	2(7.1)	4(14.3)	3(10.7)
Pusan	20(100)	5(25.0)	5(25.0)	4(20.0)	2(10.0)	3(15.0)	1(5.0)
Inchon	15(100)	6(40.0)	3(20.0)	3(20.0)	1(6.7)	2(13.3)	0(0.0)
Kyongsangbuk-Do	12(100)	5(41.7)	3(25.0)	2(16.7)	1(8.3)	0(0.0)	1(8.3)
Taegu	12(100)	4(33.3)	2(16.7)	4(33.3)	2(16.7)	0(0.0)	0(0.0)
Chungchongnam-Do	12(100)	4(33.3)	5(41.7)	0(0.0)	3(25.0)	0(0.0)	0(0.0)
Chollanam-Do	9(100)[+]	2(22.2)	3(33.3)	2(22.2)	1(11.1)	1(11.1)	0(0.0)

(Note) . Land : insufficient industrial land and premises
    . Transport : inconvenient transport
    . Workforce : lack of workforce availability
    . Productivity : low productivity of labour
    . Wage : high wage levels
    . Militancy : high militancy of labour
[+] Due to rounding errors, the actual sum of these rows are not 100.
* Other minor factors except these six important locational factors included in these table are ignored from the consideration.

Secondly, among the attractive locational factors, the factors related to labour supply were found to be the crucially important locational factors for the Japanese companies in Korea. Abundant workforce availability, low wage levels and high labour productivity all took the highest positions in the list of attractive locational factors. However, these factors were not so predominant in the regression results in the previous chapter, even though the labour factor was proved relatively influential. This seems to be caused by the evenly high correlation coefficients of each variable including the labour factor with dependent variables. The survey results in this chapter show definitely that a low-cost and highly productive workforce has played a decisive role in the location of Japanese companies in Korea.

An interesting finding concerning this labour factor is that, in contrast to the diminishing emphasis of Japanese companies on this factor, complaints about this factor, including both high wage levels and high militancy of labour, are conversely growing. At the same time, the availability of industrial land and premises and convenient transport were proved to be another two important locational factors in Korea. However, the presence of Japanese companies were not indicated as an important locating factor in contrast to the regression results.

This can be said to be caused by the concentration of Japanese companies in the two prosperous regions and, therefore, the high correlation coefficient between these two resulting from the concentration rather than from the direct influence of the existing companies upon the newcomers.

Thirdly, regarding government assistance, the managers in the Japanese companies in Korea responded, surprisingly enough, that government assistance was substantial and that the main measures of assistance were advice and the provision of industrial land and premises. The role of financial aid was said to be minimal. However, considering the sharply worsening appraisal of the government assistance among those arriving recently, it seems possible to estimate that the development of industrial estates by the Korean government for economic development and provision of these sites to Japanese companies mainly in the 1970s brought about this good assessment of the role of government assistance by Japanese companies, especially by those arriving in the earlier stage of economic development.

Fourthly, like the Japanese companies in the UK, those in Korea also searched for their locations among the neighbouring developing countries rather than comparing locations both in developed and in developing countries. This is further evidence showing the locational pattern of Japanese companies following the global managerial strategy characterised by the determination of destination at an earlier stage of location decisions and, then, close scrutiny among the locations in either the neighbouring developing or developed countries. The abundance of low-cost and highly productive labour and the availability of industrial land and premises were found to be the main reasons leading these companies to choose Korea and to reject other countries.

And, fifthly, the examination of alternative locations in Korea confirms the preference of Japanese companies for locating in the two prosperous regions, Seoul and Kyongsangnam-Do, and further in Kyonggi-Do (and to a degree in Pusan), and the importance of the three locational factors, i.e. favourable labour force, industrial land and premises and convenient transportation.

In conclusion, from the examination of the responses of the managers, it seems certain that Korea was chosen among developing countries mainly due to low-cost and highly productive labour and industrial estates at the initial stage of location decisions and that the two prosperous regions in Korea were highly preferred to other regions under similar criteria.

In aggregate, the previous argument, that the locations of Japanese subsidiaries are decided initially, at the worldwide level, by the aim of cultivating a targeted market under the framework of the global strategy and, then, by the scrutiny of various locational factors at regional level, maintains its validity in this Korean case analysis.

8.3 Comparison between the Two Countries

Up until now the responses of the managers of Japanese companies operating in the two host countries, the UK and Korea, have been examined separately. The rest of this chapter is allocated to identifying the general features of the locational behaviour of Japanese MNCs by clarifying the similarities and differences in the location decisions between the two host countries. For this purpose, a table consisting of the items which were proved important by the respondents is constructed (Table 8.39).

This table is insufficient to reveal all the sophisticated features of the empirical evidence which were discussed in this chapter. Nonetheless, by reference to the listed findings in this table, the examination of the similarities and differences of the location decisions in the two host countries becomes feasible.

8.3.1 Similarities and differences of the location decisions in the two host countries

Similarities

Through the examination of questionnaire and interview answers, some similarities in the location decisions in the two countries can be extracted.

Firstly, sufficient industrial land and premises played an important role in the location of Japanese companies in the two countries. The importance of this factor was indicated in the responses of attractive locational factors in the present location and of the main government assistance given.

In this regard, the emphasis of the Korean government on this factor seems to be justified, even though this measure has been used mainly for the purpose of national economic development policy rather than regional assistance (see 4.2.2.1 and 8.2.2.4). At the same time, convenient transport was also found to be significant in the location of Japanese companies even in developed countries like the UK. From this finding, it seems possible to mention that these factors are necessary, if not sufficient, conditions for the location of Japanese companies. On the other hand, familiar language was listed as one of the most important locational factors in both countries due to the fact that English is taught as the second language in Japan and that Korea and Japan are closely connected historically including in language.

Secondly, concerning the role of government assistance, the managers of Japanese companies in the two countries alike assessed this assistance as having a 'substantial' influence. This implies that the promotional activities of central and local government can produce a remarkable success in attracting Japanese companies into certain areas, especially in the case of Korea. The finding that the advice of central government or local authorities as a form of assistance took one of the highest positions in both countries supports this assertion.

Table 8.39 The comparison of main survey findings in the two host countries

Questions	U K	Korea
Main market	1) Main manufacturers in this or adjacent country 2) Foreign consumer market 3) Local consumer market	1) Local consumer market 2) Main manufacturers in this or adjacent country 3) Foreign consumer market
Push factors	1) Trade barriers of other countries 2) High rate of the yen 3) Lack of big markets in Japan	1) Labour shortage in Japan 2) High wage level compared to other countries 3) High rate of the yen
Attractive locational factor	1) Closeness to a big market 2) Familiar language 3) Sufficient industrial land and premises	1) Abundant workforce available 2) Low wage level 3) Sufficient industrial land and premises
Unsatisfactory locational factors	1) Lack of manufacturing suppliers or subcontractors 2) High wage level 3) High rate of crime	1) Inconvenient transport 2) Lack of workforce available 3) High militancy of labour
Influence of government assistance	1) Very substantial 6.5% 2) Substantial 22.6% 3) Moderate 24.2% 4) Minimal 41.9% 5) No answer 4.8%	1) Very substantial 18.9% 2) Substantial 11.3% 3) Moderate 20.8% 4) Minimal 41.5% 5) No answer 7.5%
Measures of government assistance	1) Financial aid 2) Advice 3) Land and premises	1) Advice 2) Land and premises 3) Speed of decision
Alternative locations	1) Germany 18.4% 2) Spain 14.6% 3) France 13.6% 4) US 7.8% 5) Singapore 4.9%	1) Taiwan 17.2% 2) Thailand 15.3% 3) Malaysia 14.8% 4) Singapore 7.7% 5) US 7.7%
Causes of rejection	1) Unfamiliar language 2) High wage level 3) Lack of workforce available	1) Low productivity of labour 2) Lack of workforce available 3) Insufficient industrial land and premises

Thirdly, among the factors which caused the rejection of alternative countries, those related to labour supply were found to be highly important. Even though the emphasis of Japanese companies on the labour factor has been less strong in the case of the UK compared to that of Korea, the labour factor, including wage levels, workforce available, militancy, etc. was proved to be non-negligible in either country to location choice.

And, finally, the choice of these two countries was made at the earlier stage of the location decision rather than after comparing all the possible alternative locations all over the world. The totally different alternative countries considered by the Japanese companies in the two countries make this assertion possible. This is thought to be caused by the fact that the circumstances, or resources, of these countries which will be exploited, such as market potentiality or low-cost labour, are obvious from the beginning. The global strategy of Japanese companies in placing their subsidiaries all over the world seems to come closer into sight through this finding.

Differences

Although a set of similarities can be found and discussed as above, differences rather than similarities are predominant in the locational pattern of Japanese companies in the two countries.

Firstly, while the largest share of the Japanese companies operating in the UK aim to supply their products to main manufacturers in this or adjacent countries, those in Korea aim to supply the local consumer market first. The proportion of the companies supplying their products in local and foreign consumer market is 50.7% (UK) and 66.9% (Korea) each. The dominant role of the consumer market in Korea is thought to result from the lack of major Japanese manufacturers in the country, e.g. Toyota, Nissan, Sony, NEC, etc., and, thus, no need to establish component manufacturers there.

Secondly, the market factor including the trade barriers of other countries and the lack of a big market in Japan played the pivotal role for the Japanese companies operating in the UK to make these companies invest outside their own territory, while the issues related to labour dominated those operating in Korea. This finding shows that Japanese companies invest in overseas countries to make use of, or exploit, the politico-economic circumstances in the targeted countries.

Thirdly, as a natural consequence of the above finding, Japanese companies emphasised factors related to the market in the UK, while those in Korea emphasised the importance of the factors related to labour for location decisions. The overriding importance of the labour factor in Korea for Japanese companies is proved once again by the increasing complaint among these companies in parallel with the growing wage level and militant activities of labour in Korea.

Fourthly, there is a significant difference in the types of government assistance given to Japanese companies. While financial assistance was remembered as the most important measure for the Japanese companies arriving in the UK, advice and the provision of industrial land and premises were among those in Korea. With regard to this, the growing complaints about the government assistance in Korea among Japanese companies and, more profoundly, the aggravating regional problems reflect the necessity to diversify policy measures, including financial assistance, to make regional policy work better.

And, fifthly, a significant difference exists in the alternative countries considered. The Japanese companies operating in the UK looked for their sites mainly among European countries, while those in Korea made comparison predominantly among Asian developing countries. This is thought to show the earlier decision as to destination within the framework of the MNCs' global strategy, as discussed above.

8.3.2 Conclusion

As expounded above, a number of similarities and differences can be found in the locational pattern of Japanese companies in the two host countries through the examination of survey answers. However, there is a kind of consistency in these various findings. This is that a Japanese company which decides to invest in overseas countries tends to behave according to a pre-determined rule of action.

All the location decision procedure such as the recognition of some push factors in Japan, the choice of a country among alternative countries, the decision as to which region among alternative locations through the comparison of locational factors including government assistance were consistent showing the clear-cut contrast between developed countries represented by the UK and developing countries like Korea. Therefore, it seems valid to argue that the locational behaviour of Japanese companies all over the world is determined and undertaken within the framework made by the global strategy of these internationalising, and already internationalised, companies.

Based on the findings in this chapter and the previous two chapters, the next part explores the implication of the locational behaviour of Japanese companies for government regional policy. First of all, the next chapter incorporates the findings, or empirical evidence, shown in this and the two previous chapters and attempts to interpret the results. The policy implication is discussed in chapter eleven and the conclusion will follow in the last chapter.

9 The interpretation of the empirical evidence within the context of a worldwide managerial strategy

9.1 Introduction

The previous three chapters have portrayed the geographical features of Japanese MNCs in the two host countries and have identified the specific factors which have been shown to influence substantially the actual location decisions of these companies.

A question needs to be answered clearly through, or in relation to, this empirical evidence: what is the exact relationship between the regional policy of the host government and the actual location choices of Japanese companies? This question comprises two contradictory aspects: the first is that of how far the Japanese companies are influenced by the host government's regional policy in making their locational decisions, and the second is the reverse of this, that of what the implications of the locational pattern of these Japanese companies are for the host government's policy.

The former can be approached by examining the changing context of regional policy and the response of the Japanese companies to these changes as reflected in their locational behaviour in the two host countries. The latter, by contrast, needs the exploration of the policy alternatives which should be considered by the host governments in order to encourage the activities of Japanese companies with the hope, eventually, of alleviating regional problems through the increased operations of these Japanese companies. (This assumes, of course, in each case, that Japanese inward investment is welcome for this or other reasons[1].) In considering these two aspects, however, it seems necessary to reconsider the nature and the global strategy of Japanese MNCs in general before hand[2]. This is because the managerial strategy of Japanese companies is thought to have dominated the explicit locational behaviour of the companies so far and likely as well to determine the future activities of these companies[3].

Therefore, this chapter delves into this issue first. Of course it is unlikely that the findings in a geographical analysis can expound thoroughly on the managerial aspects or the global strategy of these companies. Sometimes moreover locational decisions are made outside the existing managerial concept and thinking. However, despite this limitation, it is necessary to examine the managerial aspects of Japanese companies as the basis for understanding the motives of their specific geographical decisions more clearly as mentioned above and, thus, an attempt will be made here to interpret the empirical evidence from the viewpoint of the worldwide managerial strategy of Japanese concerns. On the other hand, conversely, it can be said that the managerial strategy of these companies at the worldwide level is explored by scrutinizing the empirical evidence in the two representative host countries.

9.2 The Main Findings of the Empirical Analyses

First of all, in this section, the main findings in the three empirical analyses (from chapter seven to chapter nine) are summarised in turn. (The main findings from the empirical analyses can be summarised as in Table 9.1.) During the process, another regression result produced formerly by using the same method, but with fewer variables and a shorter time span of analysis, will be introduced (9.2.2) and compared with the new regression results described in chapter eight. This effort is made in order to explore more clearly the changes in the geographical context of the two host countries and the responses of Japanese companies during the late 1980s[4].

9.2.1 The main findings from the descriptive analysis

The examination of the geographical distribution of Japanese companies in the two host countries using descriptive statistics manifested some distinguishing features.

Firstly, as the most significant difference in the geographical distribution of Japanese companies in the two host countries, Japanese companies are scattered widely across the whole country in Britain, whereas those in Korea are heavily concentrated in the two prosperous regions, Seoul and Kyongsangnam-Do.

Secondly, as an historical trend at the national level, the arrival of Japanese companies in Britain has been steadily accelerating, while that in Korea can be named as indicating either a cyclical increase or a stagnating stage. At the regional level, Japanese companies in Britain have preferred the non-

239

prosperous and less congested areas, while those in Korea have maintained the tendency of concentration in developed areas.

Table 9.1 Comparison of the main findings from the empirical analyses

Classification	Britain	Korea
[Descriptive analysis]		
1. Historical trend	Steadily increasing in numbers	Cyclical increase or stagnating stage
2. Geographical distribution	Widely dispersed between regions	Heavily concentrated
3. Ownership	100% ownership in	Mainly joint the main ventures
4. Size		Large Small
5. Industrial field	More in electronics	More diversified
[Regression analysis]		
1. Key locational factors	Presence of Japanese	Ditto companies Supply of labour
2. Role of public policy	Important role	Minimal role
3. Main variables of labour supply	A large number of unemployed and labour non-militancy	Abundance of highly skilled labour
4. Consideration of location factors	A wide range of factors	Largely dominated by polarisation
[Survey analysis]		
1. Choice of the host country	At an earlier stage of decision making	Ditto
2. Main market	Other main manufacturers	Customer markets in Korea and other countries
3. Main push factors	Market factors	Low cost labour
4. Alternative countries	Neighbouring European countries	Neighbouring Asian countries
5. Government assistance measures	Financial aid and advice	Advice, industrial land and premises

Thirdly, most of the Japanese companies in Britain are owned wholly by the parent companies in Japan in contrast to those in Korea which are established mainly as joint ventures.

Fourthly, in terms of size, Japanese companies in Britain are three or four times larger than those operating in Korea. And, small companies in both countries tend to be more concentrated in the prosperous regions than the large ones.

And, fifthly, the companies operating in the field of electronics take a larger share of the total Japanese companies in Britain than in Korea.

In short, the geographical distribution of Japanese companies in Britain is distinguished by the characteristics of a wider dispersion, a sharper increase in numbers, a predominance of whole ownership, and being larger in size and with more weight of electronics companies than is the case in Korea.

9.2.2 Main findings from the regression analysis

Here, as discussed above, the previous regression result, which was presented in 1988, is examined first and, then, compared with the new regression results.

9.2.2.1 The findings in the previous regression analysis

The previous regression analysis consisted of static and change analysis and index analysis. This analysis was undertaken with four dependent and fifty-six independent variables for Britain and four dependent and fifty-seven independent variables for Korea (Han,1988). The time span of the analysis was 1981-1987 in the British case and 1981-1986 in the Korean case. Except for these differences, the other analytical methods were the same as in the new analysis described in chapter six and chapter eight.

Regression results for Britain

The major findings of the previous regression analysis for the British case were: Firstly, through the static and change analysis, it was found that the locational behaviour of Japanese companies was highly correlated with 1) the supply of labour, in particular with its non-militancy; 2) the eligibility of the area for regional assistance; and 3) the existence of leading Japanese companies, either in the manufacturing sector or in other sectors, already operating in the area.

And, secondly, the index analysis showed that labour supply was the most important geographical factor followed by public policy and linkages.

In aggregate, labour supply represented by the non-militancy of labour, regional assistance and the presence of leading Japanese companies were found to be the most influential locational factors for Japanese companies in the UK.

Regression results for Korea

By contrast, the major findings for the Korean case were: Firstly, the static and change analysis threw up accessibility to highly skilled labour, as reflected in the supply of training facilities, as the crucial factor for the location of Japanese companies in Korea and the availability of industrial estates and the existence of leading Japanese companies as the second and the third.

And, secondly, in the index analysis, it was found that availability of land and premises was the most important locational factor and, after that, labour supply and the linkage factor followed.

In short, the number of training facilities representing skilled labour supply, the availability of industrial land and premises and the presence of Japanese companies proved to be the critical factors for the location of Japanese companies in Korea.

Comparison between the two countries

The above results demonstrated that the two host countries had in common the most important locational factors at a wider level, namely the supply of labour, government assistance and the existence of Japanese companies in the area.

However, the similarities at a wider level contain some differences in detailed aspects. These differences are: 1) in Britain, the non-militancy of labour was the most influential locational factor, while the abundance of skilled labour was the most significant in Korea; 2) Japanese companies in Britain were found to be more concerned about the existence in the location of leading Japanese companies, whereas those in Korea were highly correlated with the abundance of manufacturing suppliers; and 3) differently from those in Britain, the Japanese companies in Korea tended to be more subject to a limited number of specific locational factors.

9.2.2.2   The findings from the new regression analysis

The new regression analysis comprised three kinds of regressions; namely static and change analysis, index analysis and sub-period analysis. The time span of the first two regressions was 1981-1990 and those for the sub-period analysis were 1981-1986 and 1987-1990. The dependent and independent variables are the same as those of the previous analysis except for the increase of independent variables, i.e. the addition of five variables in the British case and eight in the Korean case respectively. The regression results for the two countries can be summarised by these two features, similarities and differences.

Firstly, the most significant feature showing the similarities between the two host countries is the key role played by the two locational factors, i.e. the presence of Japanese companies and the supply of labour.

And, secondly, the main differences between the two countries are: 1) that public policy is one of the important locational factors in Britain compared to having a minimal role in the case of Korea; 2) that, among the variables forming labour supply, a large number of unemployed and labour non-militancy are found to be most significant in Britain, while the abundance of labour, coupled with highly skilled labour, seems to be the most influential in Korea, even though this gap is getting narrower; 3) that, in contrast to the Japanese companies coming to Britain, which take into account a wide range of locational factors, those in Korea tend to be ruled by the dominant Korean geography, i.e. centralisation and polarisation, that is to say, concentration in Seoul and Kyongsangnam-Do (including Pusan) regions.

9.2.2.3 Comparison and comment

By comparing and incorporating these regression results, a group of important locational factors and the changes in the relative importance of these factors are made manifest[5].

The first thing which should be mentioned is that two locating factors, the presence of leading Japanese companies and labour supply, have played the central role consistently in the location of Japanese companies in the two countries. However, the importance of the features, or variables, comprising these two variables has been far from consistent. In Britain, the non-militancy of labour and its productivity were emphasized by the Japanese companies arriving in the earlier period, while the distaste for the areas with high unemployment rates became noticeable among the companies arriving more recently. This is thought to reflect the transition in the kind of labour necessary for Japanese companies from non-militant to highly-skilled, competent labour. It may also indicate the reduction in labour militancy throughout Britain in the 1980s enforced by unemployment and Thatcherite anti-trade union legislation.

By contrast, in Korea, the accent of Japanese companies has changed from being on highly-skilled labour to the availability of abundant labour. Another change is the shift in the linkage factor emphasised from the local availability of manufacturing firms to the more specific presence of Japanese companies. These changes demonstrate the narrowing gap between the two countries in terms of the influential locational factors for Japanese companies and the changing geographical context in the two countries.

On the other hand, the role of government assistance has been the most distinguishing aspect which shows a sharp contrast in the two host countries. Government assistance has always been one of the crucial factors for the location of Japanese companies in Britain, while its role has been minimal and reflected only a little in the availability of industrial land and premises in the case of Korea. However, a kind of change has also been occurring in this respect. In Britain, the main instrument of government assistance has been transferred from central government financial aid to companies to more general public expenditure for economic development and promotional activity. In Korea, by contrast, the meek influence of government assistance has been further eroded by the diminishing role of government in providing industrial estates.

Overall, although the presence of Japanese companies and labour supply played a central role in the location decisions of Japanese companies in both host countries, some substantial differences and changes over time caused by the different geographical context in these countries were revealed in these previous and new regression analyses.

9.2.3 The main findings from the survey analysis

The main findings from the survey analysis in the two host countries can also be examined by looking at the similarities and differences between the two.

Similarities

Firstly, sufficient industrial land and premises were important for Japanese companies in both countries.

Secondly, the assessments of the managers in the two countries about the government assistance were the same that its role was 'substantial'.

Thirdly, the factors relating to labour supply were similarly important for the location of Japanese companies in the two countries, albeit its importance is more essential in the case of Korea.

And, fourthly, location in both these countries has been chosen at an earlier stage in location decision making in these companies for the placement of subsidiaries. These two countries tended in each case to be the MNC's first and, often, only choice. And the alternatives considered were limited to the neighbouring developed or developing countries in both cases too.

Differences

Firstly, the main market for the Japanese companies in Britain was other main manufacturers in contrast to those in Korea, where it was the consumer market in Korea and overseas countries.

Secondly, the market factor was found to be crucial both for the outward movement and for the location decision of Japanese companies in Britain, while the factors relating to low-cost labour were central for those in Korea.

Thirdly, as a natural consequence of the targeting on specific markets, the alternative countries considered as locations by the Japanese companies in Britain were concentrated in European countries, while those in Korea have been mainly Asian developing countries.

And, fourthly, the primary assistance measure provided for those coming into Britain has been financial aid, while that in Korea was industrial land and premises.

9.2.4 Summary of the findings

From the above findings from the empirical analyses, some of which are complementary to each other and some in contrast, a consolidated picture of the empirical evidence can be drawn.

Firstly, as to the spatial distribution of the companies, the empirical evidence has shown that the Japanese companies in Britain are more evenly distributed spatially, larger in size, more biased towards the electronics industry and on an sharply increasing, rather than a diminishing or a stagnating, trend in numbers arriving compared to those in Korea.

Secondly, regarding the influential locational factors at regional level, it has been found in the regression analysis that labour supply, especially the non-militancy and competence of labour, government policy conducive to the investment of Japanese firms in the form of financial aid and public expenditure and the presence of operating Japanese companies in the host area are the salient locational factors which have been considered by the Japanese companies coming into Britain. In contrast, the availability of abundant skilled labour, the number of Japanese and indigenous manufacturing firms and the extent of industrial estates in which all kinds of government assistance has been available, even though its importance has been diminishing, have been influential in the case of Korea.

And, thirdly, the views of the managers through the questionnaire and interview survey have clarified the fact that the Japanese companies in Britain are aiming mainly to supply products to other main manufacturers, have been motivated to invest overseas and to locate in this country by the market factor within the framework of their parent's global strategy, have substantially benefitted from the financial aid of the British government and have considered a limited number of alternative countries in Europe. In contrast, those in Korea are targeting the consumer market in Korea and foreign countries, have been influenced crucially by the availability of low-cost and highly-skilled labour, have received advice and sites on industrial estates from the Korean government and have searched for alternative locations in Asian developing countries.

From these findings, it is possible to conclude that the important geographical factors which have influence on the locational decisions of Japanese companies in the two host countries are closely related to the overall geographical context of each of the host countries, and that the Japanese companies adopt different policies according to the different existing circumstances in the two host countries in making their locational decisions. In other words, they choose those places where the overall locational environments are substantially more advantageous rather than other areas while also comparing various kinds of geographical factors across many possible areas.

9.3 The Locational Behaviour of Japanese Multinational Companies in Terms of Their Managerial Strategy

9.3.1 The worldwide managerial strategy of Japanese MNCs

9.3.1.1 The changing foreign activities of Japanese capital

As expounded in chapter three, the overseas activities of Japanese manufacturing companies have intensified in number and scale during the last decade. In particular, the mid-1980s witnessed the sharp acceleration of this trend. With the advent of this new economic power in the field of international investment, various views about the nature of Japanese management have been formulated, especially in relation to its managerial advantages. In some developed countries, the applicability of Japanese-style management to their own industry has been studied fervently. However, as stressed in chapter two (1.3.3), without a sufficient preparatory consideration of the nature of Japanese companies and of their broad strategies, this approach bears a danger of overlooking both the unique features of Japanese-style management (Briggs,1988,pp.24-29) and the undesirable consequences which have been experienced by its practice in neighbouring countries (Lubis,1985,p.28).

It is difficult to describe the nature of Japanese capital definitively in a limited space. Nonetheless, in brief, Japanese capital, particularly in the post-war era, can be characterized as reflecting the integration of industry with banking groups under the auspices of the government (Yoshida,1987,p.7; Ackroyd et al.,1988,p.13; Glasmeier and Sugiura,1991,pp.396-401; above 1.4.1). Being collectivistic in nature, or consensus-orientated in euphony, Japanese companies have shown a kind of unified managerial strategy, most of which has been largely consistent with the government industrial policy (Trevor,1983,p.xvi and 1987,p.10; Dicken,1988,pp.641-644; Okimoto,1989, p.226; James,1989, p.3; Billet,1990,p.13)[6]. As a writer properly put it:

> "The rise of [Japanese] companies was due partly to a particularly Japanese style of production organization; not flexible specialization but a highly organized version of mass production which rested upon a precisely defined role for the Japanese state" (Sadler,1992,p.253).

Therefore, it is impossible to understand fully their managerial strategy without taking into account the priority given to the national interest ahead of the profit of private concerns that holds sway in Japanese life. The activities of Japanese companies all over the world, operating according to their global strategy, can also be understood in this context[7].

Regardless of the extent to which government policy is involved, it seems certain that Japanese companies have a well designed and organized worldwide managerial strategy that has determined the destination and the characteristics of Japanese FDI. Today, the worldwide activities of Japanese capital based on their managerial strategy is being materialized under the banner of *globalisation*[8]. Specifically, the recent globalisation of Japanese companies is said to be being pursued: 1) to mitigate the future impact of exchange rate fluctuations; 2) to avoid possible trade frictions; 3) to complement Japanese export decline; and 4) to specialise the function of each subsidiary and, therefore, to maximise the company's aggregated product (Industrial Bank of Japan [IBJ],1989,p.19). A writer depicts the worldwide activities of Japanese companies as follows:

"By coupling their increasing standardized products to meet growing convergencies in consumer preferences with global sourcing, manufacturing and shipping systems, Japanese firms were able to move gradually towards integrating their core activities - production, finance, technology, management, human resources and marketing - into a global network" (James,1989,p.97).

However, the actual forms and destinations of the FDI based on this global strategy vary according to the circumstances which each company confronts. For decades, for Japanese capital, Asian countries particularly have long been regarded both as markets and as resource suppliers which are convenient and indispensable for the national economic growth of Japan (Yoshihara, 1986,pp.83-110). In this regard, the recent upsurge of Japanese FDI in North America and Europe, including the UK, can be conceived of as a major change in the managerial strategy of Japanese companies and in Japanese government economic policy. Therefore, this changing pattern of Japanese FDI is worth scrutinizing to grasp the changing global strategy of Japanese companies more clearly.

9.3.1.2 From developing to developed country-orientated FDI

The classification of FDI according to its destination seems to be the most appropriate approach to explaining both the traditional global strategy of Japanese MNCs and the recent shift in the pattern of Japanese FDI all over the world (Dicken,1988, pp.646-650). In other words, assuming that FDI is classified into two kinds, namely developing country-orientated FDI and developed country-orientated FDI, it is apparent that the recent trend of Japanese FDI can be named as a shift of weight from the former to the latter at least to the end of 1980s (2.3.2.1)[9]. More specifically, the developed country-orientated FDI is characterised principally by the passiveness in its motive (see below), by the magnitude in its investment size and by the high level of its technology (KIET,1984,pp.43-46)[10].

Motive

First of all, Japanese FDI in these days has been motivated by the need to respond to the increasing trade barriers in developed countries rather than by the more positive objectives which caused the main stream of Japanese FDI in Asian countries. These positive objectives included expansion of profit or raw materials supply.

For a substantial period of time, the Japanese economy has depended for its maintenance and growth upon external trade with foreign countries; in other words, it has been an export- orientated economy. During the process, the necessity to utilize the cheap labour force and natural resources in neighbouring countries has been widely recognized[11]. As a result, they have been able to establish a well formed division of labour that includes these Asian countries.

In contrast, for the Japanese people, developed countries, such as the US and European countries, had been considered initially only as the markets for completed products rather than as either the providers of resources or the sites for production plants. This means that there was a sharp distinction between the production and marketing functions in Japanese industry, i.e. production occurred in Japan and in the neighbouring Asian countries on the one hand and marketing in the developed European countries and the US on the other.

However, what appeared to the West to be the over-success of Japan at the expense of the wealth of other developed countries brought about the huge trade deficits and de-industrialization in these countries. Hence, it has resulted in these trade barriers. Confronting this situation, the Japanese government and industry changed their industrial and managerial strategy to invest directly in the market countries (Dunning,1990a,p.209; Heitger and Stehn,1990,p.13)[12]. Therefore, contrary to the case of Japanese FDI in the Asian countries, that in developed countries these days is basically caused passively by this deteriorating circumstance in Japanese overseas markets (although a more positive motive has also been found in the investment of Japanese companies in these developed countries as described below).

In consequence, there has been a fundamental dissimilarity in the two kinds of FDIs. The Japanese FDI in the Asian developing countries has been aimed at obtaining access to cheap labour and natural resources and at improving the value-added and sophistication of the Japanese domestic economy and its industry by transferring low technology industry to these countries. The Japanese FDI in developed countries, in contrast, has been in

248

the main motivated deliberately to circumvent the growing trade barriers in these market countries (IBJ,1989,pp.16-18). This, it is apparent, entails a shift in the type of overseas investment from what may be called Japanese-style FDI to MNC-style FDI. This differs from the argument of Kojima which emphasizes the unique feature of Japanese FDIs in contrast to the usual MNC-style FDI of other developed countries (Kojima,1979,1986).

Size

Secondly, as well as differences in Japanese investment motivation between Asian and Western countries, the size of Japanese subsidiaries established in developed countries is considerably larger than those in developing countries (IBJ,1989,p.14). This fact became evident in the comparison between Korean and British experiences described in chapter seven. In the case of developing country-orientated FDI, most subsidiaries and their products have had no threatening competitors in the host countries, especially in terms of technology. Therefore, even though they begin to operate on a small scale, there has been no significant disadvantage in continuing to be small in terms of the management of production and marketing.

In addition, since these products are exported to other developed market countries, there has been no need to maintain a large firm size. This is because, with regard to the latter, traditionally, the exporting to, and marketing of, the products in developed countries have been undertaken by 'Sogo shosha' instead of by the manufacturing companies themselves (Franko,1983,p.64)[13]. For all these reasons, the small size of the Japanese subsidiary unit has remained feasible in developing countries like Korea.

By contrast, in developed country-orientated FDI, since the competition with indigenous manufacturers and other foreign firms is severe, a small size of investment is unsuitable. The high fixed cost caused by being a foreign concern coupled with the need to override the challenge of indigenous competitors remains as a burden for the subsidiary. Furthermore, unlike the Japanese companies in the Asian developing countries, those in developed countries tend to implement complex functions simultaneously from the design of new products to assembly (although Japanese companies have been criticized in that they have been too slow in implementing this integrated function even in developed countries). Therefore, the investment size of Japanese companies in developed countries has tended to be larger than that in developing countries. Even the investment size of the component manufacturers, which invest in developed countries in order to supply their products to the main Japanese customers there, has tended to be larger than that in developing countries.

Technological level

Thirdly, Japanese MNCs in developed countries are also differentiated from those in developing countries by their superiority in technology. In developing countries, the issue of technology has two facets. On the one hand, there is no doubt about the dominance of Japanese companies in technology. How and to what extent this excellent technology can be transferred to host country-owned businesses is the major issue of concern to these developing countries. Conversely, however, by combining with the cheap labour and resources of the host countries, Japanese products, even though they are made by low level technology in these countries, are still able to be more than competitive in the international market (Onida,1983,pp.149-154).

By contrast, in developed countries, where indigenous companies possess their own higher technology, the possession of more advanced technology than that of indigenous firms appears to be critical for the success of Japanese subsidiaries. Furthermore, Japanese companies are placed at a relative disadvantage in securing low cost labour and materials compared to indigenous competitors by their lack of local experience. In consequence, the Japanese subsidiaries in developed countries tend to equip themselves with higher technology than is the case of those in developing countries.

Organization, etc.

And, fourthly, on similar grounds, another kind of difference between the two is found in the type of division of function. In the case of Japanese companies operating in the developing countries, being export-orientated, the division of labour is decided by the process of production practised among Asian countries which is unlike that in developed countries including Britain. Those subsidiaries in developed countries tend to be managed more independently from headquarters and to show the division of labour appropriate to the specific, higher technology and complete products made.

One thing to be noted in the developed country-orientated FDIs is that the investment decisions involved are largely based on the popularity, or the marketability, of the products in the specific host country with this identified ordinarily through a feasibility survey. In other words, in investing directly in developed countries, Japanese companies have shown a tendency to place their plant sites in the market countries where their exported products have already dominated the market and this is done for the most part in order to minimize the risk of failure (KIET,1986,pp.43-44; Heitger and Stehn,1990,p.3; Dunning,1990b,p.169). This means that the location decisions of Japanese investments at the national level have substantially to do with the competitiveness of their products, or the possession of ownership advantages, as in Dunning's framework, in the market countries (Thomsen and Nicolaides,

1991,pp.39-44).

The above points can be said to be the main causes and features of the recent shift of Japanese FDI from developing country- orientated to developed country-orientated FDI and to bring out the main differences between the two FDIs. As reasoned earlier, Japanese manufacturing companies operating in Korea and those in Britain are considered respectively to be typical of these two kinds of FDI. For the Japanese companies coming into Korea, the relatively high skill level of the existing labour force in conjunction with the low wages in Korea have made the possibility of exporting the goods produced to developed countries world wide the main target as well as the seizure of the Korean market itself (KTA,1987,p.62). By contrast, Japanese companies in Britain have aimed specifically at the domination of British and EC markets from within. Exporting to countries other than EC member countries was seldom one of the main objectives of these companies (Morris, 1988,p.38).

In short, this changing pattern of Japanese FDI, i.e. from developing to developed-orientated FDI which encompasses the changes in management style, technology level and organizational structure, etc., represents the diverging global strategy of Japanese MNCs to exploit the given circumstances in the world economy to the maximum level[14].

However, it seems to be insufficient to explain the overall changes in the global strategy of Japanese MNCs simply in the context of the drastically changing world economy, which is often called 'post-Fordism' or 'disorganised capitalism' and is characterised by flexibility and diversification as described in chapter two. In other words, more flexible and diversified managerial strategies are in addition expected to be pursued by Japanese MNCs in order to mitigate unpredictable dangers in the turbulent world economy.

Trade barriers to the products of affiliates and rapid alteration of consumer taste in market countries and a sharp fluctuation in the host country economy are representative examples of change which could be overcome by adopting a more flexible global strategy. This is even more the case when taking into account the leading role of Japanese capital in introducing the forces of change, or innovation, in the world economy.

Therefore, in interpreting the empirical evidence mainly according to the above classification of the pattern of Japanese FDI, it must be envisaged that further efforts will be made in the meantime to find a more flexible managerial strategy by Japanese MNCs.

9.3.2 Interpretation of the empirical evidence in terms of this managerial strategy

Given the nature of Japanese FDI and the managerial strategy of Japanese companies described above, the concern of this analysis now turns to the issue of how far the findings of the descriptive, regression and survey analyses in the previous chapters correspond with this main Japanese managerial strategy.

Briefly speaking, most of these findings in the empirical analyses fit in with and support the worldwide managerial strategy of Japanese companies mentioned just above. This consistency between the empirical evidence presented in the previous chapters and worldwide managerial strategy of Japanese companies is explained in turn below.

In the first place, confronting the growing trade barriers of market countries, Japanese industry, which has long been accustomed to production under its own control either in its own country or in neighbouring low cost countries and to export to market countries, has begun to recognize the necessity of direct investment in the market countries. The answers made by the managers of the Japanese companies in this country explicitly showed that the trade barriers of market countries have been the dominant push factor for these companies (8.1.2.2).

Britain has been one of the major destinations of these Japanese investments seeking new manufacturing sites in developed countries. This success of Britain in attracting the Japanese companies is the result of a number of advantages such as the use of the English language, the favourable response of successive UK governments towards Japanese investments, the less competitive status of indigenous British industry and the attractiveness of well arranged regional incentives (Trevor,1987,p.13; Morris,1988,p.34), i.e. a combination of political, economic and cultural factors (Jones and North,1991, p.110). The findings of survey analysis in this study proved almost precisely the importance of these same factors, i.e. closeness to a big market, familiar language, sufficient industrial land and premises, government assistance, etc. for the attraction of Japanese companies in this country (8.1.2.3).

Therefore, it can be said that the growth of Japanese FDI in the UK these days has been affected more directly by the trade conflict of Japanese industry with developed countries rather than either by the rapid escalation of the yen or by the increasing cost of production in the previous sites in the home country or in neighbouring countries[15]. In short, the recent influx of Japanese manufacturing companies into the UK forms a part of their changed worldwide managerial strategy which attempts to circumvent the strengthening trade barriers of developed countries while maintaining the aim of profit maximization.

One thing which should be emphasized in addition to this argument is that the empirical evidence shown so far seems to suggest a step further in the development of the managerial strategy of these companies. As expounded in chapter nine (8.1.2.2), a large number of Japanese companies in this country have been found to be investing to capture European markets positively according to a globalisation strategy along with the passive reaction against the increasing trade barriers of these countries. At the same time, those in Korea have also begun to target the Korean market as well as the developed market countries (8.2.2.1). These changes seem to mark a significant readjustment of the worldwide managerial strategy of Japanese MNCs.

In other words, either the traditional strategy, which was characterised by the minimisation of production cost by using low-cost labour and materials in Asian countries [cost orientated] and the securing of the market for the sale of the products in the developed market countries, or the passive reaction to external circumstances by establishing their subsidiaries in the market countries to circumvent the trade barriers of these countries [market orientated], have begun to shift towards a new managerial strategy. This aims to capture the targeted market areas like the EC, east Asia, etc. by means of a quick response to the demand of consumers by localising manufacturing and supplying functions as near as possible to the market [globalisation orientated]. As two managers interviewed put it:

" There were no trade barriers from the EC countries. ... The EC market is strong [i.e. large enough and full of competition]. So we came here to build a customer market by designing and producing according to the customers' taste" (The manager in company B).

"The direct contact with customers is the most important to secure markets" (The manager in company F).

In short, the late 1980s witnessed the appearance of, say, 'an *international division of market* ' or '*the diversified MNC-style FDI*' in the managerial strategy of Japanese MNCs targeting specific markets within the framework of the global network[16]. The importance of Asian regional markets and national markets, along with the regional supply system, has also been accentuated in a recent study by the UN (1991) with the concepts of 'regional core networks' and 'regional insiders'. The study stated that:

" .. there is evidence that Japanese [MNCs] are building regionally-integrated, independently sustainable networks of overseas investments .." (p.42).

" While Japanese [MNCs] are still attracted to the developing Asian nations by low-cost labour, rapid demand growth in the region has increasingly been an important motive. ... Rationalized, export-oriented strategies that take advantage of low labour costs are yielding to rationalized market-oriented investments, aimed at capturing regional market share ..." (p.60)[17].

In short, targeting much smaller and more specific market areas than a broad market area like 'developing countries' as a whole is also thought to be an aspect of this diversified global strategy of Japanese MNCs. This fact seems to be the supporting evidence of the flexible change in the managerial strategy of Japanese MNCs as mentioned just above and of the afore-mentioned (1.3.2) role of Japanese capital as a main factor in worldwide structural change.

The second point to be mentioned is the technological level of subsidiaries, which was discussed in chapter three (2.3.2.2) and this chapter. Although the reputation for quality of Japanese products is being maintained, the challenge of European companies operating in the same fields requires the Japanese companies investing in Britain to produce more advanced products and to improve product quality in these subsidiaries continuously and promptly. As a result, such fields as industrial electronics and vehicles, and their R&D functions, which need much higher levels of technology than others, have provided a much larger part of the Japanese investments in Britain than is the case in Korea.

In practice, the proportion in numbers of Japanese companies in the fields of electronics, heavy machinery and vehicles is much higher in the case of Britain (66.6%) than in the Korean case (52.6%) (6.1.3 and 6.2.3). These are all fields in which the competition between manufacturers all over the world is severer than in other manufacturing fields and, thus, high technology is essential for survival[18]. This higher proportion of Japanese companies operating in high technology industry in Britain than in Korea complies with the global managerial strategy of Japanese companies described above. Furthermore, the growing R&D facilities of Japanese companies in Britain in contrast to the scarcity of this kind of activities in Korea is thought to be another example supporting this argument.

Thirdly, the investment size of Japanese concerns in the UK has been considerably bigger than that in Korea. In order to survive in competition with indigenous companies operating in the same fields, Japanese companies in Britain have had to reduce fixed cost per product, which is ordinarily disadvantageous for foreign firms and, thus, had to aim for economies of scale with a bigger size[19].

Along with the increased magnitude in the size of subsidiaries in Britain, the availability of a sufficient potential labour force emerges as one of the important factors to be considered. In the early 1980s, since the British workforce was well trained and evenly distributed, attention to those facets was reduced and the only other thing to be assessed in Britain was the militancy, or the productivity, of labour (European Company Services,1983,p.5). However, with the decrease of militant labour activity throughout the 1980s, the concern of Japanese managers has moved to the availability of the competent labour which is essential for maintaining the high productivity and competitiveness against indigenous firms or other foreign companies. The findings of the regression analysis, especially the sub-period

254

analysis, showing the change of important variables among those comprising the labour factor, illustrate this (7.1.3.4)[20]. Regarding this, a manager commented that on a point already made above:

"There were, and still are, enough labour force at the low wage level in Milton Keynes. However, these days, with the growth of companies in this area, a shortage of labour is heard" (The manager in company C).

By contrast, in developing countries as represented by Korea, the magnitude and skill level of the labour force and its distribution have been the dominant factors in the location of Japanese companies. The militancy of labour seldom emerged as a crucial factor, for the labour force in Korea and other developing countries has been less well organized and their industrial activities have been strictly controlled and restricted by the government. However, the democratisation of Korean politics and society in the late 1980s has brought about a dramatic change in this picture (Lie,1991, pp.506-510). The soaring wage level and the growing radical activities of labour have become the cause of growing complaints among Japanese managers in Korea. The manager of a company, which is located in Kyongsangnam-Do in Korea, responding to the questionnaire, wrote that:

"When we came here first, this site was very advantageous with low wage level, broad industrial lands available and ambitious government assistance. These days, with the growing industrial disputes and the disinterest of the government, this advantage has been diluted."

Since Korea is still treated as a developing country, especially from the Japanese managers' standpoint, it has to contribute to the global managerial strategy of Japanese companies with low-cost and relatively highly skilled labour. Thus, this instability in the labour factor has provoked the interest of Japanese managers in the availability of skilled labour in Korea and has provided the excuse to move their production sites to the south-east Asian countries. These features are sustained by the findings of the empirical analyses in the previous chapters in the substantial importance of the labour factor in the regression and survey analyses (7.2.1.6, 7.2.2.2 and 8.2.2.2) and the grumbles of the managers in Korea about the growing militant labour (8.2.2.3), and are consistent with the points made in this chapter.

And, fourthly, there is the linkage issue. In general, there is no constraint with regard to the proportion of local content required for Japanese manufacturing companies in developing countries. Furthermore, a large part of the products of these companies have tended to be either components of other products or intermediate goods rather than completed ones. And, even when they are sold in local markets, the challenge from indigenous firms is not so severe as in developed countries. Therefore, Japanese companies in these countries only need to concern themselves about the skilfulness of the workers they employ and the transfer of technology to sub-contractors[21].

By contrast, in developed countries, faced with the problems of severe competition and local content regulation, Japanese companies have had to spend much time on securing reliable local sub-contractors and on constructing a long-term cooperative relationship with them. In addition, there exist other problems such as the quality of the supplied parts, the system and promptness of delivery and so on (Kono,1984,p.42).

Confronting these problems, Japanese companies, as an alternative, began to induce compatriot sub-contractors from Japan to move in alongside them. Japanese sub-contractors themselves by the early 1980s have also had a strong inclination to advance into foreign countries by using their accumulated capital as a stepping stone. Among the Japanese companies that have come into Britain, Diaplastics, Optec Dai-Ichi Denko, Kiyokuni Industry, etc. can be recognized as this kind of sub-contractor (see 6.1.4).

Naturally, these incoming Japanese sub-contractors have a strong tendency, even requirement, to locate near their main Japanese customers (Young and Stewart,1986,p.86; Jones and North,1991, p.108)[22]. This fact, in addition to the widely-agreed cultural gap and just-in-time delivery system, is another important cause explaining the clustering of Japanese subsidiaries in certain areas of developed countries which differentiates these companies from those in developing countries. This contrast between developing and developed countries has been relevant in the cases of Korea and Britain at least until the first half of the 1980s. Thus, in this period, the findings in the previous chapters relating to the more overriding tendency for the concentration of Japanese companies near to other Japanese firms in Britain compared to those in Korea, in which the overall geographical tendency and the existence of indigenous manufacturing firms are also important for the Japanese companies, can be explained by these causes.

However, a drastic change in the socio-economic context in Korea, and to a certain extent in Britain as well, has made this plain distinction increasingly irrelevant. As discussed above, the global strategy of Japanese MNCs began to show a more flexible reflection against the changing context of the host economy by transforming the functions of subsidiaries and swiftly switching from one targeted market to another. The growing importance of customer markets (8.2.2.1) and the strengthening of the tendency of concentration of these Japanese companies (7.2.1.6) in Korea (even though this concentration is interpreted as mainly the product of the overwhelming force of Korean geography) are likely to be the signals of this developing global strategy of Japanese MNCs confronting the changing geographical context in their market areas[23].

In short, most of the locational characteristics of Japanese companies, both in developing countries and in developed countries, are the consequences of the worldwide managerial strategy of these companies. Under this flexible managerial strategy, a certain country, whether it is a developing or developed country, is assigned to a range of tasks for the operation of the global network involving production and marketing. And this assigned task is changed flexibly according to the changing circumstances in which each country is situated.

" The managers of the large Kaisha understand that if they want to continue as or become global competitors, they must establish manufacturing, marketing and research and development bases throughout the world" (Higashi and Lauter,1990,p.384).

In addition, these locational characteristics are the outcomes of, more broadly, the Japanese economy confronting deteriorating trading circumstances in the international economy. Therefore, to identify the geographical implications of the locational decisions of Japanese companies in the past and to predict their locational behaviour in the future, it is necessary to take into account the status of the Japanese economy within the world economy in addition to considering the geographical aspects of their production locations.

The locational pattern of Japanese MNCs in Britain and in Korea should also be explained as a reflection of the integration of the geographical context of each country with the forces of the international economy in which Japanese industry acts. In this respect, the assertions of structuralists such as Massey and Meegan (1985) are worth recalling. As expounded in chapter four, they argued that any change in either the regional or national economy should be interpreted and confronted in the context of the world economy and international market forces. Their views are valuable especially when the policy implications of the geographical characteristics of the Japanese subsidiaries are discussed as in this study.

9.4 Summary

The global managerial strategy of Japanese MNCs has shown a series of changes in accordance with the changing circumstances which these companies confront, including the changes in the world economy and the fluctuations of the politics, economy, etc. in the host countries.

Until the first half of the 1980s, Britain and Korea had played reliable roles for Japanese MNCs as one of the market countries and sourcing countries respectively according to a global framework, which was constructed by the worldwide managerial strategy of Japanese MNCs. The empirical evidence, found clearly in the regression analysis on the first sub-period and the answers made by the managers in Japanese companies that arrived in the two countries during this period, complies with this framework.

257

However, this traditional dichotomy between the sourcing countries in Asia and the market countries in America and Europe has been transformed into the massive influx of FDI in market countries at the expense of the Asian developing countries mainly due to the trade barriers laid down by the market countries. The accumulated ownership advantages of Japanese MNCs has supported this transformation. The sharp increase of Japanese subsidiaries in Britain since 1987, which was described in Chapter Six in detail, and the replies of managers indicating the trade barriers as the prime reason to move out from Japan and to invest in this country, are the evidence of this change.

The empirical evidence demonstrated in this study has been consistent with this managerial transformation of Japanese MNCs throughout the 1980s. In addition, the empirical evidence in chapter nine has revealed a step further in the evolution of the global strategy of Japanese MNCs. This evolution can be epitomised as *the division of the world market into smaller market areas* and *the flexible utilisation of the circumstances in each market area* in order to provide foreign customers with quick delivery and better services. Both the investment of the Japanese companies in the UK regardless of whether the immediate threat of trade barriers in market countries is present or not and the transformation of those companies in Korea from taking advantage of a traditional cost factor to targeting the local market according to the changing context of the economy in the host country can be said to be representative symptoms of this development. Therefore, it seems proper to argue that:

"In order to reap the great potential gain from innovations, firms need rapid access to local markets and an information network of local customers. A local presence promotes such a strategy. ...[Japanese MNCs'] technological and managerial assets enable them to produce behind trade barriers that the EC has erected against them but they would still come to Europe even if no such barriers existed" (Thomsen and Nicolaides, 1991,p.126).

In other words, with the changing circumstances in the world economy and in host countries, the worldwide managerial strategy of Japanese MNCs has demonstrated a remarkable flexibility. This is thought to be sufficient for them to accustom themselves to the drastically changing world economy, which is called 'disorganised capitalism' or 'post-Fordism'. On the other hand, this highly flexible global strategy of Japanese MNCs commits the world economy to being transformed further in the direction of flexibility and diversification.

In this regard, a little change in the regional policy of host country is expected to be reflected in the flexible managerial strategy of Japanese companies. Conversely, a sensitive transformation of Japanese MNCs provides significant implications for the host government's regional policy. These issues are considered in depth in the next chapter.

258

10 The implications of the locational behaviour of Japanese companies for regional policy in the host countries

As expounded at the beginning of the previous chapter, this chapter investigates the relationship between the host government regional policy and the locational behaviour of Japanese companies on the basis of the discussion of managerial strategy. For the purpose, this chapter will examine first the changing context of regional policy and the response of Japanese MNCs. This issue is discussed with reference to the experiences of Britain and Korea, most of which emerged and were described in the previous chapters. After that, the manifest implications of their activities for the regional policy of the host governments will follow as the latter part of this chapter.

10.1 Regional Policy and the Response of Japanese Multinational Companies

10.1.1 The role of regional policy for the location of Japanese subsidiaries : Empirical results

The concept, evolution and effect of regional policy in the two host countries were expounded in chapter five. Regional policy has been shown by many authors to have influenced the location of firms in Britain (see 3.4.2). Most studies have estimated the extent of the influence by reference to the changes in employment, industrial movement and investment volume between the period when regional policy was implemented and the other period when it was not active or not so active (Moore et al.,1986,p.13; Moore et al., 1991,p.1003; and above 4.2.2.5).

These studies have stressed the point that the financial assistance given by the British government has had a marked role in the movement of firms into designated AAs and on the growth of investment there and, as a result, also on the increase in employment in these AAs. Similarly, the importance of regional policy in attracting the overseas investment of foreign firms into the host country has been widely recognized in most countries.

However, since regional policy measures, at least initially, are planned and introduced mainly in relation to indigenous firms rather than foreign ones, there exist some limitations on estimating the exact extent to which regional policy affects the location of inward investments in each host country (Bennett and Krebs,1989,p.202). Nonetheless, the importance of regional policy for the incoming Japanese MNCs in the two host countries has been supported to a certain extent again in this study by the regression and survey results, even though the importance was not crucial or essential.

In the regression results, the correlation coefficients between the location of Japanese concerns and the regional policy in Britain measured by the total TTWAs qualifying for regional assistance in each county, by the public expenditure for economic development and promotion and by the amount of regional assistance paid, were found to range from 0.20 to 0.45. These figures are considered to be relatively high in this kind of analysis. Also in the case of Korea, the total government investment in industrial estates up to 1988, which was chosen as the explanatory variable to represent the degree of regional policy, and the stock of industrial estates, which was thought to be closely related to regional policy, showed high levels of correlation with dependent variables ranging from 0.31 to 0.79.

Therefore, in the macro-level analysis, regional policy was pointed out as an influential factor in the location choice of Japanese subsidiaries in both host countries, especially in Britain (7.1.1.6 and 7.1.2.3). However, in order to estimate the degree of influence more clearly and, thus, to enhance the relevance of this argument, this conclusion, based on the macro-level analysis, needed to be complemented and interpreted by the micro-level results obtained from direct contact with the Japanese companies concerned. The questionnaire and interview surveys in this study were undertaken for this reason.

The importance of government assistance, which comprised various policy measures including financial aid and public expenditure for economic development and promotion, was affirmed once again in the survey results. In Britain, Japanese companies assessed the government assistance as a *relatively substantial* influence and indicated financial aid and advice as the most important policy measures (8.2.2.4). Likewise, the government assistance in Korea also was appraised as a *substantial* influence by the Japanese companies operating there, and advice and government-provided land and premises were listed as the most influential measures (8.3.2.4).

Overall, the macro- and micro-analyses in this study revealed that regional policy in both countries has had a close relationship with the location decisions of Japanese companies. However, an interesting contrast concerning this issue was that British regional policy maintained its effectiveness throughout the 1980s in the face of changing economic circumstances, while Korean regional policy, which had been implemented mainly within the framework of national economic development, has lost its effectiveness especially since the mid-1980s with the changing force of the national and international economy[24]. The rest of this section demonstrates additionally some more visible features, which are considered to reinforce this conclusion. These mainly focus on the locational behaviour of Japanese companies in the changing context of host government regional policy.

10.1.2 The response of Japanese MNCs to the changing regional policy in Britain

10.1.2.1 Regional policy in transition in the 1980s

The changing context of regional policy in Britain was described previously (chapter five). In short, regional policy has given way to national economic policy and urban policy since the late 1970s mainly due to the aggravating economic situation and the Conservative government's policy.

Apart from these changes in domestic circumstances, the growing influence of international market forces, appearing in the form of pressure for restructuring and de-industrialization, and the impact of EC policy on the approaches of member states to their regional problems, have often been listed as the major external forces which have brought about a significant change in the basis on which British regional policy has been maintained (Martin and Hodge,1983,pp.137-149). Furthermore, a more fundamental change in the structure of the world economy, which is often called the emergence of 'post-Fordism' or 'disorganised capitalism', has inevitably disturbed the basis of government policy for solving regional problems. These changing circumstances have influenced every aspect of regional policy.

In general, the designation of AAs, financial assistance, the offer of serviced industrial sites, improved infrastructure and the industrial development control have been listed as the main instruments of regional policy (Townroe,1986,p.357). Among these, the first two relating to AAs and financial assistance rather than the others were considered to be more relevant for assessing the responsiveness of individual firms to regional policy. However, drastically changing circumstances demand the involvement of other policy instruments in measuring the relationship between government regional policy and the locational decisions of firms. In this respect, the response of Japanese companies to the shift in regional policy is discussed below by taking all these policy measures into account, even though the main focus is on the changes in the first two measures.

10.1.2.2 Assisted areas, financial assistance and the location of Japanese companies

Considering the findings in the regression and survey analyses, it is expected that the diagrams showing both AA status and the arrival of Japanese companies in each area may reveal a certain consistency between the changes of these two. The following figures 10.1 to 10.3 show the comparable changes of the two. As these Figures illustrate, large numbers of incoming Japanese companies have placed their investments in the AAs.

Numerically, the numbers of incoming Japanese companies locating in assisted and non-assisted areas respectively at the time of their arrival can be displayed as in Table 10.1. In total, 57.5% of the Japanese manufacturing companies arriving in Britain have placed their units in AAs. Regardless of the growing number of Japanese companies coming into this country, the preference of these companies for location in AAs has shown no sign of decline.

Conversely, when the number of Japanese companies in AAs is grouped into three periods, i.e. pre-1981, 1981-1986 and 1987-1990, the trend shows an upward movement from 52.4% to 53.7% and then to 59.7%. If the change in the boundaries of the designated AAs in 1984, which resulted in a substantial decrease of the total AA area, is taken into account, the tendency of the incoming Japanese companies to locate in the AAs can be said to have increased more markedly in recent years.

Table 10.1 Japanese companies in AAs and non-AAs by date of arrival*

(%)

Year	Total	AAs	Non-AAs
-1979	17(100)	9(52.9)	8(42.1)
1980	4(100)	2(50.0)	2(50.0)
1981	2(100)	2(100)	0(0.0)
1982	2(100)	1(50.0)	1(50.0)
1983	3(100)	2(66.7)	1(33.3)
1984	9(100)	6(66.7)	3(33.3)
1985	10(100)	6(60.0)	4(40.0)
1986	15(100)	5(33.3)	10(66.7)
1987	29(100)	16(55.2)	13(44.8)
1988	16(100)	11(68.8)	5(31.2)
1989	29(100)	21(72.4)	8(27.6)
1990	45(100)	23(51.1)	22(48.9)
Total	181(100)	104(57.5)	77(42.5)

Computed from the reports of IBB and AJEI, *Regional Trends* and *Employment Gazette*.

Fig. 10.1 The AAs in 1979 and the locations of Japanese Companies arriving before 1981.

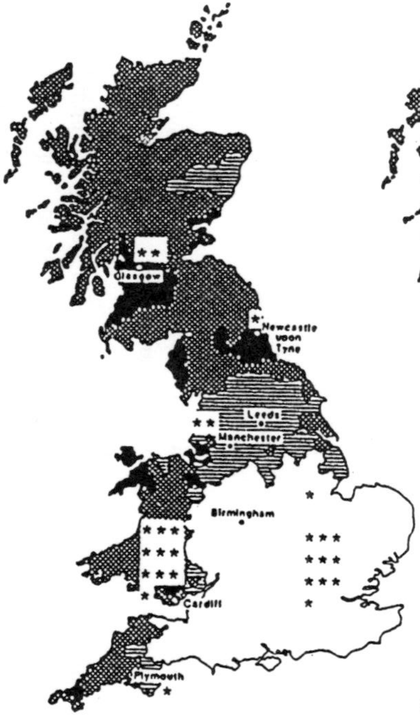

Fig. 10.2 The AAs in 1982 and the locations of Japanese Companies arriving 1982-1984.

Fig. 10.3 The AAs in 1984 and the locations of Japanese Companies arriving 1985-1990.

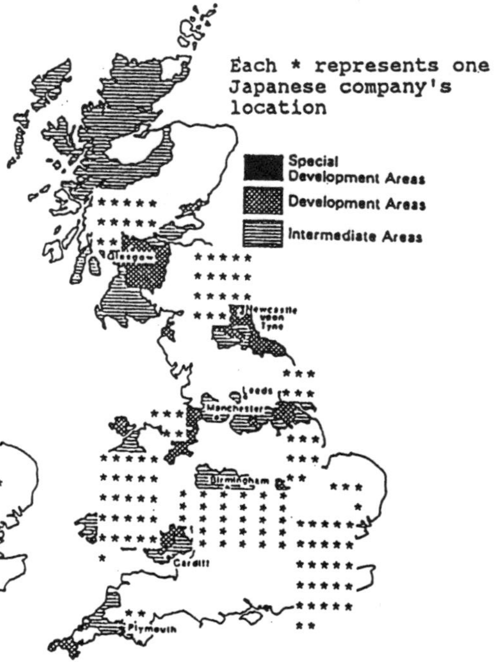

Each * represents one Japanese company's location

Special Development Areas

Development Areas

Intermediate Areas

(Note) These maps showing AAs are taken from Martin (1985, p.382).

263

As noted earlier, the total coverage of the AAs has changed from 40% of the UK working population in 1979 to 27.5% in 1982, and to 35% in 1984 (4.2.2.4). The match between the trend in the total coverage of AAs and that of the proportion of Japanese companies located in the AAs shows an interesting facet when displayed in Figure 10.4. As seen in this figure, the two trends show a reverse direction with a larger proportion of Japanese companies locating in the AAs during the period when the AAs were narrowed down and with a smaller proportion when the coverage of AAs was widening.

Figure 10.4   The coverage of AAs and the proportion of Japanese companies in the AAs

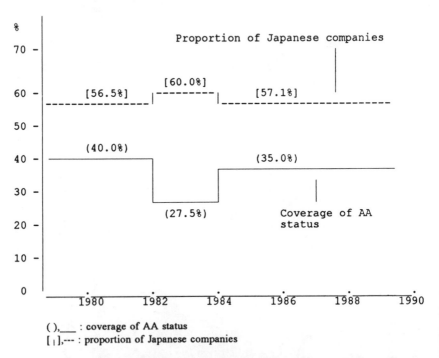

( ),___ : coverage of AA status
[₁],--- : proportion of Japanese companies

This means that the locational decisions of incoming Japanese companies have tended to respond consistently and more sensitively to the changes in the host government's regional policy.

On the other hand, the response of Japanese companies to changing regional policy can also be approached by an examination of the record of financial assistance awarded to the Japanese companies. Table 10.2 shows the amount of financial assistance sourced from RDG, RSA, ERDF and the sectoral assistance under section 8 of the Industrial Development Act 1972 and

264

1982 which Japanese companies have received.

Table 10.2   Financial assistance received by Japanese companies

Year	Total companies (cumulative)(a)[+]	Numbers of recipients £ 000(%)	Amount received(b) £ 000	Average (b/a) £ 000
1975	7	2(28.6)	167	23.9
1976	9	5(55.6)	1,213	134.8
1977	12	3(25.0)	1,348	112.3
1978	14	2(14.3)	562	40.1
1979	17	5(29.4)	1,449	85.2
1980	21	7(33.3)	1,713	81.6
1981	23	8(34.8)	7,396	321.6
1982	25	8(32.0)	2,412	96.5
1983	28	8(28.6)	10,137	362.0
1984	37	9(24.3)	7,258	196.2
1985	47	11(23.4)	14,423	306.9
1986	62	15(24.2)	20,877	336.7
1987	91	19(20.9)	12,893	141.7
1988	107	29(27.1)	67,244	628.4
1989	136	28(20.6)	21,170	155.7
1990	181	21(11.6)	13,722	75.8
Total	[181]	180(27.1)	183,984	[193.7]

[+] Column 1, the cumulative total Japanese companies in Britain, represents total potential recipients at each date, not necessarily located in AAs.
Source : Compiled from the *British Business* (1975-1989) and *Employment Gazette* (1990-1991).

Even though these figures are subject to the drawbacks of omission caused either by the firm's non-accessibility to or the small amount of, financial assistance, e.g. under £ 25,000 in RDG and under £ 5,000 in RSA, or by accident, they seem to be sufficient to express the overall trend of the financial assistance taken by Japanese subsidiaries.

According to this table, the number of recipient companies and the total amount of assistance received have both increased steadily along with the increase in the number of Japanese companies coming into this country. The sharp increase in the total amount received in 1988 was caused by the inclusion of the record amount of assistance to Nissan Motor Co. The average percentage of the total Japanese companies who were recipients in each year was 27.1%. On average, each Japanese company in this country has received over £ 193,000 per year and the amount is doubled when only those companies which are located in the AAs are taken into consideration.

Some Japanese companies received small amounts of grant or assistance many times over a long period, while others received a large amount of

265

assistance once or twice. NEC Semiconductors (UK) Ltd., Sony (UK) Ltd., etc. are examples of the former, while Yamazaki Machinery UK Co. and Komatsu Co. (UK) Ltd. are included in the latter group.

As in the case of the relationship between AA status and the number of Japanese companies located there, if an allowance is made for the diminishing size of regional financial assistance, the proportion of Japanese companies receiving financial assistance can be said to have increased considerably compared to indigenous firms. In practice, the British government has pursued the reduction of expenditure in the form of a regional assistance package from £ 842m in 1978/9 to £ 400m in 1987/8 (also see 4.2.1.4). This means that government regional assistance has been cut by 52.5% during the ten years from 1979 to 1988.

During the same period, by contrast, the proportion of Japanese companies receiving financial assistance was reduced by only 2.3 percentage points and, since then, the proportion has converged around 20%. This fact substantiates the argument that government financial assistance has been one of the influential factors for the Japanese companies coming into this country (and that FDI in AAs and elsewhere is favoured by the British government in terms of its financial assistance). The importance of financial aid for attracting Japanese companies into targeted areas found in the survey analysis in Chapter eight (8.2.2.4) is closely related to this situation.

In addition to this evidence, another matter to be considered is the recent role of other spatial policy measures aside from traditional regional policy, e.g. New Towns[25], Enterprise Zones, Urban Development Corporations' designated areas, Free Ports and Steel Closure Areas. Various kinds of assistance have been forwarded to these areas, in particular in the 1980s. If these areas are included in the wider category of AAs, the number of Japanese companies in the areas, where government assistance is available, is considered to reach over two thirds of total Japanese companies in this country.

With the diminishing emphasis on the spatially drawn AAs and the changes in the characteristics of the regional problem, the diversification of spatial policy measures has been, and is likely to become, intensified. Also it is the policy of the Invest in Britain Bureau (IBB) that foreign investment will be welcomed in the region most appropriate for the incoming concern (European Company Services,1983,p.28). In other words, the sources of financial assistance available for Japanese companies have become more flexible, varied and less focused on the official AAs.

The locational decisions of incoming Japanese companies have followed this trend. These companies have settled down not only in the designated AAs but also in the newly drawn areas. Of course not all the newly arriving Japanese companies have sought these preferential areas. Toyota, which placed its site just outside the AAs, is an illustrative example. Despite these exceptions, it seems true that Japanese firms coming into this country have been substantially responsive to the changes in spatial policy. In fact these new policy initiatives appeared to be influential factors on the location decisions of Japanese companies in the regression analysis in Chapter seven (7.1.2.3). In particular, the remarkably high correlation coefficient between public expenditure in EZs and the locations of Japanese companies implies that the locational pattern of Japanese companies has moved along with the diversified policy initiatives of the British government, although it was thought that abundant workforce and government assistance were the underlying forces behind this relationship.

From the discussion so far, the importance of government assistance, which is in the form of either financial aid in traditional AAs or newly introduced assistance measures, in attracting Japanese companies into certain areas has been confirmed again[26], even though its effectiveness tends to be amplified by another favourable locational factor, the existence of large numbers of unemployed. For Japanese MNCs coming into Britain, with location in Britain constituting an inferior position relative to indigenous competitors, government assistance, especially financial aid, is thought to be essential to their competitiveness and influential in their choice of sites in a market country which is full of competition and uncertainty.

In practice, many managers of Japanese companies operating in Britain have confessed that the financial assistance was the main, if not the only, factor in their location choice. The decision makers of Sekisui (UK) Ltd., NEC Semiconductors, Toshiba Consumer Products (UK) Ltd., etc. were reported as saying that the financial incentives offered by the British government were the most important locational factor in choosing the sites for their plants within Britain (*British Business*, 26 Sep. 1980, 8 May 1984 and 28 Nov. 1986). Other companies such as Citizen Watch (*Financial Times*, Jul. 29 1987) and Aiwa (UK) Ltd. (*British Business*, 12 Sep. 1980) also stressed the importance of this factor for their companies, even though they did not put the factor in the first position.

However, strangely enough, in the interview survey undertaken for this study, the managers appraised somewhat negatively the role of financial aid from the British government. In contrast, the non-financial assistance of the promotional bodies received a high mark from these managers. Nonetheless, the empirical evidence in the regression analysis in chapter eight, the questionnaire answers in chapter nine and the clustering of Japanese companies in AAs as discussed in this chapter obviously demonstrate the substantial influence of the assistance of the British government, with the financial aid in the designated AAs as the main factor. In fact, some managers interviewed expressed their opinion of the importance of government assistance for the locational decisions of their companies. For instance:

"As a matter of fact, I am not satisfied with this site. I don't know why the

267

former manager chose this place. Probably the DTI assistance and R&D grant influenced his decision" (The manager in company T).

"The present site is not in the assisted areas. Therefore, there was no financial aid from the British government. However, we have got a plan to build some additional facilities in the assisted areas. And it will enable the company to apply for the financial aid" (The manager in company O).

In aggregate, it can be concluded that Japanese companies investing in Britain can be said to be very responsive to the British government's incentives, mainly in the form of financial aid, and the locational patterns of these companies have become more diversified in accordance with the changing form of spatial policy measures in Britain.

10.1.3   The response of Japanese MNCs to the changing regional policy in Korea

10.1.3.1   Regional policy in transition

It has been noted earlier that regional policy in Korea has basically pursued two different, and often conflicting, objectives, i.e. national economic growth and balanced regional development. Among the two, the prime emphasis of government efforts has mainly been placed on the former. As a result, in proportion to the rapid development of the national economy during the last three decades, the disparity between regions has deepened and widened (chapter five). The geography of Korea, which is characterized by polarisation, or the widening gap between regions and between sectors, can be said to be a typical consequence of the spatial policy based on growth pole theory (however, without considering the necessity to disseminate these growth poles for regional balance) (Cho,1991,p.11)[27].

Therefore, the alleviation of regional disparity and the more equitable distribution of national wealth became an urgent matter to be tackled after the end of the 1970s. This required the redirection of the government concern, which had been heavily biased in favour of national economic development at any cost, towards balancing development between the regions. The Korean government began to introduce several policy measures to meet this urgent need. In particular, the Second Comprehensive National Land Development Plan (1982-1991) and the Sixth Five Year Economic Development Plan (1987-1991) listed these policy initiatives explicitly.

The main therapies involved are the construction of infrastructure such as roads and industrial estates in the peripheral regions, the dissemination of business service activities, e.g. banking and R&D facilities, into these lagging regions to support the activities of local concerns, and the strengthening of the regulatory control over development in Seoul MPR (Economic Planning Board,1985,p.307). On the same basis, government assistance towards industry has changed its direction from the prosperous regions, Seoul MPR and Kyongsangnam-Do province, to underdeveloped regions such as the Cholla provinces (Chollabuk-Do and Chollanam-Do). And this shift in regional and industrial policy is expected to continue for the time being in line with the democratization in politics.

10.1.3.2 Changed policy concern and the location of Japanese subsidiaries

The response of Japanese companies to the changing government policy in Korea is difficult to identify clearly, especially given the predominating trend of polarisation in Korea. Furthermore, there is not sufficient data available about either the financial assistance or the tax exemptions provided by the government.

Table 10.3 Japanese companies in the IEs and non-IE areas by date of arrival (%)

Period	Total	IEs	Non-IEs
Total	299(100)	119(38.9)	180(60.2)
Before 1981	103(100)	57(55.3)	46(44.7)
1981-1986	72(100)	19(26.4)	53(73.6)
1987-1990	124(100)	43(34.7)	81(65.3)

Computed from the Ministry of Finance, Korea (1991).

One method of estimating Japanese response to the changing policy concern involves an examination of the relationship between the locations of Japanese companies and those of industrial estates and Free Port Zones (IEs) in each Do. Since the designated IEs in each region have been the key instrument of regional and industrial policy in Korea, the extent to which Japanese companies locate in these areas seems to have significance for this analysis. The following table shows the locations of Japanese companies in Korea when they are grouped by the IEs and non-IES.

This table clearly reveals the fact that the proportion of Japanese companies located in the IEs has declined steadily since the beginning of 1980s. In particular, the proportion fell sharply in the first half of 1980s. This situation has two aspects: the one is that there is not enough room in the IEs available for the newly arriving Japanese companies and the other is that Japanese companies are no longer attracted by the incentives offered by the Korean government which have been concentrated in the IEs. Instead, they are

269

more influenced by other locational factors such as labour supply and market accessibility.

Firstly, in terms of absolute area, there still remain large vacant areas in the total IEs. 62.0 km^2 (28.3%) out of the total 219.2 km^2 of industrial land in IEs were still available at the end of 1990 (Ministry of Trade and Industry,1990). The problem is that, among the IEs, those which have been more preferred by the Japanese companies, e.g. the Korea Export Industrial Estate in Seoul, Masan Free Export Zone in Kyongsangnam-Do, etc., are fully occupied already. Therefore, most newly developed IEs, which are mainly located far from either Seoul or Pusan and Kyongsangnam-Do, have shown a weak performance in attracting mobile firms including Japanese companies.

The second point is related to the first one to a certain extent. In parallel with the declining attractiveness of IEs, which is mainly caused by the exhaustion of spare land in popular IEs, other geographical factors have come to be more influential in the locational choice of Japanese companies. As illustrated in chapters eight and nine, factors such as abundance of skilled labour, accessibility to a big market, etc. appeared to be more important than other factors including the variables related to regional policy.

This situation was depicted in chapter nine while discussing the findings of the questionnaire survey. Furthermore, the empirical evidence of the present study is supported by another similar piece of research undertaken by the Korea Trade Association (KTA). The latter study was based on a survey which was held with the participation of 281 foreign firms, of which Japanese firms provided 59.6% (171 firms). The KTA study came up with the finding that government assistance (14.1% in the total respondents) was less influential in location choice for the foreign firms than other factors such as marketability of products in the Korean market (21.3%), low cost wage labour (20.0%) and high profitability (17.7%) (KTA,1987,pp.62-63). The findings of the two empirical analyses are almost identical and are consistent with the diminishing number of Japanese companies located in the IEs in which various kinds of government assistance are easily obtained.

The above causes, in conjunction with each other, have brought about the weak responses of Japanese companies to the changes in the government objectives. Thus, these causes generate serious doubt about the effectiveness of the traditional spatial policy, which has emphasized migration control in Seoul MPR, and about the intensive government assistance to the firms in some designated IEs, in relieving regional problems. This locational pattern of Japanese companies, which is inconsistent with the anticipation of the Korean government, can largely be attributed to the following points:

The first to be mentioned is that, although the policy demand of balanced regional development and of an equitable distribution of national wealth has been recognized widely, there has been no substantial change in policy measures to meet it. The primacy of national economic policy over regional policy has been maintained, and government assistance has continued to concentrate on a small number of IEs. With this tardy policy response to the new circumstances, it may be unrealistic to expect a considerable change in the locational pattern of firms including Japanese companies. In other words, the traditional spatial policy which had been devoted to national economic development cannot be effective any more in targeting the policy in a different direction.

The second point is that the Japanese companies have behaved precisely according to the established Japanese worldwide managerial strategy ignoring the change in policy concern in Korea. Since the Japanese companies coming into Korea are more interested in the availability of skilled labour and in the possibility of capturing the Korean and foreign market than in any other factors, it is thought that the change in regional policy concern has had no significant influence on their locational pattern. This has been expounded in chapter nine.

Furthermore, unlike the Japanese companies operating in the developed market countries, those in Korea have not experienced any significant threat from indigenous competitors and, thus, they have been able to manage their companies in Korea without depending heavily on the assistance, i.e. mainly tax cuts, from the Korean government. The concentration of those Japanese companies in the designated IEs in the 1970s can be interpreted in such a way that the IEs at the time were located within and near Seoul and Kyongsangnam-Do surrounding Pusan, where many other locational factors such as labour, infrastructure, accessibility, etc. were also favourable to Japanese companies compared to other areas, and that this location in the designated IEs was the most advantageous for the Japanese companies at that time irrespective of regional policy.

Consequently, the relationship between regional policy and the locational patterns of Japanese companies in Korea can be summarized by the unchanging policy measures, despite both the desperate demand for changes in the direction of regional policy and the lowered response of Japanese companies to this policy. This shows the difference in the Korean case from the British experience as the latter can be characterized by both diversifying spatial policy measures and high responsiveness of Japanese companies to this change.

10.2 Policy Implications

The interpretation of the empirical evidence about the locational behaviour of Japanese companies (which was found in the descriptive, regression and survey analyses, in relation to the existing host government regional policy) has illuminated one aspect of the relationship between host government policy and the locational choice of Japanese companies. Another aspect that should be mentioned is the implication for the host government's regional policy of the locational pattern of Japanese companies, which behave according to a well-formed worldwide managerial strategy constructed by the integrated force of industry and banking groups and, eventually, the Japanese government.

As emphasised several times previously, each national economy has become increasingly tied into the drastically changing international economy. Therefore, individual governments have to coordinate their economic or industrial policies with both the framework of and change in the world economy (UN,1991,p.85). Regional policy also cannot be implemented without considering the forces emanating from the changing world economy. The more a national economy is open to the world, the more has the nation's regional policy to be tuned to these forces of the changing international economy. As expounded already, Japanese capital, especially in the 1980s with its accumulated fortune, began to play a key role in the arena of world economy in the form of MNCs and FDI (1.3.2 and 9.3.2). This means that the overseas activities of Japanese capital have a significant implication both for economic policy and for the regional policy of host countries.

Regarding the attraction of Japanese FDI, there remain some debatable issues to be settled in the two host countries. In Britain, warnings about the problem of the branch plant economy, or external control, are still aired by some critics. In Korea, the resentment towards Japanese capital is deeply rooted among Korean people remembering the atrocities of Japanese imperialism. In spite of these kinds of difficulties, there is a realistic necessity to invite Japanese capital into the two host countries. That is the need to stimulate the national economy and to solve the regional problem in each country by attracting in and taking advantage of the growing economic power of Japanese MNCs.

Basically, to recover and maintain the strength of the national economy may be the best policy for the host country when the host government tries to take advantage of the multinational concerns (Armstrong and Taylor,1989,p.37). This is even more the case in relation to the Japanese FDI which targets mainly the host country market[28]. However, apart from such a long-term economic strategy, there exist a number of issues to be considered in each host country as the immediate matter of concern for this study. Therefore, the implications for British and Korean policies are discussed below in turn.

10.2.1 Implications for British regional policy

It was mentioned above (10.1.2.1) that the regional policy measures in Britain have been modified and diversified in line with changing circumstances domestically and externally. And,the empirical evidence in this study revealed that these diversified policy measures have been successful in attracting

272

Japanese companies. In other words, confronting the changes in the host government policy, the response of Japanese companies to these policy measures has been maintained at a high level.

Indeed, it can be said that Japanese companies have taken full advantage of the financial assistance offered under various schemes by the British government. Among those schemes traditional regional policy has played a central role. This is not saying that there are no problems in British regional policy. Since regional policy is primarily aimed at indigenous firms rather than those from foreign countries, the relative success in attracting foreign, in particular Japanese, firms hardly guarantees the satisfactory solution of overall regional problems. In other words, the attraction of mobile foreign firms contributes to the mitigation of the gap between regions in part, and the evaluation of regional policy in relation to the induction of foreign firms should be confined to that part[29]. Given this limitation, a number of issues are worth considering regarding the attraction of mobile Japanese projects.

10.2.1.1 Effective promotional activities

The first issue that should be considered is that the attracting force of British regional policy has been, and furthermore will be, weakened by the abolition of RDG in 1988. In contrast to the original RDG scheme, the revised RDG scheme, which was introduced in 1984, was appraised as being relatively effective in its job-creation and additionality (Wren,1989a,p.134 and 1989b,pp.510-512; Swales,1989,p.367). Although Japanese companies in general tend to have close contact with the Department of Trade and Industry and local authorities before they make their final decisions and, during the process, they are guaranteed to receive financial assistance of some kind[30], the elimination of the automatic grant is expected to lessen the predictability for incoming Japanese companies about the financial assistance available and, thus, to make it more difficult for the British government to persuade Japanese companies to settle in Britain and especially in the AAs.

Certainly, the continued preference of Japanese companies for the AAs, irrespective of changing spatial policy in Britain, can be attributed to the intensified activities of promotional bodies led by IBB[31]. The abolition of RDG means that there will need to be more increased effort to win the competition with other countries for the attraction of mobile Japanese concerns. Regarding this, the following issues should also be emphasized.

Coordinated activities

In conjunction with such an intensified marketing activity, the ramified promotional efforts of authorities at various levels to try to induce Japanese firms into their own boundaries require to be coordinated (not before time).

Although this issue has been put forward by many authors (Hood and Young,1983; Armstrong,1986; Armstrong and Taylor,1987,1988; Dicken and Tickell,1992), no substantial improvement has been achieved. In order to enhance the effectiveness of their marketing activities, the collaboration of the authorities involved, rather than competition between them, through the strengthened activities of representatives (e.g. IBB or other independent bodies) is sensible as soon as possible.

The empirical evidence in this study explicitly demonstrated the main features of the worldwide managerial strategy of Japanese MNCs. Among those, *the division of the world market into smaller market areas* and *the flexible utilisation of the circumstances in each market area* appeared as the most prominent two. The continuation of these strategies by Japanese companies will result in an increase in the proportion of the local market in the marketing activities of the Japanese subsidiaries operating in each host country compared to that of exporting to neighbouring countries. In other words, when the activities of Japanese subsidiaries is divided into two kinds, i.e. the activities for capturing local markets and those aiming to subjugate markets in adjacent countries, the former activities are likely to grow more rapidly. The national level investment decision of a company which aims mainly to capture a specific host country market will be little influenced by the promotional activities of individual authorities or institutions. Only the investments which concentrate their major efforts on the capturing of a market area comprising several host countries are thought to be affected by the promotional activities either of the host government or of the host regions in deciding on a specific host country and are worth endeavouring to attract to this country. With the rapid growth of Japanese FDI aiming to capture local markets, the role of local or regional level promotional activities will decrease in attracting the Japanese investments into this country, although its role in distributing the investments among regions or areas will remain meaningful.

This means that the competitive bidding at regional or local level to attract the Japanese companies seems to be meaningless or harmful for the national interest if the companies have no alternative but to choose this country. In this respect, the need to coordinate the marketing activities between regions at the central government level will become even more important[32]. The competitive promotional activity between institutions at various levels including local authorities can cause a zero-sum game between regions and, consequently, can be detrimental to the aggregate performance of British regions by increasing the cost of their marketing effort.

The coordination between promotional activities is much more important considering the necessity to trace and predict the overall locational pattern of Japanese companies, targeting specific market areas or local markets, and to provide more favourable conditions for these Japanese companies. Without the coordination of local activities, or the enhancement of local solidarity in

Cooke's frame, it will be highly unlikely that the game will shift from a zero-sum game towards a positive-sum game (Cooke,1989,p.248). Furthermore, this coordination between local activities under the auspices of central government seems to be appropriate for the era of 'post-Fordism'[33].

The pursuit of flexibility and diversification in economic initiatives at local level has its own justification to meet the highly flexible international market forces like Japanese capital. However, to achieve an expected goal in aggregate, an effective coordination of these diversified activities from the central government is indispensable, so far as this coordination does not paralyse or suffocate the innovative activities in each locality (Nolan and O'Donnell,1991,pp.122-123)[34].

> " We will accept that no system can be perfect and that neither local government nor regional administrations have unlimited resources and a free hand to pursue their own policies without reference to other administrations" (Chisholm,1990,p.175).

In short, ramified efforts at local or regional level are insufficient to find, to interpret and to grasp the managerial strategy of Japanese MNCs and bear the danger of lessening the total national benefit through over-competition among the local areas. The national goal, i.e. the positive effects of Japanese FDI on the British economy, should also be put together with the interest of specific areas, especially that of local authorities[35]. In other words, the national context, i.e. the role of the state, as well as the global context needs to be taken into account in deciding the direction and strategies of localities (Imrie,1991, pp.450-451; Sadler,1992,pp.255-267).

Integration of functions

With regard to this, it is worth considering that the institutions which will undertake promotional activities need to be given both functions of regional development and of marketing for an area with a somewhat broader boundary. The following comment provides an indication of this:

> "The local authority is a political body rather than a working body. As a matter of fact they lack staff and money. Staffs [in the local authority and development corporation] often contact each other to discuss present issues. But most of promotional activities have been undertaken by this [development corporation]" (the official in the TDC).

As revealed in this comment, a series of consolidated functions from the development of an area to the marketing of the developed land and even to the provision of financial assistance to the incoming firms can be made more suitable and efficient for overall regional development[36]. This argument is inevitably related to the discussion about the establishment of regional level organisations in England similar to the regional development agencies in Scotland and Wales. Although there are some critics of the establishment of development agencies in England on the grounds of either the difficulty in allocating the benefits from the location of MNCs among constituent authorities (Dicken and Tickell,1992) or the more attractive conditions of prosperous regions in England compared to AAs (Armstrong and Taylor,1989), etc., well-organised planning and control from the central government (DTI) can prevent these kinds of problems and maximize the goal of the national interest with well balanced regional development[37].

10.2.1.2 Dissemination of benefits

Another matter to which the British government should direct its effort is the dissemination of the benefits resulting from the location of Japanese companies in one area to other areas and to other regions. As explained previously, Japanese companies, especially those arriving recently, have shown a tendency to cluster around the main Japanese manufacturers. This tendency is likely to continue as far as the unique features of Japanese management are maintained, in particular the just-in-time system which requires the component suppliers to locate close to their main customers. This clustering tendency of Japanese companies in certain areas results in a great boost to the economies of the host regions[38], whereas the other regions, which failed to attract foreign FDI, are left outside of this beneficial boundary[39].

The central government, which is ultimately in charge of the balanced economic growth between regions, and the regional institutions recommended just above should examine the potentiality of each area and make efforts to disseminate the benefits arising from the arrival of foreign firms to areas outside the host regions. This could be done by, for instance, supporting the growth of indigenous firms in the neighbouring regions with financial aid, technical advice, etc. and by promoting the supplier relationship between these indigenous firms and the Japanese concerns. These kinds of coordinating effort need to be continued until the problem of regional disparity disappears from the immediate agenda of the British government.

10.2.1.3 Infrastructure

The third issue to be emphasized is the importance of infrastructure. As found in Chapter eight (8.2.2.3), the accessibility of an area, in particular through motorways and trunk roads, and industrial land and premises still have considerable influence on the location choices of Japanese MNCs. The provision of this infrastructure in parallel with the financial assistance is thought to be more effective in advertising the advantages of an area than sole dependence on financial assistance (Chisholm,1990,p.171). In particular, considering the fact that local markets are important for the Japanese MNCs choosing their locations according to their changing global strategy, which divides the world market into a large number of small market areas, the easy connection between the plant sites and market regions through motorways and trunk roads becomes more crucial.

In addition to that, it is important to provide the necessary living facilities which will enable Japanese people to live comfortably in this country and to overcome the cultural gap. The construction of primary and junior schools for the children of Japanese managers may be a good example (*The Sunday Times*, 5 Jun. 1988).

10.2.1.4 Specialization of regions

And the last point of importance is that there should be an attempt to develop a kind of specialization between regions through the regional assistance[40]. In general, foreign firms have tended to concentrate in specific industry sectors showing a different mixture between regions (Young and Stewart,1986,p.83). Although it was not revealed clearly in the empirical analyses in this study, one can hardly deny the fact that Japanese companies also tend to locate in the areas where there are many other indigenous, Japanese and other foreign companies operating in the same field. Industrial electronics in Scotland, consumer electronics in Wales and heavy machinery and vehicles in the North are examples.

If the regional policy of the British government were to involve measures to specify an industrial field for each region, the attraction of mobile Japanese companies could become easier with the increased linkage effect in each region (Todd,1983; Pfaff and Hurler,1983). This fact has been proved by the Korean experience, where a large number of Japanese subsidiaries gathered in each specified IE in the 1970s, each IE being based on a distinct industrial sector[41]. (Of course, this policy has been attacked in that the targeted areas are too small in size and that these areas are clustered in a few prosperous regions.)

For this purpose in Britain, the formation of an industrial milieu, or growth cluster, in each region is recommended. This can be done mainly through the deployment of firms (especially by promoting indigenous firms) in inter-related industrial fields, through the transformation of these firms by means of the introduction of new technology and through the provision of sufficient competent labour and infrastructure for these firms[42]. To meet this end, all the available industrial, transportation, and employment, or training, policies, especially at regional and local level, need to be mobilized[43].

277

10.2.1.5 Conclusion

Consequently, from the discussions so far, it seems possible to conclude that, in order to enhance the attractiveness of AAs, more diversified and flexible assistance measures need to be introduced. Of course, the British government has already brought a remarkable change and diversification into regional policy as mentioned in chapter five and the previous section. However, a large part of these newly introduced policy initiatives has depended heavily on financial aid and tax cuts in a range of designated areas.

As the empirical analyses in this study revealed, sufficient industrial land and premises, convenient transport, abundance of high skilled labour, etc., which can be called long-run strategies necessitated for constructing regional milieu (targeting main industrial fields for each region), are equally important compared to the short-run promotional activities using financial incentives. By providing or improving these locational factors as well as the financial aid under the framework of spatial policy, the overall attractiveness of AAs is expected to be enhanced markedly[44]. From a similar standpoint to this, Dunning asserts that the attractive economic environment as a whole including appropriate wage and skill level, good infrastructure, favourable living circumstances, etc., mainly by the effort of the government, is more important than promotional activities in attracting Japanese FDI (Dunning,1990b,pp.177-179)

This means that, since there exist significant differences between AAs in the strength of each locational factor, policy measures which are mobilised for each AA should be specified and differentiated from those of other areas. The improvement of weak locational factors in each AA should be undertaken in parallel with the provision of financial assistance. For instance, according to the findings from the regression and survey analyses in this study, the measures such as further construction of the transport network in Scotland, Wales and the West Midlands, more development of industrial land and premises in the North and Yorkshire and Humberside and the provision of more training facilities in Scotland are desirable.

In short, all the possible measures from financial aid to infrastructure, labour training and even coordinated promotional activities should be taken into account and incorporated into the policy initiatives for a certain AA both to enhance the competitiveness of the area in general and to meet the requirements of targeted investments of Japanese MNCs in particular. This is much more the case in order to meet the flexible managerial strategy of Japanese MNCs which take advantage of all the conditions and locational factors. In this regard, it is appropriate to argue that:

" The coexistence today of different production contexts [i.e. Fordism and post-Fordism] prompts consideration of different policy implications of corporate behaviour" (Ettlinger,1990,p.70).

Consequently, regional policy needs to be more flexible and more coordinated in terms of both measures and participating bodies to meet and to take advantage of the flexible managerial strategy of Japanese MNCs.

10.2.2 Implications for the Korean regional policy

Unlike the British case, regional policy in Korea has been maintained without any considerable change in its measures. The urgent need for balanced regional development has been widely agreed, but without supporting policy initiatives. Consequently, doubts about the effectiveness of regional policy have been raised on various grounds. The continuing concentration of population and industry in the two prosperous areas, Seoul and Kyongsangnam-Do including Pusan, and the widening gap between regions provide the most vivid evidence showing the poor performance of regional policy in Korea.

By the same token, the usefulness of the traditional regional policy that concentrates government assistance in some designated IEs in attracting incoming Japanese companies to those areas began to fall from the mid-1970s and in particular in the early 1980s as shown just ahead. Irrespective of the changes in the policy concern, Japanese companies in Korea have chosen to concentrate their plant sites in the two prosperous regions. To make matters worse, the policy objectives of the Korean government have not been robust and consistent enough to take advantage of Japanese FDI for alleviating regional problems. The policy has often become ambiguous according to the changes in how people regard foreign capital, especially Japanese capital. A policy implication from this situation is that the diversification of policy measures and the firm implementation of these decided policy measures are necessary and urgent. The policy initiatives which need to be introduced for the purpose can be listed as follows.

First of all, a fundamental change in the structure of Korean government policy, especially in relation to economic policy and regional policy, is required. In other words, the ramified spatial and industrial policy implemented by numerous ministries needs to be integrated in the hands of one powerful body, like the DTI in Britain. In order to tackle more efficiently the emergent regional problem, which has been neglected for a long time in order to rapidly achieve the goal of national economic growth, it is necessary to reinforce the power of the ministry in charge of regional development planning and policy.

At the same time, the regulations concerned with national land planning and regional planning should be placed ahead of, or at least parallel with, those on national economic growth. As a matter of fact, this reversal has not been achieved partly due to the quiescent belief of policy makers that the concentration of industry and population in certain areas is inevitable, or even

279

necessary, for further economic development and, thus, the regional problem should be endured for the time being. However, this argument, based on agglomeration economies, has its own limit in that it overlooks the detrimental effect of concentration for economic development itself. Needless to depend on the theory of decreasing marginal efficiency, it is certain that the over-concentration phenomenon in Korea has reached a level to hamper economic development through the delivery delays, high wage cost, militant activities of labour, and high prices for industrial land and premises. This situation has become the main reason causing the lowered competitiveness of Korean products and the retreat of foreign MNCs from Korea. Therefore, without fundamental change in the policy structure and in the thinking of policy makers, the regional problem in Korea will continue, and will even be aggravated.

Secondly, various kinds of infrastructure should be constructed in the lagging regions, in particular in Cholla and Kangwon Dos. These regions are quite poor in accessibility including motorways, trunk roads, seaports and airports and universities. Although successive Korean governments have pledged to build the necessary infrastructure in these regions, their performance has been far from satisfactory. Considering the fact that many Japanese companies invest in Korea in order to capture big markets in Korea on the one hand and to export the products to other countries on the other, as expounded in chapters nine and ten, the existence of well developed transport networks, seaports and airports are crucial to attract these companies to a region.

Thirdly, to confront the limitation of the traditional IE-centred regional policy, a different kind of approach in regional policy needs to be introduced like the British case. Since linkage issues, especially the relationship with indigenous manufacturing companies in Korea, have been important for the locational choice of Japanese firms, confirmed in the survey analysis, the present assistance system of sticking to limited areas of IEs is ineffective in attracting the mobile Japanese firms as well as indigenous firms. As an alternative, the introduction of wide-drawn AAs, like those previously in Britain, is worth considering.

And, lastly, in implementing regional policy, the participation of the provincial government and local authority seems to be desirable. Since Korea has been one of the most centralised countries in the world in terms of the power of the central government, the role of local authorities has been minimal. This means that individual regions have been excluded from regional policy initiatives. In order to attract Japanese FDI into lagging regions and, thus, to take advantage of the investments for the purpose of developing these regions, local authorities should begin promotional activities of some kind for their own areas. The political democratisation since the late 1980s and the local autonomy from 1990 are thought to provide a good opportunity for local authorities to do these positive activities.

In short, a comprehensive policy initiative reaching various fields and various institutions is necessary in order to induce incoming Japanese companies as well as mobile indigenous firms into lagging regions and, eventually, to achieve the goal of a balanced regional development. In addition, regional policy in Korea also needs to be more diversified and flexible to take advantage of inward Japanese investments and, ultimately, to solve the severe regional problems[45]. To achieve that goal, a more fundamental restructuring in policy structure and process should be initiated.

10.3 Summary

The two host countries examined in this study are different in the type of the regional problem they face, in the policy measures depended on for policy support and in the issues to be improved to achieve the goal of regional policies. Nonetheless, in deciding policy towards the investment of Japanese companies, both countries are in a similar position. They have in common the need to attract Japanese investment to take advantage of that investment for the growth of the national economy and the improvement of the industrial structure on the one hand, and for the alleviation of regional problems on the other.

Among these, the latter, the relationship between the regional problem and policy and the locational decisions of incoming Japanese companies, has been the major issue of concern in this study. From the previous discussions, it has been found that the locational pattern of Japanese companies in the changing context of regional policy was significantly different in the two host countries and that the implications of these locational patterns were also dissimilar.

Briefly speaking, in Britain, the concept and the measures of regional policy have changed significantly over the last decades and, against these changes in regional policy, the Japanese companies coming into this country have responded with a consistent strategy. As a result, the British government has been and will be able to take into account the contribution of incoming Japanese companies to the objectives of regional policy in a positive way.

To enhance this positive effect to the greatest extent, a strengthening of the activities of the promotional bodies led by the IBB and the coordination of the conducive initiatives of various authorities, an increase in the provision of infrastructure in AAs and the specialization of each region in terms of an industrial field are suggested. In addition, more basically, it is proposed that all the possible policy measures need to be mobilised and coordinated flexibly in order to meet the flexible managerial strategy of Japanese MNCs.

By contrast, regional policy in Korea has been sluggish to reflect the increasing policy demand, namely the urgent requirement of a more balanced regional development. Naturally, as a result, it has been impossible to expect

281

the Japanese companies to follow the Korean government's intention and, thus, to contribute to the mitigation of the disparity between regions. Therefore, without any drastic change, the present regional policy may lose ground even further.

To confront this problem, four alternatives are recommended, namely the reorganization of the government function to give priority to balanced regional development; more intensive construction of infrastructure, in particular the transport network, seaports and airports and universities, in the lagging regions; the broadening of the target areas in which government assistance is available; and the positive participation of local authorities in regional development and promotional activity.

One important matter derived from the discussion so far is that the experience of one host country can offer an alternative or complementary policy measure to the other, e.g. the concentration of government assistance in a specified industrial field in each region for Britain and the introduction of wide-drawn AAs and the activities of local authorities for Korea.

11 Final conclusion

11.1 Theoretical Framework : Overview

The locational decisions of manufacturing firms in general are made after examining various kinds of socio-economic and geographical factors relating to the host areas considered. Recently, with the growing internationalization of industry, foreign factors, i.e. the changes in the international economy in which individual companies and national economies are incorporated and operating, have intensified their influence on the locational choices of manufacturing firms in each country and across the world.

However, internally within a business, every decision of each concern is related basically to the managerial objectives of the company whether explicit or implicit (and increasingly nowadays these objectives are very explicit). This means that the actual decisions of manufacturing (and other) firms are influenced not only by external factors at both national and international level, but also by the established and dynamic managerial strategies of the companies themselves.

From this viewpoint, the locational choices of manufacturing firms moving into foreign countries need to be understood as the products of the interaction between these forces, namely the changing circumstances in the international and national economy which the companies face, the managerial strategy of these companies at the worldwide level and the socio-economic and geographical factors in the chosen location relative to others.

The present study has tried to explain the locational behaviour of Japanese manufacturing companies in host countries as the outcome of the interaction between these forces. One thing should be mentioned is that Japanese MNCs have acted recently as leading motivators in the international economy in line with their growing wealth. Therefore, the global managerial strategy of these companies, which itself is also continuously influenced by the changes in the international economy, has emerged as an important foreign factor, or international market force, for the host countries (Young et al.,1988,pp.8-9).

In this regard, the aim the present study has pursued can be simplified into the study of the interrelationship between the worldwide managerial strategy of Japanese MNCs expressed in their locations and the major geographical factors in host countries. In particular, among the various kinds of locational factors, this study concentrated its main focus on the host government's spatial or regional policy.

Britain and Korea were selected to be analyzed as the host countries representing developed countries and Asian developing countries respectively. Both countries have in common their importance as host countries for Japanese FDI. However, there are many differences in economic and geographical circumstances between these two countries. In particular, a considerable gap in the nature of regional policy has been recognized between these countries.

In Britain and in Korea, government regional and industrial policy has been one of the influential factors in the locational choices of manufacturing firms. However, the individual geographical circumstances which define the regional policy of each host country have brought about differences in the extent and direction of policy initiatives between the two countries. The dissimilarities in regional policy, which are a key factor of the different geographical context in the two countries, can be listed as follows.

Firstly, regional policy in Britain has been implemented more systematically and over a longer period than that in Korea. The improvement of the economic situation in lagging and depressed regions has been pursued by successive British governments without any considerable challenge from critics. In Korea, by contrast, there has been a much more substantial conflict between the two government policy objectives, namely national economic growth and balanced regional development[46]. For the purpose, regional policy in Korea has depended for a long time on a growth pole strategy (concentrating in only a few prosperous regions), which recently by contrast has been claimed to be unsuitable for Britain[47].

Secondly, the performance of regional policy in the two countries has been significantly different. In Britain, many researchers have reported the successful effect of regional policy on the movement of mobile firms into designated AAs and the growth of investment and employment in these areas (Chapter four). By contrast, in Korea, in spite of the continuous concern of the government with the regional imbalance problem, there has been no noticeable report indicating the success of regional policy. This unsatisfactory performance on the part of regional policy in Korea is due to the organizational problem which the government policy structure generates: i.e. the supremacy of the objective of national economic growth with the growth pole strategy contributing to the attainment of that national goal.

And, thirdly, there is another difference in the regional problem and policy between the two countries. This is in the response of the two governments to the drastic change in the circumstances of regional policy in the 1980s. The British government has responded promptly by cutting the scale of existing policy measures and by introducing new policy initiatives, apart from the question of the effect of these initiatives. However, the Korean government has been sluggish in introducing the necessary policy transformation to fulfil the mounting policy demand. Therefore, compared to the swiftly changing spatial policy in Britain, that of Korea has been maintained without sufficient reform in its content in the 1980s.

Given these different contexts of regional policy, the locational behaviour of incoming Japanese manufacturing companies has received increasing attention in the two countries. This is because the Japanese MNCs, with their overwhelming competitiveness and accumulated wealth, are thought to be able to influence substantially the regional and national economy in the two host countries.

In particular, it has been assumed that Japanese companies have had unique features in choosing their plant sites. This study has been designed, firstly, to identify these features, especially in relation to the changing geographical factors, particularly the given host government's regional policy, by investigating the experiences of the two host countries, secondly, to interpret the results in terms of the Japanese companies' managerial strategy at the international level, and, thirdly, to make use of these strategies of Japanese MNCs for the objectives of regional policy.

11.2   Methodology Reconsidered

In this study, the empirical evidence on the locational behaviour of Japanese companies in the two countries, in relation to changing circumstances, has been traced through the descriptive, regression and survey analyses. The descriptive analysis was introduced to portray the general features of the locational pattern of Japanese companies establishing plants in the two host countries (Chapter six). The regression analysis was implemented as a macro-level analysis to identify the principal specific geographical factors influencing the locational choices of these Japanese companies (Chapter seven). And, then, the survey analysis was undertaken at a micro-level to find the managerial strategy of Japanese companies in the drastically changing world economy and the geographical factors which attracted Japanese managers in deciding their locations (chapter eight).

The numbers of Japanese companies involved were 181 in Britain and 299 in Korea. These were the total number of Japanese companies that arrived in Britain and Korea respectively up to the end of 1990. With the various statistics relating to these companies, the descriptive analysis investigated the historical trends in incoming Japanese companies, their ownership and geographical distribution, their industrial sector and their size distribution in the two host countries.

In implementing the regression analysis, 61 variables for the British case and 65 variables for the Korean case were selected initially to represent the major locational factors, namely labour supply, public policy, land and premises availability, accessibility, linkages and environmental circumstances. These locational factors, or independent variables, were chosen taking into account the estimated two year time lag with the dependent variables. Thus, most of these independent variables were based on figures for the period from 1979 to 1988. These independent variables were regressed against the chosen set of dependent variables. The dependent variables were the number of Japanese companies and their employment (investment in the case of Korea). By using these dependent and independent variables, a stepwise regression analysis was undertaken to identify the important locational factors.

The regression involved three different stages, namely 1) the static and change analysis using the static figure at a fixed date and the changes in the variables during a given period of time; 2) the index analysis integrating the variables involved in the static and change analysis; and 3) the sub-period analysis comprising the regressions of two sub-periods, i.e. 1981-1986 and 1987-1990, to show the changes in the influential location factors between these periods. By comparing the results of these four stages of regression, a set of important locational factors were identified (Chapter seven and 9.2.2).

The regression analysis of this study, however, has a number of limitations. These limitations can be identified as follows:

Firstly, there has been the problem of the lack of data resources. The difficulty in obtaining suitable data resources is the most significant obstacle in implementing this analysis. In particular, the access to Korean data corresponding to the British case was very restricted and, as a result, the explicability of the findings of the regression analysis can be said to have been constrained[48].

Secondly, being a cross-section analysis, this regression analysis is unsuitable to show fully the exact relationship between the variables, especially the relationship between the increase in the volume of employment in Japanese companies and the changes in the regional policy over a given period of time. In other words, this regression explained only the relative importance of regional policy among various kinds of locational factors either at a fixed time or during a given span of time. Therefore, it has been impossible to compare the degree of relationship between variables directly by comparing the produced correlation coefficients. In order to produce a more objective measure of relationship between the variables, a group of time-series analyses for a longer period is necessary.

And, thirdly, this regression analysis was basically a macro- analysis using published aggregate statistics. In order to estimate the extent and causality of the relationship between the locational behaviour of Japanese companies and the locational factors of the host areas more specifically and, thus, to enhance the relevance of the findings in this analysis, another kind of analysis at the micro-level was needed. Accordingly, this study introduced another kind of empirical analysis, the micro-level survey analysis.

The survey analysis was undertaken in the form of mail questionnaires and interviews. Among all the Japanese companies operating in the two host countries 62 (34.3%) companies in Britain and 106 (35.5%) companies in Korea responded with useful answers. Among these, 20 companies established in Britain allowed the access of the interview researcher and, thus, 20 interview surveys were completed.

In conducting the survey, the managers of Japanese companies were requested to answer five questions relating to, namely, the main market for their products, the push factors in Japan which resulted in the outward investment of these companies, the attractive or unsatisfactory locational factors, the influence of the host government assistance and alternative locations considered. The answers of the managers were coded, classified and analyzed by means mainly of descriptive statistics. The results produced in this way were compared with the regression results to search for the important factors for the location of Japanese companies and to infer the global strategy of these companies.

In short, by utilising both macro- and micro-analyses, the findings of this study has been able to show not only the general trend but also the precise extent of the relationship between the locational pattern of Japanese manufacturing companies and the socio-economic and geographical factors of the areas considered with these factors headed by the availability of regional policy.

11.3 Findings and Policy Implications

The main findings of these descriptive, regression and survey analyses were summarised already in Chapter nine (9.2). Briefly, once again, the findings can be summarized as follows:

Firstly, the Japanese companies in Britain were more evenly distributed spatially, larger in size, more biased towards the electronics industry and on an markedly increasing trend in numbers arriving in contrast to those in Korea.

Secondly, the regression analysis showed that labour supply, especially the non-militancy and competence of labour, government incentives comprising financial aid and public expenditure and the presence locally of leading Japanese companies were the important locational factors in Britain. In contrast, the number of Japanese manufacturing firms nearby, the abundance of labour and the availability of industrial estates were influential in the case of Korea.

Thirdly, the questionnaire and interview survey demonstrated the fact that

287

the Japanese companies in Britain were targeting mainly to supply products to other main manufacturers, were motivated to invest overseas by the market factor under their global strategy, were provided with the financial aid of the host government and considered a limited number of alternative countries in Europe. In contrast, those in Korea were targeting the consumer market in Korea and foreign countries, were influenced crucially by low-cost and highly-skilled labour, received advice and sites on industrial estates from the Korean government and searched for alternative locations in Asian developing countries.

And, finally, in relation specifically to regional policy, most Japanese companies coming into Britain have preferred or been induced to locate in AAs or peripheral regions where various kinds of government assistance were available. By contrast, in Korea, Japanese companies have continued to place their factories in the two prosperous regions regardless of government concern (in rhetoric rather than policy design however).

In short, Japanese companies have shown sharply different locational patterns in the two host countries where, admittedly, the geographical contexts have been significantly different from each other. In other words, the Japanese companies were found to have adopted different policies according to the different circumstances in making their locational decisions in order to choose those places where the overall locational conditions were the most advantageous and, thus, to utilize the existing circumstances in the host countries to the greatest extent.

An important argument of this thesis has been that these findings about the different locational behaviour of Japanese companies in the two host countries need to be considered in terms of the managerial strategy of Japanese MNCs at the worldwide level. This is because, as mentioned just ahead, the various activities of each MNC in general are undertaken within the framework of the global management strategy of that MNC. The features of the managerial strategy of Japanese MNCs, which were revealed when focusing on their different behaviours in developed countries and in developing countries, can be summarized by the following four aspects: 1) Japanese FDI has been in the process of moving from neighbouring Asian countries to developed market countries; 2) the Japanese companies in developed countries have tended to equip themselves with large scale investment and high technology; 3) the Japanese companies in developed countries have tended to show a division of labour concentrating on more specific and complete products and to lead a group of supplier companies; and, 4) Japanese MNCs have begun to invest in overseas countries regardless of the existence of trade barriers according to their globalisation strategy.

Comparing these features with the above findings of the empirical analyses, it becomes evident that the locational behaviour of Japanese companies in each host country is consistent with, and is able to be explained by, the worldwide managerial strategy of these Japanese companies: i.e. the division of the world market into smaller market areas and the flexible utilisation of the circumstances in each market area. Of course, this claim needs a little caution. Since only the two countries, namely Britain and Korea, have been involved in this study as the host countries for the Japanese FDI representing developed and developing countries. An additional effort to include more examples in other host countries in the two categories is necessary if this claim is to be validated to apply in any circumstance.

Nonetheless, within this framework, the varied responses of Japanese companies to the changes in, and to the changing context of, regional policy in the two host countries can be interpreted as the result of the managerial strategy of Japanese companies which is applied in different ways to accommodate the companies to the fresh circumstances. An important question, thus, is whether the regional policy of a host country can be well coordinated with the global managerial strategy of these companies, as the most dramatic international market force, or not.

In this regard, the success of British regional policy in attracting mobile Japanese firms into designated AAs and, thus, in utilizing these companies to alleviate regional problems can be attributed to the concomitance of, or the flexible response of, the content of British regional policy with the managerial objectives of the Japanese MNCs seeking their plant sites in Britain and, thus, in developed countries.

By contrast, the Korean government has failed to take advantage of incoming Japanese companies for achieving the goal of its regional policy. No doubt, this has been caused by the lack of government effort in coordinating these two influential forces. As a result, Japanese companies operating in Korea these days play a negative role rather than positive one in the achievement of the goal of government regional policy. With regard to the policy implication of the empirical evidence, an interesting finding is that the experience of one host country can provide a relevant policy alternative to the other.

In short, it is possible to conclude that Japanese MNCs are highly responsive and flexible to changes in the locational factors in host countries within the framework of their worldwide managerial strategies in order to maximize their own profit and, ultimately, to enable their national economy to overcome obstacles in the international arena. Another and final conclusion of this study is that there should be a renewed emphasis on the importance of the changes in international market forces, including the activities of foreign MNCs, in discussing the direction and measures of regional policy in each country, especially in this era of, so called, 'post-Fordism' or 'disorganized capitalism'.

As final words, this study has tried to link directly the geography of host countries (regional policy) and the worldwide strategy of MNCs (Japanese capital). On the one hand, the worldwide managerial strategy of Japanese MNCs has been inferred through the examination of their locations in specific areas, which are represented by a bundle of geographical factors. On the other hand, the implications, or the utilities, of this worldwide strategy have been investigated for the sake of an improved geography of host countries and host areas.

This approach needs to be differentiated from other approaches to the study of regional policy in that the policy direction has been looked for through the analysis of the influence of all the geographical factors reflected in the locational behaviour of MNCs. Also this study can be said to be singular among the studies on Japan and her capital in that it illuminates the global strategy of Japanese capital by reference to the locational behaviour of multinationalized Japanese companies in the changing geography of host countries instead of the popular issues like the unique characteristics of management style and its sociological background, etc[49]. From the meaningful findings of this study, it can be concluded that the activities or influence of international market forces can be, and should be, understood and utilized in terms of the geography of individual nations, and vice versa.

Notes

Introduction

1. Here, FDI is a type of financial flow abroad in the management process. FDI is distinguished from indirect investment, or portfolio investment, in that FDI aims at controlling the management, or production process, of the firm invested in. For more about FDI, see Chapter two.
2. Of course, 'a large market share', rather than 'high profit', has been the prime target for most Japanese companies. However, in the late 1980s, the importance of higher and short-term profit began to take an equivalent position to market share in the managerial objectives of Japanese management (Higashi and Lauter,1990,p.374).
3. Dicken explains that the capitalist market system is the *general* structure which involves MNC activities (Dicken,1992, pp.120-121).
4. Regarding the importance of manufacturing in regional growth, see Harris (1987).

Chapter One : The World Economy in a Changing Context

1. These may combine effectively into one overall structural change - hence the single noun is adopted below on many occasions.
2. As for the period of postwar boom, it is generally asserted that the period continued until the first oil crisis in 1973. However, since the symptoms of the recession in the 1970s and 1980s began to appear from the mid-1960s, this study takes the mid-1960s as the watershed dividing the boom and recession (Storper and Scott,1989,p.21; Dunford,1990,p.317; Nolan and O'Donnell,1991,p.112; Sadler,1992,p.1).
3. This problem, which the capitalism based on Keynesian economics implies, is well expounded by Hunt (1981).
4. However, because of the magnitude of the US, the economic policies of the American government still have substantial importance in world economy.
5. This means that services are integrated with manufacturing in the *Material Production* arena among the four arenas of the service function, which are highly interrelated and combined encompassing manufacturing and other services, in Wood's framework. The other arenas are the *Domestic, Public* and *Capital Circulation* arenas (Wood,1991,pp.68-69).
6. See Braverman H., *Labour and Monopoly Capital* (Monthly Review Press,New York,1974).
7. By contrast, Painter examines the crisis of Fordism in local government production such as health care and education mainly based on the framework of Aglietta and throws a question mark over the emergence of a 'post-Fordist' society (Painter,1991,pp.29-43).

8. Bagguley names Piore and Sabel as institutionalists and classifies their argument within the bounds of post-Fordism. However, scholars following their view resist being included in this school in that flexible specialization, differently from post-Fordism, which sees production or the productive system as 'integrated and coherent totalities', is a complex of 'social and political identities' which cannot be derived from a given structure of production (Hirst and Zeitlin,1991,p.2 and p.8).

    Nevertheless, the argument of flexible specialization can be included within the broader boundary of post-Fordism in that flexible specialization is based fundamentally on the mode of production in contrast with mass production.

9. It is even assessed as 'an optimistic vision to counter the gloom of the restructuring and crisis debates' (Dicken and Lloyd, 1990,p.393).

10. There are views, mainly from Marxists, that see that these forms of change involve or reflect a kind of management effort to exploit labour to the maximum degree.

11. Concerning the exact period of a long wave, scholars diverge. This is caused by the fact that Kondratiev himself did not present a fixed theory of this. While Peter Hall (1988,p.56) suggests 55 years, Brown (1984,p.92), Marshall (1987,p.2) and Knox and Agnew (1989,p.86) argue 50 years. This study, following the statistical test of Beenstock (1983,p.144), takes 50 years as a cycle of the long wave.

12. Castells summarized the features of the restructuring that emerged in the late 1980s as being : 1) the reversal of the capital-labour power relationship which appeared most eloquently in the diminishing trade union movement; 2) a changed form of government intervention from political legitimation and social redistribution to political domination and capital accumulation; and 3) the acceleration of internationalization in every part of economic process to get a higher profit (Castells,1989,pp.23-27).

13. See Yannopoulus (1990). However, Julius argues that the influence of the European single market in 1992 and the fear of protectionism on the growth of FDI in the 1980s has been insignificant. Instead, she emphasizes the significance of the liberalisation of the service sector and the political and economic context in Japan resulted from its large trade surplus (Julius,1990,pp.31-36).

14. This issue is investigated further in Chapter two.

15. Here, 'information industry' means the industry which produces high-technology devices using information technology, e.g. telecommunication facilities, microprocessor and microcomputer.

16. Regarding the spatial redistribution of facilities and employment following the transformation of the French automobile industry, see Oberhauser (1990,pp.219-228).

17. In terms of GNP, the 1937 level was already restored in 1952 (Macpherson,1987,p.11).

18. However, as to the leading role of the Japanese government in the economic development process, there exists controversy as mentioned below.

19. Munday divides the factors involved in the recovery of the Japanese economy into external elements and internal elements. The external elements consisted of an open world trading system, a fixed exchange rate and a fluent supply of raw materials including oil, while the internal elements include the co-operative efforts of policy makers and industry, a high level of personal savings, a good education system and an identifiably distinctive management system (Munday,1990,pp.2-9).

20. As to the Japanese government policy, see Okimoto, *Between MITI and Market* (Stanford University Press,1989).

21. Regarding the debate on this issue, see D. Friedman, *The Misunderstood Miracle* (Cornell University Press,Ithaca,1988), Introduction.

22. The issue of the nature of Japanese capital is discussed in more detail in Chapter nine (9.3.1).

23. In some aspects, the Japanese invasion of the Korean peninsular in the late sixteenth century can also be interpreted in this way.

24. As to the influences and pressures of other countries on Japanese capital, see Sakamoto, *Japan and the Internationalization of Capital* (A paper presented in the 'Conference on Internationalization of Japan in Comparative Perspective, Sheffield University,1989,pp.1-4).

25. Bolwijn and Brinkman classify the flexibility in Japanese manufacturing into three parts; namely volume flexibility, mix flexibility and start-up flexibility (Bolwijn and Brinkman,1987, pp.30-31).

    On the other hand, Aoki labels the prevalent organizational and operational features of Japanese companies as the J-mode in contrast to the H-mode of traditional organization (Aoki,1990, pp.1-29).

26. Some authors refuse to accept the cultural influence on the success of the Japanese economy (Friedman,1988,p.230; Porter,1990, p.420). And the culture may be changing adversely to Japanese capital.

    However, the peculiarities of Japanese culture and system cannot, and should not, be ignored. That the Japanese style management and management-labour relationship have not been easily transplanted to Korea and China because of their uniqueness in spite of the similarities in these countries' origins and Confucian traditions expresses the significance of this aspect eloquently. The difference between Japan and neighbouring countries is most apparent in the management-labour relationship (see Macpherson, 1987,pp.11-14).

27. Oberhauser also expressed almost the same opinion (Oberhauser,1990,p.218).

28. The low level of satisfaction among Japanese managers about their management system compared to their British counterparts supports this argument (*ESRC Newsletter*, Feb. 1992).

29. In contrast to the fluctuating and tripolarising international economy, international politics, with the collapse of the communist bloc, has settled down with the US remaining as the world's single superpower (*Financial Times*, 16 Mar. 1992).

Chapter Two: The Nature and Influence of Multinational Companies

1. Nester names the p/olicy of the Japanese government after the Second World War as a 'neo-mercantilist trade policy' on the ground that it pursued the greatest national wealth but without depending on military power (Nester,1990,pp.xi-xiii).

2. Hedland calls the recent structure of MNCs, which is characterised by many centres of different functions all over the world, the 'heterarchy' (Hedland and Rolander,1990,pp.24-26).

3. On the other hand, Storpford and Turner classify the historical phase of British MNCs into the following four stages; namely before the First World War, the inter-war period, from the end of the war to the 1960s or the early 1970s and the present (Storpford and Turner,1985,p.45).

4. For instance, the negative relationship between the level of political repression in the under-developed host countries and the location of MNCs based on developed countries in the period of 1975-1986 has been reported (Billet,1990,pp.29-53).

5. In total world stocks of FDI, the share of the US, which was 11.2% in 1975, increased to 29% in 1985. The inward stock of FDI into the US multiplied over 7 times, from 27.7 to 209.3 billion dollars, during the period of 1975-1986 (UN,1988,p.25 and p.526).

6. However, recently, the share of developing countries in the global total inward investment began to rise once again in the late 1980s and, especially, in 1990 (*Financial Times*, 16

Jun. 1992).

7. In fact, strictly speaking, these theories can be called 'theories about the FDI made by MNCs'. However, here, the term the 'theories about the MNC' is taken on the ground that

> "a theory of [FDI] is also a theory of the [MNC] as an actor in the world economy...,
> [because FDI] is not simply an international transfer of capital but rather the
> extension of an enterprise from its home country into a foreign host country"
> (Root,1990,p.618).

8. This part is mainly from Parry (1980, Chapter two) and Cantwell (1991). However, Cantwell divides the MNC theories into four groups according to their focusing points are either firm-specific or macroeconomic: the market power theory; the internalisation theory; macroeconomic developmental approaches; and competitive international industry theory. In his explanation, the eclectic theory is not treated as a separate theory of MNC, since it encompasses all the aspects of the above four approaches and can be used at both the level of a specific firm and of the macro-economy (Cantwell,1991,pp.17-18).

On the other hand, as mentioned in Introduction, Santiago illustrated the way that studies of FDI have developed in three different ways (Introduction).

9. The PLC model explains the basic evolution of the international production of innovations from export to direct investment as a sequence of development, i.e. the phases of innovation, expansion, maturity and decline (Lambooy,1986, pp.156-158).

10. Cantwell refuses to include this approach in the category of internalisation theory. According to him, the competitive international industry approach is quite different from internalisation or transaction cost theory in that, unlike the latter which regards ownership advantages as given, in the former approach, the acquisition of ownership advantages is the prerequisite for or essence of firms to survive in the oligopolistic market in the world *(ibid,*pp.45-52).

However, the competitive international industry approach also can be included in the broad internalisation theory in that, firstly, it basically postulates the internalisation of markets through the possession of ownership advantages and, secondly, both are similarly based on the oligopolistic rivalry between MNCs in the world market rather than on the perfect competition between them.

11. Since the mid-1980s, Dunning has referred to the eclectic paradigm rather than eclectic theory on the ground that his framework covers all the motives of international production and, thus, encompasses all the different theoretical viewpoints (Dunning,1991,p.133).

12. Dicken regards this approach as the integration of three principles originated from the organization theory, trade theory and location theory (Dicken,1992,p.126).

13. In particular, the empirical study of Al-Eryani *et al.* reports that legal constraints, tax and custom regulations, anti-dumping and antitrust legislation, etc. have been the most influential factors for US-based MNCs in using transfer pricing.

14. However, this presumption is often disputed in that, first, there is not necessarily any significant taxation differentials between major market countries to justify transfer pricing and that, second, individual subsidiaries normally resist accepting the higher prices planned by their headquarters in order to increase their own subsidiary's profit performance (Ghertman and Allen,1984,pp.87-88).

15. Dicken sees the nation state and the MNC as the two main actors in the current world economy (Dicken,1992,Ch.4).

16. Porter (1990) and Rugman and Verbeke (1990) also emphasize the role of home state policy in either enhancing or protecting the international activities of MNCs, although their arguments originate from rather different points of departure.

17. For instance, one writer analyzes the host government policy about foreign investment by dividing it into four groups; namely, the policy related to entry (regulation about ownership), to operations (local content), transfer of capital (profit and tax) and inducement (competitive bidding) (Dicken,1992,pp.155-157).
18. This overseas investment, however, was not in reality all by MNCs in manufacturing.
19. Regarding the opposite view to this effect, see Dicken (1992,p.403).
20. Conversely, the negative effect of FDI on the balance of payments of the host country is also claimed by authors (Jenkins, 1987,p.112). The cases of Australia in the 1960s (Fieldhouse, 1986,p.2) and the US in the 1980s (Hipple,1990,pp.500-502) are representative examples.
21. In terms of manufacturing production, foreign-owned firms accounted for 20% of total manufacturing production in the UK in 1987 (*Lloyds Bank Economic Bulletin*, Jun. 1990).
22. The estimates of net inward and outward direct investment are made based on the statistical inquiries of the DTI, the Bank of England and the Association of British Insurers (*British Business*, 3 Jul. 1987,pp.38-39).
23. These figures include unremitted profits, and a minus sign indicates net disinvestment overseas.
24. This perhaps reflects both the nature of regional incentives in AAs and the distribution of opportunities for takeover.
25. In fact there was a decrease in 1986 when political instability in Korea slowed up the inflow of foreign investment.
26. The importance of the non-manufacturing sector in Japanese FDI showed a sharp decline in comparison to that of the manufacturing sector in 1990 and 1991. High interest rates and a weak stock market have been indicated as the main reasons (*Financial Times*, 15 Jul. 1991; *JEI Report*, 19 Jun. 1992).
27. This issue is investigated further with regard to the globalization strategy of Japanese MNCs in Chapter nine.
28. More on the managerial strategy of Japanese MNCs is displayed in Chapters six and nine
29. This figure has been lowered to 15.3% in 1990 and, further, to 15.2% in 1991.
30. A recent survey undertaken by the Export-Import Bank in Japan illuminated that the abundant supply of low-cost labour was the main reason of the Japanese FDI in Asian countries (37.4%), standing out from those cases in the US (1.1%) and Europe (0%) (*Financial Times*, 15 Jul. 1991).
31. The global strategy of Japanese MNCs which brings about the recent changes in their geographical distribution is explored in detail in Chapters nine and ten.
32. However, more recently, MNCs are increasingly decentralizing their R&D activities, especially production support laboratories, around the world (Caves,1982a,p.256; Dicken,1992, pp.198-201).
33. Those with either a total number of employees of 300 or fewer or a paid-up capital worth 100m yen or less.
34. However, Kojima's approach is also criticized on the ground that it is appropriate only to the early stage of Japanese FDI. This was characterised by investment in the adjacent cheap-labour cost countries and the promotional policy of the Japanese government resulting in the overseas investment of small-sized firms, and, thus, has a significant limitation in portraying the general features of MNC activity (Clegg,1987,pp.27-30).

Chapter Three : The Causes and Effects of Industrial Location

1. The explanation of structural theory here includes the political economy's view.
2. Major assumptions of Weber's model can be listed as follows (Bale,1976,p.82): firstly,

most raw material supplies are localised; secondly, product markets are identical at each point; thirdly, transport costs are dependent upon the weight of the products and the distance they are transported; fourthly, markets are organised under the conditions of perfect competition; and, finally, man (the industrial decision-maker) is fully rational and informed of all the facts and conditions relevant to his plant, market and industry.

With these assumptions, Weber tried to construct a theory of minimum transport cost. During the process, Weber introduced the concept of the material index which is the ratio of the weight of localised raw material inputs to the weight of finished product. According to the magnitude of this index, an industry is determined to be either raw material oriented (where the index is bigger than 1) or market oriented (the index is smaller than 1). Also, in addition, by using isodapanes, Weber expected manufacturers to seek a still better location where labour cost savings or agglomerate economies are also possible (Smith,1981, pp.70-74).

3. T. Palander, unlike Weber who sought an optimum location by using the transport cost based on its weight, explained the optimum location by using transport cost directly. A. Lösch tried to produce a general equilibrium model of location based on distributional efficiency involving the concept of demand and maximum profit (Smith,1981,pp.84-90). On the other hand, Christaller constructed a refined system of hexagonal market areas to explain the distribution of market centres by introducing the terms of threshold and range (Healey and Ilbery,1990,pp.22-23; Dicken and Lloyd,1990,pp.25-30).

4. Smith lists A. Weber, T. Palander, E.M. Hoover, etc. as being included in the former strand, while grouping H. Hotelling, E.H. Chamberlain, A.F. Smithies, etc. in the latter.

5. See also Beckman (1968). On the other hand, Walker and Calzonetti show that cost minimization cannot be a general objective of plant location through their empirical analysis (Walker and Calzonetti,1989,p.23).

6. In particular, Dicken (1971) and Krumme (1969,1985) are the representative critics. Regarding the criticism from a different standpoint, see Massey (1973,1979b).

7. In particular, H.A. Simon, R.M. Cyert and J.G. March.

8. See also McDermott and Taylor (1982). From the same standpoint, Dicken regards the global strategy of MNCs as the product of the interrelationship between the co-ordination of a firm's activities (organizational decision) and geographical location (geographical decision) (Dicken,1992,pp.194-196). He argues that:

> "Both internalized and externalized relationships are the threads through which the global economy is integrated, linking together both organizations and geographical areas in complex interrelated and overlapping divisions of labour" *(ibid*,p.226).

9. Boddy regards this point as 'the growing concern to relate locational behaviour and employment impacts to organizational structure and corporate strategy'(Boddy,1987,p.57).

10. But this is still controversial, just the same as there are still those with faith in neoclassical theory. See Massey and Meegan eds. (1985).

11. For example, the study of Glasmeier and McClusky (1987) exploring the forces causing the spatial and organizational tendencies of the auto parts industry in the US.

12. The locational pattern and evidence on locational factors in this study is mainly British (not Korean nor Japanese). This is because the materials concerned with this issue can be more easily obtained in Britain than in other countries and that the British case is thought to be applicable to general circumstances.

13. The empirical evidence on the importance of market accessibility for the Japanese companies coming into the UK is discussed further in Chapter nine. Also, see *Financial Times* (30 Apr. 1992) for the case of Sony.

14. Regarding the impact of tax on industrial location, see Newman and Sullivan (1988). By

contrast, Schmenner *et al.* (1987), Rabino (1989) and Ziegler (1990) argue that the influence of tax is negligible.

15. Indeed regional policy in Britain is now a minor affair though much less so for foreign inward investment. This is partly because a range of newer spatially discriminating policies addressing inner city problems have been introduced. Some account of these are taken in this study.

16. The report produced by Henry *et al*, which is based on a series of cross sectional survey data collected in 1987, shows the positive effects of the construction of the Channel Tunnel on commercial and industrial locations in Kent (Henry *et al.*,1989, pp.431-445). On the other hand, infrastructure has been found to be a significant factor for the relocation of corporate headquarters in the US (Holloway and Wheeler,1991,p.72).

17. Opposition to this argument comes from Chisholm (1990, pp.144-147). Massey *et al.* have recently discussed this in relation to science parks, finding weaker connections than expected (Massey *et al.*,1992,pp.34-40).
    On the other hand, regarding the positive effects of research parks on the environment for small firm growth in the US, see Kysiak (1989).

18. Glasson classifies this factor basically into two kinds, i.e. physical environment and built environment. However, he adds the socio-economic structure of a region to these as another aspect forming environment (Glasson,1992,p.508).

19. However, some defects of this technique including a loss of information and the lack of measures for testing its assumptions are indicated by Holden *et al.* (1989,pp.15-34). See also Wren and Waterson (1991,p.116).

20. Also, see Lever (1991,p.983) for the case of Glasgow. Fothergill and Gudgin explain this situation of urban-rural shift and the resulting problem of regional inequality mainly by reference to the constraints for the expansion of factories (Fothergill and Gudgin,1982).

21. The impact of MNC activities on the host country economy was delineated in the previous Chapter (1.2.3).

22. Concerning this issue, an interesting finding of the West Midlands Development Agency (WMDA) is that the employment size of overseas companies in the West Midlands region grew remarkably, from 6,300 to 17,800, after their arrival. This implies the fact that the arrival of MNCs can bring about long-term employment creation in the host region (WMDA,1990,pp.51-52).

23. The higher technology level of MNCs compared to that of indigenous companies was found in a number of survey results including that of DTI (1983) and Hamilton (1985).

24. The fore-mentioned WMDA survey report showed that over 70% of MNCs operating in the West Midlands region purchased local products and, accordingly, there was a high linkage effect of MNC operations (WMDA,1990,p.53). Other writers analyzed the similar impact of the arrival of Nissan Motor Co. on the North region (Peck,1990,pp.354-357; Sadler,1992,pp.196-209).

25. About the general strategy of MNCs in the international market, see Adam (1975) and Dicken (1992).

26. See Young, Hood and Hamill (1988) and Chapter one (1.4.2).

Chapter Four : Regional Policy and the Location of Multinational Companies

1. Smith classifies regional problems, which are the target that regional policy aims to get rid of or mitigate, into three; namely problems in underdeveloped regions, depressed regions and congested regions. Among these, the first two are usually recognised as the main regional problems in each country. He argues that the former, which is caused by reasons connected with location, can be resolved mainly by the improvement of links

including transportation and communications, while the latter, which are brought about by structural causes, can be tackled by means of the development of new industry, the assistance to industry to decelerate its decline, etc. (Smith,1989,pp.79-80).

2. Martin and Tyler assert that this economic consideration as well as social consideration is one of the main premises on which the post-War regional policy has been based (Martin and Tyler,1992, p.144). The relevance of this economic consideration, however, has been weakened with the aggravating national economic situation.

3. However, it is generally indicated that the political considerations in implementing British regional policy have given way to economic considerations since the late 1970s. Social considerations have been important throughout.

4. During the process, Sir John Toothill's report in 1961 demanding change in the focus of regional policy from lessening the unemployment level in designated regions to creating an environment for industrial development in these regions is worth noting (Parsons,1988,p.115).

5. However, it is asserted that regional disparity has been widening not only during the depressed years from the late 1970s to the early 1980s (Townroe and Martin,1988,p.7) but even during the period of recovery in the late 1980s (Pattie and Johnston,1990,pp.288-289).

6. However, in the case of defence-orientated industry among the high technology industries, the effect of the support including the procurement expenditure is being doubted because of its poor output in commercial fields (Oakey,1991).

7. This figure has been changed to £ 264.4m in 1991/92 (*Financial Times*, 11 Jun. 1992). In constant 1989/90 prices, the average annual expenditure on regional industrial policy including investment incentives and regional business development incentives has decreased from £ 653m (1979/80-1984/85) to £ 222m (1985/86-1990/91) (Martin and Tyler,1992,p.149).

8. With regard to this, it is worth noting that Mr. Heseltine, the environment secretary in 1991, declared the necessity of some measures in the regions with high unemployment rate against the policy of Mr. Lilley, then the trade and industry minister (*Economist*, 20 Apr. 1991).

9. In this regard, the shape of regional development policy in the 1990s is required to move towards:

> "a more flexible, decentralized approach, geared to regional innovation, technology services rather than manufacturing, indigenous rather than inward investment, programmes rather than projects, and small/intermediate rather than large firms" (Stohr quoted in Glasson,1992,p.512).

10. However, in evaluating regional policy, a number of practical problems, such as data availability, displacement impact, attribution problem, time scale, etc., have also been indicated (Storey,1990,pp.675-676; McEldowney,1991,p.262).

   Likewise, Willis and Saunders list displacement effect, replacement effect and multiplier effect as the main problems in measuring the employment effect of financial aid (Willis and Saunders,1988,pp.83-87).

11. In his 1989 study, Wren, based on the survey of 29 assisted firms in Cleveland county, concludes that the RDG scheme in regional policy had been an effective measure in job creation and casts a doubt on the wisdom of its abolition.

12. For instance, Fingleton and Tyler investigate the effect of regional policy between 1972-1981 by reference to the cost-effectiveness of relocation and concluded that the effect of regional policy was poor, while that of the IDC control was significant (Fingleton and Tyler,1990,pp.433-445).

Similarly, in the case of the US, it is often reported that financial incentives including tax advantages have little impact on the location decisions of manufacturing companies (Ziegler, 1990,pp.25-30).

13. In the UK, congestion and concentration in London were also an element in British regional policy but not the major issue.

14. In particular, the concentration of main universities in Seoul area has accelerated this trend and, thus, is being indicated as one of the most crucial reasons for the extreme regional imbalance in Korea.

15. These cities are similar in character to the New Towns in the UK.

16. In the fore-mentioned Smith's perspective, a large part of the regional problem in Korea is concerned with the problems of underdevelopment and congestion caused by reasons connected with geographical location and, as such, a large portion of policy effort has been poured into solving these problems.

17. Chollabuk-Do means the north Cholla-Do, while Chollanam-Do refers to the south Cholla-Do. The names of other regions also are made in this way. (See Map 4.2.)

18. However, regional income disparity has not been used often as an explicit policy target to be tackled. It is likely that, because the income balance problem is too tricky to take as the main policy objective, the government instead has taken the spatial equalization of population and industry as the primary objective of regional policy (Hwang,1984,p.351).

19. The statistics for regional product per capita after 1986 are not available. Therefore the present research proceeds with its analysis based on pre-1986 data.

20. Seoul's population changed from 5.5 million (17.6% of the total population) in 1970, 6.9 million (19.9%) in 1975, 8.4 million (22.3%) in 1980 and 9.6 million (23.8%) in 1985.

21. Regional product remained stable but had to be shared amongst fewer people because of outward migration.

22. In contrast, local industrial estates are appraised as having succeeded in drawing some population and industry into the peripheral regions. These local sites contained 870 plants and 170,000 employees by 1981 (Korea Research Institute for Human Settlement,1982).

23. However, to a less extent, the latter aim and consequent conflict has also been present at times in the UK as has the purpose of population dispersal from the cities to overspill towns in the surrounding region.

24. To some extent, British regional policy shares this problem in that various kinds of policy measure have been initiated from the different perspectives of either the Department of the Environment or the DTI, or even the Treasury (let alone the Department of Employment with its concern for employment and unemployment).

25. Hansen et al. properly observes that:

" ... shifts in regional policy ... do not take place in isolation. They are parts, and major parts, of the periodic- perhaps even cyclical- shifts in socioeconomic policy in general, and in the socioeconomic philosophy that lies behind it" (Hansen et al.,1990,p.5).

Also, the importance of socioeconomic structure for implementing regional policy is emphasized by Ashcroft et al. (1991,pp.404-405).

26. On the other hand, a qualitative analysis questions the effectiveness of British regional policy in the 1980s in that the regional incentives, despite their initial success in attracting a large MNC (Nissan), have failed to maintain the pace in attracting continuous MNC investment (Amin and Tomaney,1991, pp.479-481).

27. The general impact of the MNC location on the economy of the host region was explained in the previous Chapter (3.4). The question examined here is related to whether

the location of MNCs will improve or aggravate regional problems.

28. The financial assistance here includes not only regional policy implemented by section 7 of the legislation, but also incentives to inward investment into Britain under section 8. The latter dissipates regional assistance as it can be given outside AAs but usually tops up regional assistance for foreign firms. Moreover, its content can be varied to suit the particular foreign firm.

29. They estimate that the total value of RSA offered to seven Japanese projects reached £ 1.9m, some 7 percent of the total capital investment of these companies. This means that Japanese MNCs were paid on average around 27-29 percent (20-22 percent in RDG and 7 percent in RSA) of their total investment.

30. 14 out of 23 firms employing 87% of the total labour force examined were located in the AAs (Dunning,1986,p.25). Further, he investigates the extent to which investment incentives including regional aids have influenced the location of Japanese MNCs in the UK and in the AAs.

31. Contrary to these findings, an analysis of the locational pattern of Japanese companies in the US reports that financial incentives have had little influence on the location decisions of these companies and that the closeness to customer firms has been the most crucial locational factor (Kenny and Florida,1992,pp.21-38). However, this conclusion seems to be unsuitable for small countries like the UK, where the matter of distance cannot be a significant issue for a location decision.

Capter Five : Methodology

1. Here, structural location theory is regarded as being included in the behavioral approach. This is because the two approaches share many parts of their methodology, even though their standpoints in interpreting the phenomenon are not identical.

2. Basically, there can be a disagreement with the way of approach taken in this study to find the 'causes' of geographical changes on the ground. It could be argued that macro-level analysis is more related with 'outcomes' than with 'causes' of changes in contrast to micro-level analysis which aims to investigate 'causes' in its nature (Massey and Meegan,1985,pp.6-8). However, in my opinion, as micro-level analysis needs to organize a set of target variables through the examination of which the 'causes' of geographical change are ultimately revealed, so the variables or factors in the macro-level analysis can also be organized and constructed to find the actual 'causes' of geographical changes. From this standpoint, the present study carries out both strands of these approach in order to reach the more relevant 'causes'.

3. Rather than the UK as Northern Ireland has been excluded.

4. This part is mainly from Keeble, 1976, Chapter four.

5. These periods are chosen for the reason that, firstly, there has been a remarkable change in the inward investment of Japanese MNCs in the two host countries in the 1980s, and especially from 1987 in the UK and that, secondly, as a more practical reason, to keep consistency and to compare with the previous regression analysis which is introduced in Chapter nine (9.2.2.1).

6. In the case of Korean data, there are some differences from this time span mainly due to the difficulty in obtaining the relevant data resources.

7. The static and change analyses in this study, however, are undertaken by using the same set of independent variables involving static and change figures. This measure is adopted mainly in order to enhance the explicability of the variation in each dependent variable.

8. For example, in estimating the transportation factor of an area, he will take into account the availability of all the possible transportation methods such as railways, airlines,

seaport traffic, motorways and so on and will draw a conclusion by comprehending all these measures.

9. Therefore, the R^2 value obtained in this kind of cross-sectional analysis is much lower than that in the case of time-series analysis (Pindyck and Rubinfeld,1991,p.62).

10. In other words, searching for the variables which explain significantly the zonal variation in the dependent variables is one of the main objectives.

11. The F value is usually expressed as the ratio of explained to unexplained variance. If the F value for given degrees of freedom is below the critical level, the importance of the variables involved can be said to be negligible.

12. In short, the analysis of residuals is implemented to examine whether the relations between independent and dependent variables are truly linear and whether there are any significant independent variables excluded, etc. prior to the determination of the final optimum regression model.

13. In general studies, the critical level of this t-value is 0.05, although it can be changed. This study also adopts mainly this critical t-value of 0.05. In Minitab statistics programme, the default F-values for the entrance and removal of independent variables (i.e. Fenter and Fremove values) are set by this criteria.

14. There are a few missing cases relating to Scottish data. For the purpose of using regression analysis, these missing cases are replaced by the mean value of the remaining cases as mentioned before (5.3.2).

15. These variables are chosen for the analysis of the whole period, 1981-1990. The regression result using these variables is contrasted with, or complemented by, the results of regressions using the variables of the two sub-periods.

16. The major seaport mentioned here means the nearest seaport which takes over a 2% share in the total seaport traffic in Great Britain.

17. The definition of a major airport is one which has regular passenger lines to other countries.

18. These X_{41} and X_{42} variables, which show the figures in 1979 instead of those in 1988 in contrast to X_{43}, are used in order to avoid the duplication of the figures of independent variables with those of dependent variables. The Korean case (X_{38} and X_{39}) is also the same with this.

19. The cultural properties mean the valuable assets and materials inherited which include old buildings, precious metals, porcelain, etc. These properties are designated and protected by the central government and local authorities.

Chapter Six : Empirical evidence I : The Geographical Distribution of Japanese Multinational Companies in the Two Host Countries

1. However, included in the 181 are 16 companies which set up a *second, third* or even *fourth* plant in other places than their initial site. Therefore, strictly speaking, the total number of subsidiaries established or acquired is 160, whereas the number of locations is 181. Furthermore, in the 160, 8 companies which are operating activities on the fringe of manufacturing are involved, as mentioned in the previous chapter.

   On the other hand, all companies are assumed to be subsidiaries and the terms subsidiary and branch are treated as interchangeable; thus all are also considered as branch plants.

2. The issue of difference between the ranks of each region for the number of companies and for the number of employees is examined in the following size distribution analysis.

3. In tables and figures, the abbreviated forms of SE, WM, NW, EM, Y&H, SW and EA are used instead of the South East, West Midlands, North West, East Midlands, Yorkshire

and Humberside, South West and East Anglia respectively.

4. Apart from these sources, chairman's reports and annual statements to shareholders of each company where obtained have been used, especially in the case of employment size.

5. In this Figure 6.3, the regions other than the five dominant ones are not included.

6. In the case of companies still in the process of construction or preparation, their planned employment size is counted.

7. The mean size of employment 30 is the figure for the local units in manufacturing industries. It becomes 33 when it is calculated in terms of legal units.

8. However, since this company consist of lots of branches performing sales, training, technical services, etc., the present study counted the number of employees working in the four main manufacturing plants of this company. Therefore, the employment size of this company analyzed in this study is 3,800 instead of 6,000.

9. As indicated in the previous chapter, the employment size discussed here is the current employment size which is, therefore, the total of initial employment plus any growth after start up. This figure is used mainly for the convenience of analysis.

10. Specifically, the industrial and consumer electronics group comprises classes 33 and 34 in the 1980 SIC order, and light engineering comprises classes 31 and 37. Chemicals and plastics consists of classes 25 and 48, and heavy machinery and vehicles including components involve classes 32, 35 and 36.

11. Among the thirty-nine Japanese companies grouped in this field, fourteen companies are car and car components manufacturers.

12. For instance, following the locationing of Nissan in Washington in the North, many Japanese component suppliers placed their plants in the North region. These component suppliers are TI Nihon, Ikeda Hoover, Nissan Yamato, SP Tyres, Calsonic, Hashimoto, etc. (Peck,1990; Jones and North,1991).

13. For instance, with the leading role of Sony and Matsushita Electric (UK) in south Wales, Electronic Harness, Diaplastics, Matsushita electronic components, Orion, etc. chose the region as their plant sites.

14. But its share of Japanese companies is close to its share of national employment (Table 6.1). This is discussed further in Chapters nine and ten.

15. The four minor regions, which have less than 2% of the total Japanese companies in Korea, are excluded from the figure for the convenience of the analysis.

16. The definition of small, medium and large size companies in terms of investment size, or capital employed, has not been made in a consistent measure. For instance, the Wilson Committee defined the companies with a capital employed in 1975 of less than £ 250,000 as a small company. By contrast, *Business Monitor* classifies companies into large (having a capital employed over £ 4.16m), medium (over £ 100,000 up to £ 4.16m) and small (up to £ 100,000) companies (Storey *et al.*,1987,pp.22-27; *Business Monitor* MA3,1984,p.2).

17. See Chapter four (4.2.2.2).

18. But this trend is also explicable by the limited time for growth in more recent arrivals though it is not thought this is applicable.

19. If Kyonggi-Do and Inchon are included in the broad Seoul metropolitan region (MPR), as discussed in Chapter four, this feature becomes even more apparent.

Chapter Seven : Empirical Evidence II : Factors Influencing the Locational Choices of Japanese Multinational Companies - Regression Results

1. However, this cut-off level was loosened in cases where the results of the stepwise regression were thought to be insufficient in explaining the contents or changes of

dependent variables. For example 7.2.1.5.

2. In this study, the variables transformed into either logarithm or square root are given in brackets, i.e. $X_n(\log)$ and $X_n(\text{sqrt})$.

3. Average size of the ten zones in Britain which were designated initially was 2.12 km^2 (523 acres), or 0.06% of the average size of each county $3,566.56 \text{ km}^2$).

4. The number of Japanese companies operating in EZs was inaccessible in published data. Therefore, each local authority or an appropriate institution in charge of EZs was contacted. Those nine companies are in Telford (2 companies), Gillingham (2), Salford (1), Dundee and Arbroath (2) and Speke (2).

5. Regarding this, there can be an argument that it is better to continue this analysis without excluding these multicollineared variables or introducing any further method like ridge regression. This argument can be made by the fact that, firstly, since partial remedial efforts such as the exclusion of highly correlated variables revealed in the pair-wise correlation matrix and the use of stepwise regression have already been made, these variables showing multicollinearity are not thought to be a crucial problem for the analysis and, secondly, that almost all the data in this kind of analysis in social science cannot be immune to a certain extent of interaction between variables.

   However, in this study, the analysis will be carried out excluding these correlated variables in the equation on the ground that another two regression analyses, index analysis and sub-period analysis, will follow and, thus, that the influence of these variables which are excluded here can be taken into account or reflected in the following analyses.

6. As said above (7.1.1.1), the meaning of this variable is analyzed further in 7.1.1.5.

7. These two variables have been added to the regression to find a more reliable relationship between the location choices of Japanese companies and the eligibility of each county for regional assistance. These figures are obtained by adding up all the RDG paid to companies over £ 25,000 during the period of 1979-1988. *British Business* is the source of these figures.

8. In fact, over half of the Japanese companies coming into Britain have chosen AAs at the time of their arrival (see 10.1.2).

9. This interpretation seems to be possible unless the Japanese actually *used* the regional level data first. However, considering the initial contact of the Japanese companies with DTI and local authorities before choosing a specific site, data at the county level rather than broader regional level is thought to be used for their decision.

10. This variable (X_{75}) is the sum of the number of areas in each county in which various kinds of financial assistance are available. The numbers of areas which have been designated under all these schemes by the end of 1985 are counted. This variable is important for it shows the shift of government emphasis from traditional regional policy to these new policy initiatives. This data is obtained from the *Industrial Development Guide 1986* (which ceased publication after that).

11. The source of these two variables is the British Rail Passenger Time Table 1987/1988. If there is no inter-city railway line from London passing through the county, the shortest time necessary for arriving in that county by changing trains is calculated for variable X_{76}. X_{77} is obtained by adding up the number of inter-city railway trains starting from London and passing through the county.

12. This variable, X_{78}, is calculated from the average regional house price at mortgage completion stage which is obtained from the *Compendium of Building Society Statistics* 1984 and *House Prices in 1990* (1991). This is regional level data. This aggregate data is included due to the lack of relevant data at county level. Thus, the extent to which this variable can explain the dependent variable is rather limited.

13. The index analysis presented here can be thought to be a changed version either of discriminant analysis or of factor analysis, in particular the factor analysis based on an R-type matrix, extracted by principal-component solution, then rotated to oblique factors (Kim,1975,pp.468-478; Aaker and Day,1990, pp.543-562).

However, even though the techniques employed in this study are similar to those in discriminant analysis or factor analysis, the index analysis needs to be distinguished from the two analyses in that the method in this index analysis attempts to group numerous variables into six fixed locational factors contrary to the ideas of the latter analyses which emphasize the identification of significant variables constituting a given factor.

14. However, this issue is beyond the focus of this analysis and, therefore, no further discussion will be made on that.

15. This interpretation is consistent with the finding of Chapter six (6.3.1).

16. For instance, the independent variable X_6 (% point change in unemployment rate 1979-1988) is divided into that of 1979-1984 and of 1985-1988.

17. This may simply have been due to little expenditure taking place in the first year or two of the zones' existence.

18. This minimal influence of the variable regarding EZs (X_{21}) can be said to support strongly the argument that the location choice of Japanese companies is not due directly to the existence of EZs but other factors concealed behind this variable.

19. The change in unemployment rate (X_6) has negative correlation coefficients, in contrast to the total unemployment rate (X_5), with dependent variables.

20. However, there is more relevant reason for this high correlation coefficient and R^2 value. This is the overall geography in Korea as mentioned below in this chapter.

21. This variable was taken to indicate that a relatively skilled labour was available in the Do.

22. Often, the high correlation coefficients come from the smaller size of observations leading to, so to speak, aggregation effect. The aggregate effect poses a substantial limitation to the effort to compare the extent to which each explanatory variable covers the variation of a dependent variable (Clark and Hosking, 1986,pp.404-408).

However, the high correlation coefficients of the variables for the Korean case in this study are more likely to be caused by the over-concentration tendency in the Korean geography.

23. This issue will be discussed once again in Chapter seven.

Chapter Eight : Empirical Evidence III : Factors Influencing the Locational Choices of Japanese Multinational Companies - Survey Results

1. As was described in Chaptersix, this number refers to the sum of locations rather than that of companies and, furthermore, involves the number of companies which are implementing R&D or sales as a prior stage before implementing manufacturing. The companies which were either located in Northern Ireland or uncontactable by the Post Office were excluded from the present study.

2. The Telford Development Corporation was disbanded on 30 September 1991.

3. For instance, Warwickshire in this country versus Bourgogne in France or Lombardy in Italy. Also see Chapter two (2.5).

4. This issue is further investigated in the next section and the following chapters.

5. Of course, a high unemployment rate is still found to be significantly related with the overall locations of Japanese companies in the whole period, even though the increase of the unemployed acts as a negative cause for the attraction of Japanese companies in this country. (See 8.1.3.4)

6. The importance of the low wage level in the UK in attracting foreign companies into this country has been indicated by many authors including Sadler (1992,p.127).

7. In particular, the comment of the Japanese prime minister, Mr Kiichi Miyazawa, on 3rd of February 1992, denouncing the lack of work ethic among the US workers, following the same kind of criticism made by Mr Yoshio Sakurauchi, Japanese House Speaker, in January, which irritated the politicians and industrialists in the US and provoked the repulsion from the US side (*Newsweek*, 17 Feb. 1992,pp.28-29).

8. In Korea, there is no consistent criterion of investment size to define SMEs. In fact, the companies which are categorized as SMEs according to the definition of *Business Monitor* in the UK (up to £ 4.16m) is too big to be called a SME in Korea. Therefore, the current study takes $ 2m to define small and medium sized companies in Korea based on the following estimation:

    1) considering the cases of the assistance of European Coal and Steel Community, of the cost limit per job in providing RDG according to the criterion made in 1984 and of the definition of Industrial Development Authority in Ireland, it is reasonable to estimate that £ 10,000 is needed to create a job (Curran *et al.*,1986,p.50; Kennedy and Healey, 1985,p.11) and, hence, £ 2m (or about $ 3.4m) is necessary to create up to 200 jobs;

    and 2) in this investment size to create a SME, it is estimated that around 60% of the necessary amount (i.e. $ 2m) is financed by Japanese FDI, considering the fact that, until recently, most Japanese FDI in Korea have been undertaken in the form of joint ventures with Korean firms.

9. This is an evidence exhibiting the limitation of regression analysis in portraying the accurate causal relationship between dependent and independent variables (see 6.3.3).

10. Regarding the problem of insufficient infrastructure in Korea, see *Financial Times* 1 May 1992 and 27 May 1992.

11. All the companies in Britain which assessed the government assistance as being 'very substantial' and all but one which assessed the assistance as being 'substantial' received financial aid from the British government.

Chapter Nine : The Interpretation of the Empirical Evidence within the Context of a Worldwide Managerial Strategy

1. See Chapter two (2.2.2.2). Regarding the problems which the welcome policy of the UK government bears, see Sugden (1990).

2. See Introduction.

3. The general features of Japanese MNCs were examined briefly in Chapter two. This chapter concentrates its focus on the worldwide managerial strategy of these companies which can be found in their distinguishable activities in developed countries and developing countries.

4. The previous regression analysis was implemented in 1987 and 1988 and its results were fully described in my proposed M. Phil. dissertation. (See M. H. Han, *Locational behaviour of Japanese multinational companies in the changing context of regional policy*, M. Phil. dissertation [not awarded due to transfer to Ph. D], CURS, The University of Birmingham,1988.)

5. The results obtained from the new regressions, in particular those from the first sub-period analysis, are not identical with those from the previous regressions. These differences in results are thought to result from a little adjustment in methodology in implementing the new regression. The main issues in the methodology which were modified and are thought to be the cause of the different results are: 1) the addition of a few more independent variables; 2) the adjustment of time span, especially that of

Britain; and, 3) the exclusion from the dependent variables of the companies that had retreated from Britain and Korea after the time when the previous analysis was undertaken. Given these differences, this study goes on with the discussion taking the results of the previous regression into account as supplementary evidence to the findings in the new regression analysis, which form the major part of the discussion.

6. Opposition to this argument is also strong. See Porter (1990, p.420) and Chapter one (1.4.1).

7. However, the managers of the twenty companies interviewed in Chapter eight denied any support from or discussion with the government officials in investing offshore, when they were asked about the relationship between the company decisions and government policy. Only two or three managers admitted that they received some general information about EC and the UK.

8. The 'globalisation' was found to be the most important reason for Japanese MNCs to invest in Europe in a survey conducted by JETRO in 1990 (Thomsen and Nicolaides,1991,p.49).

9. However, recent evaluation of the yen has caused a little change in this trend.

10. The classification of FDI into these two types is almost similar to another classification, i.e. market-based FDI and cost-based FDI, which is more popular among scholars. (See Matsumoto in Sumitomo-Life Research Institute [SARI],1990,p.57; Thomsen and Nicolaides,1991,p.49; Dicken,1992,pp.125-126)

11. Furthermore, as the Japanese once invaded and colonized many Asian countries before and during the Second World War, the Japanese have been well aware of every detail of these countries' potential (Lubis,1985).

12. The Asian countries, however, have remained as the main Japanese production sites but in a somewhat changed form, i.e. there has been an increase in the export of capital goods by Japanese firms to these Asian countries and, using the Japanese capital goods and technology on behalf of Japanese MNCs, in the export of goods produced by the firms of these Asian countries to market countries.

13. However, recently, with the growth of FDI of manufacturing companies in market countries, the sales of products has tended to be undertaken by the manufacturing companies themselves rather than by 'Sogo shosha'(James,1989,pp.13-14; Dicken,1992,p.641). As a matter of fact, it was reported that 247 Japanese manufacturing companies had more sales affiliates (466) than manufacturing affiliates (206) in the EC in March 1989 (Kame and Totsuka,1990, p.45). Moreover, during an interview with the manager of the company H, it was found that its parent company, which is the one of the biggest 'Sogo shosha' in Japan, is trying to expand or diversify its operating field from traditional general trading by participating in the manufacturing sector.

14. Regarding the changing strategies of Japanese companies coupled to the internationalizing Japanese economy, see Higashi and Lauter (1990,pp.373-389).

15. This argument that the trade conflict of Japan with European countries is the fundamental cause of Japanese FDI in Europe was also claimed in the study of Roger Strange based on the thirty six personal interviews with Japanese managers (*ESRC Information Bulletin*, 18 Jan. 1989). See also Yannopoulos (1990) regarding the impact of EC formation on the FDI flow into the EC countries.

16. This finding is also consistent with the result of statistical analysis made by Flaherty and Raubitschek. They argue, based on the analysis of IC companies in Europe, that MNCs establish international manufacturing configurations to be more competitive than others (Flaherty and Raubitschek,1990,pp.321-322).

17. Regarding the importance of the local market for Japanese FDI, see also Thomsen and Nicolaides (1991,pp.94-96).

18. Thus, technological leadership is also part of the Japanese managerial strategy.
19. On the same ground, the large size of Japanese companies along with the high technology level of these companies in the US has also been reported in a study (Kim and Lyn,1990,p.47).
20. This fact is affirmed by the comment of the Northern Development Company (*Financial Times*, 4 Jun. 1992).
21. The high local linkages of MNCs including Japanese firms in Korea has been indicated (Dicken,1992,p.398).
22. This is also evident in case of the US, where some 300 Japanese component manufacturers have followed their main assemblers (Sadler,1992,p.129).
23. This finding has a consistency with the report of Billet which shows the significance of the size of the domestic market factor for the Japanese investment in Asia (Billet,1990,p.105).

Chapter Ten : The Implications of the Locational Behaviour of Japanese Companies for Regional Policy in the Host Countries

1. In other words, in Britain, the extent to which the Japanese companies were satisfied with government assistance showed no significant change throughout the whole period of the 1980s while in Korea satisfaction diminished sharply in the latter half of 1980s.
2. This was first established however in 1946.
3. The importance of regional assistance for the location of Japanese companies in Britain was confirmed in a report of Cambridge Econometrics based on a similar approach to the present study (1992,p.33).
   On the contrary, some researchers report the low responsiveness of Japanese MNCs to regional incentives, especially in the case of the US (Billet,1990,p.60; Jones and North,1991,p.109). In a similar vein, a recent study about the foreign companies operating in the West Midlands region reports that this factor has not been central for the location decision of foreign companies (KPMG Peat Marwick and WMDA,1992,p.9).
4. Regarding the growth pole theory, see Darwent (1969), Moseley (1974), Dewar, Todes and Watson (1986), etc. Also it has been indicated that this polarisation problem is shared by many other developing and under-developed countries (Kirkpatrick *et al.*,1984, pp.221-228).
5. This overall creative atmosphere is also a basis for industrial development and rejuvenation in developed countries (Chapman and Walker,1990,p.218).
6. However, the extensive linkage effect arising from the arrival of foreign firms also needs to be taken into consideration (although this, strictly speaking, should be distinguished from the direct effect of regional policy on the attraction of these firms).
7. The above research of KPMG Peat Marwick and WMDA reports that foreign companies have contacted various institutions to receive location assistance as follows: Department of Trade and Industry (37%), local authority (25%), WMDA (18%) and Telford Development Corporation (14%) (KPMG Peat Marwick and WMDA,1992,p.10).
8. This is the representative of the British government, which contacts many would-be Japanese investors.
9. It is also the policy of the EC to restrain member countries from providing excessive assistance as a form of competitive bidding to attract foreign investment (Chisholm,1990,p.172; Wren, 1990,p.58).
10. Post-Fordism requires the amalgamation of the centralisation force with that of decentralisation in business organisation, in managerial system and in the spatial economy

at local, regional and national level (Amin and Robins,1990,p.28; Chapter one).

11. In the case of Japanese capital, its strength originated, as stressed above (1.4.3), not only from flexibility or disorganized features of the socio-economic structure and management in Japan. The more fundamental source of its competitiveness is the highly organized social structure and moral system which integrates these highly flexible individual activities including managerial strategy. The most significant problem with this Japanese capital is, as was already discussed, the sacrifice of individuals for the sake of the objectives of total organization.

12. Warning about the possibility of a zero-sum game between the promotional activities of local authorities to attract mobile companies into their own boundary by offering incentives competitively was also given in the United States (Walker and Greenstreet,1991,pp.13-30).

13. This is consistent with the characteristics of local government in a post-Fordist society portrayed by Painter (1991, p.40).

14. This issue has been advocated by the Labour party in relation to the revitalisation of regional policy (Mawson and Miller,1986,pp.246-251).

15. The representative example of the regional impact caused by the location of large Japanese companies is the case of the North, which is experiencing the clustering of large numbers of indigenous and Japanese suppliers to Nissan and the massive increase of employment in the region (*The Times*, 12 Feb. 1992; *Financial Times*, 18 Feb. 1992).
   On the other hand, conversely, there is a different strand of reports indicating a minimal impact from the location of Japanese companies on the host region economy (Jones and North,1991,p.122; Williams *et al*,1991,p.340).

16. This is one of the main reasons causing each region to take part in the competitive bidding to attract foreign companies in its own territory.

17. Of course, this does not mean to follow exactly the proposals of 'industrial districts' and 'flexible specialisation' in the post-Fordist approaches. Compared to these 'industrial districts', the specialized regions in this study are wider in their boundary and more influenced by central or local government (see below).

18. In Korea, especially in the 1970s, each IE was developed in such a way to induce the firms in the same industrial sector to locate in the specified IE; for example, Changwon IE for heavy machinery and Kumi IE for electronics, etc.

19. See Castells (1989,pp.82-103), Mansley and Rhodes (1990, p.11), Chapman and Walker (1990,p.229) and Glasson (1992,p.524). Regarding the requirement of skilled labour and the training of this labour in developing new technology firms, see Foley *et al*. (1992,pp.65-68).

20. This effort is more imperative considering the completion of the internal market in Europe, which is expected to result in the drawing of all kinds of resources such as materials, labour, capital, etc. into some favourable regions in Europe as a whole (Begg,1990,pp.90-91).

21. In this regard, the recent upsurge of local economic initiatives is worth noting, for local authorities are in such a position that they can integrate and improve these locational factors most directly. However, most of these activities including promotional activities need to be coordinated and expanded to a wider level as discussed so far.

22. Similarly, but from a rather different point of departure, Townroe has stressed a need for flexibility in policy design, implementation and management to counter the over-concentration problem in developing countries including Korea (Townroe,1989, pp.143-144).

Chapter Twelve : Final Conclusion

1. In reality, the former has been the main focus of government concern in Korea leaving the latter far behind during the last three decades. As discussed in Chapter four, this problem has been recognized in Britain as well. However, the conflict between the two major policy objectives has been more prominent in Korea than in Britain. In Britain, national economic growth took over as a main objective really only around 1965 and since 1975, but this is controversial (Jones,1986).

2. Though there was a brief period when growth poles were influential; vestiges remain in EZs, New Towns, etc.

3. The use of investment instead of employment in Japanese companies in Korea and the examination at the Do level rather than the smaller Gun level provide representative examples of this lack of available data. In the British case also, the difficulty in obtaining suitable data to represent locational factors directly forced this analysis inevitably to rely on other indirect variables which were less closely related to the locational features.

4. Regarding the general direction of researches on MNCs, see Eden (1990).

Appendices

Appendix 1 : Derivation and Sources of Variables (British Case)

1. Dependent Variables

A dependent variable is expressed as a figure of either the number of companies or the employment size of these companies derived from statistics for total manufacturing in each county. The magnitude of a variable is represented in the form of either an absolute figure or a percentage change between two dates.

Y_1 (the number of Japanese manufacturing companies in each county in 1990) comprises the number of Japanese companies in all the fields of manufacturing in each county at the end of 1990. Several companies in the process of preparing for, or proceeding with, the construction of their plants are counted as being established in 1990 in so far as the content of their investments is fixed and announced to the public and they are able to be contacted. By contrast, seven Japanese companies located in Northern Ireland are excluded as mentioned in the geographical scope of the methodology. Therefore, in total, 181 companies form the variable Y_1 in Britain.

Y_2 (the change in the number of Japanese manufacturing companies in each county 1981-1990). Strictly speaking, this dependent variable indicates the increase in the number of Japanese companies from the beginning of 1981 to the end of 1990. Since 21 companies were already operating in 1980, total companies involved in this variable are 160.

Y_3 (the total numbers employed by Japanese manufacturing companies in each county in 1990) shows the total number of employees working in the Japanese companies investigated. (Japanese staff are included in the figures.) The increase of employment in later years after initial location is, as mentioned in chapter six, added to the employment size of the year established in order to maintain the consistency with the number of companies. Therefore the dependent variable Y_4 (the absolute change in the total numbers employed by Japanese manufacturing companies in each county 1981-1990) contains purely the employment size of the companies established since 1981. The figure of Y3 in total is 59,123, while Y_4 is 48,013.

The figures from Y_1 to Y_4 are obtained from the reports of IBB, JETRO and Anglo-Japanese Economic Institute (AJEI).

2. Independent Variables

X_1 to X_8 are measures of the potential labour force of the area which could be directly employed by an incoming Japanese company. In particular, the variables X_7 and X_8 (average of and absolute change in the numbers employed in the manufacturing sector 1979-1988), which covers the employment in division 2, 3 and 4 in the 1980 SIC, are included on the ground that they are thought to provide the most direct measure of labour potential for Japanese manufacturing companies considering coming into this country and looking for a specific location. The self employed are not included.

X_1 and X_2 (total numbers and absolute change in the working population of both sexes between 1979 and 1988) relate to the total working or economically active population over school leaving age irrespective of age, including both the employed and the unemployed, across all industries including non-manufacturing. However, the self employed, HM forces or employees in domestic service have been excluded in these figures. X_3 (total numbers unemployed 1979-1988) is the numbers of 'official' unemployed, ignoring the change in definition to claimants that took place in 1982. The figure, therefore, under-estimates the actual change but will do so across all the areas roughly proportionately.

The figures for X_1, X_3 and X_7 are the calculated average of the numbers from 1979 to 1988 even though the statistics were published in later years. In contrast, X_2, X_5 and X_6 are the differences during the period. The sources of these figures are *Regional Trends* 1978-1990 and the *Employment Gazette* 1979-1988.

X_9 and X_{10} (average gross weekly earnings and the absolute change in these earnings 1979-1988) are the values which help predict the possible cost of labour in the area though excluding employers' national insurance contributions, etc. The figures are for average total male earnings (including overtime, etc.) before tax (for manual and non-manual workers combined). Although the average wage level in the manufacturing sector seems a more relevant indicator of this factor, the lack of published data at the county level prevents use of this. *Regional Trends* 1981-1989 and the *New Earnings Survey* 1979-1988 show the figures.

X_{11} to X_{14} are the measures of the education level or skill level of the potential workforce in the area. X_{11} (average percentage of pupils aged 16 staying on at school 1979-1988) is the average figure of ten years' statistics at the time of decision making from 1981 to 1990 with two years' time gap i.e. 1979-1988. It is represented by the average percentage of all 16 year olds staying on at school. X_{12} (% point change in pupils aged 16 staying on at school) is the change in the percentage during the time of 1979-1988. These figures are obtained from *Regional Trends* 1982-1990.

X_{13} and X_{14} (average of and absolute change in the number of institutions for further education 1979-1988) are additional variables introduced for the same purpose. The *Education Statistics* 1984/1985 and 1988/1989 of the Chartered Institute of Public Finance and Accountancy (CIPFA) and its Scottish branch are the source of these statistics.

X_{15} and X_{16} (total number of and absolute change in the working days lost by stoppages of work due to industrial disputes 1979-1988) express the state of labour relations and the militancy of labour in the area. Since readily available statistics about the stoppages of work due to labour disputes at county level are rare, the records of prominent stoppages solved in every quarter in each county are summed up to compute the total working days lost in each county over the years 1979-1988. The quarterly data in the *Employment Gazette* 1979-1988 are used for these variables.

X_{17} and X_{18} (gross value added in the manufacturing sector per employee and its absolute change 1981-1988) are the variables to represent the productivity of labour in the area. Once again, the lack of statistics available at county level keeps the study from using the more direct indicator, net output per employee in the manufacturing sector. So, instead, gross value added in manufacturing at county level is used. Furthermore, only the data from 1981 are accessible during the whole period of 1979-1988 in *Regional Trends* 1984-1991.

The explanatory variables from X_1 to X_{18} are, thus, factors to indicate the labour supply conditions in an area and are computed as either an annual average figure or a percentage change for the accessible years between 1979 to 1988.

X_{19} and X_{20} (total of and the % point change in the proportion of the TTWAs qualifying for regional assistance 1979-1988) are measures of the area's eligibility for the financial assistance offered to parts of the county through regional policy. The proportion of TTWAs qualifying for regional assistance in each area in each year are summed up to calculate the average proportion of the area with AA status for the seven years. During the calculation, no discrimination is made between SDA, DA and IA in their status. Therefore, the figures produced represent purely the proportion of the areas that comprises an AA. When only a part of a TTWA is designated as an assisted area, the figure is rounded up according to the ratio of that area against the total area of the county. For the calculation, the map of 280 local labour market areas (LLMAs) in Champion and Green (1985), the table of proposed changes in AAs in the Institute of Chartered Accountants (1979) and the map of assisted areas in *Regional Trends* 1985-1988 are referenced.

This may seen a strange and inadequate measure, especially when the impact of policy is important to the thesis objective. However, at a later stage, consideration is given to the AA status of the locations actually chosen by Japanese companies (chapter eight).

X_{21} (public sector investment in enterprise zones from designation in the area to 1988) is a variable showing the investment size or support of government to assist the group of areas designated as enterprise zones. The cumulative total amount of investment from the designation to 1988 is used for the analysis. *Regional Trends* 1987-1991 is the source of this variable.

X_{22} and X_{23} (average of and absolute change in the public expenditure for economic development and promotion per 1,000 population 1979-1988) are the variables introduced for the same purpose as X_{21}. With the increasing role of local initiatives in economic development in each region, this variable is expected to reveal the significance of the activities of the public sector. The *Planning and Development Statistics* 1979/80-1988/89 of CIPFA contain the figure. Statistics of economic development and promotion expenditure in Scotland are not available from these sources. Thus, this variable is omitted for Scottish counties.

X_{24} and X_{25} (average of and absolute change in total rate poundage 1979-1988) are chosen to show the extent of the local tax burden for enterprises in the area. Total rate poundage consists of rate poundages for district purposes plus county and police authority precepts. The precepts other than these, e.g. water, land drainage, etc., are excluded. Local rates are chosen for the reason that it is likely to imply more regional characteristics than any other tax measures. The *Rate Collection Statistics*, the *Rating Review* and the *Scottish Local Government Financial Statistics* 1979/80-1988/89 of CIPFA and its Scottish branch and *Regional Trends* 1981-1989 are the sources of these variables. (NB. The dates chosen happily avoid the problem of the switch to community charge even in Scotland.)

The above variables from X_{19} to X_{25} are locational factors capable of being influenced by the public sector. The statistics of the IDC control are not considered, since it was placed in abeyance in 1981. These variables are also presented as either annual averages or the percentage change during the period chosen.

X_{26} to X_{28} depict the availability of industrial land and premises in a selected area. X_{26} and X_{27} (total of and absolute change in the stock of commercial and industrial floorspace 1979-1988) comprise all the stock of floorspace both industrial and commercial floorspace and that of warehouses. *Regional Trends* 1979-1982, the *Commercial and Industrial Floorspace Statistics* 1982-1986, the *Digest of Welsh Statistics* 1983-1985 and the *Rate Collection Statistics* 79/80-88/89 and *Rating Review* 79/80-88/89 published by CIPFA and its Scottish branch are the sources of these figures.

X_{28} (rent per square foot per annum for industrial premises in 1988) represents the cost of securing industrial sites and premises in each county. The variable is expected to be associated to a great extent with the price of industrial land. A five years' figure (1984-1988) is used mainly due to the difficulty of access to the data of this kind. The *Property Rent Indices and Market Editorial (PRIME)* published by Healey and Baker is the source of this variable.

X_{29} to X_{38} are the variables reflecting transportation usage and market accessibility. X_{29} and X_{30} (total of and absolute change in foreign and domestic seaport traffic 1979-1988) involve an attempt to measure the size and usage of the various ports of Great Britain. This has been done by assuming that a bigger volume of goods traffic indicates better and more used facilities. So the statistics of domestic and foreign seaport traffic going through each port has been used as published in *Transport Statistics* between 1978 and 1988. Each county has been credited with the amount of traffic going through its ports. Thus, a county with 2 or 3 ports scores high and the West Midlands with no ports scores 0 on this variable.

X_{32} and X_{33} (total of and absolute change in air passengers through a custom airport 1979-1988) are basically applying the same approach to airports. These figures are extracted from the *Civil Aviation Monthly Statistics* 1978-1982 and the *UK Airports* 1983- 1988. One problem in calculating this variable is that there is no relevant criteria for allocating the air passengers (ignoring goods traffic) using an airport between neighbouring counties.

Therefore, in this study, the passengers using an airport are plainly regarded as being the residents of the county in which the airport is located. This criterion is adopted on the ground that, in the first place, an arbitrary allocation of the numbers is dangerous in statistical terms and that, secondly, the number of passengers using the airport located in other counties is not so enormous compared to the resident-passengers of the airport. The resulting inaccuracy will most affect the 39 counties without custom airports whose resident passengers disperse to a variety of airports.

X_{31} and X_{34} (distance to the nearest major seaport and airport) are to find the influence of the accessibility to major seaports and airports in each area. These figures are derived from the *Complete Atlas of the British Isles* (1965) of the Readers Digest Association.

X_{35} and X_{36} (total of and absolute change in length of motorways and trunk roads 1979-1988) represent the highway transportation of the area measured by the length of different kinds of roads. Among various levels of roads, only motorways and trunk roads are considered in that they seem more significant for industrial use than others. The figures are computed from the *Highway and Transportation Statistics* 1979/80-1988/89 published by CIPFA and the *Scottish Abstract of Statistics* 1980-1989.

X_{37} (the number of railway stations in the area) is to indicate the availability of railway facilities in each area. All the stations located in each county are counted for this figure. For the purpose, the *Ordnance Survey: Atlas of Great Britain* (1982) and *British Rail Passenger Timetable* (1991) are used.

X_{38} (population of the conurbations within 100 miles radius of the area) is the summed population of the conurbations among the eight major conurbations within 100 miles radius from each county. X_{38} is included in considering market accessibility since the conurbations located within this boundary are considered to provide most of the British market for the newly arriving Japanese companies. The distances are calculated from the road mileages between major towns in the *Complete Atlas of the British Isles* (1965) of the Readers Digest Association and *Regional Trends* 1990.

X_{39} and X_{40} (total number of and absolute change in manufacturing firms in the host county 1979-1988) are measures of the existence of would-be suppliers or subcontractors in the area and the figures are represented by the average during the ten year period. These variables are necessary in that incoming Japanese companies generally need a number of local companies as their suppliers of local intermediate products. The figures are obtained from the *Annual Census of Production PA 1003* 1979-1990.

X_{41} to X_{44} are included in order to examine the unique clustering feature of Japanese companies which is thought to be caused by the significant differences in language and culture between them and the host countries. The existence of Japanese companies and Japanese people are investigated in two ways. The one measures the number of Japanese manufacturing companies which were established before 1979 (X_{41} and X_{42}) to examine the inducing force of the existing manufacturing companies and the second one uses the number of Japanese companies operating in other sectors in static and change figures (X_{43} to X_{44}). In the latter case, manufacturing companies are excluded in order to prevent the companies from being counted in both sides of the equations. The reports of JETRO and the *Japanese Addresses in the UK* (1991/92) of AJEI are the sources of these figures.

X_{45} and X_{46} (percentage of and % point change in the employees in the service sector including banking, finance and business services in the county in 1988 and between 1979-1988) is the variable to examine the importance of these fields of the service sector for the locational choice of Japanese manufacturing companies. The number of employees in division 8 & 9 in 1980 SIC order are computed for these variables. These variables are obtained from *Regional Trends*.

Through the examination of the variables from X_{39} to X_{46}, it seems possible to estimate the extent to which Japanese companies emphasize linkage matters.

X_{47} and X_{48} (the proportion of and % point change in proportion of the agricultural area to the total area 1979-1988) are measures of the preferences of Japanese companies for green sites or beautiful scenery. The decrease of the agricultural area is regarded as indicating the growth of the built-up areas in the county. The total agricultural area counted here consists of crop and grass areas. The *Agricultural Statistics United Kingdom* 1979-1988, the *Welsh Agricultural Statistics* 1980-1989 and the *Scottish Abstract of Statistics* 1986-1989 provide the data.

On the same ground, the density of population in an area and its absolute change (X_{49} and X_{50}) are considered. The figures are calculated from the *Regional Trends* 1981-1990 and the *Scottish Abstract of Statistics* 1981-1985. As different indicators showing the preference of Japanese companies for beautiful scenery, the total national park area in the county (X_{51}) and the number of public parks in the county in 1988 (X_{52}) are introduced into the regression. The *Municipal Yearbook* 1987-1991 and the *Digest of Countryside Recreation Statistics* 1979 for X_{51} and the *British Outdoor Amenities Directory* 1989/90 for X_{52} are referenced for the calculation of these variables.

X_{53} and X_{54} (total amount of and absolute change in public expenditure per head on leisure and recreation facilities 1979-1988) are included to examine the extent of leisure and recreation facilities in the area. All public expenditures including those on various sports facilities are calculated by the figure of pound per head. The *Leisure and Recreation Statistics* 1979/80-1988/89 published by CIPFA provides the data. The compatible sources for the Scottish data are available in the *Rating Review* 1981/82-1988/89 by CIPFA Scottish branch.

For the same purpose, the number of golf courses in the area (X_{55}) is chosen as an explanatory variable. The figures are obtained from the *Leisure and Recreation Statistics* 1979/80-1988/89 of CIPFA and the Scottish Tourist Board.

X_{56} and X_{57} (total of and absolute change in the reported serious crime per 1,000 population 1979-1988) are taken as indicators showing the livability of an area for Japanese employees. The occurrence of crime is expressed by the cases per 1,000 persons. The *Criminal Statistics, England and Wales* 1979-1988 and the CIPFA *Police Statistics* 1979/80-1988/89 are the sources for England and Wales, whereas the *Scottish Abstract of Statistics* 1980-1985 are for Scotland. However, the Scottish data after 1985 are unavailable in the published statistics and, thus, are treated as missing.

X_{58} and X_{59} (total of and absolute change in the stock of dwellings 1979-1988) are variables to show the relative abundance of houses in an area. *Regional Trends* 1981-1990 is the source of these variables.

X_{60} and X_{61} (the amount of and absolute change in the mean re-registered rent 1979-1988) are the values to investigate the cost, or abundance, of housing for Japanese and other employees. The registered rent here refers to the rent determined by the Rent Assessment Committee under the Rent Act 1971 when an application is made by the landlord, the tenant or both. While the figures of England and Wales are extracted from the *Housing and Construction Statistics* 1978-1988, those of Scotland are obtained from the *Rating Review* 1981-1988 published by CIPFA Scottish branch.

The variables from X_{47} to X_{61} explain the relationship between the living and working circumstances of areas and the locations of Japanese companies. In the cases of X_{51} and X_{52}, the static figure at a particular point of time can provide a relevant criterion, while the average values and change figure during the period being studied are desirable forms for other variables.

Appendix 2 : Derivation and sources of variables (Korean case)

1. Dependent Variables

Y_1 (the number of Japanese manufacturing companies in each Do in 1990) is the figure for the total number of Japanese manufacturing companies operating at the end of 1990. The companies that retreated from Korea before 1990 are excluded from consideration. On the other hand, the data about the companies in process of preparing for operation in Korea have not been accessible and, thus, are also excluded from this analysis. In total, 299 companies are included in the variable Y_1.

Y_2 (the absolute change in the number of Japanese manufacturing companies in each Do 1981-1990) represents the increase of Japanese manufacturing companies in Korea since 1981. 198 companies form the variable Y_2.

Instead of the employment size of Japanese manufacturing companies in Korea which is not available to the public, this study uses the investment of the Japanese manufacturing companies operating in Korea as the dependent variable Y_3.

Y_4 (the absolute change in the investment of Japanese manufacturing companies in each Do 1981-1990) is the increase of their investment over the time studied. These dependent variables from Y_1 to Y_4 are acquired from the Ministry of Finance in Korea.

2. Independent Variables

Like the British case, X_1 to X_9 are variables for measuring the potential labour force in the Do. However, there are some differences in the concept of these variables between the two countries. For instance, X_1 and X_2 (total number of and absolute change in the working population of both sexes in each Do 1979-1988), unlike their British counterparts, include the self-employed population. However, this kind of difference is ignored in this study. With one year's data of the numbers unemployed in 1988 (X_3), which is not accessible before 1986 in Korea, four other variables from X_4 to X_7 are used to explain the availability of labour in the Do. The *Yearbook of Labour Statistics* 1980-1989 (X_1, X_2, X_8 and X_9), the *Yearbook of Regional Statistics* 1990 (X_3) and the *Korea Statistical Yearbook* 1980-1990 (from X_3 to X_7) are the sources of these variables.

X_{10} and X_{11} (average wage levels in the manufacturing sector and its % change

1979-1988) are derived from the *Social Indicators in Korea 1985* and the *Yearbook of Regional Statistics* 1988-1990. There is no discrimination between male and female wage levels in these figures.

X_{12} and X_{13} (average percentage of students attending colleges and universities and % point change in total population in the area 1979-1988) are variables to indicate the education level of the workforce in each Do. The *Statistical Yearbook* of each Do in each year and the *Yearbook of Regional Statistics* 1988-1990 are the sources of these variables.

On the same ground, X_{14} and X_{15} (the number of vocational training facilities and its absolute change 1979-1988) are included in the regression. The *Yearbook of Labour Statistics* 1980-1989 are the sources of these variables.

X_{16} and X_{17} (the proportion of union numbers in total employees in the manufacturing sector and its % point change 1979-1988) are chosen to represent the militancy of labour in the Do area instead of the working days lost by stoppages of work, mainly due to the lack of data. These variables also are calculated from the *Yearbook of Labour Statistics* 1980-1989.

X_{18} and X_{19} (gross value added per employee in the manufacturing sector and its absolute change 1979-1988) are to show the productivity of labour in the Do. The *Mining and Manufacturing Statistics* 1981-1985 and the *Yearbook of Regional Statistics* 1988-1990 are the sources of these variables.

X_{20} (total government investment in industrial estates before 1988) is the variable chosen for indicating the public assistance available to industry in the Do. Since there is no designated assisted areas in Korea, the total amount of public expenditure on industrial estates in each local authority area is summed up for this variable. This variable is calculated from the *Industrial Estate Statistics* of Ministry of Trade and Industry (1990).

X_{21} and X_{22} (local tax collected per person and its % change 1979-1988) are the variables to investigate the influence of differences in the tax burden between regions. Like the British case, local taxes among various tax measures are chosen on the ground that they can reveal the differences between regions more clearly than any others. These figures are obtained from the *Local Finance Statistical Yearbook* 1990 and the *Yearbook of Regional Statistics* 1988-1990.

Variables from X_{20} to X_{22} are related to the influence of public policy on the locational decisions of Japanese companies. X_{23} to X_{28} are the variables to indicate the availability of land and premises in each area.

X_{23} and X_{24} (total of and absolute change in the stock area of industrial estates 1979-1988) are acquired by summing up all the areas designated and developed as industrial estates in each region. In Korea, these designated industrial estates are closely related to regional policy receiving financial assistance and tax holidays. These figures are obtained from the *Investment Guide to Korea* of Ministry of Finance (1990) and the *Industrial Estate Statistics* of Ministry of Trade and Industry (1990).

X_{25} and X_{26} (total of and absolute change in the stock of commercial and industrial floor space 1979-1988) are involved to indicate the availability of existing premises for incoming Japanese companies. The figure is obtained from the *Yearbook of Regional Statistics* 1988-1990 and the *Urban Area Statistics* 1989.

X_{27} and X_{28} (average annual increase of land price and its % point change 1979-1988) comprise the prices of all kinds of land including the land for industrial, commercial and domestic use. These statistics are obtained from the *Trend of Land Price* of Ministry of Construction (1989).

X_{29} to X_{34} depict transportation usage and the market accessibility of each Do. As the indicator of seaport traffic in the region, the data of total registered vessels for foreign and domestic seaport traffic is used (X_{29} and X_{30}). Similarly, total foreign and domestic air passengers through custom airports are summed up to derive the variable X_{29}. The data for these variables are obtained from the *Yearbook of Transportation* 1980-1989.

X_{32} and X_{33} (total of and absolute change in the length of motorways and trunk roads in the Do 1979-1988) are obtained from the *Yearbook of Construction Statistics* 1990 and the *Yearbook of Regional Statistics* 1988-1990, while the number of railway stations (X_{34}) and the total population of major cities within the area of 100 miles radius (X_{35}) are counted from the figures in the *Yearbook of Transportation* 1980-1989 and the *Digest of Local Authority Boundary* 1990.

X_{36} to X_{45} are the variables showing the importance of the linkage factor to Japanese manufacturing companies coming into Korea. The *Yearbook of Labour Statistics* 1980-1989 is the source of X_{36} and X_{37} (total of and % change in the number of manufacturing firms 1979-1988), while X_{38} and X_{39} (the number of Japanese companies in the Do at the end of 1979 and their investment in 1979) and X_{40} and X_{41} (the number in 1988 of and absolute change in the Japanese companies in other fields 1979-1988) are computed from the report of the Ministry of Finance. X_{42} and X_{43} (total establishments and numbers employed in the fields of banking, finance and business services in the Do in 1988), and X_{44} and X_{45} (total of and absolute change in loans and discounts of deposit money banks in the Do 1979-1988) are sourced from the *Yearbook of Labour Statistics* 1980-1989 (X_{42} and X_{43}) and the Bank of Korea (X_{44} and X_{45}) respectively.

X_{46} to X_{65} are the variables to examine the environmental circumstances in the host area. X_{46} and X_{47} (urban park area and total area of national park in the Do in 1988) are the aggregation of designated urban park areas and national park areas in each Do. The figures are obtained from the *Yearbook of Construction Statistics* 1990.

X_{48} and X_{49} (total of and absolute change in forestry growing stock in the Do 1979-1988) are sourced by the *Korea Statistical Yearbook* 1980-1990 and the *Yearbook of Regional Statistics* 1988-1990. X_{50} (the number of golf courses in the Do in 1988) is concerned with the leisure and recreation facilities for employees in the Do. This is sourced from the *Yearbook of Regional Statistics* 1988-1990.

From X_{51} to X_{56} (stock of dwellings, the ratio of dwellings to households and total houses constructed, and their changes in the Do 1979-1988) are concerned with housing for employees. The Ministry of Construction and the *Housing Handbook* of Korea Housing Corporation (1990) are the sources of these figures. X_{57} and X_{58} (the proportion of dwellings equipped with a water supply system and its % point change in the Do 1979-1988) are directly related to the living circumstances for employees. The number of telephone facilities and their absolute change in the Do (X_{59} and X_{60}) are included by the same token. The *Korea Statistical Yearbook* 1980-1990 and the *Yearbook of Regional Statistics* 1988-1990 are the sources of these figures.

X_{61} and X_{62} (reported serious crime per 1,000 population in the Do and its absolute change 1979-1988) are also derived from the *Korea Statistical Yearbook* 1980-1990 and the *Yearbook of Regional Statistics* 1988-1990.

To appraise indirectly the attractiveness of the Do for the Japanese companies seeking for better environment places, the number of cultural properties (X_{63}), the number of hotels and restaurants (X_{64}) and numbers employed in hotels and restaurants (X_{65}) are included. The *Yearbook of Regional Statistics* 1988-1990 and the *Korea Statistical Yearbook* 1980-1990 are the providers of these figures.

Appendix 3 : Questionnaire form

Dear : Chief Executive or Manager

Re : Industrial survey of Japanese companies

1st Aug. 1991

You are politely invited to complete and return this questionnaire. It will be used to analyze the important factors which influence the locational decision-making of Japanese companies.

This forms part of my research work at the Centre for Urban and Regional Studies, University of Birmingham.

Your reply to this questionnaire will be treated as confidential and its use strictly limited to the purpose of the research. Your firm will not be identified in the report of the research. Your answering and returning of the questionnaire would be greatly appreciated and a post-paid label is enclosed to assist safe return. Thank you.

Man - Hee Han

The Centre for Urban and Regional Studies
The University of Birmingham
Edgbaston, Birmingham, B15 2TT

Question to Subsidiary and Branches of Japanese Companies Located in the U.K   [Confidential]

1. What is the profile of your firm?

Your firm is a part of a Japanese company. Please provide the following profile information about your firm (the information is to relate to the plant at the address below)

    o name _____

    o address(plant)_____

    o year of the arrival of this branch in this country
      19_____

    o total investment(established year) £_____million

    o total employees _____ (of whom_____ are Japanese)

    o What is the main market for your firm? Please tick.

     . local consumer market   [   ]

     . main manufacturers in this or adjacent country [   ]

     . foreign consumer market   [   ]

2. What were the main reasons or push factors in Japan which made your firm invest outside Japan? Please rank *three* factors in order of importance, marking them 1,2,3.

    o high rate of the yen   [   ]

    o labour shortage in Japan   [   ]

    o high wage level compared to other countries'   [   ]

    o high land price in Japan   [   ]

    o trade barriers of other countries   [   ]

    o others.   [   ]

     Please write down _____

3. Attractive or unsatisfactory locational factors :

3a) What were the main locational factors or attractive things which made the firm choose the present location? Please mark *three* factors in the list(a) below in order of importance.

3b) What were the factors which seemed least satisfactory in the present location at the time of the decision? Please tick *all* such factors in the list(b) below.

	most attrac- tive(a)	least satis- factory(b)
o low wage level	[ ]	[ ]
o abundant workforce available	[ ]	[ ]
o low militancy of labour	[ ]	[ ]

	most attrac- tive(a)	least satis- factory(b)
o high productivity of labour	[ ]	[ ]
o regional assistance from government and local authority	[ ]	[ ]
o sufficient industrial land and premises	[ ]	[ ]
o convenient transport	[ ]	[ ]
o closeness to a big market	[ ]	[ ]
o existence of manufacturing suppliers or subcontractors	[ ]	[ ]
o presence of Japanese companies in the area	[ ]	[ ]
o the 'greenness' or amenity of the area	[ ]	[ ]
o abundant leisure and recreation facilities	[ ]	[ ]
o low rate of crime	[ ]	[ ]
o abundant houses for employees in the area	[ ]	[ ]
o promotion activities of local authorities	[ ]	[ ]
o single market in Europe in 1992	[ ]	[ ]
o familiar language	[ ]	[ ]
o others.	[ ]	[ ]

Please write down _____

4. Was central or local UK government assistance in the form of

regional policy important?

4a) To what extent did government assistance influence the location choice of your firm? Please tick one.

o very substantial   (over 76%)   [   ]
o substantial   (51-75%)   [   ]
o moderate   (26-50%)   [   ]
o minimal   (0-25%)   [   ]

4b) What kind of assistance was this? Please tick all the assistance obtained.

o financial aid   [   ]
o land and premises   [   ]
o advice   [   ]
o planning permission   [   ]
o speed of work   [   ]
o others   [   ]
   Please specify_____

5. Alternative locations

5a) Which alternative areas in the world were considered when the locational decision was made? Please tick.

o Asia   o America   o Europe
. Taiwan   [   ]   . US   [   ]   . Germany [   ]
. Hong Kong [   ]   . Mexico   [   ]   . Spain   [   ]
. Singapore [   ]   . Brazil   [   ]   . France [   ]
. Korea   [   ]   . Canada   [   ]   . Eire   [   ]
. Malaysia [   ]   . Argentine [   ]   . Italy   [   ]
. Others _____   . Others _____   . Others _____

o Other continents _____ o None   [   ]

5b) Which alternative areas in the UK were considered when the locational decision was made?

o Southeast [   ] o Southwest   [   ] o East Anglia [   ]
o W Midlands [   ] o E Midlands [   ] o Northwest   [   ]
o North   [   ] o Wales   [   ] o Scotland   [   ]
o N. Ireland [   ] o Yorkshire and Humberside   [   ]

o None   [ ]

5c) Which factors were considered important enough to cause rejection of the above alternative areas? Please tick all the factors of importance in the following list.

	(5a) in the world	(5b) in the UK
o high wage level	[ ]	[ ]
o lack of workforce available	[ ]	[ ]
o high militancy of labour	[ ]	[ ]
o low productivity of labour	[ ]	[ ]
o lack of regional assistance	[ ]	[ ]
o insufficient industrial land and premises	[ ]	[ ]
o inconvenient transport	[ ]	[ ]
o far from big market	[ ]	[ ]
o lack of manufacturing suppliers or subcontractors	[ ]	[ ]
o non-existence of Japanese companies in the area	[ ]	[ ]
o the lack of 'greenness' or amenity of the area	[ ]	[ ]
o insufficient leisure and recreation facilities	[ ]	[ ]
o high rate of crime	[ ]	[ ]
o insufficient houses for employees in the area	[ ]	[ ]
o lack of promotive activities of local authorities	[ ]	[ ]
o unfamiliar language	[ ]	[ ]

o others(please specify) _____

5d) Did you consider any other area within the present region of the UK ? If so, please write down the area and the reasons.

(area)_____

(reason)_____

_____

_____

6. I would like to visit your company to discuss this matter more deeply with the person who answered this questionnaire. Could you allow me to have such an opportunity?

(Yes   /   No   )

o If yes, please indicate the following:

Person to meet:_____
Phone number :_____
Office hours   :_____

THANK YOU VERY MUCH

Please return this questionnaire using the enclosed post-paid label to :
Appendix 4 : Interview Questions

Interview Questions

I. Profile of the Firm

1. Please tell me the history of your firm, especially since the 1970s.

2. Would you please explain the organizational structure of your firm as a whole (at present and at the time when you decided to invest in the UK)

a. What is the organizational structure of this plant?

b. Is this plant owned wholly(100%) by the parent company?

3. How many overseas subsidiaries have you got at present?

a. Where are those? Is there any other subsidiary in this country apart from this plant?

b. Among those, which one do you suppose is the most successful in terms of productivity and profit?

4. What is the main product of this plant?

a. What is the main product of your parent company?

b. What is the relationship between the two in terms of products?

5. Where are the main competitors for the parent company around the world?

   a. Are they the same competitors for this plant?

6. You answered that your main market is the (consumers, manufacturers) in (this country, foreign countries).
   Where are the main consumers of your products?

   a. If you provide manufacturers, which kind of firms are those?

   b. Are those mainly Japanese firms or local firms?

II. Push Factor in Japan.

1. Was there any assistance from your government when the parent company in Japan invested in overseas countries?

   a. What kind of assistance was it?

2. What extent the high rate of the yen influenced your overseas investment?

3. When did the parent company in Japan begin the export of its products to foreign countries?

   a. And when was it to EC countries?

4. Was there any serious trade barriers from the EC countries to the products of the parent company in Japan?

   a. Which country was the most strict in trade conflict?

5. There have been news several times regarding the shortage of labour in Japan. Is it so bad?

6. Are there any industrial estates provided by the Japanese government?

   a. If not, the high price of industrial land seems to be the serious problem for individual companies. How can individual companies in Japan get their own sites?

7. Did your company decide to invest in foreign countries following its main customers?

    a. If so, was there any previous request from the customers?

    b. Or, was the decision made without previous negotiation with the customers?

III. Location Factors

1. Was there enough labour available for your firm in this area when you decide the location?

    a. What aspect of the labour force in this area was the most advantageous for your firm? (e.g. low wage level, low labour disputes, high level of techniques)

    b. Was there any disadvantageous aspect of the labour force in this area?

    c. What proportion of your employees is from this region(county)?

    d. How many trade unions are there in your firm?

    e. Have you ever experienced severe labour disputes with workers since the opening of this plant?

2. What is the size of land and premises?

    a. Was this building newly built by your firm or purchased from others?

    b. Who is the previous owner of the land, local government or individuals?

3. What is the output of this plant per day? (How many units of products do you make in this plant in a day?)

    a. Where are the major suppliers of your products?

    b. Could you tell me the proportion of your purchase from local firms in total output?

    c. What is the main route from your suppliers to your firm?

    d. You said that your main customers are in _____. What is the main route from your firm to your customers?

e. Is there any problem in the capacity of motorways and trunk roads around here?

f. Which airport, and seaport, do you use to export products?

4. How many Japanese firms were here at the time of the opening of this plant?

a. How many Japanese firms have arrived here since this plant was opened?

b. Are there any schools around here for the children of Japanese workers?

5. You replied that there are _____ Japanese employees in this firm. Have they been settled down already?

a. Were there enough houses for the employees in this area?
   Or, did you build those for yourself?

b. What do you think of the level of living cost in this area compared to London or Birmingham?

c. Are there any golf courses around here?

d. Are there enough facilities for recreation or sports in this area?

e. Do you think that the attractiveness of the landscape or amenity in this area influenced the locational decision of your firm?

IV. British Regional Policy

1. What was the role of the British government when you were considering overseas investment?

2. Which institution in the British government did you contact with when you proceeded the investment decision? Was it IBB?

3. You answered that your company received financial aid from this government. Was it RDG or RSA?

a. Could you tell me the amount of the aid that you received?

b. If none, have you ever asked for any financial assistance to the government?

4. What was the role of local government for your decision?

5. Was there any thing that you demanded to the British government, but not fulfilled by them at that time?

V. Alternative Locations

1. How many alternative countries did you consider when you decide the location of this plant?

a. If there is none, did your company decide to invest in the UK from the beginning?

2. Then, how many alternative locations in this country did you consider at that time?

3. How much time did it take for your firm to make the decision?

VI. Others

1. Please state any problems or difficulties you have had in managing this plant.

a. Has there been any problem with the location?

b. Would you choose this site and place if you were coming again now?

Appendix 5. Indices of Locational Factors (Britain)

1. Y₁

County	Labour Supply X_a	Public Policy X_b	Land & Premises X_c	Accessibility X_d	Linkages X_e	Environments X_f
Cleveland	0.2065	0.0406	-0.1389	-0.0325	-0.1532	0.1743
Cumbria	-0.3730	0.2572	-0.0963	0.0272	-0.2068	-0.1485
Durham	0.1143	-0.0431	-0.0623	-0.0833	0.1790	0.0004
Northumber	-0.0790	-0.0494	-0.1597	-0.0793	0.0206	-0.0951
Tyne & Wear	0.2889	0.6400	0.0362	0.0119	0.0344	0.2738
Humberside	0.1357	0.1467	-0.0057	0.0273	-0.1355	0.0473
N Yorkshire	-0.0925	-0.1154	-0.0606	0.0642	-0.2110	-0.1374
S Yorkshire	0.2271	0.2159	0.0409	0.0361	0.1133	0.1445
W Yorkshire	0.2917	0.1206	0.1728	0.1029	0.2047	0.2050
Derbyshire	0.0101	-0.0803	0.0041	0.0717	0.0489	0.0420
Leices	-0.0193	-0.0895	0.0373	-0.0039	0.0628	0.0712
Lincolns	-0.0010	-0.1464	-0.0705	-0.0011	-0.2183	-0.1690
Northants	-0.0959	0.1191	0.0407	-0.0519	0.0088	-0.0831
Notts	0.0571	-0.0452	0.0593	0.0264	0.0597	0.1021
Cambs	-0.1112	-0.1230	0.0182	0.0033	0.0041	-0.1358
Norfolk	-0.0468	-0.1462	0.0625	-0.1510	-0.1612	-0.1267
Suffolk	-0.1440	-0.1508	0.0175	-0.1740	-0.0790	-0.0038
Bedfords	-0.1122	-0.1244	0.0502	0.0209	-0.0076	-0.0650
Berkshire	-0.1485	-0.1566	0.2298	0.0512	0.3052	-0.0247
Bucks	-0.1979	-0.1630	0.2277	0.0536	0.6163	-0.0836
E Sussex	-0.0791	-0.1283	0.2207	0.0729	-0.1274	0.1287
Essex	0.0783	-0.1375	0.2748	0.1030	0.0851	0.0980
G London	0.4706	0.1080	0.5922	0.3493	0.5713	0.6400
Hampshire	0.0720	-0.1356	0.2109	0.0724	0.4687	0.0876
Herts	-0.0897	-0.1493	0.3403	0.1215	0.1850	0.1075
I of Wight	-0.2212	0.0103	-0.2826	-0.0860	-0.4448	-0.1841
Kent	0.0037	0.0236	0.1595	0.1521	0.0292	0.0639
Oxfordshire	-0.1735	-0.1641	-0.0831	0.0001	0.0055	-0.1597
Surrey	-0.2038	-0.1520	0.0141	0.1085	0.5696	0.0179
W Sussex	-0.2203	-0.1559	0.2638	0.0587	-0.0186	0.0063
Avon	0.0028	-0.1466	0.1295	-0.0201	-0.0785	0.0692
Cornwall	0.0174	-0.0352	-0.0952	-0.1913	-0.4465	-0.2095
Devon	0.0671	-0.1150	0.1254	-0.1394	-0.1396	-0.0526
Dorset	-0.1155	-0.1595	-0.0275	-0.1666	-0.1920	-0.0356
Gloces	-0.1399	-0.1496	-0.1047	-0.0787	-0.0337	-0.1349
Somerset	-0.1597	-0.1456	-0.0945	-0.1945	-0.1464	-0.2030
Wiltshire	-0.1237	-0.1259	0.0620	-0.0435	-0.0339	-0.0988
H & Worces	0.0140	-0.1142	-0.0026	0.0028	-0.0073	-0.1205
Shropshire	-0.0225	0.0355	-0.1527	0.0294	-0.0185	-0.1780
Staffords	0.0777	-0.1175	0.0199	0.0305	0.0073	0.0134

County	Labour Supply X_a	Public Policy X_b	Land & Premises X_c	Accessibility X_d	Linkages X_e	Environments X_f
Warwicks	-0.1106	-0.0908	-0.0984	0.0490	-0.0116	-0.0855
W Midlands	0.6291	0.1643	0.2500	0.3046	0.2821	0.2766
Chesire	0.1241	0.0615	0.0180	0.0977	0.2412	0.0485

County	Labour Supply X_a	Public Policy X_b	Land & Premises X_c	Accessibility X_d	Linkages X_e	Environments X_f
G Manches	0.3607	0.1880	0.2190	0.3560	0.2032	0.3238
Lancashire	0.1280	-0.0129	0.0845	0.0799	-0.0031	0.1233
Merseyside	0.4587	0.3246	0.0402	0.1213	-0.0219	0.2873
Clwyd	0.0418	0.3439	-0.1439	-0.0299	-0.1487	-0.0571
Dyfed	0.0133	0.1313	-0.1633	-0.1356	-0.2588	-0.2355
Gwent	0.0708	0.0195	-0.1241	-0.1037	0.4095	0.1213
Gwynedd	-0.0143	-0.0503	-0.1887	0.0631	-0.3901	-0.1458
M Glamorgan	0.1202	0.0816	-0.1237	-0.1267	0.3384	0.1495
Powys	-0.2645	-0.1308	-0.2723	-0.0230	-0.2569	-0.3755
S Glamorgan	-0.0249	0.1315	-0.1051	-0.0325	0.0925	0.0536
W Glamorgan	0.0184	0.1309	-0.1690	-0.2798	-0.0599	0.1493
Borders	-0.3551	*	-0.2373	-0.2244	-0.2150	-0.3114
Central	-0.0384	*	-0.1909	-0.0422	-0.2117	0.0582
D&Galloway	-0.0968	*	-0.2345	-0.1127	-0.3434	-0.3555
Fife	-0.0179	*	-0.1176	0.0018	-0.1749	0.0207
Gramphian	0.0349	*	0.0035	0.0191	-0.1587	-0.1116
Highlands	0.0541	*	-0.1706	-0.1057	-0.2602	-0.1863
Lothian	0.2736	*	0.0289	0.1965	0.2044	0.1632
Strathclyde	0.6841	*	0.1780	0.3580	0.5660	0.7072
Tayside	-0.0217	*	-0.1020	-0.0420	-0.1867	-0.0747
Islands	-0.2463	*	-0.3554	-0.4880	-0.3526	-0.3889

(Note) The public policy index for Scotland is treated as missing due to inaccessibility of the data representing the public expenditure for economic development and promotion (X_{22}) in this region.

2. Y₂

County	Labour Supply X_a	Public Policy X_b	Land & Premises X_c	Accessibility X_d	Linkages X_e	Environments X_f
Cleveland	0.2189	0.0530	-0.1497	-0.0326	-0.2343	0.1723
Cumbria	-0.0908	0.2684	-0.1051	0.0289	-0.2286	-0.1452
Durham	0.0845	-0.0489	-0.0697	-0.0848	0.1256	0.0018
Northumber	-0.1088	-0.0520	-0.1714	-0.0775	-0.0888	-0.0967
Tyne & Wear	0.2762	0.6558	0.0501	0.0138	0.0141	0.2737
Humberside	0.1121	0.1506	0.0069	0.0281	-0.1438	0.0477
N Yorkshire	-0.1265	-0.1201	-0.0679	0.0639	-0.2081	-0.1334
S Yorkshire	0.2734	0.2372	0.0564	0.0325	0.0972	0.1462
W Yorkshire	0.2825	0.1403	0.1971	0.1017	0.2584	0.2073
Derbyshire	0.0078	-0.0826	0.0192	0.0684	0.0172	0.0439
Leices	-0.0355	-0.0920	0.0555	-0.0092	0.0668	0.0720
Lincolns	-0.0595	-0.1527	-0.0783	-0.0023	-0.2100	-0.1642
Northants	-0.1223	0.1343	0.0549	-0.0570	0.0203	-0.0804
Notts	0.0674	-0.0447	0.0786	0.0237	0.0453	0.1031
Cambs	-0.1729	-0.1277	0.0353	0.0009	0.0096	-0.1306
Norfolk	-0.0768	-0.1523	0.0817	-0.1387	-0.1745	-0.1209
Suffolk	-0.1767	-0.1573	0.0349	-0.1623	-0.0563	-0.0021
Bedfords	-0.1494	-0.1292	0.0640	0.0163	-0.0403	-0.0625
Berkshire	-0.1841	-0.1635	0.2053	0.0483	0.3829	-0.0213
Bucks	-0.2420	-0.1703	0.1741	0.0500	0.6571	-0.0804
E Sussex	-0.1129	-0.1333	0.1978	0.0724	-0.0849	0.1276
Essex	0.0573	-0.1431	0.2928	0.1035	0.1072	0.1009
G London	0.6733	0.1339	0.5732	0.3406	0.7747	0.6356
Hampshire	0.0257	-0.1411	0.2257	0.0730	0.3359	0.0904
Herts	-0.0930	-0.1556	0.2966	0.1184	0.2372	0.1076
I of Wight	-0.2623	0.0142	-0.2998	-0.0894	-0.4113	-0.1848
Kent	0.0536	0.0386	0.1821	0.1524	0.1026	0.0683
Oxfordshire	-0.2163	-0.1714	-0.0914	-0.0028	0.0147	-0.1548
Surrey	-0.2329	-0.1586	0.0102	0.1066	0.6329	0.0226
W Sussex	-0.2700	-0.1627	0.2248	0.0578	0.0185	0.0088
Avon	-0.0040	-0.1528	0.1449	-0.0195	-0.0792	0.0720
Cornwall	-0.0134	-0.0393	-0.1040	-0.1766	-0.2359	-0.2040
Devon	0.0281	-0.1213	0.1446	-0.1252	-0.0860	-0.0481
Dorset	-0.1550	-0.1666	-0.0333	-0.1549	-0.1110	-0.0333
Gloces	-0.1792	-0.1559	-0.1139	-0.0818	-0.0540	-0.1307
Somerset	-0.1976	-0.1517	-0.1033	-0.1828	-0.1441	-0.1982
Wiltshire	-0.1618	-0.1308	0.0676	-0.0464	-0.0371	-0.0956
H & Worces	-0.0292	-0.1183	0.0133	0.0019	0.0370	-0.1160
Shropshire	-0.0588	0.0512	-0.1642	0.0267	0.0269	-0.1749
Staffords	0.0721	-0.1219	0.0357	0.0267	-0.0306	0.0167
Warwicks	-0.1318	-0.0934	-0.1074	0.0440	0.0054	-0.0829
W Midlands	0.6623	0.1903	0.2771	0.2943	0.3218	0.2779
Cheshire	0.0619	0.0338	0.0350	0.0960	0.2536	0.0503

County	G Manches	Lancashire				
G Manches	0.4539	0.2095	0.2443	0.3467	0.2662	0.3244
Lancashire	0.1594	-0.0016	0.1017	0.0790	0.0141	0.1254

County	Labour Supply X_a	Public Policy X_b	Land & Premises X_c	Accessibility X_d	Linkages X_e	Environments X_f
Merseyside	0.4288	0.3212	0.0501	0.1203	-0.0430	0.2862
Clwyd	0.0129	0.3548	-0.1464	-0.0308	-0.1527	-0.0563
Dyfed	-0.0131	0.1427	-0.1752	-0.1228	-0.3515	-0.2317
Gwent	0.0399	0.0110	-0.1342	-0.1064	0.3539	0.1183
Gwynedd	-0.0575	-0.0515	-0.2018	0.0657	-0.3725	-0.1464
M Glamorgan	0.0959	0.0784	-0.1338	-0.1153	0.2382	0.1477
Powys	-0.3134	-0.1376	-0.2891	-0.0225	-0.3393	-0.3746
S Glamorgan	-0.0624	0.1386	-0.0933	-0.0318	0.0945	0.0531
W Glamorgan	0.0103	0.1384	-0.1667	-0.2707	-0.1197	0.1450
Borders	-0.4054	*	-0.2525	-0.2323	-0.3176	-0.3123
Central	-0.0630	*	-0.2040	-0.0468	-0.2952	0.0538
D&Galloway	-0.1409	*	-0.2496	-0.1160	-0.3527	-0.3554
Fife	-0.0407	*	-0.1274	-0.0007	-0.2575	0.0144
Gramphian	-0.0136	*	0.0202	0.0171	-0.1221	-0.1116
Highland	-0.0065	*	-0.1828	-0.0923	-0.2402	-0.2059
Lothian	0.1826	*	0.0461	0.1853	0.2028	0.1577
Strathclyde	0.7695	*	0.2027	0.3515	0.5735	0.6497
Tayside	-0.0392	*	-0.1112	-0.0429	-0.2328	-0.0789
Islands	-0.2920	*	-0.3759	-0.4793	-0.4482	-0.3905

3. Y₃

County	Labour Supply X$_a$	Public Policy X$_b$	Land & Premises X$_c$	Accessibility X$_d$	Linkages X$_e$	Environments X$_f$
Cleveland	0.2306	0.4563	-0.0622	-0.0869	-0.1932	0.3526
Cumbria	-0.3594	0.3501	-0.0258	0.0048	-0.1897	-0.2047
Durham	0.1201	0.0980	0.0032	-0.1587	0.2756	0.0568
Northumber	-0.0647	0.0267	-0.0800	-0.1215	-0.0255	-0.0265
Tyne & Wear	0.3535	0.6809	0.0541	-0.0159	-0.0471	0.4810
Humberside	0.1364	0.1943	0.0158	-0.0081	-0.1374	0.0456
N Yorkshire	0.1409	-0.1005	0.0044	0.0388	-0.1770	-0.2987
S Yorkshire	0.2765	0.3872	0.0533	-0.0001	0.0019	0.1574
W Yorkshire	0.2977	0.1777	0.1332	0.0977	0.0986	0.2211
Derbyshire	0.0072	-0.1057	0.0149	0.0374	-0.0438	-0.0165
Leices	-0.0595	-0.1670	0.0140	-0.0673	-0.0132	0.1334
Lincolns	-0.0296	-0.2436	-0.0022	-0.0561	-0.1782	-0.3633
Northants	-0.1053	0.0887	-0.0128	-0.1285	-0.0433	-0.2201
Notts	0.0172	-0.0742	0.0380	-0.0163	-0.0279	0.1114
Cambs	-0.1507	-0.2151	-0.0062	-0.0401	-0.0520	-0.2307
Norfolk	-0.0681	-0.2484	0.0394	-0.0545	-0.1563	-0.3254
Suffolk	-0.1650	-0.2551	0.0005	-0.0873	-0.0891	-0.0103
Bedfords	-0.1006	-0.2171	-0.0084	-0.0185	-0.0807	-0.2098
Berkshire	-0.2089	-0.2635	0.0355	0.0225	0.2315	-0.0734
Bucks	-0.2255	-0.2727	-0.0136	0.0277	0.4604	-0.2315
E Sussex	-0.1126	-0.2227	0.0314	0.0584	-0.1067	0.1587
Essex	0.0508	-0.2360	0.3822	0.1009	0.0073	-0.0059
G London	0.5790	0.0202	0.3260	0.4846	0.3953	0.7496
Hampshire	-0.0056	-0.2333	0.1064	0.0551	0.3084	-0.0199
Hertfords	-0.1536	-0.2529	0.0900	0.1269	0.0805	0.0630
I of Wight	-0.1987	-0.0234	-0.1853	-0.1701	-0.3021	-0.1032
Kent	-0.0443	-0.0668	0.1058	0.1735	0.0044	-0.0523
Oxfordshire	-0.2110	-0.2742	-0.0149	-0.0526	-0.0509	-0.2343
Surrey	-0.2418	-0.2568	0.0679	0.1139	0.9664	0.0221
W Sussex	-0.2533	-0.2624	0.0375	0.0383	-0.0465	0.0452
Avon	-0.0414	-0.2491	0.0518	-0.0551	-0.1011	0.1411
Cornwall	0.0134	0.0758	-0.0252	-0.1192	-0.1941	-0.4250
Devon	-0.0017	-0.0917	0.0652	-0.0414	-0.1053	-0.1635
Dorset	-0.1460	-0.2677	0.0321	-0.0761	-0.1207	-0.0109
Gloces	-0.1531	-0.2307	-0.0332	-0.1335	-0.0877	-0.2173
Somerset	-0.1893	-0.2476	-0.0246	-0.1175	-0.1411	-0.3421
Wiltshire	-0.1580	-0.2193	-0.0276	-0.1176	-0.0799	-0.0339
H & Worces	-0.0496	-0.1908	0.0000	-0.0180	-0.0351	-0.2271
Shropshire	-0.0334	-0.0128	-0.0742	-0.0056	-0.0444	-0.2387
Staffords	0.0608	-0.2073	0.0283	-0.0077	-0.0712	-0.1066
Warwicks	-0.1257	-0.1688	-0.0277	0.0235	-0.0546	-0.1540
W Midlands	1.0246	0.1713	0.1873	0.4175	0.1367	0.3318
Cheshire	0.1340	0.1289	0.0163	0.0867	0.2134	-0.0665

G Manches	0.3870	0.2487	0.1590	0.4846	0.1034	0.3791
Lancashire	0.1071	-0.0030	0.0912	0.0669	-0.0436	0.0556

County	Labour Supply X_a	Public Policy X_b	Land & Premises X_c	Accessibility X_d	Linkages X_e	Environments X_f
Merseyside	0.5508	0.3820	0.0692	0.1282	-0.0788	0.4915
Clwyd	0.0482	0.4454	-0.0797	-0.0783	-0.1464	-0.0046
Dyfed	-0.0038	0.2689	-0.0831	-0.0329	-0.2653	-0.2847
Gwent	0.0645	0.1207	-0.0496	-0.1713	0.4427	0.3549
Gwynedd	-0.0157	0.0388	-0.1050	0.0516	-0.2783	-0.0277
M Glamorgan	0.1100	0.2354	-0.0493	-0.0165	1.1239	0.4198
Powys	-0.2635	-0.1511	-0.1765	-0.0591	-0.2578	-0.2013
S Glamorgan	-0.0265	0.2756	-0.0962	-0.0736	0.4030	0.2525
W Glamorgan	0.0405	0.1730	-0.1143	-0.2375	-0.1296	0.4547
Borders	-0.3510	*	-0.1474	-0.3458	-0.2445	-0.1557
Central	-0.0173	*	-0.1080	-0.0728	-0.2306	0.3282
D&Galloway	-0.1483	*	-0.1450	-0.1909	-0.2661	-0.2454
Fife	-0.0285	*	-0.0460	-0.0122	-0.2074	-0.0052
Gramphian	-0.1876	*	-0.0152	0.2280	-0.1276	-0.1460
Highland	-0.0642	*	-0.0908	0.0101	-0.2024	-0.3194
Lothian	0.0732	*	0.0252	0.2939	0.2429	0.1482
Strathclyde	0.4734	*	0.1355	0.5224	0.4976	0.2127
Tayside	-0.0137	*	-0.0329	-0.0805	-0.1922	-0.0145
Islands	-0.2394	*	-0.2476	-0.5442	-0.3249	-0.1517

4. Y_4

County	Labour Supply X_a	Public Policy X_b	Land & Premises X_c	Accessibility X_d	Linkages X_e	Environments X_f
Cleveland	0.2456	-0.0061	-0.1312	-0.1290	-0.2552	0.2770
Cumbria	-0.4327	0.2473	-0.1006	-0.1184	-0.2493	-0.1654
Durham	0.1247	0.0002	-0.0727	-0.1290	-0.0724	0.0415
Northumber	-0.0882	-0.0225	-0.1446	-0.1457	-0.3162	-0.0407
Tyne &.Wear	0.4052	0.7843	0.0285	-0.1148	0.0663	0.4525
Humberside	0.1496	0.1801	-0.0131	-0.0554	-0.1400	0.1000
N Yorkshire	-0.1608	-0.0989	-0.0712	-0.0799	-0.2263	-0.2003
S Yorkshire	0.3231	0.3971	0.0329	-0.0243	0.1933	0.1894
W Yorkshire	0.3619	0.2098	0.1837	0.0503	0.5293	0.2807
Derbyshire	0.0095	-0.0943	-0.0039	-0.0296	0.0859	0.0373
Leices	-0.0633	-0.1297	0.0233	0.0521	0.1901	0.1532
Lincolns	-0.0387	-0.2069	-0.0797	-0.1079	-0.2285	-0.2549
Northant	-0.1211	0.1707	0.0205	-0.0527	0.0766	-0.1693
Notts	0.0200	-0.0593	0.0455	0.0270	0.1208	0.1496
Cambs	-0.1699	-0.1749	0.0060	-0.0511	0.0514	-0.1439
Norfolk	-0.0798	-0.2061	0.0472	-0.1417	-0.1842	-0.2360
Suffolk	-0.1861	-0.2123	0.0062	-0.1404	-0.0327	0.0310
Bedfords	-0.1098	-0.1767	0.0276	0.1020	-0.0128	-0.1923
Berkshire	-0.2300	-0.2202	0.1407	-0.0270	0.2587	-0.0659
Bucks	-0.2546	-0.2288	0.1107	-0.0067	0.3387	-0.2115
E Sussex	-0.1313	-0.1820	0.1341	-0.0587	-0.0695	0.1517
Essex	0.0660	-0.1944	0.2835	0.0929	0.2023	0.0982
G London	0.7365	0.1537	0.8036	0.8722	1.3877	0.8806
Hampshire	0.0034	-0.1919	0.1868	-0.0652	0.2231	0.0532
Herts	-0.1614	-0.2103	0.2306	0.0314	0.3626	0.1003
I of Wight	-0.2393	0.0048	-0.2065	-0.1029	-0.3837	-0.2197
Kent	-0.0512	0.0339	0.1537	-0.0265	0.1936	0.0486
Oxfordshire	-0.2355	-0.2302	-0.0901	-0.0626	0.0597	-0.1801
Surrey	-0.2641	-0.2139	0.0038	0.0033	0.3096	0.0126
W Sussex	-0.2831	-0.2192	0.1560	0.3489	0.0635	0.0440
Avon	-0.0450	-0.2067	0.0996	-0.0668	-0.0591	0.1588
Cornwall	-0.0031	0.0509	-0.0997	-0.2296	-0.2569	-0.3821
Devon	-0.0095	-0.1099	0.1043	-0.0921	-0.0690	-0.0550
Dorset	-0.1691	-0.2241	-0.0403	-0.1100	-0.1033	0.0136
Gloces	-0.1723	-0.1909	-0.1070	-0.0587	-0.0294	-0.1657
Somerset	-0.2167	-0.2053	-0.0992	-0.1540	-0.1432	-0.2772
Wiltshire	-0.1792	-0.1788	0.0301	-0.1003	-0.0077	-0.0212
H & Worces	-0.0607	-0.1528	-0.0101	-0.0567	0.0901	-0.1466
Shropshire	-0.0516	0.0796	-0.1402	-0.0418	0.0769	-0.1921
Staffords	0.0722	-0.1675	0.0108	-0.0216	0.0213	-0.0222
Warwicks	-0.1472	-0.1314	-0.1022	0.0226	0.0458	-0.1035
W Midlands	1.2496	0.2681	0.2994	0.5456	0.7061	0.4170
Cheshire	0.1580	-0.1436	0.0081	-0.0270	0.1013	0.0057

338

G Manches	0.4695	0.3027	0.2419	0.7020	0.5542	0.4465
Lancashire	0.1264	0.0183	0.0835	0.0852	0.1122	0.1458

County	Labour Supply X_a	Public Policy X_b	Land & Premises X_c	Accessibility X_d	Linkages X_e	Environments X_f
Merseyside	0.6383	0.2962	0.0341	0.0786	-0.0006	0.4755
Clwyd	0.0353	0.4449	-0.1257	-0.1003	-0.1528	-0.0567
Dyfed	-0.0207	0.1924	-0.1468	-0.1386	-0.3508	-0.2762
Gwent	0.0614	0.0676	-0.1211	-0.0876	-0.0512	0.2158
Gwynedd	-0.0376	0.0263	-0.1617	-0.1217	-0.3633	-0.1437
M Glamorgan	0.1101	0.1419	-0.1208	-0.0948	-0.2018	0.2442
Powys	-0.3119	-0.1527	-0.2023	-0.1115	-0.3429	-0.3032
S Glamorgan	-0.0397	0.2040	-0.0819	-0.1231	-0.0983	0.1550
W Glamorgan	0.0368	0.1167	-0.1325	-0.1483	-0.0993	0.2362
Borders	-0.4037	*	-0.1867	-0.0547	-0.3279	-0.2888
Central	-0.0327	*	-0.1629	0.0144	-0.3108	0.1218
D&Galloway	-0.1833	*	-0.1854	-0.0920	-0.3515	-0.3565
Fife	-0.0453	*	-0.1164	-0.0067	-0.2781	-0.0410
Gramphian	-0.2136	*	-0.0056	0.4317	-0.1173	-0.1637
Highland	-0.0859	*	-0.1512	-0.1310	-0.2061	-0.4817
Lothian	0.0842	*	0.0188	0.5128	0.0259	0.1179
Strathclyde	0.5558	*	0.1967	0.5214	0.3021	0.1856
Tayside	-0.0260	*	-0.1050	-0.0815	-0.2537	-0.1111
Islands	-0.2884	*	-0.2324	-0.5728	-0.4002	-0.3747

Appendix 6. Indices of locational factors (Korea)

1. Y_1

County	Labour Supply X_a	Public Policy X_b	Land & Premises X_c	Accessibility X_d	Linkages X_e	Environments X_f
Seoul	0.9455	0.8452	0.4809	0.2417	1.8684	1.0259
Pusan	0.1400	-0.2534	-0.0025	0.1576	0.3133	-0.1288
Taegu	-0.1243	0.0588	-0.4696	-0.1709	-0.2066	-0.4071
Inchon	0.0755	0.2431	-0.1826	0.0581	-0.1985	-0.2610
Kyonggi	1.0498	1.4340	0.6440	0.0488	0.6228	0.2710
Kangwon	-0.5096	-0.4798	-0.4021	0.0159	-0.5541	-0.1180
C C Buk	-0.5121	-0.4429	-0.3320	0.0095	-0.5476	-0.4265
C C Nam	-0.3423	-0.2894	-0.2268	0.0356	-0.4227	-0.0839
C L Buk	-0.4908	-0.6080	-0.1668	-0.1712	-0.2711	-0.3728
C L Nam	-0.1876	-0.5214	0.1309	-0.1036	-0.3908	0.1146
K S Buk	-0.0492	-0.1668	0.2447	0.0086	-0.1942	0.2270
K S Nam	0.4520	0.5565	0.9033	0.2199	0.6123	0.4816
Cheju	-0.4448	-0.3762	-0.6207	-0.3502	-0.6297	-0.3217

2. Y_2

County	Labour Supply X_a	Public Policy X_b	Land & Premises X_c	Accessibility X_d	Linkages X_e	Environments X_f
Seoul	0.9428	0.8844	0.5989	0.4643	1.4001	1.0090
Pusan	0.0474	-0.2492	0.0124	-0.0801	0.3129	-0.0662
Taegu	-0.0571	0.0682	-0.3310	-0.0649	-0.3102	-0.3741
Inchon	-0.0884	0.2451	-0.1213	-0.1290	0.0746	-0.0935
Kyonggi	1.4470	1.4065	0.5411	0.2249	0.9897	1.1677
Kangwon	-0.6906	-0.4822	-0.2900	0.0519	-0.4025	-0.3027
C C Buk	-0.3965	-0.4455	-0.2256	0.1947	-0.6516	-0.4515
C C Nam	-0.3008	-0.2873	-0.1367	0.2211	-0.5077	-0.1870
C L Buk	-0.4406	-0.6172	-0.1459	-0.2051	-0.2315	-0.3189
C L Nam	-0.4496	-0.5310	0.0741	-0.1847	-0.4741	0.0352
K S Buk	-0.0485	-0.1651	0.1096	-0.0452	0.0586	-0.0529
K S Nam	0.4493	0.5480	0.5184	-0.1450	0.6099	0.0622
Cheju	-0.4127	-0.3752	-0.6030	-0.3027	-0.8697	-0.4266

3. Y_3

County	Labour Supply X_a	Public Policy X_b	Land & Premises X_c	Accessibility X_d	Linkages X_e	Environments X_f
Seoul	0.4844	0.2724	0.2863	-0.0754	0.7890	0.5511
Pusan	-0.1194	-0.2048	0.1145	0.1876	0.1512	-0.1414
Taegu	-0.2796	0.0635	-0.4063	-0.2145	-0.0883	-0.2973
Inchon	0.1728	0.2603	-0.1282	0.0051	-0.1001	-0.4218
Kyonggi	0.3018	0.8979	0.4474	-0.0555	0.1949	0.3563
Kangwon	-0.3417	-0.3616	-0.4494	0.0434	-0.4763	0.0109
C C Buk	-0.5830	-0.2725	-0.2395	-0.1665	-0.2667	-0.2015
C C Nam	-0.3792	-0.1825	-0.1776	-0.1165	-0.2037	-0.0669
C L Buk	-0.3954	-0.3375	-0.2223	-0.1184	-0.1208	-0.3016
C L Nam	0.0150	-0.2366	0.2093	0.0832	-0.1905	0.1755
K S Buk	0.3096	-0.0416	0.0321	0.0815	-0.0949	-0.1150
K S Nam	0.8158	0.4728	1.0453	0.5753	0.7603	1.1563
Cheju	-0.0011	-0.3296	-0.5129	-0.2301	-0.3538	-0.7024

4. Y_4

County	Labour Supply X_a	Public Policy X_b	Land & Premises X_c	Accessibility X_d	Linkages X_e	Environments X_f
Seoul	1.0434	0.3320	0.2439	0.0704	0.9223	0.6961
Pusan	-0.0491	0.0295	0.0773	0.3315	0.2027	0.1424
Taegu	-0.2735	0.1145	-0.2764	-0.1916	-0.0934	-0.4304
Inchon	-0.0374	0.3388	-0.0364	0.1134	-0.0939	-0.0555
Kyonggi	0.2459	0.3277	0.3684	-0.1055	0.0816	0.5239
Kangwon	-0.2769	-0.3416	-0.2837	-0.2496	-0.2058	-0.0908
C C Buk	-0.7307	-0.1625	-0.1513	-0.1482	-0.2505	-0.2765
C C Nam	-0.2969	-0.1109	-0.0585	-0.1243	-0.1729	-0.1362
C L Buk	-0.4255	-0.1343	-0.0633	-0.1054	-0.1101	-0.3250
C L Nam	0.3463	-0.1025	0.1776	0.1624	-0.1239	0.2341
K S Buk	0.2359	-0.0385	0.1811	0.1107	-0.0575	0.1091
K S Nam	0.5042	0.1793	0.5458	0.2721	0.1505	0.2505
Cheju	-0.2880	-0.4313	-0.7259	-0.1351	-0.2489	-0.6400

Bibliography

Aaker D.A. and Day G.S. (1990) : *Marketing Research* (John Wiley & Sons, Chichester).

Abdallah W.M. (1989) : *International Transfer Pricing Policies* (Quorum Books, Westport Conn.).

Abumere S.I. (1978) : 'Multinationals, Location Theory and Regional Development: Case Study of Bendel State of Nigeria', *Regional Studies*, 12, pp.651-664.

Achen C. (1982) : *Interpreting and Using Regression* (Sage, Beverly Hills).

Ackroyd S., Burrell G., Hughes M. and Whitaker A. (1988) : 'The Japanisation of British Industry?', *Industrial Relations Journal*, 19.1, pp.11-23.

Adam G. (1975) : 'Multinational Corporations and Worldwide Sourcing', see Radice H. (ed.).

Aglietta M. (1979) : *A Theory of Capitalist Regulation* (New Left Books, London).

Agricultural Statistics United Kingdom : HMSO, Annual Publication.

Ahiakpor J.C.W. (1990) : *Multinationals and Economic Development* (Routledge, London).

Akira I. (1971) : 'The Failure of Military Expansionism', in Morley J.W. (ed.) *Dilemmas of Growth in Pre-War Japan* (Princeton University Press, Princeton).

Al-Eryani M.F., Alam P. and Akhter S.H. (1990) : 'Transfer Pricing Determinants of US Multinationals', *Journal of International Business Studies*, 21.3, pp.409-425.

Aliber P.Z. (1985) : 'Transfer Pricing: A Taxonomy of Impacts on Economic Welfare', see Rugman A.M. and Eden L. (eds.).

Allen J. (1988a) : 'The Geography of Service', see Massey and Allen (eds.).

Allen J. (1988b) : 'Towards a Post-Industrial Economy?', see Allen J. and Massey D. (eds.).

Allen J. and Massey D. (eds.) (1988) : *The Economy in Question: Restructuring Britain* (Sage, London).

Allen K., Begg H., McDowall S. and Walker G. (1986) : *Regional Incentives and the Investment Decisions of the Firm*, Department of Trade and Industry (HMSO, London).

Alperovich G. and Katz E. (1988) : 'The Location decision and Employment Suburbanization', *Urban Studies*, 25.3, pp.243-247.

Amin A. and Goddard J. (eds.) (1986) : *Technological Change, Industrial Restructuring and Regional Development* (Allen and Unwin, London).

Amin A. and Robins K. (1990) : 'The Re-emergence of Regional Economies? The Mythical Geography of Flexible Accumulation', *Environment and Planning D*, 8.1, pp.7-34.

Amin A. and Tomaney J. (1991) : 'Creating an Enterprise Culture in the North East? The Impact of Urban and Regional Policies in the 1980s', *Regional Studies*, 25.5, pp.479-488.

Annual Census of Production : See *Business Monitor*.

Annual Report on Residents Income : Ministry of Home Affairs, Korea, Annual Statistics (1966-1980) (Korean Version).

Aoki M. (1990) : 'Toward an Economic Model of Japanese Firm', *Journal of Economic Literature*, XXVIII, pp.1-27.

Archer B.H. (1970) : *Location of Industry for a Rural Environment*, Research Paper 3, University College of North Wales.

Armour A.J.L. (ed.) (1985) : *Asia and Japan* (Athlone, London).

Armstrong H. (1986) : 'The Division of Regional Industrial Policy Powers in Britain: Some Implications of the 1984 Policy Reforms', *Environment and Planning* Ch. 4.3, pp.325-342.

Armstrong H. and Taylor J. (1985) : *Regional Economics and Policy* (Phillip Allen, Oxford).

Armstrong H. and Taylor J. : *Regional Policy: The Way Forward* (Employment Institute, London, 1987).

Armstrong H. and Taylor J. (1989) : *Regional Policy and the North-South Divide* (Employment Institute, London).

Arther D. Little Ltd. (1986) : *A Survey of Foreign Firms in Wales: Their Assessment of the Welsh Workforce*, WINVEST, Welsh Development Agency.

Ashcroft B. (1982) : 'The Measurement of the Impact of Regional Policies in Europe: A Survey and Critique', *Regional Studies*, 16.4, pp.287-305.

Ashcroft B. and Ingham K. (1979) : 'Comparative Adaptation and the Response to Regional Policy: A Comparative Analysis of MNC Subsidiaries and Indigenous Companies', *Regional Studies*, 13, pp.25-37.

Ashcroft B. and Ingham K. (1982) : 'The Comparative Impact of UK Regional Policy on Foreign and Indigenous Firm Movement', *Applied Economics*, 14, pp.81-100.

343

Ashcroft B., Love J.H. and Malloy E. (1991) : 'New Firm Formation in the British Counties with Special Reference to Scotland', *Regional Studies*, 25.5, pp.395-409.

Ashcroft B. and McGregor P.G. (1989) : ' The Demand for Industrial Development Certificates and the Effect of Regional Policy', *Regional Studies*, 23.4, pp.301-314.

Ashcroft B. and Taylor J. (1977) : 'The Movement of Manufacturing Industry and the Effect of Regional Policy', *Oxford Economic Papers*, 29, pp.84-101.

Ashcroft B. and Taylor J. (1979) : 'The Effect of Regional Policy on the Movement of Industry in Great Britain', see MacLennan D. and Parr J. (eds.).

Atkinson J. (1989) : *Management Strategies for Flexibility and the Role of the Trade Unions*, Institute of Manpower Studies.

Auty R.M. (1990) : 'The Impact of Heavy Industry Growth Poles on South Korean Spatial Structure', *Geoforum*, 21.1, pp.23-33.

Bagguley P. (1989) : *The Post-Fordism Enigma: Theories of Labour Flexibility*, Working Paper 29, Lancaster Regionalism Group, Feb.

Balchin P.N. (1990) : *Regional Policy in Britain* (Paul Chapman, London).

Balchin P.N. and Bull G.H. (1987) : *Regional and Urban Economics* (Harper & Row, London).

Bale J. (1976) : *The Location of Manufacturing Industry* (Oliver and Boyd, Edinburgh).

Bank of Japan (1991) : *Comparative Economic and Financial Statistics*.

Bank of Korea (1991) : *Annual Statistics of Overseas Investment* (Korean Version).

Bartlett C.A., Doz Y. and Hedland G. (eds.) (1990) : *Managing the Global Firm* (Routledge, London).

Bassett K., Boddy M., Harloe M. and Lovering J. (1989) : 'Living in the Fast Lane: Economic and Social Change in Swindon', see Cooke P. (ed.).

Beal T. (1982) : *The Implications for the South of Recent Developments in Japan's Direct Foreign Investment*, Department of Political Studies, Sheffield City Polytechnic.

Beckmann M. (1968) : *Location Theory* (Random House, New York).

Beenstock M. (1983) : *The World Economy in Transition* (George Allen and Unwins, London).

Begg H. and McDowall S. (1987) : 'The Effect of Regional Investment Incentives on Company Decisions', *Regional Studies*, 21.5, pp.459-470.

Begg I.G. (1990) : 'The Single European Market and the UK Regions', see Cameron G. et al. (eds.).

Begg I.G. (1991) : 'High Technology and the Urban Areas of Great Britain: Developments in the 1980s', *Urban Studies*, 28.6, pp.961-981.

Begg I.G. and Cameron C. (1988) : 'High Technology and the Urban Areas of Great Britain', *Urban Studies*, 25.5, pp.361-379.

Bennett R.J. and Krebs G. (1989) : 'Regional Policy Incentives and the Relative Costs of Capital in Assisted Areas in Britain and Germany', *Regional Studies*, 23.3, pp.201-218.

Best M.H. (1990) : *The New Competition* (Polity Press, Cambridge).

Beyers W.B. (1981) : 'Alternative Spatial Linkage Structures in Multinational Economic Systems', see Rees J, Hewings G. and Stafford H. (eds.).

Billet B.L. (1990) : *Investment Behaviour of Multinational Corporations in Developing Areas* (Transaction Publishers, New Brunswick N.J.).

Birkin M. and Wilson A. (1986) : 'Industrial Location Models 1: A Review and An Integrating Framework', *Environment and Planning A*, 18.2, pp.175-205.

Blackaby F. (ed.) (1979) : *De-Industrialisation* (Heineman, London).

Blackbourn A. (1978) : 'Multinational Enterprises and Regional Development: A Comment', *Regional Studies*, 12, pp.125-127.

Blackbourn A. (1982) : 'The Impact of Multinational Corporations on the spatial organisation of Developed Nations', see Taylor M. and Thrift N. (eds.).

Boddy M.J. (1987) : 'Structural Approaches to Industrial Location', see Lever W.F. (ed.).

Bolwijin P. and Brinkman S. (1987) : 'Japanese Manufacturing: Strategy and Practice', *Long Range Planning*, 20.1, pp.25-34.

Bradbury J. (1985) : 'Regional and Industrial Restructuring Process in the New International Division of Labour', *Progress in Human Geography*, 9.1, pp.38-63.

Branson W.H. (1970) : 'Monetary Policy and the New View of International Capital Movements', *Brookings Papers on Economic Activity*, 2.

Braverman H. (1974) : *Labour and Monopoly Capital* (Monthly Review Press, New York).

British Shopping Developments : Hillier Parker, Annual Publication (1987-1989).

Brown M.B. (1984) : *Models in Political Economy* (Penguin, Harmondsworth).

Brech M. and Sharp M. (1984) : *Inward Investment: Policy Options for the UK* (Routledge and Kegan Paul, London).

Briggs P. (1988) : 'The Japanese at Work: Illusions of the Ideal', *Industrial Relations Journal*, 19.1, pp.24-30.

British Business : Department of Trade and Industry, Weekly Publication (1971-1987).

British Outdoor Amenities Directory : John S Turner & Associates Ltd, Annual Publication.

British Rail Passenger Timetable : British Rail, Annual Publication.

Buck T. and Atkins M. (1976) : 'The Impact of British Regional Policies on Employment Growth', *Oxford Economic Papers*, 28, pp.215-222.

Buck T. and Atkins M. (1983) : 'Regional Policies in Retrospect: An Application of Analysis of Variance', *Regional Studies*, 17.3, pp.181-189.

Buckley P.J. and Casson M.C. (1976) : *The Future of the Multinational Enterprise* (Macmillan, London).

Bukharin M. (1975) : 'World Economy and National Economy', see Radice H. (ed.).

Business Briefing : British Chamber of Commerce, Weekly Publication.

Business Monitor : HMSO, Annual Publication, see *Census of Production*.

Cambridge Econometrics Ltd. (1992) : *Regional Economic Prospects*, Jan. 1992, Cambridge.

Cameron G., Moore B., Nicholls D., Rhodes J. and Tyler P. (eds.) (1990) : *Cambridge Regional Economic Review: The Economic Outlook for the Regions and Counties of the United Kingdom in the 1990* (University of Cambridge/ P A Cambridge Economic Consultants Ltd., Cambridge).

Cantwell J. (1991) : 'A Survey of Theories of International Production', see Pitelis C.N. and Sugden R. (eds.).

Carr M. (1983) : 'A Contribution to the Review and Critique of Behavioral Industrial Location Theory', *Progress in Human Geography*, 7.3, pp.386-401.

Casson M. (1981) : *Transaction Cost and Theory of the Multinational Enterprise*, Dalhousie Discussion Papers in International Business, No.8.

Casson M. (1986) : *Multinationals and World Trade* (Allen and Unwin, London).

Casson M. (1990) : *Multinational Corporations* (Edward Elgar, Aldershot).

Castells M. (1989) : *The Informational City - Information Technology, Economic Restructuring and Urban - Regional Process* (Basil Blackwell, Oxford).

Caves R. (1971) : 'International Corporations: The Industrial Economics of Foreign Investment', *Economica*, 38, pp.1-27.

Caves R. (1982a) : 'Multinational Enterprises and Technology Transfer', see Rugman A.M. (ed.).

Caves R. (1982b) : *Multinational Enterprise and Economic Analysis* (Cambridge University Press, Cambridge).

Census of Economic Activity : HMSO, Annual Publication.

Census of Production : Business Monitors, Production Series (PA 1001-1003), HMSO, Annual Publication.

Champion A.G., Green A.E., Owen D.W., Ellin D.J. and Coombes M.G. (1987) : *Changing Places* (Edward Arnold, London).

346

Champion T. and Green A. (1985) : *In Search of Britain's Booming Towns: An Index of Local Economic Performance for Britain*, Discussion Paper 72, Centre for Urban and Regional Development Studies, University of Newcastle upon Tyne.

Champion T. and Green A. (1988) : *Local Prosperity and the North-South Divide: Winners and Losers in 1980s Britain*, Centre for Urban and Regional Development Studies, University of Newcastle upon Tyne.

Chang K. (1989) : 'Japan's Direct Manufacturing Investment in the United States', *The Professional Geographer*, 41.3, pp.314-328.

Chapman K. and Walker D. (1987) : *Industrial Location* (Basil Blackwell, Oxford).

Chapman K. and Walker D. (1990) : *Industrial Location* (Second Edition) (Basil Blackwell, Oxford).

Cheshire P., Camagni R.P., Gaudemar J.P., and Roura J.R.C. (1991) : '1957 to 1992: Moving Toward a Europe of Regions and Regional Policy', see Rodwin L. and Sazanami H. (eds.).

Chisholm M. (1985) : 'De-Industrialization and British Regional Policy', *Regional Studies*, 19.4, pp.301-313.

Chisholm M. (1990) : *Regions in Recession and Resurgence* (Unwin Hyman, London).

Chisholm M. and Öppen J. (1973) : *The Changing Pattern of Employment* (Croom Helm, London).

Cho K.R. (1990) : 'The Role of Product-Specific Factors in Intra-Firm Trade of US Manufacturing Multinational Corporations', *Journal of International Business Studies*, 21.2, pp.319-330.

Cho J.S. (1991) : *Regional Disparity and Uneven Spatial Development in Korea: The Period of the Comprehensive National Physical Development Plan*, Working Paper 79, Centre for Urban and Regional Research, University of Sussex.

Chung J.W. (1991) : 'International Market Shares and Global Economic Power', *Japan and the World Economy*, 3, pp.1-16.

Chung J.W. and Kim D.Y. (1986) : 'An Interactive Causal Analysis of Price Dynamics: A Case Study of Korea', *Economic Development and Cultural Change*, 34.4, pp.837-853.

Chung B.S. and Lee C.H. (1980) : 'The Choice of Production Techniques by Foreign and Local Firms in Korea', *Economic Development and Cultural Change*, 29.1, pp.135-140.

Civil Aviation Monthly Statistics : Civil Aviation Authority, Monthly Publication.

Clark W.A.V. and Hosking P.L. (1986) : *Statistical Methods for Geographers* (John Wiley and Sons, New York).

Clegg J. (1987) : *Multinational Enterprises and World Competition* (Macmillan, Basingstoke).

Cole J. and King C. (1968) : *Quantitative Geography* (John Wiley and Sons, Chichester).

Collins L. and Walker D.F. (eds.) (1975) : *Locational Dynamics of Manufacturing Activity* (John Wiley and Sons, Chichester).

Collis C., Noon D., Gray K. and Roberts P. (1989) : *Overseas Investment to the West Midlands Region (Second Report)*, Report of the West Midlands Industrial Development Association.

Commercial and Industrial Floorspace Statistics, England and Wales : HMSO, Annual Publication.

Commission for the New Towns (1986) : *Industrial Development Guide 1986* (Longman, London).

Compendium of Building Society Statistics (1984) : Building Society Association, Irregular Publication, 5th edition.

Complete Atlas of the British Isles (1965) : Reader's Digest.

Cooke P. (1986) : 'The Changing Urban and Regional System in the UK', *Regional Studies*, 20.3, pp.243-251.

Cooke P. (1989) : 'Critical Cosmopolitanism: Urban and Regional Studies into the 1990s', *Geoforum*, 20.2, pp.241-252.

Cooke P. (ed.) (1989) : *Localities: The Changing Face of Urban Britain* (Unwin Hyman, London).

Cooper M.J.M. (1975) : *The Industrial Location Decision-Making Process*, Occasional Paper 34, Centre for Urban and Regional Studies, University of Birmingham.

Cosh A., Hughes A., Singh A., Carty J. and Plender J. (1990) : *Takeovers and Short-termism in the UK*, Industrial Policy Paper No.3, Institute for Public Policy Research, London.

Crawford P., Fothergill S. and Monk S. (1985) : *The Effect of Business Rates on the Location of Employment*, Department of Land Economy Final Report, University of Cambridge.

Criminal Statistics, England and Wales : HMSO, Annual Publication.

Criminal Statistics, Scotland : HMSO, Annual Publication.

Curran J., Stanworth J. and Watkin D. (eds.) (1986) : *The Survival of the Small Firm* (Gower, Aldershot).

Damesick P.J. (1983) : 'Towards a More Genuine Regional Policy', *Town and Country Planning*, 52.12, pp.350-351.

Damesick P.J. (1984) : 'The Future of Regional Planning and Policy in the UK: The Findings of the RSA Inquiry', *Regional Studies*, 18, pp.165-173.

Damesick P.J. (1985) : 'Recent Debates and Developments in British Regional Policy', *Planning Outlook*, 28.1, pp.3-7.

Damesick P.J. (1987a) : 'The Changing Economic Context for Regional Development in the United Kingdom', see Damesick P.J. and Wood P.A. (eds.).

Damesick P.J. (1987b) : 'The Evolution of Spatial Economic Policy', see Damesick P.J. and Wood P.A. (eds.).

Damesick P.J. and Wood P.A. (eds.) (1987) : *Regional Problems, Problem Regions, and Public Policy in the United Kingdom* (Clarendon Press, Oxford).

Darwent D.F. (1969) : 'Growth Poles and Growth Centres in Regional Planning - A Review', *Environment and Planning*, 1, pp.5-32.

Department of Trade and Industry (1983) : *Regional Industrial Policy: Some Economic Issues* (DTI, London).

Department of Employment (1984) : 'Revised Travel-to-Work Areas', *Employment Gazette*, 92.9, Occasional Supplement.

Devine P.J., Jones R.M., Lee N. and Tyson W.J. (1976) : *An Introduction to Industrial Economics* (Allen and Unwin, London).

Dewar D., Todes A. and Watson V. (1986) : *Regional Development and Settlement Policy: Premises and Prospects* (Allen and Unwin, London).

Dicken P. (1971) : 'Some Aspects of Decision-Making Behaviour of Business Organizations', *Economic Geography*, 47, pp.426-437.

Dicken P. (1976) : 'The Multiplant Business Enterprise and Geographical Spaces: Some Issues in the Study of External Control and Regional Development', *Regional Studies*, 10, pp.401-412.

Dicken P. (1986) : *Transnational Corporations and the United Kingdom Automobile Industry*, Working Paper 18, North West Industry Research Unit, University of Manchester.

Dicken P. (1988) : 'The Changing Geography of Japanese Foreign Direct Investment in Manufacturing Industry: A Global Perspective', *Environment and Planning A*, 20, pp.633-653.

Dicken P. (1990) : 'Japanese Industrial Investment in the UK', *Geography*, 75, pp.351-354.

Dicken P. (1992) : *Global Shift: Industrial Change in a Turbulent World* (Paul Chapman, London).

Dicken P. and Lloyd P.E. : *Location in Space* (Harper Collins, New York, 1990).

Dicken P. and Tickell A. (1992) : 'Competitors or Collaborators? The Structure of Inward Investment Promotion in Northern England', *Regional Studies*, 26.1, pp.99-106.

Diewert W.E. (1985) : 'Transfer Pricing and Economic Efficiency', see Rugman A.M. and Eden L. (eds.).

Digest of Countryside Recreation Statistics (1979) : The Countryside Commission, Annual Publication.

Digest of Local Authority Boundary : Ministry of Home Affairs, Korea, Annual Publication (1987) (Korean Version).

Digest of Welsh Statistics : HMSO, Annual Publication.

349

Dohse K. (1987) : 'Innovations in Collective Bargaining through the Multinationalisation of Japanese Automobile Companies: The Case of NUMMI (USA) and Nissan (UK)', see Trevor M. (ed.).

Dunford M. (1977) : 'The Restructuring of Industrial Space', *International Journal of Urban and Regional Research*, 1.3, pp.510-520.

Dunford M. (1979) : *Capital Accumulation and Regional Development in France*, Working Paper 12, Urban and Regional Studies Division, University of Sussex.

Dunford M. (1990) : 'Theories of Regulation', *Environment and Planning D*, 8.3, pp.297-321.

Dunning J.H. (1970) : *Studies in International Investments* (Allen and Unwin, London).

Dunning J.H. (1972) : *International Investment* (Penguin, London).

Dunning J.H. (1973) : 'The Determinants of International Production', *Oxford Economic Papers*, 25, pp.289-336.

Dunning J.H. (1977) : 'Trade Location of Economic Activity and the MNE: A Search for an Eclectic Approach', in Ohlin B, Hesselborn P.O. and Wijkman P.M. (eds.) *The International Allocation of Economic Activity* (Macmillan, London).

Dunning J.H. (1979a) : 'Explaining Changing Patterns of International Production: In Defense of the Eclectic Theory', *Oxford Bulletin of Economics and Statistics*, 41, pp.269-295.

Dunning J.H. (1979b) : 'The UK's International Direct Investment Position in the Mid-1970s', *Lloyds Bank Economic Review*, 132, pp.1-21.

Dunning J.H. (1984) : 'Japanese Investment in UK Industry: Trojan Horse or New Catalyst for Growth', *Multinational Business*, 4, pp.1-6.

Dunning J.H. (ed.) (1985) : *Multinational Enterprises, Economic Structure and International Competitiveness* (John Wiley and Sons, Chichester).

Dunning J.H. (1986) : *Japanese Participation in British Industry* (Croom Helm, London).

Dunning J.H. (1988a) : *Multinationals, Technology and Competitiveness* (Unwin Hyman, London).

Dunning J.H. (1988b) : 'International Business, the Recession and Economic Restructuring', see Hood N. and Vahlne J. (eds.).

Dunning J.H. (1990a) : 'US and Japanese Manufacturing Affiliates in the UK: Comparison and Contrasts', see Casson M. (ed.).

Dunning J.H. (1990b) : 'Japanese Manufacturing Investment and the Restructuring of the United Kingdom Economy', see Webster A. and Dunning J.H. (eds.).

Dunning J.H. (1991) : 'The Eclectic Paradigm of International Production: A Personal Perspective', see Pitelis and Sugden (eds.).

Dunning J.H. and Norman C. (1982) : *The Theory of the Multinational Enterprise: An Application to Multinational Office Location*, Discussion Paper 63, University of Reading.

Dunning J.H. and McQueen M. (1982) : 'The Eclectic Theory of International Enterprise and the International Hotel Industry', see Rugman A.M. (ed.).

Eatwell J. (1982) : *Whatever Happened to Britain* (Duckworth, London).

Economic Planning Agency (Japan) (1984) : *Economic Survey of Japanese Government 1983/1984*, The Government of Japan.

Economic Planning Agency (Japan) : *Japanese Economic Statistics*, Annual Report.

Economic Planning Board (Korea) : *White Paper on the National Economy*, Annual Publication (1985, 1986, 1990) (Korean Version).

Economic Planning Board (Korea) : *White Paper on Foreign Direct Investment*, Annual Publication (Korean Version).

Economist : Britain - Regional Policy Back in Fashion, 20 Apr. 1991, pp.56-57.

Eden L. (1990) : 'New Directions in International Business Research', *Research in Global Business Management*, 1, pp.163-175.

Edgington D.W. (1987) : 'Influence on the Location and Behaviour of Transnational Corporations: Some Examples Taken from Japanese Investment in Australia', *Geoforum*, 18.4, pp.343-359.

Education Statistics : CIPFA, Annual Publication.

Electronics Industries Association of Japan (1987) : *Investing in Britain: Japan's Electronics Industry*, Brochure.

Employment Gazette, Department of Employment: HMSO, Monthly Publication (1978-1991).

ESRC Information Bulletin (1989) : 'Japanese Manufacturing Investment in Europe', 18 Jan. 1989.

ESRC Newsletter (1992) : 'Japanese Managers No More Satisfied than British Managers', Feb. 1992.

Ettlinger N. (1990) : 'Worker Displacement and Corporate Restructuring: A Policy Conscious Appraisal', *Economic Geography*, 66.1, pp.67-82.

European Company Services Ltd. (1983) : *Japanese Direct Investment in the UK: A Survey*, Consultants in International Management and Marketing (European Company Services Ltd., London).

Fieldhouse D.K. (1986) : 'The Multinational: A Critique of a Concept', see Teichova A. et al. (eds.).

Financial Times : South Korea Survey, 14 May 1987.

Financial Times : Financial Times Survey: Yorkshire and Humberside, 27 Jul. 1987.

Financial Times : Foreign Investment Floods into South Korea, 8 Oct. 1987.

Financial Times : Japanese Multinationals: The Prizes and Pitfalls of Going Offshore, 24 Nov. 1987.

Financial Times : Japanese Industry: Survey, 7 Dec. 1987.

Financial Times : Industrial Aid Plans Focus on Small and Medium-Sized Groups, 13 Jan. 1988.

Financial Times : Foreign Investment in S. Korea Tripled, 23 Jan. 1988.

Financial Times : Financial Times Survey: Japanese Industry, 7 Dec. 1988.

Financial Times : Sophistication Enters the Search for Ideal Locations, 4 Jan. 1989.

Financial Times : Newcomers Who Are Welcomed but Feared, 19 Apr. 1989.

Financial Times : Financial Times Survey: South Korea, 27 Nov. 1989.

Financial Times : Financial Times Survey: South Korea, 16 May 1990.

Financial Times : East, West- Home's the Most Profitable, 2 Jan. 1991.

Financial Times : Emphasis on Design, 4 Jan. 1991.

Financial Times : Toyota Plans High European Content for Cars: Honda Chooses Suppliers for Swindon Plant, 8 Jan. 1991.

Financial Times : Japanese Go Private, 3 Mar. 1991.

Financial Times : Financial Survey: South Korea, 5 Jun. 1991.

Financial Times : Assault on Japan, 10 Jun. 1991.

Financial Times : Financial Times Survey: Japan, 15 Jul. 1991.

Financial Times : A Multinational Changing Gears, 12 Aug. 1991.

Financial Times : Financial Times Survey: Japan in the United Kingdom, 20 Sep. 1991.

Financial Times : Financial Times Survey: Tyne and Wear, 18 Feb. 1992.

Financial Times : Japan is the Catalyst for Conversion, 9 Mar. 1992.

Financial Times : After the Cold War, Economics is King, 16 Mar. 1992.

Financial Times : Financial Times Survey: Relocation in the UK, 30 Apr. 1992.

Financial Times : Financial Times Survey: Building for Asia's Future, 1 May 1992.

Financial Times : Financial Times Survey: Korea, 27 May 1992.

Financial Times : Japanese Investment in North Set to Fall, 4 Jun. 1992.

Financial Times : Boundaries of Assisted Areas to be Reviewed, 11 Jun. 1992.

Financial Times : Multinationals Switch Focus of Investment, 16 Jun. 1992.

Financial Times : Japanese Concerns Step Up Welsh R&D, 19 Jun. 1992.

Financial Times : Transnationals Pace the Growth Track, 15 Jul. 1992.

Financial Times : Japanese Managers Lament at the Loss of Old Work Ethic, 13 May 1992.

Fingleton B. and Tyler P. (1990) : 'A Cost-Based Approach to the Modelling of Industrial Movement in Great Britain', *Regional Studies*, 24.5, pp.433-445.

Firn J.R. (1975) : 'External Control and Regional Development: The Case of Scotland', *Environment and Planning A*, 7, pp.393-414.

Flaherty M.T. and Raubitschek R.S. (1990) : 'Local Presence and International Manufacturing Configurations in Technology-Intensive Industries', *Japan and the World Economy*, 2, pp.301-326.

Fletcher D.R. (1989) : *The Crisis of the Fordist Regime of Accumulation and the Rise of a Neo-Proletariat*, M. Soc. Sc Dissertation, Centre for Urban and Regional Studies, University of Birmingham.

Floyd J.E. (1969) : 'International Capital Movements and Monetary Equilibrium', *American Economic Review*, 59.

Foley P.D., Watts H.D. and Wilson B. (1992) : 'Introducing New Process Technology: Implications for Local Employment Policies', *Geoforum*, 23.1, pp.61-72.

Foot D. (1981) : *Operational Urban Models: An Introduction* (Methuen, London).

Fothergill S. and Gudgin G. (1982) : *Unequal Growth* (Heineman, London).

Fothergill S., Gudgin G., Kitson M. and Monk S. (1988) : 'The Deindustrialization of the City', see Massey and Allen (eds.).

Fothergill S., Kitson M. and Monk S. (1985) : 'The Supply of Land for Industrial Development', in Barret S. and Healey P. (eds.) *Land Policy: Problems and Alternatives* (Gower, Aldershot).

Fothergill S., Monk S. and Perry M. (1987) : *Property and Industrial Development* (Hutchinson, London).

Franko L.G. (1983) : *The Threat of Japanese Multinationals* (John Wiley and Sons, Chichester).

Friedman D. (1988) : *The Misunderstood Miracle* (Cornell University Press, Ithaca).

Frost M.E. (1976) : 'Government Action and Manufacturing Employment in the Nothern Region 1952-1971', in Masser I. (ed.) *Theory and Practice in Regional Science* (Pion, London).

Fukuda K.J. (1982) : 'Decision-Making in Organisations: Comparisons of the Japanese and Chinese Models', *Hong Kong Journal of Public Administration*, 4.2, pp.176-183.

Gaffikin F. and Nickson A. (1984) : *Job Crisis and the Multi-nationals: The Case of the West Midlands* (Trade Union Resources Centre, Birmingham).

Galbraith C.S., DeNoble A.F. and Estavillo P. (1990) : 'Location Criteria and Perceptions of Regional Business Climate: A Study of Mexican and US Small Electronics Firms', *Journal of Small Business Management*, 28.4, pp.34-47.

Gamble A. (1989) : *Internationalisation and the National Economy: The British Case*, Paper presented to the Conference on the Internationalisation of Japan in Comparative Perspective, University of Sheffield.

Ghertman M. and Allen M. (1984) : *An Introduction to the Multinationals* (Macmillan, London).

353

Giddy I. and Young S. (1982) : 'Conventional Theory and Unconventional MNEs: Do New Forms of MNE Require New Theories ?', see Rugman A.M. (ed.).

Glasmeier A.K. and McClusky R.E. (1987) : 'US Auto Parts Production: An Analysis of the Organization and Location of Changing Industry', *Economic Geography*, 63.2, pp.142-159.

Glasmeier A.K. and Sugiura N. (1991) : 'Japan's Manufacturing System: Small Business, Subcontracting and Regional Complex Formation', *International Regional Science Review*, 14.3, pp.395-414.

Glasson J. (1992) : 'The Fall and Rise of Regional Planning in the Economically Advanced Nations', *Urban Studies*, 29 3/4, pp.505-531.

Goddard J.B. and Champion A.G. (eds.) (1983) : *The Urban and Regional Transformation of Britain* (Methuen, London).

Goddard J.B. and Thwaites A. (1987) : 'Technological Change', see Lever W.F. (ed.).

Goldberg M.A., Helsley R.W. and Levi M.D. (1989) : 'The Location of International Financial Activity: An Interregional Analysis', *Regional Studies*, 23.1, pp.1-7.

Gordon I.R. (1990) : 'Regional Policy and National Politics in Britain', *Environment and Planning C*, 8, pp.427-438.

Green A., Owen D. and Hasluck C. (1991) : *The Development of Local Labour Market Typologies: Classifications of Trave-to-Work Areas*, Research Paper 84, Department of Employment.

Green W. and Clough D. (1982) : *Regional Problems and Policies* (Reinhart and Winston, Halt).

Grosse R. (1982) : 'Regional Offices in Multinational Firms', see Rugman A.M. (ed.).

Gudgin G. (1978) : *Industrial Location Processes and Regional Employment Growth* (Saxon House, Farnborough).

Haigh R.W. (1990) : 'Selecting a US Plant Location: The Management Decision Process in Foreign Companies', *Columbia Journal of World Business*, 25.3, pp.22-31.

Haigh R.W., Adams R.A., Driftmier C.A. and Welch T.K. (1989) : *Investment Strategies and the Plant Location Decision - Foreign Companies in the United States* (Praeger, New York, 1989).

Hall P. (1982) : *Urban and Regional Planning* (Allen and Unwin, London).

Hall P. (1988) : 'The Geography of the Fifth Kondratieff', see Massey D. and Allen J. (eds.).

Hall P. (1991) : 'Structural Transformation in the Regions of the United Kingdom', see Rodwin L. and Sazanami H. (eds.).

Hamilton C. (1986) : *Capitalist Industrialization in Korea* (Westview Press, Boulder).

354

Hamilton F.E.I.(ed) (1974) : *Spatial Perspectives on Industrial Organization and Decision-Making* (John Wiley and Sons, Chichester).

Hamilton F.E.I.(ed.) (1978) : *Industrial Change* (Longman, London).

Hamilton F.E.I. (1985) : *Recent Dynamics of Multinational Enterprises: Regional and Local Implications*, Working Paper 16, University of Hong Kong.

Hamilton F.E.I.(ed.) (1987) : *Industrial Change in Advanced Economies* (Croom Helm, London).

Hamilton F.E.I. and Linge G. (eds.) (1979) : *Spatial Analysis, Industry and the Industrial Environment, Vol.1* (John Wiley and Sons, Chichester).

Hamilton F.E.I. and Linge G. (eds.) (1983) : *Spatial Analysis, Industry and the Industrial Environment, Vol.3* (John Wiley and Sons, Chichester).

Han M.H. (1988) : *Locational behaviour of Japanese multinational companies in the changing context of regional policy*, M. Phil. dissertation, Centre for Urban and Regional Studies, The University of Birmingham.

Hansen N. (1988) : 'Regional Consequences of Structural Changes in the National and International Division of Labour', *International Regional Science Review*, 11.2, pp.121-136.

Hansen N., Higgins B. and Savoie D.J. (1990) : *Regional Policy in a Changing World* (Plenum Press, New York).

Harris L. (1988) : 'The UK Economy at a Cross-Road', see Allen J. and Massey D. (eds.).

Harris R.I.D. (1987) : 'The Role of Manufacturing in Regional Growth', *Regional Studies*, 21.4, pp.301-312.

Hayter R. and Watts H.D. (1983) : 'The Geography of Enterprise: A Reappraisal', *Progress in Human Geography*, 7.2, pp.157-181.

Haywood S.W. (1979) : *The Determinants of Industrial and Office Location: Survey of Estate Agents and Property Development Companies*, Research Note 1, Joint Unit for Research on the Urban Environment, University of Aston.

Hedland G. and Rolander D. (1990) : 'Action in Heterarchies - New approaches to Managing the MNC', see Bartlett C.A., Doz Y. and Hedland G. (eds.).

Healey M. (1982) : 'Plant Closures in Multiplant Enterprises - The Case of a Declining Industrial Sector', *Regional Studies*, 16.1, pp.37-51.

Healey M. (1983) : 'Components of Locational Change in Multiplant Enterprises', *Urban Studies*, 20.3, pp.327-342.

Healey M. and Ilbery B. (1990) : *Location and Change* (Oxford University Press, Oxford).

Heininger H. (1986) : 'Transnational Corporations and the Struggle for the Establishment of a New International Economic Order', see Teichova A. et al. (eds.).

355

Heitger B. and Stehn J. (1990) : 'Japanese Direct Investments in the EC - Response to the Internal Market 1993 ?', *Journal of Common Market Studies*, XXIX.1, pp.1-15.

Henderson J. (1989) : *The Globalisation of High Technology Production* (Routledge, London).

Henderson R.A. (1980) : 'The Location of Immigrant Industry within a UK Assisted Area: The Scottish Experience', *Progress in Planning, 14, Part 2* (Pergamon, Oxford).

Hennart J.F. (1989) : 'Can the New Forms of Investment substitute for the Old Forms? A Transaction Cost Perspective', *Journal of International Business Studies*, 20.2, pp.211-234.

Hennart J.F. (1991) : 'The Transaction Cost Theory of the Multinational Enterprise', see Pitelis and Sugden (eds.).

Henry A., Carruth A., Thomas A. and Vickerman R. (1989) : 'Location Choice and Labour Market Perceptions: A Discrete Choice Study', *Regional Studies*, 23, pp.431-445.

Higashi C. and Lauter G.P. (1990) : *The Internationalization of the Japanese Economy* (Kluwer Academic Publishers, Boston).

Highway and Transportation Statistics : The Chartered Institute of Public Finance and Accountancy (CIPFA), Annual Publication.

Hill S. and Munday M. (1991) : 'Foreign Direct Investment in Wales', *Local Economy*, 6.1, pp.21-34.

Hipple F.S. (1990) : 'Multinational Companies and International Trade: The Impact of Intrafirm Shipments on US Foreign Trade 1977-1982', *Journal of International Business Studies*, 21.3, pp.495-504.

Hirst P. and Zeitlin J. (eds.) (1989) : *Reversing Industrial Decline?* (Berg, Oxford).

Hirst P. and Zeitlin J. (1991) : 'Flexible Specialization versus Post-Fordism: Theory, Evidence and Policy Implications', *Economy and Society*, 20.1, pp.1-56.

Hitchens D.M.W.N, Birnie J.E. and Wagner K. (1992) : 'Competitiveness and Regional Development: The Case of Northern Ireland', *Regional Studies*, 26.1, pp.106-114.

Hoare A.G. (1983) : *The Location of Industry in Britain* (Cambridge University Press, Cambridge).

Holden D.R., Narin A.G.M. and Swales J. (1989) : 'Shift-Share Analysis of Regional Growth and Policy: A Critique', *Oxford Bulletin of Economics and Statistics*, 51.1, pp.15-34.

Holland S. (1976) : *Capital versus the Regions* (Macmillan, London).

Holloway S.R. and Wheeler J.O. (1991) : 'Corporate Headquarters Relocation and Changes in Metropolitan Corporate Dominance, 1980-1987', *Economic Geography*, 67.1, pp.54-74.

Hood N. and Vahlne J. (eds.) (1988) : *Strategies in Global Competition* (Croom Helm, London).

Hood N. and Young S. (1979) : *The Economics of the Multinational Enterprise* (Pergamon, Oxford).

Hood N. and Young S. (1983) : *Multinational Investment Strategies in the British Isles*, Department of Trade and Industry (HMSO, London).

Horaguchi H. and Toyne B. (1990) : 'Setting the Record Straight: Hymer, Internalisation Theory and Transaction Cost Economics', *Journal of International Business Studies*, 21.3, pp.487-494.

Horst T. (1971) : 'The Theory of the Multinational Firm: Optimal Behaviour under Different Tariff and Tax Rates', *Journal of Political Economy*, 79.5, pp.1059-1072.

House of Commons, Expenditure Committee (Trade and Industry Sub-Committee) (1973) : *Regional Development Incentives*, Session 1973-1974 Minutes of Evidence, Appendices and Index, 85-I, pp.525-683.

House Prices in 1990 (1991) : Nationwide Anglia Building Society, Quarterly Publication.

Housing and Construction Statistics : HMSO, Annual Publication.

Howard R.S. (1968) : *The Movement of Manufacturing Industry in the United Kingdom 1945-1965*, (HMSO, Board of Trade, London).

Howells J.R. and Charles D.R. (1989) : 'Research and Technological Development and Regional Policy: A European Perspective', see Gibbs D. (ed.).

Hudson R. (1988) : 'Labour Market Changes and the New Forms of Work in Old Industrial Regions', see Massey and Allen (eds.).

Hunt E.K. (1981) : *Property and Prophets: The Evolution of Economic Institutions and Ideology* (Harper & Row, London).

Hutton J. (1988) : *The World of the International Manager* (Phillip Allen, Oxford).

Hwang M.C. (1984) : *Regional Development* (Kyongyoungmunhwawon, Seoul) (Korean Version).

Hymer S. (1972) : 'The Multinational Corporation and the Law of Uneven Development', in Bhagwati J.N. (ed) *Economics and World Order* (Free Press, New York).

Hymer S. (1976) : *The International Operations of National Firms: A Study of Foreign Direct Investment* (MIT Press, Cambridge).

Imrie R. (1991) : 'Industrial Change and Local Economic Fragmentation: The case of Stoke-on Trent', *Geoforum*, 22.4, pp.433-453.

Industrial Bank of Japan (1988) : 'Foreign and Domestic Undergoing Structural Economic Adjustment', *Japanese Finance and Industry (Quarterly Survey)*, 74.II, pp.1-38.

357

Industrial Bank of Japan (1989) : 'Factors Behind Japanese Direct Investment Abroad', *Japanese Finance and Industry (Quarterly Survey)*, 80.IV, pp.13-24.

Industrial Development Guide : Cambridge Information and Research Services, Annual Publication (1983-1986).

Industrial Relations Services (1990) : *Industrial Relations Review and Report*, 470.

Institute of Fiscal and Monetary Policy (1986) : *Financial Statistics of Japan: FY 1986*, Ministry of Finance (Japan).

Invest in Britain Bureau : *Annual Report* (1980-1991).

Invest in Britain Bureau (1992) : *Inward Investment in the UK: A Market Report*, Irregular Publication.

Itaki M. (1991) : 'A Critical Assessment of the Eclectic Theory of the Multinational Enterprise', *Journal of International Business Studies*, 22.3, pp.445-460.

Itoh M. (1990) : *The World Economic Crisis and Japanese Capitalism* (Macmillan, Basingstoke).

James B.G. (1989) : *Trojan Horse: The Ultimate Japanese Challenge to Western Industry* (Mercury Books, London).

Japan Economic Almanac : The Nikkei Weekly, Annual Publication (1991, 1992).

Japanese External Trade Organisation (1987) : *Current Management Situation of Japanese Manufacturing Enterprises in Europe: The Third Current Situation Survey Report* (JETRO, London).

JEI Report : Japanese Economic Institute, Weekly Publication (15 Jun. 1990, 21 Jun. 1991, 26 Jul. 1991 and 19 Jun. 1992).

Jenkins R. (1987) : *Transnational Corporations and Uneven Development* (Methuen, London).

Jenkins R. (1991) : 'The Political Economy of Industrialization', *Development and Change*, 22.2, pp.197-231.

Joereskog K.G., Klovan J.E. and Reyment R.A. (1976) : *Geological Factor Analysis* (Elsevier Scientific Publishing Co., Amsterdam).

Johanson J. and Mattsson L.G. (1988) : 'Internationalisation in Industrial Systems - A Network Approach', see Hood N. and Vahlne J.E. (eds.).

Johns G. (1987) : 'Regional Policy and Industrial Strategy in the Welsh Economy', *Regional Studies*, 21.6, pp.555-567.

Jones J. (1986) : 'An Examination of the Thinking behind Government Regional Policy in the UK since 1945', *Regional Studies*, 20.3, pp.261-266.

Jones G. (1986) : *British Multinationals* (Gower, Aldershot).

Jones P.N. and North J. (1991) : 'Japanese Motor Industry Transplants: The West European Dimension', *Economic Geography*, 67.2, pp.105-123.

Juergens U. (1989) : 'The Transfer of Japanese Management Concepts in the International Industry', see Wood S. (ed.).

Julius D. (1990) : *Global Companies and Public Policy: The Growing Challenge of FDI Investment* (Royal Institute of International Affairs, London).

Jung K.H. (1990) : 'Internationalization of Korean Firms in the Global Context', see Kim D.C. and Healey G.H. (eds.).

Kafkalas G. (1982) : *Location Theory and Forms of Spatial Interaction: The Case of Non-Fuel Minerals*, Working Paper 28, Urban and Regional Studies, University of Sussex.

Kame G. and Totsuka K. (1990) : 'Japanese Manufacturing Investment in the EC: Motives and Locations', see Sumitomo-Life Research Institute.

Kamata S. (1984) : *Japan in the Passing Lane* (Counterpoint, London).

Kay N.M. (1991) : 'Multinational Enterprise as Strategic Choice: Some Transaction Cost Perspectives', see Pitelis C.N. and Sugden R. (eds.).

Keeble D.E. (1969) : 'Local Industrial Linkage and Manufacturing Growth in Outer London', *Town Planning Review*, 40.2, pp.163-188.

Keeble D.E. (1976) : *Industrial Location and Planning in the United Kingdom* (Methuen, London).

Keeble D.E. (1978) : 'Industrial Decline in the Inner City and Conurbation', *Transactions of Institute of British Geographers*, 3, pp.101-114.

Keeble D.E. (1987) : 'Industrial Change in the United Kingdom', see Lever W.F. (ed.).

Keeble D.E. (1989) : ' High Technology Industry and Regional Development: The Case of the Cambridge Phenomenon', *Environment and Planning C*, 7, pp.153-172.

Keeble D.E., Bryson J. and Wood P. (1991) : 'Small Firms, Business Services Growth and Regional Development in the United Kingdom: Some Empirical Findings', *Regional Studies*, 25.5, pp.439-457.

Keeble D.E. and Hauser D.P. (1972) : 'Spatial Analysis of Manufacturing Growth in Outer South-East England 1960-1967', *Regional Studies*, 6, pp.11-36.

Kennedy K.A. and Healey T. (1985) : *Small-Scale Manufacturing Industry in Ireland* (The Economic and Social Research Institute, Dublin).

Kenny M. and Florida R. (1992) : 'The Japanese Transplant: Production Organization and Regional Development', *Journal of the American Planning Association*, 58.1, pp.21-38.

Kim J.O. (1975) : 'Factor Analysis', in Nie N.H. et al. (eds.) *Statistical Package for the Social Sciences* (2nd ed.) (McGrow-Hill, New York).

Kim W.S. and Lyn E.O. (1990) : 'FDI Theories and the Performance of Foreign Multinationals Operating in the US', *Journal of International Business Studies*, 21.2, pp.41-53.

Kim D.C and Healey G.H. (ed.) (1990) : *Korea and the United Kingdom*, East and West Studies Series 12 (Institute of East and West Studies, Yonsei University, Seoul).

Kimura Y. (1989) : 'Firm-Specific Strategic Advantages and Foreign Direct Investment Behaviour of Firms: The Case of Japanese Semiconductor Firms', *Journal of International Business Studies*, 20.2, pp.296-314.

Kindleberger C.P. and Audretch D.B. (eds.) (1983) : *The Multinational Corporation in the 1980s* (The MIT Press, Cambridge).

Kirby A. (1983) : *The Politics of Location: An Introduction* (Methuen, London).

Kirkpatrick C.H., Lee N. and Nixon F.I. (1984) : *Industrial Structure and Policy in Less Developed Countries* (Allen and Unwin, London).

Knox P. and Agnew J. (1989) : *The Geography of the World Economy* (Edward Arnold, London).

Kogut B. (1983) : 'Foreign Direct Investment as a Sequential Process', see Kindleberger C.P. and Audretsch D.B. (eds.).

Kojima K. (1978) : *Direct Foreign Investment: A Japanese Model of Multinational Business Operations* (Croom Helm, London).

Kojima K. (1986) : 'Japanese-Style Direct Foreign Investment', *Japanese Economic Studies*, XIV.3, pp.52-82.

Kono T. (1984/1985) : 'Multinational Management', *Japanese Economic Studies*, XIII.1-2, pp.3-44.

Koo B.Y. (1984) : *Industrial Structure and Foreign Investment: A Case Study of Their Interrelationship for Korea*, Working Paper 8402, Korea Development Institute.

Koo B.Y. and Lee E.O. (1985) : *Korean Business Ventures Abroad: Patterns and Characteristics*, Working Paper 8502, Korea Development Institute.

Korea Development Institute (1988) : *Industrial Policies of Korea and the Republic of China*, Papers and Discussions from the 1988 Joint KDI/Chung-Hua Institution for Economic Research (CHIER) Conference.

Korea Economic Indicators : Economic Planning Board (Korea), Annual Publication (Korean Version).

Korea Housing Corporation (1990) : *Housing Handbook* (Korea Housing Corporation, Seoul) (Korean Version).

Korea Institute for Economics and Technology (1986) : *The Japanese Foreign Direct Investment and Management Strategy* (KIET, Seoul) (Korean Version).

Korea Institute for Economics and Technology (1984) : *The Causes for the Success of Japanese Multinationals* (KIET, Seoul) (Korean Version).

Korea Municipal Yearbook (1986) : Ministry of Home Affairs (Korea), Annual Publication (Korean Version).

Korea Research Institute for Human Settlement (1982) : *Data for the Second National Land Development Plan* (KRIHS, Seoul) (Korean Version).

Korea Statistical Yearbook : Economic Planning Board (Korea), Annual Publication (Korean Version).

Korea Trade Association (1985) : *The Alternatives to Promote the Export to Japan* (KTA, Seoul) (Korean Version).

Korea Trade Association (1987) : *A Report on the Activities of Foreign Owned Companies* (KTA, Seoul) (Korean Version).

Kotabe M. and Murray J.Y. (1990) : 'Linking Product and Process Innovations and Modes of International Sourcing in Global Competition: A Case Study of Foreign Multinational Firms', *Journal of International Business Studies*, 21.3, pp.383-408.

Kotabe M. and Omura G.S. (1989) : 'Sourcing Strategies of European and Japanese Multinationals: A Comparison', *Journal of International Business Studies*, 20.1, pp.113-130.

KPMG Peat Marwick and West Midlands Development Agency (1992) : *The 1992 Survey of Foreign-Owned Companies in the West Midlands*, First Survey Report, Birmingham.

Krumme G. (1969) : 'Towards a Geography of Enterprise', *Economic Geography*, 45, pp.30-40.

Krumme G. (1985) : 'Flexibility Views in Industrial Location and Location Decision Theory', see Rees J. Hewings G. and Stafford H. (eds.).

Kujawa D. (1986) : *Japanese Multinationals in the United States* (Praeger, New York).

Kumazawa M. and Yamada J. (1989) : 'Jobs and Skills under the Life-Long Nenko Employment Practice', see Wood S. (ed.).

Kume G. and Totsuka K. (1990) : 'Japanese Manufacturing Investment in the EC: Motives and Locations', see Sumitomo Life Insurance.

Kunio Y. (1986) : *Japanese Economic Development* (Oxford University Press, Tokyo).

Kwon W.Y. (1988) : 'Population Decentralization from Seoul and Regional Development Policy', see Richardson H.W. and Hwang M.C. (eds.).

Kysiak R.C. (1989) : 'The Impact of Research Parks on Regional Development', *Real Estate Finance Journal*, 5.2, pp.64-69.

Lambooy J.G. (1986) : 'Locational Decisions and Regional Structure', in Paelinck J.H.P. (ed.) *Human Behaviour in Geographical Space* (Gower, Aldershot).

Landaburu E. (1985) : 'Forward', see Dunning J.H. (ed.).

Lash S. and Bagguley P. (1987) : *Labour Flexibility and Disorganized Capitalism*, Working Paper 15, Lancaster Regionalism Group.

Lash S. and Urry J. (1987) : *The End of Organized Capitalism* (Polity Press, Cambridge).

Latham W.R. (1976) : *Locational Behaviour in Manufacturing Industries, Applied Regional Science, Vol.4* (Leiden, Nijhoff).

Law C.W. (1980) : *British Regional Development Since World War I* (Methuen, London).

Lecraw D.J. (1985) : 'Some Evidence on Transfer Pricing by Multinational Corporations', see Rugman A.M. and Eden L. (eds.).

Lee H.Y. (1989) : 'Growth Determinants in the Core-Periphery of Korea', *International Regional Science Review*, 12.2, pp.147-163.

Lee K.S. (1988) : 'An Evaluation of Industrial Location Policies for Urban Deconcentration in Korea', see Richardson H.W. and Hwang M.C. (eds.).

Leisure and Recreation Statistics : CIPFA, Annual Publication.

Lever W.F. (ed.) (1987) : *Industrial Change in the United Kingdom* (Longman, London).

Lever W.F. (1991) : 'Deindustrialization and the Reality of the Post-industrial City', *Urban Studies*, 28.6, pp.983-999.

Lever-Tracy C. (1990) : 'Fordism Transformed? Employee Investment and Workplace Industrial Relations at Ford', *The Journal of Industrial Relations*, 32.2, pp.179-196.

Lewis J. and Townsend A. (eds.) (1989) : *The North-South Divide* (Paul Chapman, London).

Lie J. (1991) : 'The Prospect for Economic Democracy in South Korea', *Economic and Industrial Democracy*, 12, pp.501-513.

Lloyd P.E. and Shutt J. (1985) : 'Recession and Restructuring in the North West Region 1974-1982: The Implications of Recent Events', see Massey D. and Meegan R. (eds.).

Lloyds Bank Economic Bulletin (1990) : 'UK Open for Business', 138.

Local Government Comparative Statistics : CIPFA, Annual Publication.

Local Finance Statistical Yearbook : Ministry of Home Affairs (Korea), Annual Publication (Korean Version).

Lovering J. (1990) : 'Fordism's Unknown Successor: A Comment on Scott's Theory of Flexible Accumulation and the Re-emergence of Regional Economics', *International Journal of Urban and Regional Research*, 14.1, pp.159-174.

Lubis M. (1985) : 'Japan from Economic Power to Cultural Inspiration?', see Armour A.J.L. (ed.).

Lund P.J. and Gleed R.H. (1979) : 'The Development Area Share of Manufacturing Industry Investment 1966-1969', *Regional Studies*, 13, pp.61-72.

MacKnight S. (1987) : 'Japan's Foreign Direct Investment Takes Off', *JEI Report*, 25B, pp.8-12.

MacLennen D. and Parr J. (eds.) (1979) : *Regional Policy: Past Experience and New Directions* (Martin Robertson, London).

Macpherson W.J. (1987) : *The Economic Development of Japan C. 1868-1941* (Macmillan, Basingstoke).

Magee S.P. (1977) : 'Information and the Multinational Corporation: An Appropriability Theory of Direct Foreign Investment' in Bhagwati J.N. (ed.) *The New International Economic Order* (MIT Press, Cambridge).

Magee S.P. (1981) : *The Appropriability Theory of Multinational Corporation Behaviour*, Discussion Paper 51, International Investment and Business Studies, University of Reading.

Magee S.P. and Young L. (1983) : 'Multinationals, Tariffs and Capital Flows with Endogenous Politicians', see Kindleberger C.P. and Audretch D.B. (eds.).

Major Statistics of Korean Economy : Economic Planning Board (Korea), Annual Publication (Korean Version).

Malizia E. and Marimpietri A. (1982) : 'Contrasts in the Locational Attractiveness of the South East to New Manufacturers', *The Review of Regional Studies*, 12.2, pp.9-24.

Mandel E. (1975) : 'International Capitalism and Supernationality', see Radice H. (ed.).

Mansley N. and Rhodes J. (1990) : 'Economic Performance and Prospects in the Regions', see Cameron G., Moore B., Nicholls D., Rhodes J. and Tyler P. (eds.).

Marquand J. (1980) : *Measuring the Effects and Costs of Regional Incentives*, Government Economic Service Working Paper 32, Department of Industry.

Marsh P., Barwise P., Thomas K. and Wensley R. (1988) : *Managing Strategic Investment Decisions in Large Diversified Companies*, Centre for Business Strategy, London Business School.

Marshall M. (1987) : *Long Waves of Regional Development* (Macmillan, Basingstoke).

Martin R.L. (1985) : 'Monetarism Masquerading as Regional Policy? The Government's New System of Regional Aid', *Regional Studies*, 19.4, pp.379-388.

Martin R.L. (1988a) : 'Industrial Capitalism in Transition: The Contemporary Reorganization of the British Space-Economy', see Massey D. and Allen J. (eds.).

Martin R.L. (1988b) : 'The Political Economy of Britain's North-South Divide', *Transactions of Institutions of British Geographers*, 13, pp.389-418.

Martin R.L. (1989a) : 'The Reorganization of Regional Theory: Alternative Perspectives on the Changing Capitalist Space Economy', *Geoforum*, 20.2, pp.187-201.

Martin R.L. (1989b) : 'The Political Economy of Britain's North-South Divide', see Lewis J. and Townsend A. (eds.).

Martin R.L. and Hodge J.S. (1983) : 'The Reconstruction of British Regional Policy: The Crisis of Conventional Practice', *Environment and Planning C*, 1.2, pp.133-152.

Martin R.L. and Tyler P. (1992) : 'The Regional Legacy', in Michie J. (ed.) *The Economic Legacy 1979-1992* (Academic Press, London), pp.140-167.

Martinussen J. (1988) : *Transnational Corporations in a Developing Country: The Indian Experience* (Sage, New Delhi).

Massey D. (1973) : 'Towards a Critique of Industrial Location Theory', *Antipode*, 5.3, pp.33-39.

Massey D. (1979a) : 'In What Sense a Regional Problem?', *Regional Studies*, 13, pp.233-245.

Massey D. (1979b) : 'A Critical Evaluation of Industrial Location Theory', see Hamilton F.E.I. and Linge G. (eds.).

Massey D. (1984) : *Spatial Division of Labour, Social Structures and the Geography of Production* (Macmillan, London).

Massey D. (1987) : 'The Shape of Things to Come', see Peet R. (ed.).

Massey D. (1988) : 'What's Happening to UK Manufacturing?', see Allen J. and Massey D. (eds.).

Massey D. and Allen J. (eds.) (1988) : *Uneven Re-Development: Cities and Regions in Transition* (Hodder and Stoughton, London).

Massey D. and Meegan R. (1979) : *The Geography of Industrial Organisation*, Progress in Planning, 10.3 (Pergamon, Oxford).

Massey D. and Meegan R. (1982) : *The Anatomy of Job Loss* (Methuen, London).

Massey D. and Meegan R. (eds.) (1985) : *Politics and Method* (Methuen, London).

Massey D., Quintas P. and Wedd D. (1992) : *High Tech Fantasies, Science Parks in Society, Science and Space* (Routledge, London).

Maswood S.J. (1989) : *Japan and Protection* (Routledge, London).

Matsumoto K. (1990) : 'The Impact of FDI on Japan's Trade Balance with the EC', see Sumitomo Life Research Insurance.

Mawson J. and Miller D. (1986) : 'The Alternative Regional Strategy: A New Regional Policy for Labour', in Nolan P. and Paine S. (eds.), *Rethinking Socialist Economics* (Polity, Cambridge).

McBee M. (1987) : 'The Changing Face of Foreign Direct Investment in Japan', *JEI (Japanese Economic Institute) Report*, 42A, pp.1-7.

McCallum J.D. (1979) : 'The Development of British Regional Policy', see MacLennan D. and Parr J. (eds.).

McDermott M.C. (1989) : *Multinationals: Foreign Divestment and Disclosure* (McGraw-Hill, London).

McDermott P. (1977) : 'Capital Subsidies and Unemployed Labour: A Comment on the Production Function Approach', *Regional Studies*, 11, pp.203-210.

McDermott P. and Taylor M. (1982) : *Industrial Organization and Location* (Cambridge University Press, Cambridge).

McEldowney J.J. (1991) : 'Evaluation and European Regional Policy', *Regional Studies*, 25.3, pp.255-260.

McGreevy T.E. and Thomson A.J. (1983) : 'Regional Policy and Company Investment Behaviour', *Regional Studies*, 17.5, pp.347-358.

McNee R.B. (1974) : 'A Systems Approach to Understanding the Geographic Behaviour of Organisations, Especially Large Corporations', see Hamilton F.E.I. (ed.).

Meegan R. (1988) : 'A Crisis of Mass Production?', see Allen J. and Massey D. (eds.).

Mendenhall W. and Sincich T. (1989) : *A Second Course in Business Statistics: Regression Analysis* (Dellen, San Francisco).

Middlesex Polytechnic, London Industry and Environment Research Group (1979) : *A Conceptional Framework for Analyzing Industrial Change*, Occasional Paper 2, Middlesex Polytechnic.

Mills E. and Song B.N. (1977) : *Korea's Urbanisation and Urban Problems 1945-1975* (Korea Development Institute, Seoul).

Mining and Manufacturing Statistics : Economic Planning Board (Korea), Annual Publication (Korean Version).

Ministry of Construction, Korea (1981) : *The Comprehensive Urban Policy in the 1980s* (Korean Version).

Ministry of Construction, Korea (1986) : *Land Policy in Korea* (Korean Version).

Ministry of Construction, Korea : *Trend of Land Prices*, Quarterly Publication, 1989 3/4 (Korean Version).

Ministry of Finance, Korea : *Report of Foreign Direct Investment*, Annual Publication (1987, 1991) (Korean Version).

Ministry of Finance, Korea : *Foreign Investment Statistics*, Unpublished Statistics (1987, 1990) (Korean Version).

Ministry of Finance, Korea (1990) : *Investment Guide to Korea*, Irregular Publication.

Ministry of Finance, Korea (1991) : *Guidelines for Foreign Investment*, Irregular Publication.

Ministry of Finance, Korea : *List of Foreign Invested Companies*, Unpublished Data (1986, 1991) (Korean Version).

Ministry of Trade and Industry, Korea (1990) : *Industrial Estates Statistics*, Irregular Publication (Korean Version).

Moore B. and Rhodes J. (1973) : 'Evaluating the Effect of British Regional Policy', *Economic Journal*, 83, pp.87-110.

Moore B. and Rhodes J. (1976) : 'Regional Economic Policy and the Movement of Manufacturing Firms to Development Areas', *Economica*, 43, pp.17-31.

Moore B., Rhodes J. and Tyler P. (1986) : *The Effects of Government Regional Economic Policy*, Department of Trade and Industry (HMSO, London).

Moore B., Tyler P. and Elliot D. (1991) : 'The Influence of Regional Development Incentives and Infrastructure on the Location of Small and Medium Sized Companies in Europe', *Urban Studies*, 28.6, pp.1001-1026.

Morgan A.D. (1979) : 'Foreign Manufacturing by UK Firms', see Blackaby F. (ed.).

Moriarty B.M. (1983) : 'Hierarchies of Cities and the Spatial Filtering of Industrial Development', *Papers of the Regional Science Association*, 53, pp.59-82.

Morishima M. (1991) : 'Information Sharing and Firm Performance in Japan', *Industrial Relations*, 30.1, pp.37-61.

Morris J. (1988) : 'The Who, Why and Where of Japanese Manufacturing Investment in the UK', *Industrial Relations Journal*, 19.1, pp.31-40.

Moseley M. (1974) : *Growth Centres in Spatial Planning* (Pergamon, Oxford).

Munday M. (1990) : *Japanese Manufacturing Investment in Wales* (University of Wales Press, Cardiff).

Municipal Yearbook : Municipal Journal Ltd., Annual Publication (1987-1991).

Muramatsu M. and Krauss E.S. (1987) : 'The Conservative Party Line and the Development of the Patterned Pluralism', in Yamamura K. and Yasuba Y. (ed.) *The Political Economy of Japan, Vol. 1: The Domestic Transformation* (Stanford University Press, Stanford), pp.516-554.

Murray R. (1975) : 'The Internationalisation of Capital and the Nation State', see Radice H. (ed.).

Murray R. (1991) : 'The State After Henry', *Marxism Today*, pp.22-27.

National Audit Office (1986) : *Department of the Environment, Scottish Office and Welsh Office: Enterprise Zones*, Report by the Comptroller and Audit General, HMSO.

Nester W.R. (1990) : *Japan's Growing Power over East Asia and the World Economy* (Macmillan, Basingstoke).

New Earnings Survey : HMSO, Annual Publication.

Newby H., Bujra J. and Littlewood P. (eds.) (1985) : *Restructuring Capital: Recession and Reorganization in Industrial Society* (Macmillan, Basingstoke).

Newman R.J. and Sullivan D.H. (1988) : 'Econometric Analysis of Business Tax Imports on Industrial Location: What do we Know and How do We Know It?', *Journal of Urban Economics*, 23, pp.215-234.

News Week : 'Are Americans Really Lazy?', 17 Feb. 1992, pp.28-29.

Nielsen L.D. (1991) : 'Flexibility, Gender and Local Labour Markets - Some Examples from Denmark', *International Journal of Urban and Regional Research*, 15.1, pp.42-54.

Nolan P. and O'Donnell K. (1991) : 'Flexible Specialisation and UK Manufacturing Weakness: A Comment on Hirst and Zeitlin', *The Political Quarterly*, 62.1, pp.106-124.

Nonaka I. (1990) : 'Managing Globalization as a Self-renewing Process: Experiences of Japanese MNCs', see Bartlett C.A., Doz Y. and Hedland G. (eds.).

Norcliffe G.B. (1975) : 'A Theory of Manufacturing Places', see Collins L. and Walker D.F. (eds.).

Nye J.S. (1983) : 'The Multinational Corporations in the 1980s', see Kindleberger C.P. and Audretsch D.B. (eds.).

O'Donovan I. (1984) : *Ethnity and Migration: A Study of the Irish in Britain*, Ph.D Thesis, Department of Psychology, University of Birmingham.

O'Farrell P.N. (1980) : 'Multinational Enterprises and Regional Development: Irish Evidence', *Regional Studies*, 14, pp.141-150.

O'Farrell P.N. (1985) : 'Manufacturing Employment Change and Establishment Size', *Area*, 17.1, pp.35-43.

O'hUallachain B. (1985) : 'Spatial Patterns of Foreign Direct Investment in the US', *Professional Geographer*, 37.2, pp.154-162.

O'hUallachain B. (1986) : 'The Role of Foreign Direct Investment in the Development of Regional Industrial Systems: Current Knowledge and Suggestions for a Future American Research Agenda', *Regional Studies*, 20.2, pp.151-162.

Oakey R.P. (1991) : 'High Technology Industry and the 'Peace Dividend': A Comment on Future National and Regional Industrial Policy', *Regional Studies*, 25.1, pp.83-86.

Oberhauser A.M. (1990) : 'Social and Spatial Patterns under Fordism and Flexible Accumulation', *Antipode*, 22.3, pp.211-232.

Odland J. (1988) : *Spatial Autocorrelation* (Sage, Newbury Park).

Office of Population Census and Surveys (1986) : *Labour Force Survey 1983-1984* (Series LFS, No 4) (HMSO, London).

Ogata S. (1989) : *Growing Interdependence and Internationalisation*, Paper for Silver Jubilee Conference on the Internationalization of Japan in Comparative Perspective, University of Sheffield.

Ohmae K. (1985) : *Triad Power* (Free Press, New York).

Ohmae K. (1990) : *The Borderless World* (Collins, London).

Okimoto D. (1989) : *Between MITI and the Market* (Stanford University Press, Stanford).

Onida F. (1983) : 'Japan and Italy: Old and Newly Emerging Roles in the International Division of Labour', in Fodella G. (ed.) *Japan's Economy in a Comparative Perspective* (Paul Norbury Publications, Tenterden).

Ordnance Survey: Atlas of Great Britain (1982) : Ordnance Survey and County Life Books.

Ozawa T. (1979) : *Multinationalism, Japanese Style: The Political Economy of Outward Dependence* (Princeton University Press, Princeton).

Ozawa T. (1985) : 'Japan', see Dunning J.H. (ed.).

Padget C. : *The Effects of Regional Policy*, Discussion Paper 28, University of Reading.

Painter J. (1991) : 'Regulation Theory and Local Government', *Local Government Studies*, 17.6, pp.23-44.

Palloix C. (1975) : 'The Internationalisation of Capital and the Circuit of Social Capital', see Radice H. (ed.).

Park S.H. (1990) : *Regression Analysis* (Minyoungsa, Seoul) (Korean Version).

Park S.O. (1986) : 'Regional Changes in the Industrial System of a NIC: The Case of Korea', in Hamilton F.E.I.(ed.) *Industrialisation in Developing and Peripheral Regions* (Croom Helm, London).

Park S.O. and Wheeler J.O. (1983) : 'Industrial Location Policies and Manufacturing Employment Change: The Case of the Republic of Korea', *Regional Development Dialogue*, 4, pp.45-64.

Parker A.J. (1970) : *Employment Location/Allocation Models*, Occasional Papers 13, Department of Geography, University College London.

Parry G. (1980) : *The Multinational Enterprise: International Investment and Host Country Impacts* (JAI Press, Greenwich).

Parsons D.W. (1986) : *The Political Economy of British Regional Policy* (Croom Helm, London).

Parsons W. (1988) : *The Political Economy of British Regional Policy* (Routledge, London).

Pattie C.J. and Johnston R.J. (1990) : 'One Nation or Two? The Changing Geography of Unemployment in Great Britain, 1983-1988', *Professional Geographer*, 42.3, pp.288-298.

Pavitt K. (1987) : 'International Patterns of Technological Accumulation', in Hood N. and Vahlne J.E. (eds.) *Strategies in Global Competition* (Croom Helm, London).

Peck F. (1990) : 'Nissan in the North East: The Multiplier Effects', *Geography*, 75, pp.354-357.

Peet R. (ed.) (1987) : *International Capitalism and Industrial Restructuring* (Allen and Unwin, Winchester MA.).

Pettigrew P. and Dann S. (1986) : 'Streamlining Regional Industrial Aid?', *Regional Studies*, 20, pp.182-184.

Pfaff M. and Hurler P. (1983) : 'Employment Policy for Regional Labour Markets', *Environment and Planning C*, 1, pp.163-178.

Pindyke R.S. and Rubinfeld D.L. (1991) : *Econometric Models and Economic Forecasts* (McGraw-Hill, London).

Piore M.J. and Sabel C. (1984) : *The Second Industrial Divide: Possibilities for Prosperity* (Basic Books, New York).

Pitelis C.N. and Sugden R. (eds.) (1991) : *The Nature of the Transnational Firm* (Routledge, London).

Planning Directory : Hillier Parker, Annual Publication, 5 (1990).

Planning and Development Statistics : CIPFA, Annual Publication.

Police Statistics : CIPFA, Annual Publication.

Porter M.E. (1990) : *The Competitive Advantage of Nations* (Macmillan, London).

Pounce R.J. (1981) : *Industrial Movement in the United Kingdom 1966-75*, Department of Industry (HMSO, London).

Poynter T.A. (1985) : *Multinational Enterprise and Government Intervention* (Croom Helm, London).

Property Rent Indices and Market Editorial (PRIME) : Healey and Baker, Annual Publication.

Rabino S. (1989) : 'High-technology Firms and Factors Influencing Transfer of R&D Facilities', *Journal of Business Research*, 18, pp.195-205.

Radice H. (ed.) (1975) : *International Firms and Modern Imperialism* (Penguin Books, Harmondsworth).

Rate Collection Statistics, England and Wales : CIPFA, Annual Publication.

Rating Review : CIPFA, Scottish Branch, Annual Publication.

Rees J., Hewings G. and Stafford H. (1981) : *Industrial Location and Regional Systems* (Croom Helm, London).

Rees R.D. (1985) : 'Is There Still a National Economic Case for Regional Policy?', *Regional Studies*, 19.5, pp.471-475.

Rees R.D. and Miall R.H. (1979) : *The Effects of Regional Policy on Manufacturing Investment and Capital Stock within the UK* (Department of Industry, London).

Rees R.D. and Miall R.H. (1981) : 'The Effects of Regional Policy on Manufacturing Investment and Capital Stock within the UK between 1959 and 1978', *Regional Studies*, 15.6, pp.413-424.

Regional Studies Association (1982) : The Changing Environment for Regional Policy in the UK (Theme issue), *Regional Studies*, 16.5.

Regional Studies Association (1983) : *Report of an Inquiry into Regional Problems in the UK* (Geo Books, Norwich).

Regional Trends : HMSO, Annual Publication.

Reid N. (1990) : 'Comments on Japan's Direct Manufacturing Investment', *The Professional Geographer*, 42.2, pp.223-226.

Richardson H.W. and Hwang M.C. (eds.) (1988) : *Urban and Regional Policy in Korea and International Experiences* (Korea Research Institute for Human Settlements, Seoul).

Riddel R. (1985) : *Regional Development Policy* (Gower, Aldershot).

Roberts P.W. (1985) : 'Mobile Manufacturing Firms: Locational Choice and Some Policy Implications', *Regional Studies*, 19.5, pp.475-481.

Roberts P.W. and Noon D. (1987) : 'The Role of Industrial Promotion and Inward Incentives in the Process of Regional Development', *Regional Studies*, 21.2, pp.167-173.

Robinson F., Wren C. and Goddard J. (1987) : *Economic Development Policies: An Evaluation Study of the Newcastle Metropolitan Region* (Oxford University Press, Oxford).

Rodwin L. (1991) : 'European Industrial Change and Regional Economic Transformation: An Overview of Recent Experience', see Rodwin L. and Sazanami H. (eds.).

Rodwin L. and Sazanami H. (eds.) (1991) : *Industrial Change and Regional Economic Transformation* (Harper Collins, London).

Root F.R. (1990) : *International Trade and Investments* (South-Western Publishing Co., Cincinnati).

Rugman A.M. (1979) : *International Diversification and Multinational Enterprises* (Lexington Books, Lexington)

Rugman A.M. (1981) : *Inside the Multinationals: The Economics of Internal Markets* (Croom Helm, London).

Rugman A.M. (ed.) (1982) : *New Theories of the Multinational Enterprise* (Croom Helm, London).

Rugman A.M. and Eden L. (eds.) (1985) : *Multinationals and Transfer Pricing* (Croom Helm, London).

Rugman A.M., Lecraw D.J. and Booth L.D. (1986) : *International Business: Firm and Environment* (McGraw-Hill, Singapore).

Rugman A.M. and Verbeke A. (1990) : *Global Corporate Strategy and Trade Policy* (Routledge, London).

Ryu C.S. (1986) : *Econometrics* (Pakyoungsa, Seoul) (Korean Version).

Sadler D. (1992) : *The Global Region: Production, State Policies and Urban Development* (Pergamon, Oxford).

Sadri S. and Williamson C. (1989) : 'Management and Industrial Relations Strategies of Multinational Corporations in Developing Countries', *Journal of Business Research*, 18, pp.179-193.

Sakamoto K. (1989) : *Japan and the Internationalization of Capital*, Paper for Silver Jubilee Conference on the Internationalization of Japan in Comparative Perspective, University of Sheffield.

Sant M. (1975) : *Industrial Movement and Regional Development: The British Case* (Pergamon, Oxford)

Santiago C.E. (1987) : 'The Impact of Foreign Direct Investment on Export Structure and Employment Generation', *World Development*, 15, pp.317-328.

Sayer A. (1989) : 'Post-Fordism in Question', *International Journal of Urban and Regional Research*, 13.4, pp.666-695.

Schmenner R.W. (1982) : *Making Location Decisions* (Prentice-Hall, London).

Schmenner R.W., Huber J.C. and Cook R.L. (1987) : 'Geographic Differences and the Location of New Manufacturing Facilities', *Journal of Urban Economics*, 21, pp.83-104.

Scott A.J. (1991) : 'Flexible Production Systems: Analytical Tasks and Theoretical Horizons - A Reply to Lovering', *International Journal of Urban and Regional Research*, 15.1, pp.130-134.

Scottish Abstract of Statistics : HMSO, Annual Publication.

Scottish Housing Statistics : HMSO, Annual Publication (1983-).

Scottish Local Government Financial Statistics : CIPFA, Scottish Branch, Annual Publication.

Shigehara K. (1991) : 'External Dimension of Europe 1992: Its Effects on the Relationship between Europe, the United States and Japan', *Bank of Japan Monetary and Economic Studies*, 9.1, pp.87-102.

Shimokawa K. (1989) : *Internationalization of Japanese Business - A Case Study of the Automobile Industry*, Paper for Silver Jubilee Conference on the Internationalization of Japan in Comparative Perspective, University of Sheffield.

Slowe P. (1981) : *The Advanced Factory in Regional Development* (Gower, Aldershot).

Smidt M. and Wever E. (1990) : *The Corporate Firm in a Changing World Economy* (Routledge, London).

Smith D. (1988) : 'The Japanese Example in South West Birmingham', *Industrial Relations Journal*, 19.1, pp.41-50.

Smith D. (1989) : *North and South* (Penguin, London).

Smith B.M.D. (1971) : *Industrial Movement and Location in the West Midlands: Summary Report*, Centre for Urban and Regional Studies, University of Birmingham.

Smith D.M. (1970) : 'On Throwing Out Weber with the Bath Water: A Note on Industrial Location Linkage', *Area*, 2, pp.15-18.

Smith D.M. (1981) : *Industrial Location: An Economic Geographical Analysis* (John Wiley and Sons, Chichester).

So Y.I. (1989) : *Regression Analysis* (Changjisa, Seoul) (Korean Version).

Social Indicators in Korea : Economic Planning Board (Korea), Annual Publication (Korean Version).

Song B.N. (1984) : *Korean Economy* (Seoul, Pakyoungsa) (Korean Version).

Spencer K., Taylor A., Smith B.M.D., Flynn N. and Batley R. (1986) : *Crisis in the Industrial Heartland: A Study of the West Midlands* (Clarendon Press, Oxford).

Spiegleman R.G. (1968) : *A Study of Industry Location Using Multiple Regression Techniques*, Agricultural Economic Report 10, Economic Research Service, Department of Agriculture.

Stafford H.A. (1974) : 'The Anatomy of the Location Decision', see Hamilton F.E.I. (ed.).

Stafford H.A. (1979) : *Principles of Industrial Facility Location* (Conway Publications, Inc., Atlanta).

Statistics of Education : HMSO, Annual Publication.

Statistical Yearbook : Annual Publication (Published by Each Do in Korea) (Korean Version).

Stevens G.V.G. (1972) : 'Capital Mobility and the International Firm' in Machlup F., Salant W. and Tarshis L. (eds.) *International Mobility of Capital*, National Bureau of Economic Research.

Storey D.J. (1990) : 'Evaluation of Policies and Measures to Create Local Employment', *Urban Studies*, 27.5, pp.669-684.

Storey D.J., Keasey K., Watson R. and Wynarczyk P. (1987) : *The Performance of Small Firms* (Croom Helm, London).

Storper J.M. (1981) : 'Toward a Structural Theory of Industrial Location', see Rees J., Hewings G. and Stafford H. (eds.).

Storper J.M. and Scott A.J. (1989) : 'The Geographical Foundations and Social Regulation of Flexible Production Complexes', in Wolch J. and Dear M. (eds.) *The Power of Geography: How Territory Shapes Social Life* (Unwin Hyman, Winchester MA.), pp.21-40.

Storper J.M. and Turner L. (1985) : *Britain and the Multinationals* (John Wiley and Sons, Chichester).

Suarez-Villa L. and Han P.H. (1991) : 'Organisations, Space and Capital in the Development of Korean Electronics Industry', *Regional Studies*, 25.4, pp.327-343.

Sugden R. (1990) : 'The Warm Welcome for Foreign-Owned Transnationals from Recent British Governments', in Chick M. (ed.) *Governments, Industry and Markets* (Edward Elgar, Aldershot), pp.215-224.

Sumitomo-Life Research Institute (1990) : *Japanese Direct Investment in Europe: Motives, Impacts and Policy Implications* (Avebury, Aldershot).

Swales J.K. (1989) : 'Are Discretionary Regional Subsidies Cost-Effective?', *Regional Studies*, 23.4, pp.361-368.

Swamidass P.M. (1990) : 'A Comparison of the Plant Location Strategies of Foreign and Domestic Manufacturers in the US', *Journal of International Business Studies*, 21.2, pp.301-317.

Sweet M. (1981) : *Industrial Location Policy for Economic Revitalisation* (Praeger, New York).

Taylor M. and Thrift N. (eds.) (1982) : *The Geography of Multinationals* (Croom Helm, London).

Taylor M. and Thrift N. (1986) : *Multinationals and the Restructuring of the World Economy* (Croom Helm, London).

Teichova A., Levy-Levoyer M. and Nassbaum H. (eds.) (1986) : *Multinational Enterprise in Historical Perspective* (Cambridge University Press, Cambridge).

The Agricultural Statistics, United Kingdom : HMSO, Annual Publication (1980-).

The Anglo-Japanese Economic Institute (1991) : *Britain and Japan: An Economic Briefing*, Irregular Publication.

The Anglo-Japanese Economic Institute : *Japanese Addresses in the UK*, Annual Publication (1991/92).

372

The Bank of Korea : *The Statistical Yearbook for Foreign Investment*, Annual Publication (1991) (Korean Version).

The Bank of Korea : *Tonggye Wolbo*, Monthly Publication (Korean Version).

The Birmingham Post : Burnaston Sets Pace for Jobs in Motor Industry, 9 Aug. 1990.

The Government of Korea (1982) : *The Second Comprehensive National Land Development Plan 1982-1991* (Korean Version).

The Institute of Chartered Accountants in England and Wales (1979) : *Financial Assistance for Industry and Commerce in the United Kingdom* (Peat, Merwick, Mitchell & Co, London).

The Japan Economic Review : Monthly Publication (15 Feb. 1990 and 15 Jul. 1990).

The Observer : Toyota and Ford Rev Up the Economy, 31 May 1992, p.37.

The Sunday Times : The Rising Sons and Daughters of Japan, 5 Jun. 1988.

The Sunday Times : Inland Revenue Probes Tax Avoidance at Sony, 22 Mar. 1992.

The Times : European Car Industry (Focus), 12 Feb. 1992.

Thielemans E. (1974) : 'The Multinational Enterprise', in Wilson J.S. and Scheffer C.F. (eds.) *Multinational Enterprises: Financial and Monetary Aspects* (Leiden, Sijthoff).

Thomas I.C. (1992) : 'Additionality in the Distribution of European Regional Development Fund Grants to Local Authorities', *Local Economy*, 6.4, pp.292-310.

Thomsen S. and Nicolaides P. (1991) : *The Evolution of Japanese Direct Investment in Europe* (Harvester Wheatsheaf, Hemel Hemstead).

Todd D. (1983) : 'Area Development or Sectoral Conflict? An Example of the Discriminatory Effects of Regional Policy in Britain', *Environment and Planning C*, 1.2, pp.153-162.

Tomaney J. (1991) : *Japanese Inward Investment: North East Experiences*, Paper presented to the CLES conference on 'Japanese Inward Investment in the UK', Matlock.

Townroe P.M. (1969) : 'Locational Choice and the Individual Firm', *Regional Studies*, 3.1, pp.15-24.

Townroe P.M. (1971) : *Industrial Location Decisions*, Occasional Paper 15, Centre for Urban and Regional Studies, University of Birmingham.

Townroe P.M. (1972) : 'Some Behavioral Considerations in the Industrial Location Decision', *Regional Studies*, 6, pp.261-272.

Townroe P.M. (1976) : *Planning Industrial Location* (Leonard Hill Books, London).

Townroe P.M. (1979) : *Industrial Movement: Experience in the US and UK* (Saxon House, Farnborough).

Townroe P.M. (1985) : 'A Discriminant Analysis of the 1980 Sao Paulo Industrial Location Survey', *Environment and Planning A*, 17.1, pp.115-131.

Townroe P.M. (1986) : 'Regional Economic Development Policy in a Mixed Economy', *Journal of Regional Policy*, 6, pp.355-372.

Townroe P.M. (1989) : 'The case for Experimental, Adaptive Restraint Policies in Developing Nation Metropolitan Areas', *International Regional Science Review*, 12.2, pp.131-146.

Townroe P.M. (1991) : 'Rationality in Industrial Location Decisions', *Urban Studies*, 28.3, pp.383-392.

Townroe P.M. and Martin R. (1988) : *Regional Development in the United Kingdom in the Nineteen Nineties: An Introductory Paper*, Regional Studies Association, 1988/89 Regional Review Panel.

Townsend A.R. (1986) : 'The Location of Employment Growth after 1978: The Surprising Significance of Dispersed Centres (UK)', *Environment and Planning A*, 18.4, pp.529-545.

Townsend A.R. (1987) : 'Regional Policy', see Lever W.F. (ed.).

Transport Statistics : HMSO, Annual Publication.

Trevor M. (1983) : *Japan's Reluctant Multinationals* (Frances Pinter, London).

Trevor M. (ed.) (1987) : *The Internationalisation of Japanese Business* (Campus Verlag, Frankfurt am Main).

Trevor M. and Christie I. (1988) : *Manufacturers and Suppliers in Britain and Japan* (Policy Studies Institute, London).

Twomey J. and Taylor J. (1985) : 'Regional Policy and the Interregional Movement of Manufacturing Industry in Great Britain', *Scottish Journal of Political Economy*, 32.3, pp.257-277.

Tyler P. and Kitson M. (1987) : 'Geographical Variations in Transport Costs of Manufacturing Firms in Great Britain', *Urban Studies*, 24, pp.61-73.

Tyler P. and Rhodes J. (1986) : 'The Census of Production as an Indicator of Regional Differences in Productivity in the UK', *Regional Studies*, 20.4, pp.331-339.

UK Airports : Civil Aviation Authority, Annual Publication.

United Nations (1983) : *Salient Features and Trends in Foreign Direct Investment* (United Nations, New York).

United Nations (1988) : *Transnational Corporations in World Development: Trends and Prospects* (United Nations, New York).

United Nations (1991) : *World Investment Report 1991: The Triad in Foreign Direct Investment* (United Nations, New York)

Urban Area Statistics : Korea Land Development Corporation, Annual Publication (Korean Version).

Vernon R. (1966) : 'International Investment and International Trade in the Product Cycle', *Quarterly Journal of Economics*, 80.2, pp.190-207.

Vernon R. (1974) : 'Location of Economic Activity', in Dunning J.H. (ed.) *The Multinational Enterprise and Economic Analysis* (Allen and Unwin, London).

Wakabayashi H. (1988) : *The Development of Economic Policy and the Industrial Economy in Post-War Japan*, Discussion Paper No.89, Centre for Urban and Regional Development Studies, University of Newcastle upon Tyne.

Walker R. and Calzonetti F. (1990) : 'Searching for New Manufacturing Plant Locations: A Study of Location Decisions in Central Appalachia', *Regional Studies*, 24.1, pp.15-30.

Walker R. and Greenstreet D. (1991) : 'The Effect of Government Incentives and Assistance on Location and Job Growth in Manufacturing', *Regional Studies*, 25.1, pp.13-30.

Warren B. (1975) : 'How International is Capital ?', see Radice H. (ed.).

Watts H.D. (1987) : *Industrial Geography* (Longman, London).

Webber M.J. (1984) : *Industrial Location, Scientific Geography Series 3* (Sage, Beverly Hills).

Webber M.M. (1983) : 'The Myth of Rationality: Development Planning Reconsidered', *Environment and Planning B*, 10.1, pp.89-99.

Webster A. and Dunning J.H. (eds.) (1990) : *Structural Change in the World Economy* (Routledge, London).

Welsh Agricultural Statistics : HMSO, Annual Publication.

West Midlands Development Agency (1989) : *Overseas Investment to the West Midlands Region*, Second Report.

West Midlands Development Agency (1990) : *Benefits of Inward Investment to the West Midlands Region*, Final Report.

Westney D.E. (1990) : 'Internal and External Linkages in the MNC: The Case of R&D Subsidiaries in Japan', see Bartlett C.A., Doz Y. and Hedland G. (eds.).

Whang I.J. (1985) : 'The Role of Government in Economic Development in Korea during the Sixties and Seventies', in Korea Development Institute, *Industrialisation and Rural Change*, International Development Exchange Program (KDI, Seoul).

Wheatley M. (1991) : 'Milton Keynes: A Moving Story', *Management Today*, Anniversary Issue, pp.75-84.

Wheeler J.O. (1981) : 'Effects of Geographical Scale on Location Decisions in Manufacturing: The Atlanta Example', *Economic Geography*, 57, pp.134-145.

Wheeler J.O. and Park S.O. (1984) : 'External Ownership and Control: The Impact of Industrial Organization on the Regional Economy', *Geoforum*, 15.2, pp.243-252.

Wilkinson E. (1983) : *Japan versus Europe* (Penguin Books, Harmondsworth).

Williams K., Williams J. and Haslam C. (1991) : 'What Kind of EC Regional Policy?', *Local Economy*, 5.4, pp.330-346.

Williamson O.E. (1975) : *Markets and Hierarchies* (Free Press, New York).

Willis K.G. and Saunders C.M. (1988) : 'The Impact of a Development Agency on Employment: Resurrection Discounted?', *Applied Economics*, 20, pp.81-96.

Womack J.P., Jones D.T. and Roos D. (1990) : *The Machine that Changed the World* (Rawson Associates, New York).

Wood P.A. (1974) : 'Are Behavioral Approaches to Industrial Location Theory Doomed to be Descriptive?', in Massey D. and Morrison W.I. (eds.) *Industrial Location: Alternative Frameworks* (Centre for Environmental Studies, London).

Wood P.A. (1982) : 'Industrial Geography', *Progress in Human Geography*, 6.4, pp.576-583.

Wood P.A. (1984) : 'Regional Industrial Development', *Area*, 16.4, pp.281-289.

Wood P.A. (1987) : 'Behavioral Approaches to Industrial Location Studies', see Lever W.F. (ed.).

Wood P.A. (1988) : 'Employment Change and the Role of the Producer Service Sector', see Massey and Allen (eds.).

Wood P.A. (1991) : 'Conceptualisation of the Role of Services in Economic Change', *Area*, 23.1, pp.66-72.

Wood S. (ed.) (1989) : *The Transfer of Work ?* (Unwin Hyman, London).

Woronoff J. (1984) : *Japan's Commercial Empire* (Macmillan, London).

Wren C. (1988) : 'Closure Rates among Assisted and Non-Assisted Establishments', *Regional Studies*, 22.2, pp.107-119.

Wren C. (1989a) : 'The Revised Regional Development Grant Scheme: A Case Study in Cleveland County of a Marginal Employment Subsidy', *Regional Studies*, 23.2, pp.127-137.

Wren C. (1989b) : 'Factors Underlying the Employment Effects of Financial Assistance Policies', *Applied Economics*, 21, pp.497-513.

Wren C. (1990) : 'Regional Policy in the 1980s', *National Westminster Bank Quarterly Review*, Nov. 1990, pp.52-63.

Wren C. and Waterson M. (1991) : 'The Direct Employment Effects of Financial Assistance to Industry', *Oxford Economic Papers*, 43.1, pp.116-138.

Yannopoulos G.N. (1990) : 'Foreign Direct Investment and European Integration: The Evidence from the Formative Years of the European Community', *Journal of Common Market Studies*, XXVIII.3, pp.235-259.

Yannopoulos G.N. and Dunning J.H. (1976) : 'Multinational Enterprises and Regional Development: An Exploratory Paper', *Regional Studies*, 10.4, pp.389-399.

Yearbook of Construction Statistics : Ministry of Construction, Korea, Annual Publication (Korean Version).

Yearbook of Labour Statistics : Ministry of Employment, Korea, Annual Publication (Korean Version).

Yearbook of Population Movement : Economic Planning Board, Korea, Annual Publication (Korean Version).

Yearbook of Regional Statistics : Economic Planning Board, Korea, Annual Publication (1988-) (Korean Version).

Yearbook of Transportation : Ministry of Transportation, Korea, Annual Publication (Korean Version).

Yoshida M. (1987) : *Japanese Direct Manufacturing Investment in the United States* (Praeger, New York).

Yoshihara K. (1978) : *Japanese Investment in South East Asia* (The University Press of Hawaii, Honolulu).

Yoshihara K. (1986) : *Japanese Economic Development* (Oxford University Press, Tokyo).

Young S., Hood N. and Hamill J. (1988) : *Foreign Multinationals and British Economy* (Croom Helm, London).

Young S. and Stewart D. (1986) : 'The Regional Implications of Inward Direct Investment', see Amin A. and Goddard J. (eds.).

Ziegler J.A. (1990) : 'Industrial Location and State and Local Tax and Other Financial Incentives', *Arkansas Business & Economic Review*, 23.1, pp.25-30.

Index

Anglo-Japanese Economic Institute (AJEI) 127, 189, 263
assisted areas (AAs) 56, 77, 87-89, 91-93, 101-106, 260, 262-267, 273, 276,
          278, 280, 281, 282, 284, 288, 291
alternative locations 76, 116, 192, 204-207, 209, 211, 212, 214, 224,
          225, 226-228, 230, 232, 234, 236, 246, 287, 288
assisted areas 77, 89, 163, 262, 268
attractive locational factors 194, 199, 211, 216, 220, 231, 233
autocorrelation 111
Banwol New Town Development Plan 97
big spender 10
boomerang effect 52
branch plant economy 52, 53, 81, 272
Britain 2, 6, 9, 10, 27, 53, 56, 74, 77, 79, 82, 105, 109, 111-113,
          115, 125-130, 132-135, 137, 139, 141-145, 147, 148,
          150, 158, 160, 163, 167, 179, 185, 189, 190, 192, 193,
          195, 198, 200-202, 204, 205, 210, 212, 214, 240, 241,
          242-246, 251, 252, 254-258, 260-262, 265-268, 272,
          273, 277, 279-282, 284, 285, 287, 288, 291
     British capitalism 19
     British industry 79, 252
     British manufacturing industry 72, 79, 80
     British regional policy 88, 272
capital 2, 3, 5, 9, 11, 14, 15, 18-20, 22, 23, 26-28, 30-35, 37-42, 45,
          46, 50-55, 58, 60, 61, 63, 71-73, 80, 87, 91, 94, 136,
          144, 183, 212, 246-248, 252, 254, 256, 272, 275, 279,
          290
     capital accumulation 14, 18, 71
     capital intensive industry 80
     capital subsidies 91
     capitalist economy 8, 9, 14, 21

change analysis 79, 111, 115, 147, 149, 152, 158, 164, 165, 169, 170, 172, 176, 179, 180, 241-243, 286
classical theory 42
coefficients 110, 155, 156, 158, 167, 171, 173, 176, 178, 179, 184, 231, 260, 286
commercial treaty 27
commercialisation 24
company-specific factors 42
compatriot companies 155, 166, 199, 217, 230
consensus management 31
Conservative government 87, 88, 261
conservative policy line 29
Cooke's frame 275
core workers 16, 17
correlation coefficients 155, 156, 158, 167, 171, 173, 176, 178, 179, 184, 231, 260, 286
correlation matrix 110, 115, 148, 150, 151, 170, 171
cost-factors 194
crisis 9, 14, 15, 22
crisis of capitalism 9
crisis of Fordism 9, 15
crisis of mass production 9
cross-section analysis 164, 286
cross-tabulation 205, 209, 212, 226, 229
Daebul Industrial Estate 100
Department areas (DAs) 86, 87, 89, 91, 101, 103, 105
de-industrialization 10, 79, 249, 262
defence industry 93
defensive direct investment 58
Department of Trade and Industry 273
dependent variables 110, 111, 113, 115, 117, 120, 147, 155, 156, 158, 160-164, 167, 169, 171, 172, 176, 178, 179, 181, 184, 186, 231, 261, 286
developing countries 6, 23, 30, 40-42, 52, 53, 58, 60-64, 78, 204, 205, 206, 211, 215, 218, 225, 226, 232, 235, 236, 245, 246, 249-251, 254-258, 284, 288, 291
development areas 86, 87
disorganized capitalism 12, 18, 20
diversified MNC-style FDI 254
division of function 24, 49, 251
division of labour 11, 22-24, 26, 46-48, 50, 248, 251, 288
European Community (EC) 41, 52, 145, 203, 251, 253, 259, 262

EC market 203, 253
eclectic paradigm 42, 45
economic geography 23, 24, 26
    economic initiatives 80, 275
    Economic Planning Board (EPB) 101, 269
electronics industry 245, 287
English Estates 76
Euro-dollar 10
European Regional Development Fund 4, 88
export-led expansion 28
f value 114
f-test 114
FDI 1-4, 6, 22, 23, 25, 30, 33, 35, 37-41, 45-48, 53-64, 136, 141, 215,
        247-254, 258, 266, 272, 274-276, 278-280, 284, 288,
        291
Five Year Economic Development Plan 268
flexibility 9, 13-21, 31-35, 251, 259, 275
flexible firm 16
flexible production 17, 23
Fordism 3, 9, 12-15, 17, 18, 22, 23, 31, 35, 251, 259, 262, 275, 278,
        291
Fordist mass production 8, 17, 31, 34, 35
foreign direct investment 1, 53
Free Export zones 99
Free Port Zones 269
geographical distribution 2, 5, 59, 61, 66, 81, 125, 128, 136, 138, 141,
        143-146, 148, 189, 214, 240, 241, 285
    geographical tendency 257
geography 3, 9, 23-26, 70-72, 80, 94, 104, 176-179, 218, 228, 243,
        257, 268, 290, 291
global 2, 3, 34, 39, 40, 42, 46, 48-52, 204, 211, 212, 215, 225, 232,
        234, 235, 236, 239, 246-248, 251, 252, 254, 256-259,
        275, 277, 283, 287, 288, 290, 291
global competitors 257
    global economy 42
    global headquarters 39
    global locational behaviour 3
    global network 247, 254, 257
    global profit 49
    global sourcing 247
    global structural changes 34
    global welfare 50

globalisation 193, 211, 216, 247, 253, 288
goodness-of-fit 189
heavy and chemical industry 97
heteroscedasticity 111
high technology industry 76, 80, 93, 254
industrial and managerial strategy 249
    Industrial Bank of Japan 247
    industrial capitalism 13
    industrial classification systems 112
    industrial complexes 221
    industrial components 78
    industrial development 1, 15, 74, 77, 88, 97, 99, 168, 262, 264
    Industrial Development Act 264
    industrial development controls 1
    industrial development policy 88
    industrial disputes 118, 151-154, 157, 165, 197, 256
    industrial distribution 131, 139, 145, 190, 213
    industrial districts 16
    industrial electronics 254, 277
    industrial floorspace 118
    industrial geography 72
    industrial investment activity 87
    industrial land and premises 118, 170, 173, 179, 196, 199, 206, 207, 210, 211, 212, 218, 219, 223, 224, 226, 228, 229, 231, 232, 233, 235, 242, 244, 245, 253, 276, 278, 280
    industrial location 3-5, 11, 42, 65-71, 73, 74, 76-79, 82, 108
    industrial location analysis 66-68
    industrial location change 71, 79
    industrial location model 69
    industrial location theory 67, 68, 71, 108
    industrial milieu 277
    industrial mix 190, 213
    industrial movement 92, 93, 108, 260
    industrial obsolescence 86
    industrial organization 14, 43, 44
    industrial policy 4, 29, 32, 33, 104, 247, 269, 279, 284
    industrial premises 119, 155, 170
    industrial regions 25
    industrial relations 15
    industrial relocation 86
    industrial resources 64

industrial sectors 23, 74
industrial sites 95, 99, 262
industrial society 34
industrial specialization 18
industrial structure 1, 12, 79, 91, 281
industrial system 70
industrialization 10, 79, 249, 262
industrialized country 27
industry 4, 5, 8, 19, 20, 22-32, 52, 57-59, 62, 70-72, 74, 76, 78-81,
    85-87, 91, 93-95, 97, 98, 100, 101, 138, 139, 141, 179,
    184, 186, 190, 191, 221, 228, 229, 245-247, 249, 252,
    253, 254, 256, 257, 269, 270, 272, 273, 277, 279, 283,
    287
Industry Allocation Act 97
Institute of Fiscal and Monetary Policy 59
inter-industry linkages 81
Intermediate areas 87
internalization theory 42, 44-46, 64
international 1-3, 8-12, 14, 19-25, 27, 29, 30, 35, 36, 38, 39, 41-44,
    47, 50, 51, 53-55, 65, 71-73, 77-79, 81, 83, 88, 91, 92,
    109, 130, 246, 250, 253, 257, 258, 261, 272, 275, 283,
    284, 285, 290, 291
 international arena 291
 international capital flow 41, 54
 international competition 44, 79
 international competitiveness 55
 international demand and supply conditions 81
 international division of labour 11, 22, 24, 50
 international division of market 253
 international economic circumstances 30
 international economic structure 29, 109
 international economy 3, 10, 22, 23, 25, 27, 35, 36, 65, 71, 79,
    91, 257, 261, 272, 283
 international investment 42, 43, 246
 international management strategy 50
 international market 2, 9, 24, 25, 30, 44, 47, 72, 79, 83, 88,
    250, 258, 261, 275, 284, 290, 291
 international market structure 44
 International Monetary Fund 10, 38
 international monetary system 10
 international politics 11, 19, 35
 international trade 8, 29, 51

international trading companies 39
internationalization 10, 19, 21, 28, 30, 45, 46, 51, 283
    internationalization of capital 45, 46, 51
    internationalization of class struggle 46
    internationalization of industry 283
    internationalization of Japanese capital 28, 30
    internationalized economy 27
Invest in Britain Bureau 266
Japan 2, 4, 6, 9, 22, 26-30, 32-37, 41, 48, 53, 55-64, 66, 75, 82, 116, 128, 131, 134, 136, 192-194, 196, 206, 210, 212, 214, 215, 216, 217, 233-236, 241, 247-249, 256, 258, 287, 290
    Japan's direct investment 41
    Japan's political economy 33
    Japanese capital 2, 3, 9, 22, 26-28, 30-34, 37, 61, 63, 136, 246-248, 252, 254, 272, 275, 279, 290
    Japanese car manufacturers 53
    Japanese companies 2, 5, 6, 50, 75, 81-83, 101, 105, 106, 108, 109, 111, 112, 113, 115, 116, 119, 122, 125-139, 141-145, 148, 149, 150, 152-157, 161-172, 174, 176-186, 188-212, 214-227, 229-236, 239-259, 261-274, 276, 277, 279, 280-282, 285-288, 290, 291
    Japanese culture 83
    Japanese direct investment 59
    Japanese Economic Institute (JEI) 41, 59, 60
    Japanese economic policy 29
    Japanese economic success 29
    Japanese electronics companies 133, 135, 145
    Japanese enterprises 28, 32
    Japan External Trade Organization (JETRO) 106, 113, 127
    Japanese FDI 3, 6, 41, 57-62, 64, 215, 247-249, 251-253, 272, 274, 275, 278-280, 284, 288, 291
    Japanese government 27-29, 52, 194, 248, 249, 272
    Japanese imperialism 27, 272
    Japanese industrial policy 32
    Japanese industry 26, 28, 30, 59, 139, 249, 252, 253, 257
    Japanese inward investment 63, 137, 239
    Japanese labour practices 33
    Japanese language 226
    Japanese management 28, 31, 32, 35, 246, 276
    Japanese manufacturing industry 62

Japanese manufacturing investment 134
Japanese miracle 34
Japanese MNCs 2-5, 49, 50, 57, 61-64, 74, 76, 77, 81-85, 105,
              106, 109, 111, 113, 136, 189, 193, 204, 212,
              216, 232, 238, 239, 246, 248, 250-254, 257-261,
              267, 268, 272, 274-279, 281, 283-285, 288, 290,
              291
Japanese outward direct investment 59
Japanese overseas investment 58, 59, 75, 134, 205
Japanese overseas markets 249
Japanese parent companies 2, 113, 144, 212
Japanese people 32, 204, 248, 277
Japanese politics 29
Japanese production methods 34
Japanese products 22, 27, 145, 250, 254
Japanese projects 273
Japanese semiconductor firms 62
Japanese style management 31-35
Japanese sub-contractors 256
Japanese subsidiaries 113, 130, 136, 138, 141, 143, 144, 177,
              186, 211, 232, 249, 250, 256, 258, 261, 265,
              274, 277
Japanese trade surplus 30
Japanese worldwide managerial strategy 271
Japanese youth 34
just-in-time delivery system 256
Keynesian 8, 10, 20-22
Keynesian demand side policy 22
Keynesian economic theory 10
Keynesian mass consumption 8
Kondratiev's cycle 34
Korea 2, 5, 6, 9, 30, 36, 37, 53, 56-58, 63, 75, 76, 82-85, 94-98, 100,
              101, 102, 109, 112-115, 135-145, 169-174, 176, 177,
              179, 183-186, 205, 207, 212-236, 240-246, 250, 251,
              253, 254, 255-258, 260, 261, 268-272, 279-282,
              284-288, 291
Korea Export Industrial Estate 270
Korea Statistical Yearbook 140
Korea Trade Association (KTA) 270
Korea's trade surplus 58
Korean economic activity 136
Korean economy 6, 57, 94, 136, 137

Korean firms 57, 58
Korean government policy 279
Korean government's intention 282
Korean indigenous firms 141
Korean manufacturing industry 58
Korean market 144, 214, 216, 230, 251, 253, 270
Korean MNCs 56-58
Korean outward investment 57, 58
Korean people 82, 272
Korean politics 137, 255
Korean population 94
Korean products 280
Korean regional policy 97, 138, 185, 261, 279
Korean Research Institute for Human Settlement 99
Korean territory 82
Korean war 27
labour flexibility 19, 31
lean production 12
local content regulation 256
Local Industry Development Act 97
location 3-6, 11, 24, 26, 42, 43, 45, 47, 55, 56, 65-85, 94, 101-106,
        108, 109, 113, 115, 125, 127-129, 134, 136, 141, 149,
        150, 152, 154-157, 163, 164, 166-168, 170, 173, 176,
        177, 179, 183-186, 191, 194, 196, 197, 199, 200,
        202-204, 206-212, 214, 217, 218, 220-224, 226-229,
        231-236, 239, 241-245, 251, 255, 260-262, 267, 269,
        270, 271, 276, 283, 286, 287
    location analysis 66-68, 70, 81
    location theory 4, 42, 43, 47, 67-72, 108
    location-specific advantage 47
    locational behaviour 2-6, 71, 81, 83, 85, 101, 109, 111, 113,
        125, 140, 141, 157, 163, 164, 179, 184, 186,
        188, 230, 232, 236, 239, 242, 246, 257, 259,
        261, 271, 283, 285, 286, 288, 290
    locational change 66, 71, 73, 78
    locational characteristics 109, 257
    locational choice 66, 109, 141, 162, 163, 185, 270, 271, 280
    locational circumstances 208
    locational decision 1, 2, 69, 70, 72, 73, 78, 102, 103, 108,
        109, 112, 125, 141, 227
    locational decision-making 1, 2, 69, 70, 72, 73, 78, 102, 103,
        108

locational distribution 109, 134-136, 144, 145, 154
locational factor 4, 67, 73, 108, 109, 112, 113, 116, 149, 158-162, 176, 177, 179, 184, 207, 226, 242, 267, 278
locational factor analysis 4, 67, 73, 109, 116
locational features 2, 47, 111, 185
locational movement 4, 66, 73, 81
locational push factors 74
locational shift 1, 4, 66, 67, 74, 78-80
locational shift pattern analysis 4, 67, 78
locational shift process 66
locational strategies 57
long-wave theory 21
low technology industry 249
manufacturing industry 5, 8, 58, 62, 72, 79, 80, 85
Marxism 13
Metropolitan Population Dispersion Plan 97
metropolitan region (MPR) 94-98, 100, 136, 138, 227, 229, 269, 270
Ministry of International Trade and Industry (MITI) 29, 32
Ministry of Trade and Industry (Korea) 101, 270
MNCs 1-6, 8, 11, 18, 22, 23, 25, 30, 37-44, 46-53, 55-58, 61-64, 66, 74, 75-77, 80-85, 88, 101-106, 109, 111, 113, 136, 189, 193, 204, 212, 216, 232, 235, 238, 239, 246, 248, 250, 251, 252-254, 257-261, 267, 268, 272, 274-281, 283-285, 288, 290, 291
modes of regulation 14
motor vehicle industry 25
multicollinearity 151, 153, 162, 166, 167, 173, 175, 176
multilateralism 10
multinational companies 1, 10, 11, 21, 37, 101, 125, 135, 246
multiple regression 108, 109, 114, 115
National Comprehensive Physical Development Plan 97
National Land Use Management Act 97
neo-Fordism 12, 14
neoclassical economic theory 67-69
neoclassical economists 67
neoclassical location theory 4, 67, 68
neoclassical theorists 73
neoclassical theory 4, 72, 108
new international division of labour (NIDL) 24
New Town 97, 100
New Town overspill policy 100

newly industrializing countries (NICs) 11, 41, 52, 61, 140
numerical flexibility 17
ordinary regression procedure 111
Organization for Economic Co-operation and Development (OECD) 38
organized capitalism 13, 18-20
ownership advantage 45
pay flexibility 17
political economist 37
    political economy view 42, 45
portfolio investment 39, 47
positive-sum game 275
post-Fordism 3, 12-15, 17, 18, 22, 23, 31, 251, 259, 262, 275, 291
production locations 257
profit 1-4, 22, 25, 26, 39, 46, 48, 49, 56, 67, 68, 73, 80, 82, 247, 248, 253, 291
    profit guarantees 56
    profit maximization 1, 4, 39, 48, 73, 80, 253
profitability 40, 82, 270
psychic income 69
pull factors 4, 74-76, 82, 109, 194, 210, 217
push factors 4, 64, 74, 75, 82, 109, 116, 193, 210, 214-217, 233, 236, 241, 287
quality circles 14, 19, 31
Research and Developmemt (R&D) 30, 44, 52, 62, 63, 78, 81, 254, 255, 268
rationality maximization 4
regional 1-6, 18, 20, 21, 25, 26, 30, 33, 49, 72, 75, 77, 78, 80-95, 97, 98-106, 108, 115, 118, 121, 126, 135, 136, 138-140, 143, 154-158, 163, 170, 175, 177, 179, 180, 185, 188, 194-200, 202, 203, 206, 208, 211, 212, 217, 218, 219-222, 224, 227, 229, 230, 232, 233, 235, 236, 239, 240, 242, 245, 252, 254, 258-264, 266, 268-282, 284, 285-288, 290, 291
    regional administrations 275
    regional agencies 105
    regional aid 103, 104
    regional assistance 89, 91, 106, 115, 118, 121, 154-158, 163, 195, 197, 198, 199, 202, 206, 208, 211, 217-220, 227, 230, 233, 242, 260, 266, 277
    regional balance 87, 94, 101, 104, 105, 268
    regional development 4, 77, 88, 89, 95, 100-102, 106, 268, 270, 275, 276, 279, 281, 282, 284

387

Regional Development Grant (RDG) 77, 89, 91, 93, 105, 154, 157, 197, 264, 265, 273
regional disparity 98, 104, 268, 276
regional distribution 126, 135, 139, 143, 200, 221
regional economic indicators 92
regional economy 25, 80, 81, 85, 93, 105, 106
regional employment premium (REP) 77, 86, 87, 93
regional financial assistance 155, 163, 266
regional growth 94, 99
regional growth centres 99
regional imbalance 80, 94, 97, 99, 100, 104, 105, 284
regional incentives 85, 94, 102-105, 252
regional income disparity 98
regional industrial specialization 18
regional institutions 276
regional market 254
regional milieu 278
regional planning 95, 100, 279
regional policy 1-6, 75, 77, 80, 81, 84-89, 91-95, 97-106, 108, 136, 138, 143, 163, 164, 170, 177, 179, 185, 188, 196, 197, 202, 203, 218, 221, 222, 224, 235, 236, 239, 259-262, 264, 266, 268, 270-273, 277-282, 284-288, 290, 291
regional politics 88
Regional Studies Association (RSA) 78, 86
regional subsidies 103
regional supply system 254
regional trade blocs 30
Regional Trends 90, 263
regionalist 20
regression analysis 81, 82, 93, 108-111, 113, 115, 117, 125, 147, 163, 164, 183, 184, 188, 210, 211, 217, 218, 226, 241, 242, 243, 245, 255, 258, 267, 285-287
regression coefficients 110
regression data 210
regression equation 114, 150, 151, 153, 171, 174, 181
regression model 110, 115
regulationist school 14
relocation 86
semiconductor industry 25
sense of international vulnerability 35
service industry 93

social regulation 34
Special Development Areas (SDAs) 87, 89, 101 87
Standard Industrial Classification (SIC) 112-113
static regression 171, 184
stepwise multiple regression 108
structural approach 71, 72
      structural autonomy 81
      structural change 8-10, 12-14, 21-25, 31, 32, 34, 36, 37, 79,
           89, 254
      structural constraints 4
      structural factors 46, 73, 102
      structural theory 4, 67, 71-73
structure 1, 3, 8, 9, 11, 12, 20-22, 29, 30, 33, 34, 38, 44, 46, 64, 65,
          70, 71, 74, 79, 83, 91, 100, 109, 251, 262, 279-281, 284
t-test 114
Telford Development Corporation 191, 198
Thatcher government 19, 149
Thatcherite anti-trade union legislation 244
transfer pricing 47, 49-51
triad power 41
travel-to-work area (TTWA) 118
unfavourable locational factors 209, 228
United Nations 39
unsatisfactory locational factors 116, 192, 194, 198, 199, 211, 212,
          214, 216, 219, 220, 229, 287
Urban Development Corporations (UDCs) 88, 155, 185, 266
Urban Planning Act 97
vertical integration 49, 63, 102
Welsh Development Agency (WDA) 196, 201
West Midlands Development Agency (WMDA) 76,130, 202
world-systems theory 21
worldwide regulation 35
Yochon Industrial Estate 139
zero-sum game 274, 275

AGRICULTURAL POLICY REFORM